Lecture Notes
in Business Information Processing 303

Series Editors

Wil M.P. van der Aalst
  Eindhoven Technical University, Eindhoven, The Netherlands
John Mylopoulos
  University of Trento, Trento, Italy
Michael Rosemann
  Queensland University of Technology, Brisbane, QLD, Australia
Michael J. Shaw
  University of Illinois, Urbana-Champaign, IL, USA
Clemens Szyperski
  Microsoft Research, Redmond, WA, USA

More information about this series at http://www.springer.com/series/7911

Witold Abramowicz (Ed.)

Business Information Systems Workshops

BIS 2017 International Workshops
Poznań, Poland, June 28–30, 2017
Revised Papers

Springer

Editor
Witold Abramowicz
Poznań University of Economics
  and Business
Poznań
Poland

ISSN 1865-1348   ISSN 1865-1356 (electronic)
Lecture Notes in Business Information Processing
ISBN 978-3-319-69022-3   ISBN 978-3-319-69023-0 (eBook)
https://doi.org/10.1007/978-3-319-69023-0

Library of Congress Control Number: 2017956060

Printed on acid-free paper

This Springer imprint is published by Springer Nature
The registered company is Springer International Publishing AG
The registered company address is: Gewerbestrasse 11, 6330 Cham, Switzerland

Preface

During each edition of the BIS Conference we make efforts to provide an opportunity for discussion about up-to-date topics from the area of information systems research. However, there are many topics that deserve particular attention. Thus, a number of workshops and accompanying events are co-located with the BIS Conference. Workshops give researchers the possibility to share preliminary ideas and initial experimental results and to discuss research hypotheses from a specific area of interest. BIS Workshops are an ideal place to present research ideas.

Three workshops and two accompanying events took place during the 20th BIS Conference. We were proud to host well-known workshops such as AKTB (ninth edition) and BITA (eighth edition) as well as a new initiative, SESSISE. Each workshop focused on a different topic: knowledge-based business information systems (AKTB), challenges and current state of business and IT alignment (BITA), and sustainable energy systems, smart infrastructures, and smart environments (SESSISE).

Additionally, BIS hosted a Doctoral Consortium. It was organized in a workshop formula, thus the best papers from this event are included in the book. Moreover, all authors had the possibility to discuss their ideas on PhD theses and research work with a designed mentor.

Together with the BIS Conference, the Second Polish National Congress on Information Systems took place. It was an event organized by the Polish Scientific Society for Business Informatics addressed to academia and businesses that conduct research in the area of business informatics. The event included a keynote speech, a discussion panel, and several regular and poster sessions. The best articles presented during the congress were then invited for publication in the volume.

The workshop authors had the chance to present their results and ideas in front of a well-focused audience; thus the discussion provided the authors with new perspectives and directions for further research. Based on the feedback received, authors had the opportunity to edit the workshop articles for the current publication. The volume contains 25 articles that are extended versions of papers accepted for BIS workshops. The volume ends with an invited paper presented during a special session of the main BIS Conference: "The Evolution of Business Information Systems and the BIS." In total, there were 74 submissions for all mentioned events. Based on the reviews, the respective workshop chairs accepted 25 in total, yielding an acceptance rate of 34%.

We would like to express our thanks to everyone who made the BIS 2017 workshops successful. First of all, our workshops chairs, members of the workshop Program Committees, authors of submitted papers, and finally all workshop participants. We cordially invite you to visit the BIS website at http://bisconf.info and to join us at future BIS conferences.

June 2017   Witold Abramowicz

Contents

SESSISE Workshop

Doctoral Consortium

Second National Congress on Information Systems

The Evolution of Business Information Systems and the BIS

AKTB Workshop

AKTB 2017 Workshop Chairs' Message

Virgilijus Sakalauskas and Dalia Kriksciuniene

The 9th Workshop on Applications of Knowledge-Based Technologies in Business (AKTB 2017) was organized in Poznan (Poland) in conjunction with 20th BIS2017 conference. It continued the successful series of AKTB workshops held in Poznan, Berlin, Vilnius, Larnaca, and Leipzig (2016).

The workshop invited researchers, practitioners, and policy makers to gather for discussion on the most urgent topics where advanced IT may serve for their progress. The workshop called for sharing research knowledge of efficient computational intelligence methods for implementing business information systems in finance, health care, e-business, and other application domains. We invited papers that provide advanced services for information systems users, propose innovative solutions for smart business and process modeling, especially targeting big data issues.

AKTB 2017 continued the tradition of delivering efficient computational solutions validated by experimental research and based on in-depth knowledge of business domains using smart data.

In all, 16 articles were submitted to the AKTB 2017 workshop. Each paper was evaluated by two or three independent reviewers of the Program Committee (PC). The nine highest ranked articles were accepted for presentation during the conference and the second stage of reviewing before including them in the conference proceedings. The PC of AKTB 2017 invited one additional paper, as it discusses a very interesting topic about the process and methods for evaluation of the EU health care efficiency.

There were 19 outstanding researchers who represent prestigious scientific institutions from 13 countries joining the PC as paper reviewers. They evaluated the quality of the articles by taking into account the criteria of their relevance to the workshop topics, originality, novelty, and quality of presentation.

We appreciate the level of work and expertise of the PC members, whose reviews provided an in-depth analysis of the submitted research works and highlighted valuable insights for the authors. The high standards followed by the reviewers enabled us to ensure the high quality of the workshop event, excellent presentations, intensive scientific discussions, and added value to the workshop proceedings.

We would like to express our gratitude for the success of AKTB 2017 to all authors of submitted papers, members of the PC, the Informatics Department of Vilnius University, and the Department of Information Systems of Poznan University of Economics and Business, and to acknowledge the outstanding efforts of the Organizing Committee of the 20th International conference BIS 2017.

Organization

Chairs

Dalia Kriksciuniene   Vilnius University, Lithuania
Virgilijus Sakalauskas   Vilnius University, Lithuania

Program Committee

María Dolores Alfonso Suárez	SIANI, Spain
František Babič	Technical University of Kosice, Slovakia
Lia Bassa	Foundation for Information Society, Hungary
Regis Cabral	FEPRO, Funding for European Projects, Sweden
Ferenc Kiss	Foundation for Information Society, Hungary
Dalia Kriksciuniene	Vilnius University, Lithuania
Audrius Lopata	Vilnius University, Lithuania
Saulius Masteika	Vilnius University, Lithuania
Elpiniki I. Papageorgiou	Technological Educational Institute of Central Greece
Laima Papreckiene	Kaunas University of Technology, Lithuania
Justyna Patalas-Maliszewska	University of Zielona Góra, Poland University of Vienna, Austria
Tomas Pitner	Masaryk University, Czech Republic
Jose Raul Romero	University of Córdoba, Spain
Vytautas Rudzionis	Vilnius University, Lithuania
Virgilijus Sakalauskas	Vilnius University, Lithuania
Darijus Strasunskas	POSC Caesar Association, Norway
Leonard Walletzky	Masaryk University, Czech Republic
Danuta Zakrzewska	Institute of Information Technology Technical University of Lodz, Poland

A Framework for Optimising Business Rules

Alan Dormer[(⊠)]

Department of Information Technology, Monash University, Clayton, Australia
Alan.dormer@monash.edu.au

Abstract. There has been significant growth in the number of business intelligence platforms that support and execute business rules since the late 1990s that shows no signs of abating. This paper examines the question of how to optimize business rules that can support rather than replace the human decision maker. It presents a novel framework to combine data (including decisions and actual outcomes), a business rules engine and the human judge. Preliminary results, on real data, suggest that about 80% of cases could be determined by a rules engine with an overall increase in gross profit of about 2%.

Keywords: Business intelligence · Business rules · Analytics · Optimisation · Decision support · Services · Productivity

1 Introduction

According to Gartner, Business intelligence (BI) is an umbrella term that includes the applications, infrastructure and tools, and best practices that enable access to and analysis of information to improve and optimize decisions and performance [1]. A more comprehensive definition is: Business intelligence systems combine operational data with analytical tools to present complex and competitive information to planners and decision makers. The objective is to improve the timeliness and quality of inputs to the decision process [2]. Business rules are very common within industry, particularly the service sector. They enable consistent decision making by individuals and a degree of automation using business rules engines. Expertise and experience can be codified and used by a large number of less expect and less experience staff.

There is a natural relationship between BI and business rules. Whilst planners and decision makers use the insights directly, we can use the same insights to influence the behaviour of others of the business through the business rules that they adhere to.

This paper addresses a challenge in the services sector: that of finding a set of business rules that maximises the expected value to an organization. For example, in customer qualification (do we want to do business with this customer), segmentation (what do we want to offer this customer) and claims management, where we need to balance the wants and needs of the customer, and the profitability and reputation of the organisation.

The following section reviews relevant literature and compares and contrasts research the related field of business process optimization. In Sect. 3 we provide a

© Springer International Publishing AG 2017
W. Abramowicz (Ed.): BIS 2017 Workshops, LNBIP 303, pp. 5–17, 2017.
https://doi.org/10.1007/978-3-319-69023-0_1

definition of the problem. The framework is defined in Sect. 4 and in Sect. 5 we discuss its application. Preliminary results are described in Sect. 6.

2 Literature Review

Business rules deal with variability and uncertainty. Customers are different; outcomes are often uncertain. Yet we need consistency: if two customers meet a certain criterion for acceptance, then they should both be accepted. In the last 20 years or so there has been an increase in computerisation that enables not only consistency but monitoring, enforcement and flexibility [3]. These software systems, called business rules engines, enable organisations to build and maintain sophisticated sets of rules that can control and monitor many thousands of staff and millions of transactions, in real-time. They also enable rules to be changed to reflect changes in business circumstances. But while business rules deliver consistency, they do not automatically deliver efficiency or maximise customer service or revenue. For further information see [4].

Business processes are also important to both the services and manufacturing sectors. This is particularly important in manufacturing as many important parts of the business are about processing physical items rather than information and rules themselves are not sufficient [5]. The human resources and physical resources which are used, both cost money. This has naturally led to the concept of business process optimisation where the sequencing of tasks, allocation of tasks to machines, etc., are planned to minimise costs and/or maximise revenue [6]. Indeed manufacturing often goes a lot further and uses optimisation and forecasting techniques to maximise profit based on variable demand and anticipated demand in quite sophisticated ways [7].

Optimisation in the services sector is not so well advanced. Two notable exceptions are staff rostering [8] and supply chain optimisation [9]. Rostering is widely used for the purposes of having the right number of people (and no more than is necessary) with the right skills, in the right place at the right time. This is motivated by cost reduction, because people costs are very significant in the services sector. Supply chain optimisation is about tasks, such as supply, storage and distribution, the allocation of resources to tasks, and the order that tasks are performed.

There are significant potential economic benefits in optimising the operation of the services sector through optimal business rules, and increasing the productivity of the services sector has been identified as key challenge/opportunity [10].

So, broadly speaking, an organisation may have right number of people, with the right skills, all doing the same thing (in the same situation) by using the same business rules. But could it do better, and serve its customers better by optimising business rules?

Business rules are part of business processes, and it is important to understand the difference between them, and their respective optimisation. A business process is a collection of related, structured activities or tasks that produce a specific service or product (serve a particular goal) for a particular customer or customers. [11] Business process optimisation is considered as the problem of constructing feasible business process designs with optimum attribute values such as duration and cost [12].

A business rule is a rule that defines or constrains some aspect of business and always resolves to either true or false. Business rules are intended to assert business structure or to control or influence the behaviour of the business [13]. Our definition of BPR is: Business rules optimisation is about finding that set of business rules that maximises the expected net contribution to the organisation that uses them.

Business rules research has, up to now, focussed on the following areas:

- The efficient construction of business rules from expert knowledge [14, 15] or other data sources [16],
- The creation [17, 18], organisation [19], deployment [20] or integration [21] of business rules
- The impact or use of business rules [22–25]
- How they enforce policies [26]

There is one reference [27] that considers rules and optimisation, but in the context of rules working with optimisation (linear programming, etc.) to provide decision support; each case or situation is dealt with by rules and optimisation with a separate optimisation calculation carried out each time. We are looking at the ability to optimise the rules (in advance) so that they get the best outcome every time, without further optimisation being required.

There is a large body of research on Business Process Optimisation (BPO). A Google Scholar search for business process optimisation/optimization on 13/12/16 yielded 2502 results.

BPO research focusses predominately on the processes required to produce an outcome at minimum time and/or cost, and the way that tasks and activities are structured (ordering, linkage, etc.). In almost all cases in the literature, rules (where cases or components are directed one way or the other) are not considered.

Research on Business Rule Optimisation is limited. A Google Scholar search for business rule optimization/optimisation on 13/12/16 yielded 6 results [28, 29] relate to the interactions between participants in a communication channel (such as telephone calls or social media). [30] is about fraud prevention. [31] concerns the development of constraint based search techniques and [32] is about simulation of social economic systems within a city. Only [33] presents the problem, albeit at a very basic level. We believe that BRO represents and new area of research that is different too, yet complements, the established area of BPO.

3 Problem Definition

Examples of business rules include decisions around accepting new customers [34], paying insurance claims [35], and treating patients in hospital.

Rules provide consistency and enable organisations to employ less experienced and expensive staff to deal with variability and uncertainty. There has been significant growth in the number of software platforms that support and execute business rules since the late 1990s that shows no signs of abating [36].

Whilst business rules provide consistency and a degree of automation, there is always the question of whether they are, in some sense, correct. In the context of most organisations, correct means that the result of their consistent application is to maximise profit, minimise cost or some other key performance indicator (KPI).

In this research we propose to create a framework capable of constructing optimal business rules including important issues such as what is optimisation in this context, what information should we use to drive them, how we should construct them and how we integrate human judgement?

Many examples of business rules can be identified, ranging from commercial (deciding on a loan application or insurance claim, approving expenditure, etc.), to social such as medical diagnosis and assessing issues around child protection.

The basic idea is that we can use a computer (a business rules engine or machine) in conjunction with a human judge to make decisions. This is important; we are not seeking to eliminate the human judge as a matter of principal, we are merely using him or her when it make economic sense.

They have some concepts and features in common:

- There is a subject or CASE
- The CLASS of a CASE is an unknown variable
- We are required to make a DETERMINATION for each CASE
- Each CASE has ATTRIBUTES, features or cues that are apparent
- The ATTRIBUTES are random binary, integer and real variables
- The ATTRIBUTES cannot be assumed to be independent of each other
- It is possible to make a DETERMINATION on the CASE by observing the ATTRIBUTES
- This DETERMINATION may be made by a HUMAN judge or MACHINE
- There are BUSINESS RULES for the MACHINE
- The BUSINESS RULES are interpreted by the MACHINE, which processes each case and decides upon it or refers it to a HUMAN
- The HUMAN has some freedom to use their judgement, as well as the BUSINESS RULES, to make a DETERMINATION
- For the organisation, which is one of the STAKEHOLDERS, there are monetary consequences from both correct and incorrect DETERMINATIONS.

Table of Examples

Application	Loan approval	Child protection	Medical diagnosis
CASE	Loan applicant	Child of interest	Patient
CLASS	Good Bad	Abused At risk Not at risk	Healthy Diseased
DETERMINATION	Accept Reject	Do nothing Monitor Act	Do nothing Tests Treat
ATTRIBUTES	Credit score	Parents	Symptoms

(continued)

(*continued*)

Application	Loan approval	Child protection	Medical diagnosis
	Income Security	History Observations	Test results
BUSINESS RULES	Credit policy	Statute	Medical procedure
MACHINE	Application website	Triage	Screening test
Output from MACHINE	Accept, Reject or Refer	No case, Low priority, High priority	Negative, Positive (refer)
HUMAN JUDGE	Underwriter	Social worker	Doctor

In the cases above, the MACHINE takes one or more of the ATTRIBUTES as input and performs logical operations on the ATTRIBUTES to make a DETERMINATION on a CASE. One of the DETERMINATIONS is refer to the HUMAN JUDGE. In the loan approval application, certain CASES will be rejected automatically, others will be automatically accepted and the rest referred.

Organisations utilise processes to structure activities directed towards their objectives. Naturally an organisation may have many objectives, sometimes related to the different stakeholders in the organisation.

The activities of an organisation can be broken down into tasks, and each task requires different resources such as people, equipment, machines and time.

In this paper we consider organisations whose customers request a service. The particular objective we address is optimising the choice of which customers to accept and which to reject.

We examine the process which serves this objective: *the customer selection process*.

The outcomes of the process are (1) a set of customers (CASES) accepted (2) a set of customers who withdraw from the process (3) a total benefit from the customers served, and (4) an opportunity cost associated with the customers who are not served either because they dropped out, or because they were not selected. The process also has a cost (5) arising from the resources consumed in its component activities.

If the benefits (3) and the costs (4) and (5) can be quantified, the process is optimised when (3) − ((4) + (5)) has been maximised. In all cases we need to classify the customer (or case) as accurately as possible whilst minimising the cost of classification, the opportunity cost of rejecting a customer that we should accept and the liability of accepting a customer we should not have accepted. There are also consideration around abandoned transactions; making the customer experience more onerous by asking for too much information can results in otherwise potentially valuable customer giving upon the process. In addition we have to recognise that financial services providers have levels of engagement including on-line, customer service agents and experts, such as underwriters, each of which bring different costs and expertise to the problems.

A similar problem that can be addressed in the same way is one of approvals, particularly for purchases or commencement of a contract, where different levels of staff have different approval levels. If a purchase/project is above a particular level, it needs to go to a more senior member of staff.

For the pilot application we considered the problem of loan approval. There were 6 data items requested:

– Credit score (which is a composite of other variables including credit history) (FICO)
– Loan amount
– Debt to income (DTI)
– Years of employment (EMP)
– State
– Postcode

The complete objective function is:

(total good applications × (1 − AR) − good cases rejected) × potential profit
− cost of bad cases accepted × potential loss
− cost of determination

where AR is the abandonment rate which is a function of the amount of information requested.

For the purposes of the pilot we can assume that potential profit and potential loss are related to the size of the loan. The processing costs are a function of the amount of information, for example a familiarisation time and a time proportional to the amount of information.

4   Discussion

The customer selection process essentially involves two major subprocesses: an initial automated filtering of the customers, possibly followed by a final selection carried out by a human expert. In practice the number and availability of the experts is somewhat inflexible, so the allocation of resource to the second subprocess cannot readily be changed. Consequently the first, filtering, subprocess must adapt its outcomes: forwarding a narrower band of customers to the second process on some days to avoid overloading the experts.

In order to tackle the overall goal of optimising the customer selection process, the BRO framework must consequently address both automated and human decision-making.

To meet the overall objective of optimising the customer selection process, this research must address some traditional business process optimisation questions: resources and throughput of different activities, incurring certain resource costs and yielding certain value. It must also address issues in automated decision-making, such as decision-tree optimisation, but in the context of a decision-making process that includes delegation to a human expert. Thirdly it must address issues in human decision-making: what is the effect, on speed and accuracy of human decision-making, of sending them only the most difficult cases as opposed to a broader spread of cases? The final issue relates to the different stakeholders of the organisation. Is it important never to reject a "good" customer who might have benefitted from the service? Or is it important to process ALL the customers within a certain time? Or is it simply required to maximize the profit margin?

What we are seeking to understand is *how business rules and the process of their application can be designed and optimised, to maximise their net contribution to the business that uses them.* In this context optimisation includes:

- Costs (reduction)
- Compliance (with regulations)
- Customer service (maintain or improve)

There are different types of rules, but they share some common features:

- Humans can make decisions on their own
- The rules can help them
- Some of the rules can be executed by machine

What we are looking at comprises essentially three things

- What can the machine do, and what rules should they execute?
- How do we optimise such rules?
- How can we create a framework where humans and machine contribute to maximise net benefit?

5   The Framework

There are a number of considerations with the customer selection process that need to be addressed.

Firstly, that we have to decide on the information that we collect and analyse. Information collection may be relatively cheap and painless for the organisation; the customer either fills in a form or goes on-line and does all the work. But analysing the information may not be so cheap; if we can use a computer, costs are low; if we need to use a human to make the decision, costs can be high. In addition, there is evidence that asking for too much information can result in abandoned transactions; the customer simply gives up [37]. Whilst each piece of information will have an impact on the accuracy of the classification, it will also have an impact of the processing cost and abandonment rate. We are seeking that (minimal) subset that gives us the best expected profit. This is known as the feature selection problem in machine learning [38].

Unfortunately this is not a straightforward process. Until we define the rules we don't know how the outcome of the processing, and we cannot define the rules until we know what information we require to process. So in order to address the information question we need some way to approximate the processing step.

The second challenge is to model human judgement challenge is to model human judgement. There is a lot of research into this question in the field of psychology. The LENS model [39] has been applied to many problems involving judgement, such as medical diagnosis. Based on past performance, we can fit a model for any human judge and compare their judgement against 3 other quantities; the model of their judgement, a model of the outcome and the actual outcome. From that we can estimate their judgement on any particular case in the future. The original LENS model is linear but there are obvious extensions using polynomial regression and classifications techniques, such as decision trees [40].

The third challenge is how to build the rules, which are executed essentially for free by a computer. There are several ways to do this, for example decision trees or rule learning [41]. The subtlety in our case is that the decision is three ways; accept, reject and refer (to the human decision maker).

The final challenge is to incorporate the business rule engine (the computer) with the human judge. The key issue here is that we have to compare probabilities for each end point of the rules (the leaves of the decision tree). If we take the output of the rule we know the probability that any case will be good is determined during the build, based on the training data. Conversely, if we give the case to the human judge we can estimate their accuracy (using the judgement model) and determine is the extra cost is justified by increased discrimination or classification accuracy.

6   Preliminary Results

We tested the basic framework described with a subset of a large data set [42]. We examined the resource allocation problem, which is how many cases should be given to the human judge. For reasons of simplicity we assume that the human judge is 100% accurate; we have data on outcomes as well and this will be addressed later. We also assume that the potential profit (of taking on a good customer) and loss (from taking on a bad customer) are equal to 50% of the average loan value. These numbers are simple inputs and can easily be varied.

Initial analysis showed that the address attributes (State and Postcode) and Loan Amount did not add any value. A simple 5 level decision tree was built using the WEKA Workbench [43] with the remainder of the attributes. This is shown below:

```
FICO < 802.5

|  EMP < 0.75 : 0 (236800/649) [118014/306]

|  EMP >= 0.75

|  |  DTI < 24.99

|  |  |  DTI < 4.05 : 0 (25206/344) [12687/190]

|  |  |  DTI >= 4.05

|  |  |  |  FICO < 751.5 : 0 (44825/4009) [22450/1906]

|  |  |  |  FICO >= 751.5

|  |  |  |  |  FICO < 752.5 : 1 (520/126) [256/49]

|  |  |  |  |  FICO >= 752.5 : 0 (3716/911) [1760/445]

|  |  DTI >= 24.99 : 0 (30260/28) [15403/26]

FICO >= 802.5

|  FICO < 819.5

|  |  FICO < 803.5

|  |  |  DTI < 2.54

|  |  |  |  DTI < 0.39 : 0 (17/2) [9/4]

|  |  |  |  DTI >= 0.39 : 1 (60/27) [30/11]

|  |  |  DTI >= 2.54

|  |  |  |  DTI < 30.02 : 1 (905/27) [486/27]

|  |  |  |  DTI >= 30.02 : 0 (14/0) [8/0]

|  |  FICO >= 803.5 : 0 (864/0) [429/0]

|  FICO >= 819.5

|  |  FICO < 835

|  |  |  FICO < 820.5 : 1 (952/23) [508/6]

|  |  |  FICO >= 820.5 : 0 (40/0) [25/0]

|  |  FICO >= 835 : 1 (10491/2) [5271/2]
```

At each (of the 14) leaves of the tree we have information on the type of node (0 = bad, 1 = good) and the composition of that node (#correct, #incorrect) and the numbers in square brackets are the validation set. For example, on the first leaf we test for FICO < 802.5 and then EMP < 0.75. We determine that the node is bad with 236800 correctly classified (as bad) and 649 incorrectly classified. The problem now is to determine whether it is worth giving these cases to a human judge, and incurring a cost, or simply rejecting all of them automatically and accepting the cost of rejecting a relatively small number of good cases.

If we set the cost of a determination at 0.5% of the average loan, we find that it is optimal to assign 77% of the cases to the rules engine, and the gross profit increases by 1.8% over that obtained by using the human judge on all cases (shown below). With a determination cost of 0.25% of the average loan value, the allocation remains the same, with an increase in gross profit of 0.6%. The break-even point is reached when the cost of a determination is 0.134% of the average loan value. The profit figures below are $1,000's.

	Optimal case load		Profit
Leaf	Machine	Human	Increase
1	355769	0	15616
2	0	38427	0
3	0	73190	0
4	0	951	0
5	0	6832	0
6	45717	0	2419
7	0	32	0
8	0	128	0
9	0	1445	0
10	22	0	1
11	1293	0	78
12	0	1489	0
13	65	0	4
14	15768	0	910
Total	418634	122494	19028
	77.36%	22.64%	1.81%

The diagram shows that if we take the machine determination for leaf 1, the net saving over giving the cases to the human judge is $15,616,000. The same applies to leaves 6, 10, 11, 13 and 14. For the remainder, it is better to give the case to the human, with no net saving.

7 Conclusion

Business rules are widely used with industry yet there is virtually no research around how to create rules that in some sense optimise the expected value of their application. Conversely Business Process Optimisation (BPO) has been widely researched. There are similarities but also some essential differences. We have defined the concept of Business Rules Optimisation (BRO) in the context of their use in the services sector and created the representative example of customer selection. The framework we have developed employs ideas and techniques from machine learning and psychology, and is complementary to BPO. The frame work cannot be applied linearly as there are elements of iteration. But for each step within the framework we have identified useful techniques that could be applied to answer the key questions such as:

- What information do we ask for?
- How do we model human judgement?

- How do we build the rules?
- How do we incorporate a rules engine with a human decision maker?
- How do we modify the rules when caseload changes?

The potential of this approach is considerable. BPO has developed and created an industry without considering the impact that rules have on processes with variability and uncertainty. BRO has the potential to extend the application of optimisation to many more processes. In further work we plan to implement and validate the framework for a large credit assessment data set [38] that includes accepted and rejected customers, and outcomes. We will also consider human judgement and the ability to modify rules in real-time as the caseload changes.

References

1. Gartner Group. http://www.gartner.com/it-glossary/business-intelligence-bi/
2. Negash, S.: Business intelligence. Commun. Assoc. Inf. Syst. **13** (2004). Article 15. http://aisel.aisnet.org/cais/vol13/iss1/15
3. Andreescu, A.: Methodological approaches based on business rules. Inform. Econ. J. **12**(3), 23–27 (2008)
4. Taylor, J.: Decision Management Systems: A Practical Guide to Using Business Rules and Predictive Analytics. IBM Press, Indianapolis (2011)
5. Harmon, P.: Business process management: today and tomorrow. In: Dumas, M., Reichert, M., Shan, M.-C. (eds.) BPM 2008. LNCS, vol. 5240, p. 1. Springer, Heidelberg (2008). doi:10.1007/978-3-540-85758-7_1
6. Vergidis, K.: Business process optimisation using and evolutionary multi-objective framework. Ph.D. thesis (2008)
7. Dormer, A.: Hybrid Optimisation System for Solving Planning and Scheduling Problems. COR/INFORMS, Banff (2004)
8. Ernst, A., et al.: Staff scheduling and rostering: a review of applications, methods and models. Eur. J. Oper. Res. **153**, 3–27 (2004)
9. Zachary, H., et al.: Supply-chain optimisation – players, tools and issues. OR Insight **14**, 20–30 (2001)
10. Drucker, P.F.: The new productivity challenge. Harv. Bus. Rev. **69**(6), 69 (1991)
11. Teodoru, S.F.: Business process management integration solution in financial sector. Inform. Econ. **13**(1), 47 (2009)
12. Vergidis, K.: An evolutionary multi-objective framework for business process optimisation. Appl. Soft Comput. **12**(2), 2638–2653 (2012)
13. The Business Rules Group. Final Report, Revision 1.3, July 2000
14. Gupta, A.K., Lotlikar, R.M., Angshu, R.: System and Method for Determining Interpersonal Relationship Influence Information using Textual Content from Interpersonal Interactions. U.S. Patent Application No. 13/177,998
15. Gupta, A.K., Lotlikar, R.M., Angshu, R.: Method for Determining Interpersonal Relationship Influence Information using Textual Content from Interpersonal Interactions. U.S. Patent Application No. 13/594,963
16. Sneed, H.M., Erdos, K.: Extracting business rules from source code. In: Proceedings of Fourth Workshop on Program Comprehension. IEEE (1996)
17. Gottesdiener, E.: Capturing business rules. Softw. Dev.-San Franc. **7**, 72 (1999)

18. Shao, J., Pound, C.J.: Extracting business rules from information systems. BT Technol. J. **17** (4), 179–186 (1999)
19. Chikofsky, E.J., Cross, J.H.: Reverse engineering and design recovery: a taxonomy. IEEE Softw. **7**(1), 13–17 (1990)
20. Chisholm, M.: How to Build a Business Rules Engine: Extending Application Functionality through Metadata Engineering. Morgan Kaufmann, Burlington (2004)
21. Kardasis, P., Loucopoulos, P.: Expressing and organising business class rules. Inf. Softw. Technol. **46**(11), 701–718 (2004)
22. Rosca, D., Wild, C.: Towards a flexible deployment of business rules. Expert Syst. Appl. **23** (4), 385–394 (2002)
23. Cibrán, M., D'hondt, M., Jonckers, V.: Aspect-oriented programming for connecting business rules. In: Proceedings of the 6th International Conference on Business Information Systems, vol. 6, no. 7 (2003)
24. Gottesdiener, E.: Business rules show power, promise. Appl. Dev. Trends **4**(3), 36–42 (1997)
25. Van Eijndhoven, T., Iacob, M., Ponisio, M.L.: Achieving business process flexibility with business rules. In: 12th International Conference on Enterprise Distributed Object Computing. IEEE (2008)
26. Graml, T., Bracht, R., Spies, M.: Patterns of business rules to enable agile business processes. Enterp. Inf. Syst. **2**(4), 385–402 (2008)
27. Appleton, D.S.: Business rules - the missing link. Datamation **30**(17), 145 (1984)
28. Leite, J.C.S., Leonardi, M.C.: Business rules as organizational policies. In: Proceedings of the 9th International Workshop on Software Specification and Design. IEEE Computer Society (1998)
29. Liu, F., et al.: Risk Assessment Rule Set Application for Fraud Prevention. U.S. Patent No. 8,924,279. 30 (2014)
30. Jandir, R.: Event based propagation approach to constraint configuration problems. Master's theses, 3659 (2009). http://scholarworks.sjsu.edu/etd_theses/3659
31. Begunov, N., Moskalev, I., Klebanov, B.: City agent-based model. In: Proceedings of the 2008 Spring Simulation Multiconference. Society for Computer Simulation International (2008)
32. Boyer, J., Mili, H.: Agile Business Rule Development' Process, Architecture, and JRules Examples. Springer, Heidelberg (2011)
33. Dormer, A.: Optimising business rules in the services sector. Int. J. Soc. Behav. Educ. Econ. Bus. Ind. Eng. **6**(10), 2580–2584 (2012)
34. Graydon. https://www.graydon.co.uk/downloads/epaper-new-era-customer-acceptance-decision-model. Accessed 13 Dec 2016
35. RMS. http://www.rms.nsw.gov.au/documents/business-industry/examiners/business-rules-authorised-inspection-station-scheme.pdf. Accessed 13 Dec 2016
36. NHFP. http://www.publichospitalfunding.gov.au/Media/Business%20Rules%20Volume%202.pdf. Accessed 13 Dec 2016
37. Gartner. https://www.gartner.com/doc/1926217/vendors-business-rule-market. Accessed 13 Dec 2016
38. Salescycle. https://blog.salecycle.com/strategies/form-abandonment-can-avoid. Accessed 13 Dec 2016
39. Hall, M.: Correlation-based feature selection of discrete and numeric class machine learning. In: Proceedings ICML 2000 Seventh International Conference on Machine Learning, 29 June–02 July, pp. 359–366 (2000)

40. Brunswik, E.: The Essential Brunswik: Beginnings, Explications, Applications, New Directions in Research on Decision Making, Research Conference on Subjective Probability, Utility and Decision Making (1985)
41. Breiman, L., Friedman, J.H., Olshen, R.A., Stone, C.J.: Classification and Regression Trees. Wadsworth International, Belmont (1984)
42. Bundy, A., Siver, B., Plummer, D.: An analytical comparison of some rule learning programs. Artif. Intell. **27**, 137–181 (1985)
43. https://www.lendingclub.com/info/download-data.action

A Social Recommendation Mechanism
for Crowdfunding

Yung-Ming Li[1], Jyh-Hwa Liou[1,2(✉)], and Yi-Wen Li[1]

[1] Institute of Information Management, National Chiao Tung University,
1001 University Road, Hsinchu 300, Taiwan R.O.C.
yml@mail.nctu.edu.tw, alioujh@gmail.com,
c80617@gmail.com
[2] Center for General Education, Hsin Sheng College of Medical Care
and Management, Taoyuan, Taiwan

Abstract. In recent years, a new kind of fund-raising mode crowdfunding, is
gradually arising. Through the rapid spread of the Internet, customers can show
their creativity and ideas on the fundraising platform and attract backers to
invest extensively in support of the count painting or product development.
However, according to fund-raising platform statistics, we found that the success
rate of fund-raising plans is less than half. Therefore, the purpose of this study is
to propose a backers recommendation mechanism, which integrates information
from fundraising and social networking platforms, considering the factors of
social relationship, user preferences and background analysis, to help creators
improve the success rate of crowdfunding.

Keywords: Crowdfunding · Crowdfunding platforms · Social network · Social
relationship · Social recommendation

1 Introduction

In simple terms, crowdfunding is a new way to gain the funds to complete a specific
project. The marketplace of crowdfunding keeps growing as soon as possible and it has
reached up to 50 billion in 2013 [1]. In recent years, more and more crowdfunding
platforms have appeared, like: Kickstarter, which is the biggest crowdfunding platform
in the world, has funded $529 million USD in 2014 [1]. Besides, there are 3.3 million
people to back the projects in Kickstarter [2]. But, according to the recent statistics, the
success rate of projects are never over 50% since crowdfunding platforms appeared [3].
Even though creators prepare very well to promote their projects, they only have half of
success possibility to achieve their goals. There are lots of reasons for the frustration of
crowdfunding activity.

We want to use a phase recommendation to help the creator to break the bottleneck of
different fundraising phase with the combination of Facebook. The proposed mechanism
will solve the problems of crowdfunding with the combination of social networks via the
phase recommendation system. The issues to be conquered are as follows.

- How to find the backers who are interested in the crowdfunding projects from the
  social network?

© Springer International Publishing AG 2017
W. Abramowicz (Ed.): BIS 2017 Workshops, LNBIP 303, pp. 18–25, 2017.
https://doi.org/10.1007/978-3-319-69023-0_2

- How to reinforce the willingness of investing crowdfunding projects and improve the degree of trust.

Nowadays, everything in the Internet can be recommended for someone, so we want to develop a new application of phase recommendation systems. We develop a brand social network based recommendation mechanism to improve the diffusion of crowdfunding projects. Overall, the mechanism can reinforce the relationship of social networks and recommend appropriate backer in different phase. In the proposed mechanism, we will divide fundraising activities into different stages.

This paper is organized as follows. The basic concepts and literature related to our research topics are provided in Sect. 2. In Sect. 3, we present the system framework. Section 4 describes the processes of the experiment and discusses the empirical results. Section 5 concludes our research contributions and describes research limitations and the future works.

2 Related Work

2.1 Crowdfunding

Crowdfunding is a novel method of financing for those people who don't have independent wealth but want to complete a project [3]. Whose people originate fundraising projects in the crowdfunding platforms to show their ideas are be called creator. Conversely, whose people have willingness to invest crowdfunding projects in the websites are be called backers [4]. Basically, crowdfunding has three different types according to the feedback: lending crowdfunding, equity crowdfunding and rewards crowdfunding. Crowdfunding can help creators earn funds from the Internet [5]. Generally, the backers often are ordinary people and the money they invest is too less to affect their daily life so that most people have the ability to back some interesting projects [4]. Massolution reported that crowdfunding has reached $1.5 billion in 2013 [6]. Kickstarter, Indiegogo, and GoFundMe are all famous crowdfunding platforms in the world [7], especially Kickstarter, the site has raised $1.5 billion in funding and over $7.8 million backers to back 78 thousand successful projects [2].

2.2 Recommendation Systems

Recommendation systems aim to recommend something or someone to a specific user. In the past, recommendation system often focus on points of interest (POI) to identify top k items which satisfied user's requirement and rank it for user [8]. Then, a related research which is based on collaborative filtering recommendation appeared. There are various technique like: decision tree, clustering, regression, neural networks and association rule mining. According to the technique, recommendation system can be classified two types: a content-based and a collaborative-based systems [9].

According to the above study, we can understand that recommendation system has great development in recent years. However, most of recommendation system can't match our needs, we want to design a flexible system which can adjust the weights with different crowdfunding phases to avoid the failure of crowdfunding projects. We adopt a hybrid personalized recommendation by combing with content-based and collaborative-based on social network.

3   The System Framework

In this research, we develop a novel social-based crowdfunding recommendation mechanism that can help all participants in this crowdfunding campaign. We aim to help creators to find potential backers and reach their crowdfunding goals, through a mechanism of social network activities mining and proper recommendation lists selecting. The system architecture is shown as Fig. 1. The components included in the systems are described as follows.

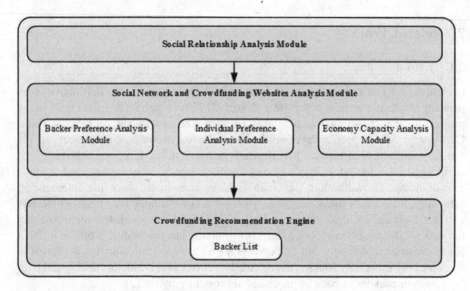

Fig. 1. The system framework

3.1   Social Relationship Analysis Module

This module will construct a creator's social network to evaluate the social distance between the creator and the backer. We compute the interaction and closeness to complete this module.

Social Interaction Analysis. There are four kinds of social data we use: (1) the number of two users tagged together in the same comments, photos, check-ins and posts, (2) the number of comments by the two users written in the each other's posts, comments, photos, status and check-ins, (3) the number of likes given by two users in the each other's' posts, comments, photos, status and check-ins and (4) the number of clubs the two user joined.

Social Closeness Analysis. In this section, we have to calculate the distance between the creator and the backer. If they have more mutual friends in the social network, we can reasonably infer they have more association.

3.2   Social Network and Crowdfunding Websites Analysis Module

Backer Preference Analysis Module. In order to understand users' behavior in the crowdfunding platforms, we collect and analyze users' activities. In Backer Preference Analysis Module, we will record and analyze a backer's activities.

In this part, we would start to collect related information from the platforms. We denote $BackerPreference(b_i, type)$ as a value that represents the score of backer's preference of a specific type in the crowdfunding websites. b_i represents a backer i and $type$ represents the project's type. The value will be used to judge the degree of recommendation in the next module.

$$BackerPreference(b_i, type) = ShareTimes(b_i, type) + TypePreference(b_i, type) \quad (1)$$

$ShareTimes(b_i, type)$ represents the total times of sharing a specific project type in social media from backer b_i. For example, if a backer b_i shared a crowdfunding project about "Art" three times on Facebook, the value of $ShareTimes(b_i, Art)$ is 3. $TypePreference(b_i, type)$ represents b_i's preference about a type in the crowdfunding platform. If the value of $TypePreference(b_i, type)$ is higher, it represents the project type is more attractive for backer b_i.

In the Social Analysis Module, we will analyze user's preference to know what project type the backer focuses on. We compute preference and similarity to complete this module.

Individual Preference Analysis Module. In order to understand backer' preference, the module will gather user's personal information from Facebook, the most popular social network in the world.

$$IndividualPreference(b_i, type) \\ = SocialPreference(b_i, type) * Similarity(\overrightarrow{b_i}, \overrightarrow{type}) \quad (2)$$

We compute the value of $SocialPreference(b_i, type)$ by the following kinds of social data: (1) check-ins: check-ins records the service of social network to exhibit what his/her does or where his/her is, (2) pages: the page is a user likes or pays attention to on social media, (3) like: the like is a button that a user can click it on social media, like: Facebook and (4) comment: the comment is a user write or give the rank on Facebook.

Facebook has their rule to classify check-ins, pages, like, and comment so we just have to transform the social data to match the TypeTree. For example, user who like to check-ins in art exhibitions, we can infer his/her might be interested in the arts. Similarly, like and pages have the own category in Facebook, we just have to make sure the category to match the TypeTree.

$$SocialPreference(b_i, type) = checkins_{type}(u_i) + page_{type}(u_i) + like_{type}(u_i)$$
$$+ comment_{type}(u_i) \tag{3}$$

$$Similarity(\overrightarrow{b_i, type}) = \overrightarrow{b_i, type} = \sum_{i=1}^{n} \overrightarrow{b_i, type_i} \tag{4}$$

Economy Capacity Analysis Module. The most important factor to consider is to make sure whether a potential backer user has the economy capacity to invest something. We will judge it through the analysis of occupation and background.

In order to understand user's economy capacity, we will ask user to fill in the questionnaire about some basic information, including: (1) ages: backer's ages, (2) educational background: backer's the higher academic degree, (3) work experience: to understand backer's income and (4) income: the salary of the backer.

3.3   Crowdfunding Recommendation Engine

After collecting enough information from the above four modules, we will use the weight values of four criteria, this mechanism can have the ability to measure the suitability-of-recommendation that the backer u_i will be recommended to invest the project p of creator u_j in a specific crowdfunding phase. We denote the suitability-of-recommendation of backer i as $Suitability(b_i, c_j, type)$. We calculate the value of $Suitability(b_i, c_j, type)$ by the aggregation of the weight value of each criterion with the corresponding score of the criterion which calculated by the social relationship, backer preference, individual preference and crowdfunding preference analysis module. The value of $Suitability(b_i, c_j, type)$ is measured as the Eq. 5.

$$Suitability(b_i, c_j, type) = W_S(i) * SocialRelationship(b_i, c_j) +$$
$$W_I(i) * IndividualPreference(b_i, type) +$$
$$W_B(i) * BackerPreference(b_i, type) +$$
$$W_E(i) * EconomyCapacity(b_i) \tag{5}$$

After calculations in the above sections, we could generate a proper list for recommendation and exhibit it for the creator. The creator will receive a recommendation list which provides basic information about the going project: (1) the distance of the going project and (2) the phase of the going project. Besides, the backer list also provides five types of backer's information: (1) name, (2) picture, (3) social relations with the creator, (4) individual preference and (5) Facebook Personal Website: to offer the contact way to creators.

4 Experiment

4.1 Experiment Design

In our experiments, we have 282 users join the system. We use Facebook PHP SDK and Graph API to access their Facebook information after they agree the authorization. In the past 12 months, they have 27636 check-ins, 81216 posts, 133104 tags, 11280 fan paged liked, 345732 likes and 225600 comments. The average number of friends of each user is 280. The user's age is 18 to 40 years old. The gender distribution is 161 males and 121 females. The education background is 164 master degree, 112 university degree and 6 high school. 141 users have 1 to 2 work experience, 68 users have one work experience and 73 has no work experience.

In the proposed mechanism, we should know to compute the importance of four factors: social relationship, backer preference, individual preference and economy capacity. Users have to answer which factor is the most important to them with respect to different scenarios. According to AHP structure, we use the fundamental scale to represent the relative importance: 1 represents "equal importance", 3 represents "weak importance", 5 represents "essential importance" and 7 represents "very strong importance".

The evaluation we use questionnaire to understand user's feeling via likeness for the invitation. The scale of the scores which used to the questions was from 1 to 5.

4.2 Experimental Results

The Evaluation of Likeness. Figure 2 shows the results of users about how much do you like this project invitation in different models and scenario. The value of every model is average score.

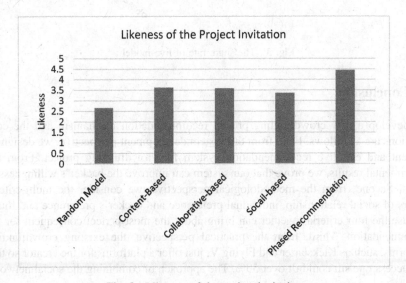

Fig. 2. Likeness of the project invitation

According to Fig. 2, we can find that the random model has the lower value of the likeness of the project invitation and the phase recommendation model has the highest value. Besides, we can understand the social relationship has more influence to user.

The Evaluation of Share Rate. After the backer receives the project invitation, they can choose to "share" the system page via the Facebook plugin function (Fig. 3). The share times can obtain from our system record and is measured as:

$$ShareRate = \frac{\Phi ShareTime}{\Phi Invitation}$$

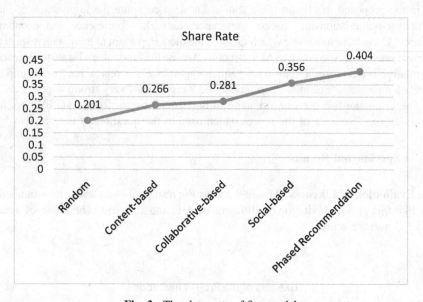

Fig. 3. The share rate of five model

5 Conclusion

We develop a new crowdfunding project recommendation mechanism and the contributions are as follows. First, from the system development perspective, we design an efficient and effective recommendation system for crowdfunding project. From the experimental results, we prove that our system can improve the backer's willingness to invest. Second, from the methodological perspective, we consider the multi-criteria factors of social relationship, individual preference and backer's preference and found that use the four criteria together can bring about the most perfect consequent for the recommendation. Third, from the practical perspective, the existing crowdfunding platforms, such as Kickstarter and Flying V, just offer a platforms for the creator so that the success rate sill couldn't over 50%. The approach of combining the social network,

Facebook, can analyze the user's preference and find the potential backer for the creator to overcome current problem of crowdfunding project.

There are some limitations in this research listed as following. First, the proposed mechanism gather related information from Facebook, however, there are more popular social network like: Twitter and Weibo. In the future, we can combine more social network to collect users' information and analyze users' preference exactly. Though more reliable sources, we could strengthen the recommendation for user. Second, our mechanism may have the problem of cold start, if the user of our system is too few, the recommendation would lose accuracy. Third, in fact, social networks only can offer a part of the interaction between two users because social network sometimes can't reflect the real world.

References

1. Entrepreneur. The Basics of Crowdfunding. Entrepreneur (2013)
2. Kickstarter. The year in Kickstarter 2014 in Kickstarter (2014). https://www.kickstarter.com/year/2014?ref=footer#intro
3. Zheng, H., Li, D., Wu, J., Xu, Y.: The role of multidimensional social capital in crowdfunding: a comparative study in China and US. Inf. Manag. **51**(4), 488–496 (2014)
4. Mollick, E.: The dynamics of crowdfunding: an exploratory study. J. Bus. Ventur. **29**(1), 1–16 (2014)
5. Chiu, C.M., Liang, T.P., Turban, E.: What can crowdsourcing do for decision support? Decis. Support Syst. **65**, 40–49 (2014)
6. Massolution.com. 2013 The Crowdfunding Industry Report (2013). http://www.crowdsourcing.org/research
7. gofundme. Top 10 Crowdfunding Sites (2014). http://www.crowdfunding.com
8. Kim, J.K., Kim, H.K., Oh, H.Y., Ryu, Y.U.: A group recommendation system for online communities. Int. J. Inf. Manag. **30**(3), 212–219 (2010)
9. Mishra, R., Kumar, P., Bhasker, B.: A web recommendation system considering sequential information. Decis. Support Syst. (2015)

Principal Sources for the Identification of Tacit Knowledge Within an IT Company, as Part of an Intelligent System

Justyna Patalas-Maliszewska[1(✉)] and Irene Krebs[2]

[1] University of Zielona Góra, Zielona Góra, Poland
J.Patalas@iizp.uz.zgora.pl
[2] Brandenburg University of Technology Cottbus-Senftenberg,
Cottbus, Germany
krebs@b-tu.de

Abstract. This article aims to present principal sources for the identification of tacit knowledge within an IT Company, as part of an intelligent system. It is stated, that knowledge workers have the specialised knowledge to come up with or formulate new ideas and that this specialised knowledge is the product of targeted education, experience and competences. Using our personnel usefulness function (Evaluation of Personnel as an Asset – EPS method), a base of knowledge workers, within an IT company is created and then, by using the FAHP method, the main sources of tacit knowledge (MTKS) from this base of knowledge workers are identified. Finally, the implementation of our approach in an information system is presented.

Keywords: Identification of tacit knowledge · EPS method · An intelligent system · An IT company

1 Introduction

The profitability of an IT company depends to a large extent on intangible resources [7]. Companies can ensure their long-term competitiveness by the acquisition, storage and transferring -or sharing- of internal knowledge. According to Chen et al. [3] a company's employees are valuable capital in the creation and acquisition of internal knowledge.

The process of knowledge management consists of three, interconnected areas: (1) the acquisition and creation of knowledge, (2) the dissemination of knowledge, (3) the use of knowledge [11]. According to the research literature, we can distinguish knowledge sources depending on stages in the knowledge management process [1, 6, 8, 14, 15, 17]. In this article, we have paid special attention to the identification of the main sources of tacit knowledge in an IT company, namely, the critical kind of knowledge which is related to employees in the first stage of the process of knowledge management. Our research methodology is based on two stages: (1) the identification of knowledge workers, (2) the identification of the principal source of tacit knowledge, using the Fuzzy Analytical Hierarchy Process (FAHP) method, implemented in our intelligent system. Knowledge workers may be practitioners, designers and commanders. Nonaka

© Springer International Publishing AG 2017
W. Abramowicz (Ed.): BIS 2017 Workshops, LNBIP 303, pp. 26–36, 2017.
https://doi.org/10.1007/978-3-319-69023-0_3

and Takeuchi [9] furthermore, they combine intellectual powers with substantial competences [4]. We argued with Nonaka and Takeuchi and with Davenport, stating that knowledge workers have the specialised knowledge to come up with or formulate new ideas and that this specialised knowledge is the product of targeted education, experience and competences. Using our personnel usefulness function: Evaluation of Personnel as an Asset method – EPA method, we first create a base of knowledge workers, within an IT company and then, by using the FAHP method, we are then able to identify the main sources of tacit knowledge from this base of knowledge workers.

The motivations for writing this paper are, firstly, IT companies because their value is based on their employees' knowledge. Secondly, this study aims to identify the most crucial source of tacit knowledge within an IT company, as this is the first step in the acquisition and storage of the unique knowledge of that company. Finally, the article presents the implementation of our methodology in an information system, as part of an intelligent system.

The structure of the article is as follows: Sect. 2 presents the results of research in the literature, vis-à-vis identification of the knowledge sources within an IT company. Section 3 explains our methodology, while Sect. 4 presents the implementation of our research results in an information system. Finally, Sect. 5 states the main conclusions and presents future research work.

2 Related Tacit Knowledge Sources in an IT Company

The managers of an IT company should pay special attention to the identification of the source of knowledge if they want to be in control of the knowledge management process. We make the distinction between knowledge which is explicit which can be presented within a company in the form of company documents, patent, reports and such like and knowledge which is tacit, that is, knowledge which is related to the employees in a company. Tacit knowledge plays a crucial role in an IT company [16]. Based on the premise, that tacit knowledge is employee-based, this paper discusses how the use of a dedicated information system can support identification of the main source of tacit knowledge in an IT company. Sources of tacit knowledge, like feedback from customers and suppliers, consultation, analysis-simulation results, observations conducted in real time, analysis of records, demonstrations and training, knowledge audits and audio or video recordings of activities by experienced employees, can all be defined [2, 5, 11].

According to the results of our research (see Fig. 1) we know that managers in IT companies are fully au fait with the importance of the sources of tacit knowledge in the context of the identification of -and capitalisation on- their know-how in completed IT projects. The research data was collected from the managers and chief executive officers of seventeen IT companies as a result of direct meetings/interviews in April-May of 2015. The importance of knowledge sources was assessed by the use of the five-point, Likert Scale in which 1 = strongly disagree and 5 = strongly agree. Figure 1 presents the principal sources of tacit knowledge in manufacturing companies and is based on the results of the research.

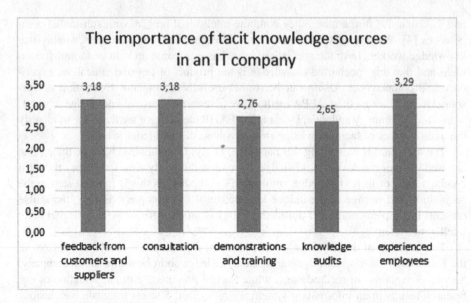

Fig. 1. The importance of tacit knowledge sources in an IT company - results of our own research

We can observe that experienced employees are most important for managers of IT companies, as a source of tacit knowledge; to this end, we have developed a two-stage framework for identifying the main source of tacit knowledge: (1) the identification of knowledge workers using the Evaluation of Personnel as an Asset method – EPA method, (2) the main source for the identification of tacit knowledge using the Fuzzy Analytical Hierarchy Process (FAHP) method.

Our work also highlights the acquisition of knowledge in IT projects, by employees who are engaged in IT projects within an IT company.

We design and develop an intelligent systems for IT companies that enable the storage and exchange of expert knowledge. In this paper, we have presented part of this system but have included the main sources for the identification of tacit knowledge. This part is based on the use of the EPA method, in order to identify knowledge workers in an IT company and select the main sources of tacit knowledge from this base of IT company knowledge workers, using the FAHP method.

3   Model of the Principal Sources in the Identification of Tacit Knowledge – The MTKS Model

The first stage involved in the proposed MTKS model is based on identification of the knowledge workers in an IT company, using the personnel usefulness function (Evaluation of Personnel as an Asset method – EPA method) [13]:

$$F_n = GK + PK + A + E + CI, \text{ where } n \in N \text{ and where} \tag{1}$$

GK = the general knowledge of the nth worker in the company.

PK = the professional knowledge of the nth worker in the company.

A = the professional abilities of the nth worker in the company.

E = the experience of the nth worker in the company.

CI = the capacity for innovation of the nth worker in the company.

To obtain values for each component of the EPA method, the employees in an IT company are required to complete web-based questionnaires.

Based on the results and on algorithmic solutions, values are created for each of the components:- $1 \leq GK \leq 5; 1 \leq PK \leq 5, 1 \leq A \leq 5, 1 \leq E \leq 5, 1 \leq I \leq 5$ for each employee [12].

Based on the solutions, each employee can then be identified as a knowledge worker, if he/she obtains $F_n \geq 17$ grading and is accepted as such, by the company's managers.

According to the second step of our MTKS model, managers in an IT company will then determine the importance of each component of the EPA method for each knowledge worker vis-à-vis their knowledge of IT projects completed in a company, according to the following rules:

- His/her general knowledge is equally important, moderately more important, much more important, most important, compared with his/her professional knowledge.
- His/her general knowledge is equally important, moderately more important, much more important, most important, compared with his/her professional abilities.
- His/her general knowledge is equally important, moderately more important, much more important, most important, compared with his/her experience.
- His/her professional knowledge is equally important, moderately more important, much more important, most important, compared with his/her professional abilities.
- His/her professional knowledge is equally important, moderately more important, much more important, most important, compared with his/her experience.
- His/her professional abilities are equally important, moderately more important, much more important, most important, compared with his/her experience.
- His/her capacity for innovation is equally important, moderately more important, much more important, most important, compared with his/her general knowledge.
- His/her capacity for innovation is equally important, moderately more important, much more important, most important, compared with his/her professional knowledge.
- His/her capacity for innovation is equally important, moderately more important, much more important, most important, compared with his/her professional abilities.
- His/her capacity for innovation is equally important, moderately more important, much more important, most important, compared with his/her compared with his/her experience.

The FAHP (Fuzzy Analytic Hierarchy Process) method was then implemented and used. The FAHP method allows the relative dominance of a particular component of the EPA method to be determined from elements which cannot be measured in the context of the selection of an employee, as the most important source of knowledge in an IT company. According to Nydick and Hill [10], a linguistic variable can be described by a fuzzy number $\tilde{a} = (l, m, u)$ of a triangular fuzzy membership function. The triangular fuzzy number $\tilde{a} = (l, m, u)$ is defined in the set $[l, u]$, and its membership function takes a value equal to 1 at the point m. The fuzzy scale of preferences is strictly defined by Nydick and Hill [10].

The model allows the identification of the main sources of tacit knowledge in an IT company from within a group of knowledge workers, in the context of the selection of those employees having appropriate knowledge regarding completed IT projects. The MTKS model, presented as part of an intelligent system for an IT company is implemented; the next section is then presented.

4 Implementation of the MTKS Model, as a Part of an Intelligent System for an IT Company

Below is an extract from the intelligent system, based on the proposed MTKS model.

Web-questionnaires on knowledge for each component of the EPA method are defined, firstly (see Fig. 2).

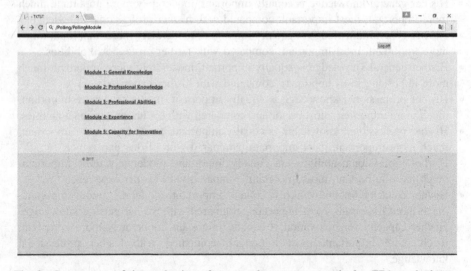

Fig. 2. Components of the evaluation of personnel as an asset method – EPA method, own research

Each employee in the IT company completes the knowledge web-questionnaires for each component of the Evaluation of Personnel as an Asset method – EPA method (see Figs. 3, 4, 5, 6, and 7). Our EPA method concept, necessitates the formulation of a different knowledge questionnaire for the various employees, according to the business processes in each company. Currently, we have created web-questionnaires according to the following business processes defined in an IT company:

- Preparation of new projects.
- Definition of the scope of new projects.
- Creation of new products.
- Improvement to existing products.
- Provision of market analysis.
- Provision of market research.
- Provision of technical research.
- Designing the concept of a new product.
- Creation of a prototype.
- Creation of the final product.
- Strategies to gain market share and best practices.
- Preparing the firm's strategy.
- Planning the firm's development.
- Management of human resources.
- Risk management.
- Control.
- Finding new projects.
- Decision making.
- Provision of support and benefits.
- Participation at meetings.
- Learning.
- Training.
- Administrative Work/Reporting.

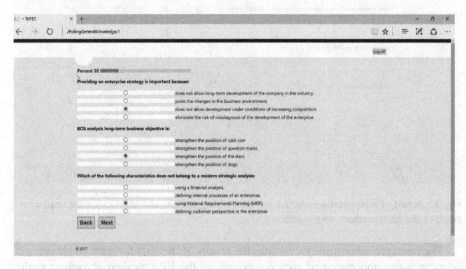

Fig. 3. A part of web-questionnaire for the component general knowledge for the implementation of the EPA method, own research

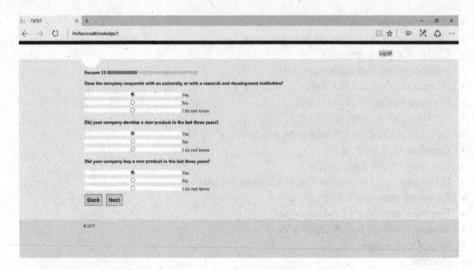

Fig. 4. A part of web-questionnaire for the component professional knowledge for the implementation of the EPA method, own research

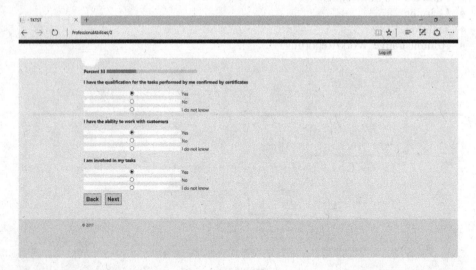

Fig. 5. A part of web-questionnaire for the component professional abilities for the implementation of the EPA method, own research

The manager subsequently evaluates the results of the tests for each employee and determines the importance of each component of the EPA method according to the defined rules – see Sect. 3. By using the FAHP method, the manager is thus able to

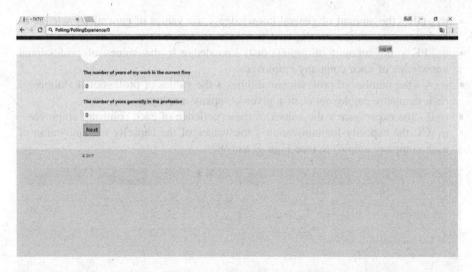

Fig. 6. A part of web-questionnaire for the component experience for the implementation of the EPA method, own research

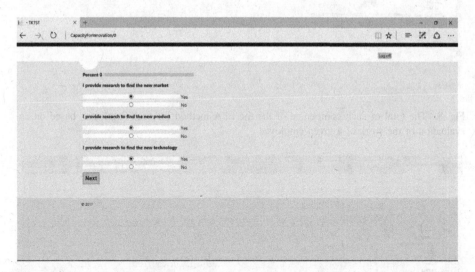

Fig. 7. A part of web-questionnaire for the component capacity for the implementation of the EPA method, own research

evaluate each component of the EPA method with regard to each employee and consequently, is then able to track/define the main sources of tacit knowledge according to the statement: $F'_n \geq 3$, where

$$F' = w_{GK}GK + w_{PK}PK + w_A A + w_E E + w_{CI}CI, \text{ where} \tag{2}$$

- $w_{GK}GK$ - the amount of general knowledge x the values of general knowledge of each company employee.
- $w_{PK}PK$ - the amount of professional knowledge x the values of professional knowledge of each company employee.
- $w_A A$ - the number of professional abilities x the values of professional abilities of each company employee, or of a given company employee.
- $w_E E$ - the experience x the values of the experience of each company employee.
- $w_{CI}CI$ -the capacity for innovation x the values of the capacity for innovation of each company employee (see Figs. 8 and 9).

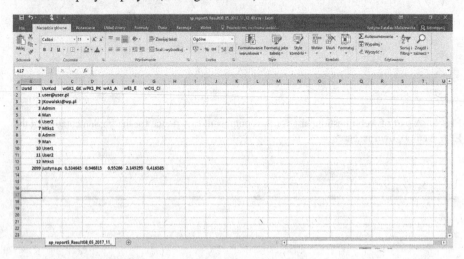

Fig. 8. The total of each component of the the the EPA method for each employee, based on an evaluation of the work of a given employee

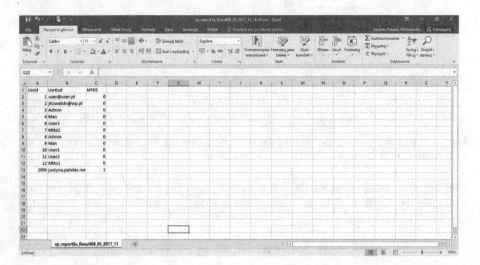

Fig. 9. The main sources in the identification of tacit knowledge in an IT company, as part of an intelligent system

The proposed approach to the identification of the main sources of tacit knowledge in an IT company allows the most important sources of tacit knowledge, in an IT company, to be defined. In a created intelligence system, the methods for acquiring tacit knowledge, vis-à-vis completed projects in a company, are implemented from the MTKS defined. These issues will be developed and discussed in our future work.

5 Conclusion

This study was motivated by the actual needs of managers of IT companies who have a strong desire to introduce new projects in order to be more innovative and competitive on the market. The object of this study was to investigate how managers can be supported in the process of the identification of the main sources of tacit knowledge in an IT company, using the MTKS model proposed. Our paper presents our approach to the identification of the main sources of tacit knowledge in an IT company as a part of an intelligent system. This concept will be further developed in our future work.

As with all studies, this study has certain limitations which further research should aim to overcome. Firstly, this study focusses on IT industries because the intention was to analyse the main sources of tacit knowledge within an IT company. It would be unwise to generalise this approach too broadly in respect of other enterprises. Furthermore, the knowledge web questionnaires were created for specific business processes. So, it would be useful to re-define these knowledge web questionnaires for other business processes. These conclusions and limitations suggest proposals for the direction of future research and the on-going development of our intelligent systems.

References

1. Bell, G.G., Zaheer, A.: Geography, networks, knowledge flows. Organ. Sci. **18**(6), 955–972 (2007)
2. Belussi, F., McDonald F., Borrás, S.: Industrial districts: state of the art review. Research report, Project West–East id: Industrial districts re-location processes. Identifying policies in the perspective of the European Union enlargement. Report (2005). http://cordis.europa.eu/docs/publications/1001/100123911-6_en.pdf. Accessed 03 Nov 2016
3. Chen, C.J., Shih, H.A., Yang, S.Y.: The role of intellectual capital in knowledge transfer. IEEE Trans. Eng. Manag. **56**(3), 402–411 (2009)
4. Davenport, T.H., Prusak, L.: Working Knowledge: How Organizations Manage What They Know. Harvard Business School Press, Boston (1998)
5. Falkenberg, L., Woiceshyn, J., Karagianis, J.: Knowledge sourcing: internal or external? In: Competitiveness and Learning 5th International Conference (2003). http://www2.warwick.ac.uk/fac/soc/wbs/conf/olkc/archive/olk5/papers/paper16.pdf. Accessed 15 Nov 2016
6. Haas, M.R., Cummings, J.N.: Barriers to knowledge seeking within MNC teams: which differences matter most? J. Int. Bus. Stud. **46**, 36–62 (2015)
7. Lev, B., Daum, J.: The dominance of intangible assets: consequences for enterprise management and corporate reporting. Measur. Bus. Excell. **8**(1), 6–17 (2004)

8. Morris, S., Hammond, R., Snell, S.: A microfoundations approach to transnational capabilities: the role of knowledge search in an ever-changing world. J. Int. Bus. Stud. **45**, 405–427 (2014)
9. Nonaka, I., Takeuchi, H.: The Knowledge-Creating Company: How Japanese Companies Create the Dynamics of Innovation. Oxford University Press, Oxford (1995)
10. Nydick, R.L., Hill, R.P.: Using the analytic hierarchy process to structure the supplier selection procedure. Int. J. Purch. Mater. Manag. **28**(2), 31–36 (1992)
11. Patalas-Maliszewska, J., Dudek, A.: A model of a tacit knowledge transformation for the service department in a manufacturing company: a case study. Found. Manag. Int. J. **8**(1), 75–188 (2016)
12. Patalas-Maliszewska, J., Krebs, I.: A model of the tacit knowledge transfer support tool: CKnow-board. In: Dregvaite, G., Damasevicius, R. (eds.) ICIST 2016. CCIS, vol. 639, pp. 30–41. Springer, Cham (2016). doi:10.1007/978-3-319-46254-7_3
13. Patalas-Maliszewska, J.: Knowledge Worker Management: Value Assessment, Methods, and Application Tools. Springer, Heidelberg (2013). doi:10.1007/978-3-642-36600-0
14. Peltokorpi, V., Vaara, E.: Knowledge transfer in multinational corporations: productive and counterproductive effects of language-sensitive recruitment. J. Int. Bus. Stud. **45**, 600–622 (2014)
15. Rosen, B., Furst, S., Blackburn, R.: Overcoming barriers to knowledge sharing in virtual teams. Org. Dyn. **36**, 259–273 (2007)
16. Seidler-de Alwis, R., Hartmann, E.: The use of tacit knowledge within innovative companies: knowledge management in innovative enterprises. J. Knowl. Manag. **12**(1), 133–147 (2008)
17. Singh, J.: Multinational firms and knowledge diffusion: evidence using patent citation data. Acad. Manag. Proc. **59**(3), 649–680 (2004)

Sentiment-Analysis for German Employer Reviews

Jennifer Abel, Katharina Klohs, Holger Lehmann,
and Birger Lantow[✉]

Department of Business Information Systems,
Faculty of Computer Science and Electrical Engineering,
The University of Rostock, Albert-Einstein-Str. 22, 18051 Rostock, Germany
{jennifer.abel,katharina.klohs,holger.lehmann,
birger.lantow}@uni-rostock.de

Abstract. This paper examines the possibilities of sentiment analysis performed on German employer reviews. In times of competition for highly skilled professionals on the German job market, there is a demand for the monitoring of social media and web sites providing employment related information. Compared to mainstream research this implies (1) a focus on German language, (2) employer reputation as a new domain, and (3) employer reviews as a new source possibly showing special linguistic characteristics. General approaches and tools for sentiment analysis and their application to German language are assessed in a first step. Then, selected approaches are evaluated regarding their analysis accuracy based on a data set containing German employer reviews. The results are used to conclude major obstacles, promising approaches and possible prospective research directions in the domain of employer reputation analysis.

Keywords: Sentiment analysis · Recruitment · Social media analysis · Employer reputation · Machine learning

1 Introduction

In 2016, 70% of German information technology companies stated that there is a lack regarding professionals on the job market[1]. The situation in other German industry branches is similar. Thus, there is a competition for skilled workforce on the job market. In consequence, the concepts of social media marketing are approaching human resources departments. The volume of user-generated content in social networks (Twitter or Facebook) as well as in Blogs increases continuously[2]. Additionally, the market of specialized portals that provide employer ratings based on user generated content is growing as well.

---

[1] https://www.bitkom.org/Presse/Pressegrafik/2016/November/Bitkom-Charts-IT-Fachkraefte-14-11-2016-final.pdf.

[2] http://epceurope.eu/wp-content/uploads/2015/09/epc-trends-social-media.pdf.

© Springer International Publishing AG 2017
W. Abramowicz (Ed.): BIS 2017 Workshops, LNBIP 303, pp. 37–48, 2017.
https://doi.org/10.1007/978-3-319-69023-0_4

Web portals like Kununu[3], Jobvoting[4], or Glassdoor[5] offer a platform for writing reviews about employers. In the course of human resources management, the monitoring of the attitude (the sentiment) towards the employer in these portals and also in the rest of the social web is an important element, which is usually controlled manually nowadays.

Next to the evaluation of (semi-)structured data from employer-review-specialized portals, there is also a need of an analysis of unstructured text-data from other sources like Facebook and Twitter. Considering the rising data volume[6], an automation of this process is desired. Here, sentiment analysis plays a major role. Sentiment analysis classifies human communication content regarding positive or negative sentiment [1]. This can be generally applied to all kinds of human communication. In the context of our work we consider textual data only. The research in this area has progressed in recent years [2]. Especially for text mining, some procedures are established and a lot of tools are available, which can be used for the task of sentiment analysis.

The goal of this paper is to examine the possibilities for an analysis of German employer reviews with reference to existing sentiment-analysis approaches. This represents a transfer to a new domain compared to known approaches like assessments of movies or products, and evaluations of brands. Besides the domain related content, a different language style in this domain may lead to different results compared to earlier research. Furthermore, there is a transfer regarding the used language. Compared to German language, English is spoken by a lot more people and shows a simpler grammar. Worldwide, English is spoken by 1.5 billion people compared to only 185 million people that speak German[7]. Thus, research and tool support mainly focuses on English language. The following research questions addressed in our paper:

1. What kind of effort is necessary to apply sentiment analysis methods to a certain language (German) and domain (Employer Reputation)?
2. How well do the selected approaches evaluate German employer ratings in comparison?
3. What conclusions can be generally drawn for the selected domain?

Generally, this study has an explorative character. Thus, the observed phenomena and problems are in focus and not the significance of differences in performance or the estimation of effort. In order to answer the research questions, this work is structured as follows. In the next section, basic approaches for sentiment analysis are briefly explained. This serves for the classification and description of available tools, and for the identification of required language specific artefacts. This is followed by an experiment (Sect. 3) and a summary together with the outlook in Sect. 4.

---

[3] www.kununu.com.

[4] www.jobvoting.de.

[5] www.glassdoor.com.

[6] http://www.smartinsights.com/social-media-marketing/social-media-strategy/new-global-social-media-research/.

[7] https://www.statista.com/statistics/266808/the-most-spoken-languages-worldwide/.

2   Sentiment Analysis Approaches

In order to classify approaches for sentiment analysis, a distinction is made regarding the object of analysis (classification level) and the used technology.

According to [3, 11] sentiment analysis approaches can be divided in the following classification levels: (1) word, (2) sentence, and (3) document. The word-level inspects individual words for their polarity and usually distinguishes between positive, negative and neutral words. At the sentence-level the polarity of each individual sentence is assessed by aggregating the words' polarities. At document level sentence polarities are aggregated for a complete document. Several rules can be applied for that aggregation. The assessment on word or sentence level can identify different sentiments in different parts of a larger structure (sentence or document).

Regarding the used technology, two main approaches for sentiment analysis exist [1]: Machine learning and the lexicon-based approach. A third technique is the hybrid approach, which is a combination of machine learning and lexicon-based techniques. This is mentioned here for completeness, but not further explained.

2.1   Machine Learning

Machine learning approaches can generally be divided into supervised and unsupervised learning. In the case of supervised learning, the goal is to learn a mapping of input values to output values while the correct output values are known [4]. This is done using a training data set. A learning algorithm learns a model by minimizing the mapping bias compared to the correct mapping provided by the training data set [5]. For the selected application domain, this approach means the generation of appropriate training data by collecting German-language employer evaluations and classifying them manually with regard to their sentiment.

Prior to the application of machine learning, generally a pre-processing of the texts is required in order to perform feature selection and feature extraction [11]. A feature in this context is an attribute (e.g. frequency of a certain term) whose value is used for classification. Pre-processing typically includes tokenization, stemming/lemmatizing, filtering stop-words, and pruning for feature selection, resulting in a word vector. For feature extraction, a measure for the importance of the single words in the vector for each text/document has to be calculated. The *Term Frequency-Inverse Document Frequency* (TF-IDF) is a metric that multiplies the two quantities Term Frequency (TF, number of term occurances) and Inverse Document Frequency (IDF, inverse of the number of documents that contain the term) and has proven to be well fitted for text classification [7]. The TF-IDF-measure is used for the evaluation in Sect. 3. For these steps, there is a good tool support. However, setting the parameters for text-pre-processing can have a large influence on the performance of machine learning technologies (see Sect. 3).

In the area of supervised learning, there are a variety of usable technologies. Popular and often supported approaches are *Bayes Classifiers*, *Support Vector Machines* (*SVM*), *Decision Trees*, and *Artificial Neural Networks* (see also [8]). The *Bayes Classification* is based on the Bayes' law, which can be used to calculate the conditional probability of an event under a particular condition. The classifier represents each object by an n-dimensional vector, where n is the number of features of an object. Accordingly, an object is assigned to the class it belongs to with the highest probability [9]. *SVMs* construct a plane which separates the instances of the classes in the feature space as best as possible. Such planes, however, are usually in a multi-dimensional space. Thus, their determination can cause large computational effort [8]. *Decision Trees* are a widespread method, which is used in many areas. The CART method, the CHAID method or the ID3 algorithm are the most common forms [10]. The advantage of *Decision Trees* is the simplicity in understanding and interpreting the results [13]. However, they are not well fitted for classification tasks with a high number of features such as natural language texts. *Artificial Neural Networks* are information-processing systems whose structure and mode of operation are similar to those of nervous systems, especially to the brain of animals and humans. There is the possibility of supervised as well as unsupervised learning. *Artificial Neural Networks* are characterized by a high computational effort.

In the case of unsupervised learning, the output values are not known and only the input values are available. Therefore, it is necessary to determine regularities in the input values [6]. These learning methods are generally unsuitable for the chosen application, because the resulting clusters do not need to have any relation to the expressed sentiment.

2.2   Lexicon-Based Analysis

Ravi and Ravi describe in [11] a lexicon as a sentiment vocabulary. Thus, the elements of a vocabulary are tagged with a polarity (positive or negative), as well as a degree of strength. The generation of a lexicon starts with a seed word, which is tested for synonyms and antonyms by means of a lexicon such as WordNet. Based on the seed, polarity and its strength can be derived for synonyms and antonyms. The idea of the lexicon-based sentiment analysis is to search for positive and negative words within a sentence and to use these occurrences for sentence classification. This should also include the sentiment strength. Sentences like: *"This book is good."* and *"This book is excellent."* could be not distinguished regarding sentiment otherwise. Therefore, strength values are used for weighting the single word sentiments. This rule cannot be applied straight forward because there are constructs like negations or amplification words. Reinforcing words such as *"very, a little, quite, ..."* have no positive or negative polarity, but they reinforce or weaken the following words in a sentence in their sentiment. The use of a negation in a sentence can lead to a negation of the complete sentence. Individual sentences containing both positive and negative parts are also problematic. These are predominantly sentences with binding words such as *"but, although"* [12]. These issues are addressed by rules that base on sentence and terms structure.

2.3   Problems of Sentiment-Analysis

There may occur various problems using the mentioned methods of sentiment analysis. A major problem of the lexicon-based approach is that it cannot be predicted how the sentiment is expressed. For example, it is difficult to define the sentiment orientation of domain specific expressions. Thus, a "long battery lifetime" is considered to be positive, but a "long waiting time" is considered negative [15]. However, a context or domain specific lexicon may help to solve this problem if the context is known.

In the case of machine learning approaches, the problem is the model fitting to a certain domain. If a system has been trained with a corpus of movie reviews, it will deliver less accurate results with regard to, for example, employer evaluations. A solution would be to train the model for all possible application domains [16]. However, this increases effort. Both methods have limited performance regarding the detection of irony and sarcasm. Even humans have difficulties here. A lot of context information has to be considered and interpreted correctly in order to detect these phenomena. For example, the simple statement "This is awesome." can be connoted positive but also negative as a sarcastic statement [17].

3   Experimental Evaluation of Analysis Methods

This study focuses on the effort for adapting or creating classifiers for the given domain and language and on the accuracy of sentiment analysis. This addresses research questions 1 and 3 presented in the introduction.

Although the used tools may have an influence on the results, the general process of implementing one of the analysis approaches for a certain application domain is tool independent as well as general assumptions regarding classification accuracy. Section 3.1 briefly describes the tool selection process and its results. The data set used for the assessment is discussed in Sect. 3.2. The actual execution of the experiment is then described (Sect. 3.3). At last, the results are evaluated (Sect. 3.4).

3.1   Sentiment Analysis Tool Selection

The search for appropriate sentiment analysis tools was based on the surveys by Ravi and Ravi [11] and Pang and Lee [18]. Additionally, a Google-search for German sentiment analysis tools has been conducted. Overall 35 tools have been found. 17 were able to process German texts. Only two met the criteria (a) availability as open source and (b) German language support. Thus, RapidMiner has been selected for the evaluation of machine learning based approaches and SentiStrength for lexicon-based approaches.

RapidMiner is an open-source data-mining-tool. It offers many different analytical methods, including simple statistical evaluations, correlation and regression analyses, classification and clustering [19]. Besides operators for data extraction and text analysis (tokenizer, stemmer etc.) there are operators provided that implemented machine learning algorithms such as *Decision Tree, Artificial Neural Nets, SVM*, and *Naïve Bayes*. An analysis at sentence and document level is possible [19].

SentiStrength is a lexicon-based application for sentiment-analysis of short texts. It was originally developed for English language. The aim of sentiment analysis with SentiStrength is to calculate a cumulative document polarity based on the polarity of single words and expressions [25]. Thus, in the lexicon, there is a word list associated with positive and negative polarity values. The result of an analysis is the strength of negative and positive polarity in a given document [21, 25]. According to [25] two scales are used, because psychological research showed that people process positive and negative sentiments at the same time. This can occur especially when a person has mixed feelings about a situation and weighs the advantages and disadvantages. Using SentiStrength, a text has a positive polarity if the analysis value is between 2 and 5 (negative between −2 and −5) [21]. Accordingly, the values 1 and −1 are neutral and are ignored in the calculation.

The lexicon originally came from manually annotated MySpace comments regarding positive/negative polarity [25]. Later, the lexicon resource has been extended with annotated data of the General Inquirer Lexicon[8] (LIWC) [15]. SentiStrength supports rules for negation and amplification of sentiments. The German version of SentiStrength was developed by Pirker and Kyewsk [21]. It is based on a translation of the LIWC data in 2011 using the Google translator. Furthermore, manual corrections and additions have been made. A similar process for creating a language specific lexicon is described by Momtazi in [12] for German language and by Cirqueira et al. for Portuguese language in [24].

3.2 Example Data Set

In order to check the correctness of sentiment analysis, an annotated data set for training and/or comparison is needed (see Sect. 2). Manual annotation is very time-consuming and contradicts the concept of automation behind the analysis approaches [22].

Thus, the employer evaluation portal Kununu has been selected as the data source. Besides a textual comment, users can rate the employers by a five-star rating scale. These ratings on a Likert scale can be used for automated annotation/classification regarding the sentiment and reduces the effort for manual coding. In contrast to the majority of social media content, comments on Kununu are rather long and contain less colloquial language. Emoticons and letter repetitions are seldom used, which therefore do not have to be considered further in automated processing. This reflects the domain specific language style.

A training data set of 1200 records was collected manually. Thelwall et al. recommend in [21] a size of 2000 records for training and evaluation. As shown later in Sect. 3.3, this number does not need to be matched to draw conclusions. Although a larger data set results in better outcomes, this effect is small. The following criteria have been applied for record selection: (1) Even distribution of comment types (pos./neg.) per employer, (2) German language comments, (3) Clear polarity regarding the star rating (see below). On average the use of 28 comments per company was noticed.

In order to classify the data regarding positive/negative polarity, the available star ratings on the basis of a Likert scale were used. The individual comments were classified as positive if the given number of stars was greater than or equal to 4. A negative classification was carried out at less than 2.5 stars. The discrepancy in the selection results from the fact that it is not possible to assign 0 stars (the minimum is 1). In

---

[8] http://liwc.wpengine.com/.

addition, significantly more comments were positively evaluated by users. The comments having a rating between 2.5 and 4 stars were not included in the training data set to draw a clear boundary between positive and negative.

As recommended by [12], an additional test data set of 120 records (equally distributed positive/negative, 10% of the training data size) has been used for the evaluation of classification accuracy.

Using machine learning, the employer name within the comments may be determined by the learning algorithm as the best discriminator for positive or negative polarity. Hence, a certain company is a "bad" employer and thus all comments including its name are negative. To avoid this overfitting of the learned model, company names have been used as stop-words and are thus filtered out for sentiment analysis. This filtering is generally not required for lexicon based approaches.

3.3 Implementation of the Experiment

As already described, several learning algorithms are available in RapidMiner. For the evaluation and comparison of the automated classification, *Naïve Bayes* and *SVM* have been selected. *Naïve Bayes* is a very efficient approach which can perform very well in certain situations while the *SVM* is outstanding regarding accuracy [13]. Considering other approaches supported by RapidMiner - decision trees show a poor performance for text analysis and artificial neural network consume a lot computing resources [13].

The pre-processing of texts was done using standard RapidMiner components. Figure 1 shows the used process. For stemming, which needs a language specific algorithm, RapidMiner implements the stemmer by Caumanns presented in [14]. The classification accuracy had a large sensitivity regarding the lower bound for the pruning step (removing infrequent terms). Including words that occurred in less than 0.5% of the comments resulted in a drop in classification accuracy. A lot of these words was equally distributed in positive and negative comments, but was used by the machine learners to determine positive polarity. The reason was the higher term frequency (TF) in positive comments due to their generally lower length. An optimum for the lower bound was manually found at 2%. Thus, all words that occurred in less than 2% of the comments have been excluded from the word vector.

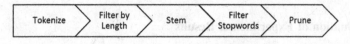

Fig. 1. Text pre-processing in RapidMiner

The provision of training data is a main driver for the effort caused by supervised machine learning. Thus, the influence of different training data set sizes on classification accuracy was investigated by learning the *SVM* and the *Naïve Bayes* classifiers with 300, 600, 900 and last 1200 records of the available training data. Furthermore, the size of the used word vector which equals to the number of features used for classification was monitored. If there is a saturation regarding the number of features, an increase of the training data set size will have little effect on accuracy.

In order to map the 2 scale rating of SentiStrength to a positive/negative classification, all comments that showed a negative polarity have been classified negative, regardless of the value in the positive scale. SentiStrength as a lexicon based tool does not need a training. Thus, the effect of the training data set size has not been evaluated. However, for the context of the given domain there are specific words that have a positive or negative polarity which is not the case in their general usage. The problem of context-relatedness has already been discussed in Sect. 2.3. For example, "pressure" is negative in a work context and "training" is positive. Thus, the effect of collecting such terms from a set of 60 comments training data and adding them to the lexicon in order to create a context specific lexicon has been evaluated. There was no change in the accuracy. Although there was a certain qualitative saturation (newly assessed comments did not provide data for new lexicon entries), the new words in the lexicon have not been found in the test data.

The accuracy of the classification results is examined by means of the three evaluation measures Recall, Precision and F-Measure [26]. They are commonly used in data analysis [23, 27–30]. The values are calculated regarding the negative polarity classification because the determination of negative comments is important in the given application domain. Calculation is based on numbers of correctly (true positive - tp and true negative - tn) and falsely (false negative - fn and false positive - fp) categorized comments. The formulas for determining the negative polarity class recall and precision values are listed below.

$$Recall = \frac{tn}{fp+tn} \quad Precision = \frac{tn}{tn+fn} \quad F-Measure = \frac{2*R*P}{P+R} \quad (1)$$

The recall measures how many of the actually negative comments in the database were found in relation to the number of all negative comments in the database. The precision is the ratio of the correctly negatively classified comments to the total number of all negatively classified comments. The F-Measure is the harmonic mean of recall and the precision. It serves as a general measure for classification performance. Figure 2 shows the resulting values for the different training set sizes. Table 1 compares the tested methods with their obtained values for Precision, Recall and F-Measure regarding negative polarity in percent.

3.4   Evaluation of Experimental Results

Looking at research question 1 - What kind of effort is necessary for an analysis of German-language texts? – a first answer is that a lexicon based approach can reach a good performance without any effort regarding the creation of a training data set or a lexicon, as long as a general language specific sentiment lexicon is available. When it comes to machine learning, a next question comes up regarding the effort - How does the size of the training data set influence the accuracy of the machine learning approaches?

There is a stable performance of *SVM* around 80% F-Measure. The *Naïve Bayes* accuracy in contrast increases with an increasing training data size but does not match the SVM performance. Based on these conclusions and the other experimental results,

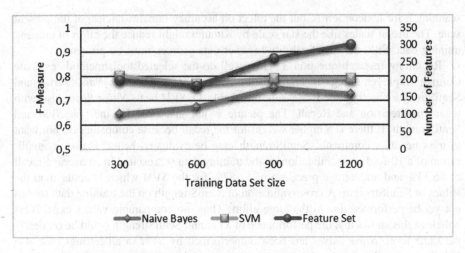

Fig. 2. F-Measure and feature set size over training data set size

Table 1. Performance of sentiment analysis approaches

	Recall	Precision	F-Measure
Naïve Bayes	66.04	81.40	72.92
SVM	71.70	88.37	79.17
SentiStrength	83.02	69.84	75.86

some qualitative assumptions regarding the application effort of the approaches can be made. For *SVM*, a small training data set already seems to allow good analysis accuracy. *Naïve Bayes* needs a larger training data set but still does not match *SVM* performance.

However, there are indicators that the performance of both *SVM* and lexicon based approach can be improved spending effort on data preparation. Looking at the development of the feature set size with regard to the training data set size (Fig. 1), there is a drop from 300 to 600 training data records. This indicates a high diversity in the data. The diversity shows this effect here because of the small sample size. Furthermore, there is an increase in the feature set size from 600 to 1200 training data records, thus no saturation can be seen. The latter again indicates a diversity in the data, assuming more relevant words in an even larger training data set. At last, the extension of the SentiStrength lexicon and the missing effect on accuracy showed, that a diverse vocabulary is used to comment on employers. The selected lexicon elements seem to be semantically relevant but have a low document frequency. The reasons could be a company specific vocabulary or different groups of portal users having different professional backgrounds.

In consequence a larger training data set needs to be used for *SVM* training or a larger amount of comments needs to be screened for relevant lexicon entries in order to have a measurable positive effect on classification accuracy. Regarding the effort of improving the accuracy, manual classification of a text seems to pose less effort than scanning it for lexicon terms, but the effect on accuracy remains unclear at the present state. The use of scales like the star scale by Kununu might reduce the effort of creating training data. Still, the transferability to other data sources must be proven.

Regarding research question 3 "How well do the selected tools/methods evaluate German employer ratings in comparison?", the *SVM* outperforms *Naïve Bayes* and SentiStrength based on the F-Measure (see Table 1). *SVM* beats *Naïve Bayes* also with regard to Precision and Recall. The picture is not that clear for the pair *SVM* and SentiStrength. If there is a higher weight for the recall because companies do not want to miss negative comments, SentiStrength may be evaluated better. However, application of a 10-fold cross-validation on the training data set resulted in an average recall of 86.33% and an average precision of 81.83% for the *SVM* which is better than the values of SentiStrength. A cross-validation of SentiStrength on the training data set has not yet be performed due to the large effort. Thus, no comparable values exist. Nevertheless, this shows that the performance of *SVM* and SentiStrength could be on nearly the same level. *Naïve Bayes* has been outperformed by *SVM* in all settings (see also Fig. 2).

4 Conclusion and Outlook

This work focused on the possibility of automated sentiment-analysis of German-language comments from the career portal Kununu. Machine learning in the form of *SVM* and lexicon based approaches in the form of SentiStrength showed a good classification performance. There are some indicators that SVM outperforms SentiStrength in the present domain. Nevertheless, following the experimental evaluation in Sect. 3, the accuracy of both methods can be improved by manually preparing data for training or by lexicon construction. However, a cost/benefit estimation seems to be difficult. The rule of thumb by Thelwall et al. in [21] that supposes 2000 records for training data set size is of little help here. Thus, future research should investigate possible guidelines. A way might be provided by the assessment of word frequencies, the use of context information for data selection or by methods for feature selection [31].

Considering the specificities of the domain, a future task will be the evaluation whether the generally shorter length of positive comments is typical for the domain.

Considering the possibility of assessing user provided classification for automated training as in the case of Kununu's star rating, the application accuracy of the trained model for other sources needs to be assessed. Some bias may be induced by the practise of users to add some positive comments to a negative rating and vice versa.

For future research, an automated content analysis in addition to the sentiment analysis may be interesting. This could help to plan actions based on the evaluation of negative comments. The structure of the comments (headlines/paragraphs) could be included in the analysis here. Furthermore, the general sentiment classification might be improved by using headlines like "Pros" and "Cons".

In principle, it remains questionable whether the achieved classification quality is sufficient for practical acceptance in the selected application area. There are therefore several directions for future investigations. On the one hand, it is necessary to determine from which classification accuracy is perceived as sufficient (beneficial) for practical use. Then it has to be clarified whether and how the accuracy (possibly by hybrid methods) can be raised to a corresponding level.

References

1. Heyer, G.: Text Mining und Text Mining Services. eDITion, 1/2010:7–10 (2010)
2. Dashtipour, K., Poria, S., Hussain, A., et al.: Multilingual sentiment analysis: state of the art and independent comparison of techniques. Cogn. Comput. **8**(4), 775 (2016)
3. Medhat, W., Hassan, A., Korashy, H.: Sentiment analysis algorithms and applications: a survey. Ain Shams Eng. J. **5**(4), 1093–1113 (2014)
4. Marsland, S.: Machine Learning - An Algorithmic Perspective. CRC Press, Boca Raton (2015)
5. Dietterich, T.G.: Ensemble methods in machine learning. In: Kittler, J., Roli, F. (eds.) MCS 2000. LNCS, vol. 1857, pp. 1–15. Springer, Heidelberg (2000). doi:10.1007/3-540-45014-9_1
6. Lämmel, U., Cleve, J.: Künstliche Intelligenz. Carl Hanser Verlag GmbH Co. KG, Munich (2012)
7. Baeza-Yates, R., Ribeiro-Neto, B.: Modern Information Retrieval. Addison Wesley, Boston (1999). (Chap. 3)
8. Cherkassky, V., Mulier, F.M.: Learning from Data: Concepts, Theory, and Methods. Wiley, Hoboken (2007)
9. Domingos, P., Pazzani, M.: On the optimality of the simple bayesian classifier under zero-one loss. Mach. Learn. **29**(2), 103–130 (1997)
10. Rokach, L., Maimon, O.: Top-down induction of decision trees classifiers - a survey. IEEE Trans. Syst. Man Cybern. Part C **35**(4), 476–487 (2005)
11. Ravi, K., Ravi, V.: A survey on opinion mining and sentiment analysis: tasks, approaches and applications. Knowl. Based Syst. **89**, 14–46 (2015)
12. Momtazi, S.: Fine-grained German sentiment analysis on social media. In: Proceedings of the 9th International Conference on Language Resources and Evaluation, pp. 1215–1220 (2012)
13. Khan, A., Baharudin, B., Lee, L.H., Khan, K.: A review of machine learning algorithms for text-documents classification. J. Adv. Inf. Technol. **1**(1), 4–20 (2010)
14. Caumanns, J.: A Fast and Simple Stemming Algorithm for German Words. Published in: Department of computer science at the free university of Berlin, pp. 1–10 (1999)
15. Thelwall, M., Buckley, K., Paltoglou, G.: Sentiment strength detection for social web. J. Am. Soc. Inform. Sci. Technol. **63**(1), 163–173 (2012)
16. Blitzer, J., et al.: Biographies, bollywood, boom-boxes and blenders: domain adaptation for sentiment classification. In: ACL, pp. 440–447 (2007)
17. Maynard, D., Greenwood, M.A.: Who cares about sarcastic tweets? Investigating the impact of sarcasm on sentiment analysis. In: LREC, pp. 4238–4243 (2014)
18. Pang, B., Lee, L.: Opinion Mining and Sentiment Analysis. Found. Trends® Inf. Retr. **2**(1–2), 1–135 (2008). 4.1.2 Subjectivity Detection and Opinion Identification
19. Land, S., Fischer, S.: Rapid miner 5 - rapid miner in academic use (2012). http://docs.rapidminer.com/resources/. Accessed 22 May 2016
20. Shalunts, G., Backfried, G.: SentiSAIL: sentiment analysis in English, German and Russian. In: Perner, P. (ed.) MLDM 2015. LNCS, vol. 9166, pp. 87–97. Springer, Cham (2015). doi:10.1007/978-3-319-21024-7_6

21. Thelwall, M., Buckley, K., Paltoglou, G., Cai, D., Kappas, A.: SentiStrength (2010). http://sentistrength.wlv.ac.uk/. Accessed 16 May 2016
22. Esuli, A., Sebastiani, F.: SENTIWORDNET: a publicly available lexical resource for opinion mining. In: Proceedings of the 5th Conference on Language Resources and Evaluation, pp. 417–422 (2006)
23. Remus, R., Quasthoff, U., Heyer, G.: SentiWS – a publicly available German-language resource for sentiment analysis. In: Proceedings of the 7th International Conference on Language Resources and Evaluation, LREC, pp. 1168–1171 (2010)
24. Cirqueira, D., Jacob, A., Lobato, F., de Santana, A.L., Pinheiro, M.: Performance evaluation of sentiment analysis methods for Brazilian Portuguese. In: Abramowicz, W., Alt, R., Franczyk, B. (eds.) BIS 2016. LNBIP, vol. 263, pp. 245–251. Springer, Cham (2017). doi:10.1007/978-3-319-52464-1_22
25. Thelwall, M., Buckley, K., Paltoglou, G., Cai, D.: Sentiment strength detection in short informal text. J. Am. Soc. Inform. Sci. Technol. 61(12), 2544–2558 (2010)
26. Hripcsak, G., Rothschild, A.: Agreement, the F-measure, and reliability in information retrieval. J. Am. Med. Inform. Assoc. 12(3), 296–298 (2005)
27. Balahur, A., Perea-Ortega, J.M.: Sentiment analysis system adaptation for multilingual processing: the case of tweets. Inf. Process. Manag. 51(4), 547–556 (2015)
28. Kumar, N., Srinathan, K., Varma, V.: Using Wikipedia anchor text and weighted clustering coefficient to enhance the traditional multi-document summarization. In: Gelbukh, A. (ed.) CICLing 2012. LNCS, vol. 7182, pp. 390–401. Springer, Heidelberg (2012). doi:10.1007/978-3-642-28601-8_33
29. Scharkow, M.: Thematic content analysis using supervised machine learning: an empirical evaluation using German online news. Qual. Quant. 47(2), 761–773 (2011)
30. Scholz, T., Conrad, S., Wolters, I.: Comparing different methods for opinion mining in newspaper articles. In: Bouma, G., Ittoo, A., Métais, E., Wortmann, H. (eds.) NLDB 2012. LNCS, vol. 7337, pp. 259–264. Springer, Heidelberg (2012). doi:10.1007/978-3-642-31178-9_31
31. Bolón-Canedo, V., Sánchez-Maroño, N., Alonso-Betanzos, A.: A review of feature selection methods on synthetic data. Knowl. Inf. Syst. 34(3), 483–519 (2013). doi:10.1007/s10115-012-0487-8

Product Knowledge Management Support for Customer-Oriented System Configuration

Alexander Smirnov[1,2], Nikolay Shilov[1,2(✉)], Andreas Oroszi[3],
Mario Sinko[3], and Thorsten Krebs[4]

[1] SPIIRAS, 14 Line 39, 199178 St. Petersburg, Russia
{smir,nick}@iias.spb.su
[2] ITMO University, Kronverkskiy pr. 49, 197101 St. Petersburg, Russia
[3] Festo AG & Co., Ruiter Straße 82, 73734 Esslingen, Germany
{oro,sni}@de.festo.com
[4] encoway GmbH, Buschhöhe 2, 28357 Bremen, Germany
krebs@encoway.de

Abstract. Due to the changes in global markets, companies strive for attracting and retaining customers in various ways. The paper investigates the problem of product configuration knowledge management in a customer-oriented way and how it has been solved. The authors' vision of required improvements in business processes and knowledge-based systems at the considered company is shared. Nevertheless, the presented work can give significant input to achieve benefits for component manufacturers that tend to become system vendors in general.

Keywords: Knowledge management · Customer view · Application view · Automation

1 Introduction

Due to the changes in global markets, companies strive for attracting and retaining customers in various ways [1, 2]. The situation is the same in every market where there is a long history in the regarding type of products. Multiple product manufacturers and vendors are present and there is not much room for new products, unless they are really innovative. The markets are shrinking and companies striving for attracting and retaining customers see service provision as a new path towards profits and growth.

Achievements in the area of artificial intelligence (AI) open new possibilities for increasing customer satisfaction from customer-driven design to reduced lead-time. The current wave of progress and enthusiasm for AI began around 2010, driven by three mutually reinforcing factors: the availability of big data from sources including e-commerce, businesses, social media, science, and government; which provided raw material for dramatically improved machine learning approaches and algorithms; which in turn relied on the capabilities of more powerful computers [3]. Therefore, adaptation of information & knowledge management in companies to the new trends is mandatory to succeed in the current situation.

W. Abramowicz (Ed.): BIS 2017 Workshops, LNBIP 303, pp. 49–58, 2017.
https://doi.org/10.1007/978-3-319-69023-0_5

Today, in the era of Internet of Things, "products generate a large amount of information during their lifecycle. … Several tools of product lifecycle management have been developed in the last years to address this issue, but they are rarely exploited by companies, especially SMEs" [4]. The presented research is aimed to address the 3Vs of big data, which are considered as major pillars of efficient information & knowledge management: volume, variety, and velocity [5]. Recently, there have appeared multiple ideas on increasing the number of Vs, however, "they only bring big data into the realm of traditional data processing and analytics" [6]. The volume and velocity in the discussed work are dealt with through incorporating software services aimed not only to complement the products (offering customers product-service systems instead of pure hardware systems) but also to accumulate usage statistics for further analysis. This makes it possible to better understand customers' needs and indirectly involve them into the product and system design processes ("customer-driven design"). The ontology-based knowledge representation facilitates solving the problem of variety.

The paper is based on the analysis and modification of the knowledge management processes related to system configuration and engineering at the automation equipment producer Festo AG & Co KG. Festo is a worldwide provider of automation technology for factory and process automation with wide assortments of products (more than 30 000–40 000 products of approximately 700 types, with various configuration possibilities) ranging from simple products to complex systems.

Around the world, 61 Festo national companies and 250 regional offices in 176 countries ensure that advice, service, delivery quality, and reliability precisely meet customer needs in all global industrial regions. Today, more than 300,000 industrial customers in 200 industry segments worldwide rely on Festo's problem-solving competency. It produces pneumatic and electronic automation equipment and products for various process industries in 11 Global Production Centres and 28 National Service Centres [7].

The paper investigates the problem of system configuration knowledge management in a customer-oriented way and the how it has been solved. Implementing such an application-system view addresses the problem of designing the customer view on system selection, configuration, and usage, i.e. defining user experience by "talking in a customer-understandable language" and addressing customer's application problems.

Obviously, considering the company's scale, processing data about products sold to each customer necessarily deals with the big data. The paper shares the vision of the authors of required improvements in business processes and knowledge-based systems at the considered company related system configurations to address the 3Vs of big data. Though the research results are based on the analysis of one company, the presented work can give significant input to achieve benefits for component manufacturers that tend to become system vendors in general.

The remaining part of the paper is structured as follows. The next section describes the research methodology applied. Then, the approach centralised around the new configuration view is proposed. It is followed by the description of the corresponding changes in company's IT systems. Section 5 presents the case study example. Section 6 outlines the major findings obtained. Some summarizing remarks are presented in the Conclusion.

2 Research Methodology

The used gap analysis methodology [8, 9] was implemented through the following steps. First, the analysis of the current organisation of the information & knowledge management in the company was carried out. Then, the expert estimation of the company benchmark was done. Based on this, the comparison of the present and future business process and knowledge management organisation was done resulting in creating corresponding process matrixes. This has made it possible to identify major gaps between the present and the future business organization, analyse these and define strategies to overcome these gaps.

Research efforts in the area of information management show that information & knowledge needs of a particular employee depend on his/her tasks and responsibilities. Even within one company representatives of different roles like product managers, sales personnel, etc. have different needs when interacting with an application like a system configurator. However, if managers or sales representatives, for example, might know about the products and are able to configure by deciding on technical facts, the customer, usually doesn't know about the technical details of the company's products or even what kind of product he/she may use to solve his/her application problem. This is the reason why technical product details should be hidden from the customer under the application layer. As a result, the customer-oriented configuration process has to be based on the system application.

3 Application View

As it was mentioned above, the customer-oriented system view comes from the application side. After defining the application area, configuration rules and constraints to the system are defined. They are followed by characteristics and system structure definition. Finally, the apps (software applications) enriching the product functionality or improving its reliability and maintenance can be defined. The same applies to the sales stage.

As a result, implementing such application-constraints-system view addresses the problem of designing the customer view on product selection, configuration and processing (defining user experience, "talking in a customer-understandable language") [10].

Based on different complexity levels, the company's products can be classified as simple discrete components, configurable products, or system configurations. The major goals are (1) reducing the effort in producing products and (2) reducing the time-to-delivery to the customer. For this purpose, three levels of complexity are differentiated:

- PTO – pick to order: A product is order-neutrally pre-fabricated and sold as a discrete product. This means that no configuration is necessary to identify the correct combination of components. The different combinations already exist and for the customer it is a selection process rather than a configuration process. No order-specific production is required.

- ATO – assemble to order: The different components a product can be composed of are pre-fabricated but the correct combination of components is left open for order clearing process. The product itself is order-specifically produced from these existing components.
- ETO – engineer to order: A product is based on a known set of pre-fabricated components (like in the ATO scenario) but the specific customer need requires additional engineering activity. In this case, new components need to be engineered, constructed, and fabricated in order to fulfil a customer order and product the order-specific product.

Both goals (reducing the effort in producing products and reducing the time-to-delivery to the customer) should be reached by having less engineering activity (ETO) but more products that can be assembled based on a pre-defined modular system (ATO). In this sense, it is intended to make use of the "economies of scale". Products of different complexity require distinct handling in the process from request to delivery.

Of course, the selection and configuration of these different types needs to be addressed accordingly. However, the customer should not be aware of this distinction. To the customer, the sales process should always "feel" the same.

As it was mentioned, different information & knowledge needs of different roles (product managers, sales personnel, customers, etc.) are the reason to hide the technical product and service details under the application layer. In addition, the selection of the right product for solving the application problem can be based on a mapping between the application layer and a (hidden) technical product layer. In the optimal case, a customer does not notice whether he/she is selecting a discrete product, configuring a complex system, and so on.

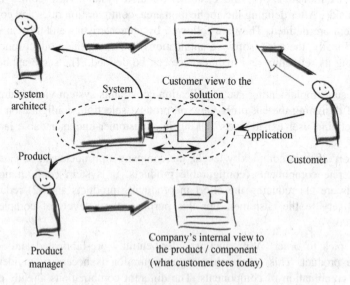

Fig. 1. The shift from the product view to the system view.

As a result, the overall concept of customer-centric view on the products has been formulated as shown in Fig. 1. It includes the introduced above new role of "System architect" responsible for the holistic view to the system and its configuration, description of its functionality and applications, and designing a customer view to it.

4 Changes in IT Systems

The changing requirements on business processes also induce changing requirements on IT systems.

In today's world, most companies do system specification with MS Word documents or similar approaches. These documents are handed over to construction. Construction hands over other data, e.g. technical characteristics via PDM systems or CAD files, to manufacturing, and so on. At the time a sales channel is set up for the new system, the initial data from product specification is lost. In the world of big data, this approach cannot survive. Thus, a new requirement for effectively setting up sales configurators and after-sales support is a continuous database. Knowledge about the system's application domain should be formally acquired already in the early phases of new system development.

A modelling environment must be capable of designing modular system and product architecture. This means that using such an environment, it must be possible to reuse single product models in the scope of system configurations and assign product or system models to application knowledge. This requires the definition of well-formed product model interfaces to allow for modularity. Such interfaces enable a black-box approach, in which all products or modules implementing this interface can be chosen for the complex product/system; i.e. they become interchangeable. For the customer the complex details of product models on lower levels of the system architecture remain invisible. The customer decides based on the visible characteristics of the black-box.

Finally yet importantly, it is also important to support multi-user activities on the different parts of product, system and application models without losing track of changes and implication that such changes have.

5 Pilot Case Study Implementing the Developed Approach

The developed approach has been verified on a pilot case for the Control cabinet system. This is a complex system consisting of a large number of different control elements, some of which are also complex systems. Due to variety of components, its functionality is significantly defined by the software control system. Control cabinets are usually configured individually based on the customer requirements since their configurations are tightly related to the equipment used by the customer.

Before the change, the customer had to compile a large bill of materials by deciding individually for every single component, in order to get the control cabinet. Now, with a holistic view to the control cabinet as to a single complex system including corresponding apps and software services, it can be configured and ordered as one product.

At the first stage, based on the demand history, the main requirements and components are defined at the market evaluation stage.

Then, at the engineering stage the components, baseline configurations based on branch specific applications as well as possible constraints are defined. This was done on the top of earlier developed ontology (see [11] for details). The ontology was built around the 4-level taxonomy based on the VDMA classification (Verband Deutscher Maschinen- und Anlagenbau, German Engineering Federation, [12]). Taxonomical relationships support inheritance that makes it possible to define more common attributes for higher level classes and inherit them for lower level subclasses. The resulting ontology consists of more than 1000 classes. The same taxonomy is currently used in the company's PDM and ERP systems. For each product family (class) a set of properties (attributes) was defined, and for each property its possible values and their codes were defined as well. The lexicon of properties is ontology-wide, and as a result the values can be reused for different families. Application of the common single ontology provides for the consistency of the product codes and makes it possible to reflect incorporated changes in the codes instantly.

Complex product description consists of two major parts: product components and rules. Complex product components can be the following: simple products, other complex products, and application data. The set of characteristics of the complex product is a union of characteristics of its components. The rules of the complex products are union of the rules of its components plus extra rules. Application data is an auxiliary component, which is used for introduction of some additional characteristics and requirements to the product (for example, operating temperatures, certification, electrical connection, etc.). They affect availability and compatibility of certain components and features via defined rules. Some example rules are shown in Fig. 2. The figure represents a valve terminal (VTUG) and compatibility of electrical accessories option C1 (individual connecting cable) with mounting accessories (compatible only with H-rail mounting) and accessories for input-output link (not compatible with 5 pin straight plug M12). These rules are stored in the knowledge base and can be later used during configuration of the valve terminal for certain requirements.

The result of this is a source information for creating a cabinet configurator tool that makes it possible for the customers to configure cabinets based on their requirements online. At this stage, such specific characteristics are taken into account as components used, characteristics and capabilities of the cabinet, as well as resulting lead time and price (Fig. 3).

Based on the customer-defined configuration the engineering data is generated in an automatic (in certain cases – semi-automatic) way, which is used for the production stage. As a result, the centralized production of cabinets is based on the automatically generated engineering file (Fig. 4).

The new business process made it possible to reduce the time from configuration to delivery from several weeks to few days (depending on the required components). The attitude of the customers is yet to be analysed since so far they have approached the new process as an experiment and not as routine work. The system maintenance has also been significantly simplified due to the system-based view. All the knowledge about this product (not only separated components) is available and can be used for modification of its configuration on customer's demand.

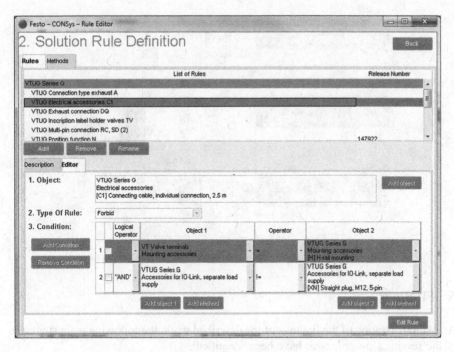

Fig. 2. Rules example.

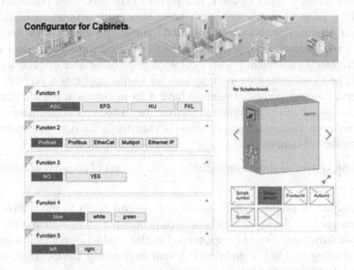

Fig. 3. Control cabinet configurator: an interface example.

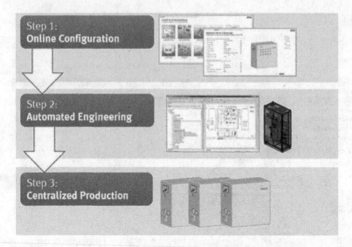

Fig. 4. Control cabinet: from online configuration to production.

6 Findings

As a summarization of the findings of the described work, the following main strategies of the servitization processes have been identified:

1. Designing customer view on product selection, configuration, and processing.

There are different types of users, like product managers, sales personnel, or customers. These users have different needs when interacting with an application like a product configurator. The customer view and the company's internal view describe two contrary views addressing the intersection between the company's product diversity and the customer's individuality with a common goal: being able to guide a customer in selecting and configuring the right system for his/her application problem. At first sight, diversity and individuality seem to have a lot in common, but the goal behind each is rather distinct. It is important to analyse the customer's context (especially for offering services): system usage, customer's industry, who does the maintenance, country-specific regulations, etc.

2. Increasing system modularity/reusability in the context of complex systems and big data.

The structure of product combinations and systems needs to modularized. Comparable modules have the key ability to be used in multiple configuration contexts. This concerns not only products and components, but also product combinations and whole systems assuming building a multilevel system engineering model. Thus, a general system model architecture needs to be set up.

3. From business processes to IT and vice versa.

Though it is reasonably considered that the changes of business processes are the driver to changes in the corresponding IT systems, the experience has shown that it is not always the case. Having defined a general strategy, the company can try to implement some pilot particular IT solutions to support existing business processes or parts of them. If such solutions turn out to be successful, they could be extended and will cause changes in the business processes.

Besides the above strategies, some more particular findings with impacts on business processes and knowledge-based systems can be identified as well.

The impacts on business processes include:

1. Aligning the business processes (improving interoperability and avoiding redundant tasks). When building a new configurator platform, it is important to align business processes like new system engineering together with the desired outcome. Doing so can help improving interoperability and avoiding redundant tasks e.g. in data maintenance.
2. Setting up sales and pricing strategies. While for tangible products, the price is typically based on the production costs plus some margin, pricing for systems is more complex and requires development of new sales strategies.

The impacts on information systems include:

1. Homogenizing and standardizing master data (increasing master data quality; e.g. for being able to compare components, which are necessary to build partially defined combinations and systems).
2. Implementing IT support for the changed processes (supporting the improved business processes).
3. Systems' needs have to be defined. This includes information and knowledge related to components/machines, software, and valid combinations of hardware and software components.
4. Statistics need to be recorded and interpreted.

7 Conclusions

The paper presents results of the ongoing shift from separate product and component to integrated systems offering. In particular, it is concentrated on improving customer experience in configuring and ordering for configurable systems. The core idea is the change from the convenient for the company view of the products to the customer-friendly view from the system application perspective, which required an introduction of a new role of "System architect". The developed business process and supporting IT systems made it possible to implement the scenario of the automated production of the customer-configured control cabinet.

The presented work is an ongoing joint research, which is still in an intermediary step of implementation. So far, a pilot case for the control cabinet product has been implemented together with the CPQ (configure – price – quote) software vendor encoway GmbH. This configuration application is already in use for selected customers. The future work will include achieving automated production of other customer-configured systems. The research is based on the study carried out in the company Festo AG&Co KG, however, the results can give significant input to achieve benefits for component manufacturers that tend to become system vendors in general.

Acknowledgment. The research was supported partly by project funded by grant # 16-07-00375 of the Russian Foundation for Basic Research and research Program I.5 of the Presidium of the Russian Academy of Sciences (State Research no.0073-2015-0006). This work was also partially financially supported by Government of Russian Federation, Grant 074-U01.

References

1. Zhang, M.-R., Yang, C.-C., Ho, S.-Y., Chang, C.H.: A study on enterprise under globalization competition knowledge management and creation overhead construction. J. Interdisc. Math. **17**(5–6), 423–433 (2014). Taylor & Francis
2. Erdener, K., Hassan, S.: Globalization of Consumer Markets: Structures and Strategies. Routledge, Abingdon (2014)
3. Artificial Intelligence, Automation, and the Economy. Report of Executive Office of the President of the United States, December 2016. https://www.whitehouse.gov/blog/2016/12/20/artificial-intelligence-automation-and-economy. Accessed 10 Jan 2017
4. Bruno, G., Korf, R., Lentes, J., Zimmermann, N.: Efficient management of product lifecycle information through a semantic platform. Int. J. Prod. Lifecycle Manag. **9**(1), 45–64 (2016). Inderscience Publishers
5. Laney, D.: 3D Data Management: Controlling Data Volume, Velocity and Variety. Gartner. http://blogs.gartner.com/doug-laney/files/2012/01/ad949-3D-Data-Management-Controlling-Data-Volume-Velocity-and-Variety.pdf. Accessed 12 Jan 2017
6. Giokas, L.: Discussion message. http://www.ibmbigdatahub.com/infographic/four-vs-big-data. Accessed 12 Jan 2017
7. Smirnov, A., Shilov, N., Oroszi, A., Sinko, M., Krebs, T.: Towards life cycle management for product and system configurations: required improvements in business processes and information systems. Procedia CIRP **48**, 84–89 (2016). Elsevier
8. Ramadi, E., Ramadi, S., Nasr, K.: Engineering graduates' skill sets in the MENA region: a gap analysis of industry expectations and satisfaction. Eur. J. Eng. Educ. **41**(1), 34–52 (2016). Taylor & Francis
9. Suriadi, S., et al.: Current research in risk-aware business process management: overview, comparison, and gap analysis. Commun. Assoc. Inf. Syst. Assoc. Inf. Syst. (AIS) **34**(1), 933–984 (2014)
10. Smirnov, A., Kashevnik, A., Shilov, N., Oroszi, A., Sinko, M., Krebs, T.: Changing business information systems for innovative configuration processes. In: Matulevičius, R., Maggi, F. M., Küngas, P. (eds.) Joint Proceedings of the BIR 2015 Workshops and Doctoral Consortium co-located with 14th International Conference on Perspectives in Business Informatics Research (BIR 2015). CEUR, vol. 1420, pp. 62–73 (2015)
11. Smirnov, A., Kashevnik, A., Teslya, N., Shilov, N., Oroszi, A., Sinko, M., Humpf, M., Arneving, J.: Knowledge management for complex product development. In: Bernard, A., Rivest, L., Dutta, D. (eds.) PLM 2013. IAICT, vol. 409, pp. 110–119. Springer, Heidelberg (2013). doi:10.1007/978-3-642-41501-2_12
12. VDMA: German Engineering Federation (2013). http://www.vdma.org/en_GB/. Accessed 5 June 2017

Transformation Algorithms of Knowledge Based UML Dynamic Models Generation

Ilona Veitaite[✉] and Audrius Lopata

Department of Informatics, Kaunas Faculty, Vilnius University,
Muitines g. 8, 44280 Kaunas, Lithuania
{Ilona.Veitaite,Audrius.Lopata}@knf.vu.lt

Abstract. The article represents knowledge based UML Dynamic models (Use Case, Activity, State Machine, Protocol State Machine, Sequence, Communication, Timing and Interaction Overview) generation process from Enterprise Model (EM), where every model generation is defined with transformation algorithm. The algorithms description is presented as Activity diagrams with depiction an explanation of essential steps.

Keywords: Enterprise modelling · Knowledge-based · IS engineering · UML · Transformation algorithms

1 Introduction

Business and IT alignment is a main concern in both fields: IT and business. There are a broad variety of models, methods and techniques i.e. Zachman framework, J. Henderson and N. Venkatraman business and IT strategic alignment model likewise numerous IS engineering frameworks. Majority of them introduces guidelines on the abstract theoretical degree only and practical realization solutions on engineering degree is nevertheless not sufficient [1, 3, 4].

The usage of formal structure called knowledge-based subsystem, which consists of Enterprise model and Enterprise meta-model, improves the quality and sufficiency of IS engineering process. The Enterprise meta-model is assumed to be the essential formal structure for domain knowledge gathering for the IS development targets. This meta-model regulates Enterprise model structure and Enterprise model accumulates knowledge that is required for whole IS development process and will be used in all stages of IS development life cycle [1, 5, 7, 8].

UML is one of the most extensive software specification standards. It is a universal IS modelling language used in a number of methodologies and enforced in well-known modelling tools [1]. The knowledge stored in Enterprise model can be applied in UML models dedicated to use in IS development life cycle stages [11, 12]. All these UML can be generated within transformation algorithms, when the necessary knowledge is gathered into knowledge repository, where it is already verified to assure automatically generated design models quality in knowledge collection into knowledge repository phase [13, 14].

© Springer International Publishing AG 2017
W. Abramowicz (Ed.): BIS 2017 Workshops, LNBIP 303, pp. 59–68, 2017.
https://doi.org/10.1007/978-3-319-69023-0_6

2 Matching Between Enterprise Model Elements and UML Elements

Enterprise meta-model is formally determined enterprise model composition, which contained of a formalized enterprise model alongside with the general principles of control theory (Fig. 1). Enterprise model is the main source of the requisite knowledge of the specific problem domain for IS engineering and IS reengineering processes [3].

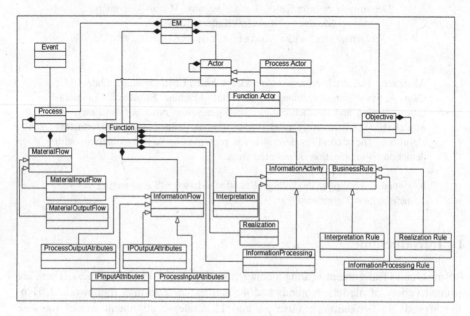

Fig. 1. Class diagram of Enterprise meta-model [3]

UML models can be generated from Enterprise model using transformation algorithms. Firstly, certain UML model must be identified for generation process, after this identification, the initial – main element of this UML model must be selected from Enterprise model. Secondly, all related elements must be selected according the initial element and all these related components must be linked between regarding constraints, necessary for UML model type identified earlier.

Information systems design methods specify the arrangement of systems engineering actions, i.e. how, in what order and what UML model to use in the IS development process and how to implement the process (Table 1). Many of them are based on diverse types of models describing differing aspects of the system properties. Sense of each model can be defined individually, but more important is the fact that each model is the projection of the system. An inexperienced specialist can use UML models inappropriately and the description of the system will possibly be contradictory, insufficient and contentious [1, 2, 6].

Table 1. Enterprise model process and function elements role variations in UML dynamic models [9, 10].

EM	UML model element	UML dynamic model	Description
Process/function	Use case	Use case model	A use case is a type of behavioural classifier that defines a unit of functionality achieved by actors or subjects to which the use case applies in combination with one or more actors
	Activity	Activity model	Describes a parameterized behaviour as correlative flow of actions
	Behavioural state machine	State machine model	Specifies individual behaviour of a part of designed system through limited state transitions
	Protocol state machine	Protocol state machine model	Expresses a usage protocol or a lifecycle of some classifier
	Message	Sequence model	Describes one specific kind of communication between lifelines of an interaction
	Frame	Communication model	Describes a unit of behaviour that concentrates on the appreciable exchange of information between connectable elements
	Frame	Interaction overview model	Describes a unit of behaviour that concentrates on the appreciable exchange of information between connectable elements

Information systems design methods specify the arrangement of systems engineering actions, i.e. how, in what order and what UML model to use in the IS development process and how to implement the process. Many of them are based on diverse types of models describing differing aspects of the system properties. Sense of each model can be defined individually, but more important is the fact that each model is the projection of the system. An inexperienced specialist can use UML models inappropriately and the description of the system will possibly be contradictory, insufficient and contentious [1, 2, 6].

This kind of system description is totally confusing, because most of the information in the models overlay and express the same things just in different approaches, as it is shown in the table (Table 1). Accordingly identification of exact UML model for generation process has high importance, because of regarding this selection depends generated element significance for system development process.

3 UML Dynamic Model Transformation Algorithms

UML Dynamic models represent the dynamic behaviour of the objects in a system, which can be described as a series of changes to the system over time [10].

3.1 UML Use Case Model Transformation Algorithm

UML Use Case model defines a collection of actions, called use cases that some system or systems, called subject, should or can operate in combination with one or more external users of the system, called actors, to contribute some appreciable and relevant outcomes to the actors or other users of the system or systems [9, 10].

In UML Use Case model generation from Enterprise model (Fig. 2) initial element is actor or subject, after generation of this element, follows selection of Enterprise model element: process or function and use case element is generated. After the generation of these two types of elements, they have to be linked to each other with some type of relationship: association, extension or inclusion, which is defined by Enterprise model element Business Rule. After all these elements are generated, there is update of actor or subject element and check are there more actor elements left in enterprise model.

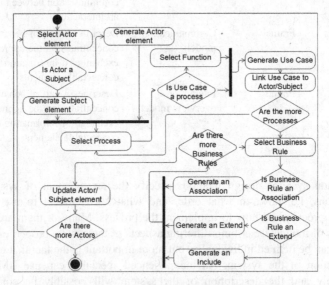

Fig. 2. UML use case model transformation algorithm

3.2 UML Activity Model Transformation Algorithm

UML Activity model describes sequence and conditions for coordinating lower-level behaviours, instead than which classifiers own those. These behaviours are generally called control flow and object flow models [9, 10].

In UML Activity model generation from Enterprise model (Fig. 3) initial element is partition, after generation of this element, follows selection of Enterprise model element: process or function and activity element is generated. Afterward the generation of these two types of elements, they have to be linked to each other. In activity models object nodes are generated from Enterprise model material or informational flow elements. And all these generated elements are connected through control nodes which are based on Enterprise model business rule elements. Later all these elements are generated, there is update of actor element and check are there more actor elements left in enterprise model.

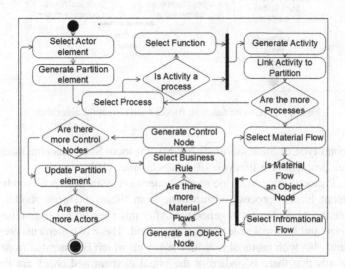

Fig. 3. UML activity model transformation algorithm

3.3 UML State Machine and Protocol State Machine Models Transformation Algorithms

UML State Machine models are used for modelling individual behaviour through definite state transitions. To express the behaviour of a part of the system, state machines can further be used to express the usage protocol of part of a system. These two types of state machines are committed to as behavioural state machines and protocol state machines. First type of State machine model describes individual behaviour of a part of designed system through limited state transitions [9, 10].

In UML Behavioural State Machine model generation from Enterprise model (Fig. 4) initial element is process or function, it means that from these enterprise model elements behavioural state machine element is generated. Subsequently this element generation second related element is simply state or composite state, which is generated from information flow. Furthermore, first two elements are linked to each other and also with pseudostate element, which is generated from business rule. After that there is update of the initials element and check are there more process elements left in enterprise model [9, 10].

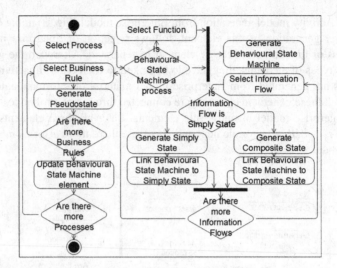

Fig. 4. UML state machine model transformation algorithm

And second type of State machines is UML Protocol State Machine model, which defines usage protocol or a lifecycle of some classifier [10].

In UML Protocol State Machine model generation from Enterprise model (Fig. 5) initials element is also process or function, from these enterprise model elements protocol state machine element is generated. After this element generation information flow is selected and Protocol state element generated. These two elements are linked to each other and also with protocol transition element, which is generated from business rule. Afterwards that there is update of the initial element and check are there more process elements left in enterprise model.

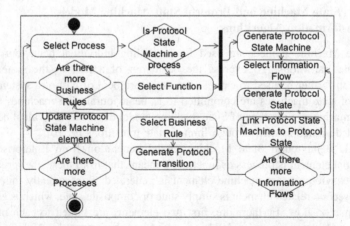

Fig. 5. UML protocol state machine model transformation algorithm

3.4   UML Sequence Model Transformation Algorithm

UML Sequence model is one of the interaction models group which concentrates on the message interchange between system participants called lifelines [9, 10].

In UML Sequence model generation from Enterprise model (Fig. 6) initial element is lifeline, after generation of this element, follows selection of Enterprise model element: process or function and message element is generated. Afterwards the generation of these two types of elements, they have to be linked to each other. In sequence models execution specification, combined fragment, interaction use, state invariant and destruction occurrence are generated from Enterprise model business rule elements. Later all these elements are generated, there is update of lifeline element and check are there more actor elements left in enterprise model.

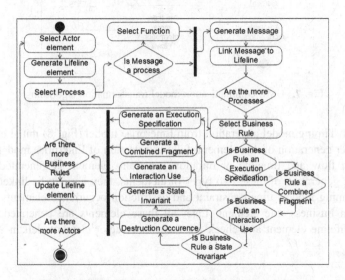

Fig. 6. UML sequence model transformation algorithm

3.5   UML Communication Model Transformation Algorithm

UML Communication Model is another one of the interaction models group, and it focuses on the interaction between participants called lifelines where the architecture of the internal structure and how this corresponds with the objects called message passing is central [9, 10].

In UML Communication model generation from Enterprise model (Fig. 7) initial element is lifeline, after generation of this element, follows selection of Enterprise model element: process or function and frame element is generated. Subsequently the generation of these two types of elements, they have to be linked to each other. In communication models message elements are generated from information flow element. Later all these elements are generated, there is update of lifeline element and check are there more actor elements left in enterprise model.

3.6 UML Timing Model Transformation Algorithm

UML Timing model is also one of the interaction models group and defines interactions when a primary purpose of the model is to reason about time. Timing models concentrate on conditions changing inside and between lifelines ahead a linear time axis [9, 10].

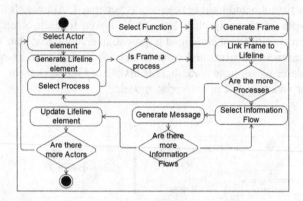

Fig. 7. UML communication model transformation algorithm

In UML Timing model generation from Enterprise model (Fig. 8) initial element is lifeline, after generation of this element, follows selection of Enterprise model element information flow and timeline or duration constraint element is generated. Subsequently the generation of these two types of elements, they have to be linked to each other. In timing models time constraint and destruction occurrence elements are generated from business rule element. Later all these elements are generated, there is update of lifeline element and check are there more actor elements left in enterprise model.

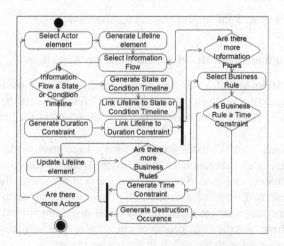

Fig. 8. UML timing model transformation algorithm

3.7 UML Interaction Overview Model Transformation Algorithm

UML Interaction Overview model is last of the interaction models group, which defines interactions through a variant of models in a way that stimulates overview of the control flow. Interaction overview models focus on the overview of the flow of control where the nodes are interactions or interaction uses. The participants like lifelines and objects like messages do not appear at this overview level [9, 10].

In UML Interaction model generation from Enterprise model (Fig. 9) initial element is process or function, it means that from these enterprise model elements frame element is generated. All other elements: duration constraint, time constraint, interaction use and control nodes, are related to the initial frame element and depends from enterprise business rule element.

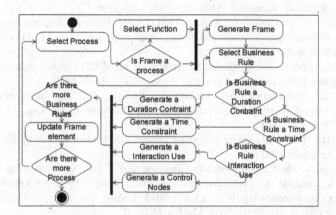

Fig. 9. UML interaction overview model transformation algorithm

4 Conclusions

In the first part of the article the matching of Enterprise model elements and UML Dynamic model elements is presented. The next part handles with detailed explanation of UML Dynamic models (Use Case, Activity, State Machine, Protocol State Machine, Sequence, Communication, Timing and Interaction Overview) transformation, that are necessary for knowledge-based IS engineering process are presented. The specified solution insures data coherence between specific design models in this manner providing more systematic IS engineering process.

The future works are: to create implementation of these transformation algorithms by knowledge-based tool's prototype, to include more detailed UML models elements application instruction into IS engineering process and to determine more validation preferences also present progressive enterprise model analysis aspects.

References

1. Butleris, R., Lopata, A., Ambraziunas, M., Veitaite, I., Masteika, S.: SysML and UML models usage in knowledge based MDA process. Elektronika ir elektrotechnika. **21**(2), 50–57 (2015). Print ISSN 1392-1215, Online ISSN 2029-5731
2. Chen, H.Y., Li, Ch., Tse, T.H.: Transformation of UML interaction diagrams in to contract specifications for object-oriented testing. Postprint of Article in Proceedings of the 2007 IEEE International Conference on Systems, Man, and Cybernetics (SMC 2007). IEEE Computer Society, Los Alamitos (2007)
3. Gudas, S., Lopata, A.: Meta-model based development of use case model for business function. Inf. Technol. Control **36**(3) [8] (2007). ISSN 1392 – 124X·2007
4. Henderson, J., Venkatraman, N.: Strategic alignment: leveraging information technology for transforming organizations. IBM Syst. J. **38**(2), 472–484 (1999)
5. IEEE Computer Society: Guide to the Software Engineering Body of Knowledge SWEBOK. Version 3.0. (2014). Paperback ISBN-13: 978-0-7695-5166-1
6. Nikiforova, O., Kozacenko, L., Ahilcenoka, D.: UML sequence diagram: transformation from the two-hemisphere model and layout. Appl. Comput. Syst. **14**, 31–41 (2013/14). doi:10.2478/acss-2013-0004
7. Lopata, A., Ambraziunas, M., Gudas, S.: Knowledge based MDA requirements specification and validation technique. Transform. Bus. Econ. **11**(1), 248–261 (2012)
8. Lopata, A., Ambraziunas, M., Gudas, S., Butleris, R.: The main principles of knowledge-based information systems engineering. Electron. Electr. Eng. **11**(1), 99–102 (2012). ISSN 2029-5731
9. OMG UML: Unified Modelling Language version 2.5. Unified Modelling (2017). http://www.omg.org/spec/UML/2.5
10. UML diagrams: The Unified Modeling Language (2017). http://www.uml-diagrams.org/
11. Lopata, A., Veitaite, I.: UML diagrams generation process by using knowledge-based subsystem. In: Abramowicz, W. (ed.) BIS 2013. LNBIP, vol. 160, pp. 53–60. Springer, Heidelberg (2013). doi:10.1007/978-3-642-41687-3_7
12. Veitaitė, I., Ambraziūnas, M., Lopata, A.: Enterprise model and ISO standards based information system's development process. In: Abramowicz, W., Kokkinaki, A. (eds.) BIS 2014. LNBIP, vol. 183, pp. 73–79. Springer, Cham (2014). doi:10.1007/978-3-319-11460-6_7
13. Veitaitė, I., Lopata, A.: Enterprise model, MOF and ISO standards based information system's development. XX tarpuniversitetinė magistrantų ir doktorantų konferencija. Informacinės technologijos 2015. Konferencijos pranešimų medžiaga. Vilniaus universitetas (2015). ISSN 2029-249X
14. Lopata, A., Veitaite, I., Žemaitytė, N.: Enterprise model based UML interaction overview model generation process. In: Abramowicz, W., Alt, R., Franczyk, B. (eds.) BIS 2016. LNBIP, vol. 263, pp. 69–78. Springer, Cham (2017). doi:10.1007/978-3-319-52464-1_7. ISBN 978-3-319-26762-3

Analysis of Users Buying Behaviour to Improve the Coupon Marketing

František Babič[(⊠)] and Ľudmila Pusztová

Department of Cybernetics and Artificial Intelligence,
Faculty of Electrical Engineering and Informatics,
Technical University of Košice, Košice, Slovak Republic
{frantisek.babic,ludmila.pusztova2}@tuke.sk

Abstract. The paper describes a data-mining case study devoted to an analysis of the users buying behaviour with the aim to improve the effectiveness of the relevant coupon marketing campaign. A coupon represents a ticket or number in an electronic form that we can use for a financial discount when purchasing a product. We can use this type of marketing to increase the number of the new customers and to reward the current ones. In our case, we used the datasets available within DMC 2015 and implemented the analytical process in accordance to the CRISP-DM methodology. Based on initial form of data, we focused mainly on pre-processing phase to extract hidden information, potentially useful for better prediction. For this purpose, we used decision trees algorithms like C4.5, C5.0, Random forest, CART and Logistic model tree. The obtained results were plausible and in some cases more accurate as other already published.

Keywords: Transaction · Coupons · Data mining · Decision trees

1 Introduction

Nowadays, sellers in-store or via e-shop are trying to affect the possible target group for their products with different ways. The coupons represent one of the most successful methods how to influence the consumer purchasing decisions. The Shoppers Trend Report 2014 [19] says that 96% of consumers in USA use coupon. PRRI-US 2017 Coupon and promo code Use Study [15] presents that 92% of respondents reported using coupons in the past year, e.g. 87% for Millennials, 91% for Generation Xers and 96% for Baby Boomers. The Millennials represent a demographic cohort with the early 1980s as starting birth years and the mid-1990s to early 2000s as ending birth years. The Generation Xers has a date of birth between the early-to-mid 1960s and early 1980s, and Baby Boomers were born between the years 1946 and 1964. These results confirmed the importance of coupon marketing regardless of age. The main difference is a form of coupon suitable for the relevant target group, e.g. the younger customers prefer an electronic form received within email on by their mobile phones. The sellers and marketers can easily track the coupons by redemption rate and redemption location. In advanced form, they can use them to collect customer data. In combination with purchase transactions, this data represents an important source that can answer the questions like who typically uses coupons or who will make purchase without usage a

© Springer International Publishing AG 2017
W. Abramowicz (Ed.): BIS 2017 Workshops, LNBIP 303, pp. 69–78, 2017.
https://doi.org/10.1007/978-3-319-69023-0_7

coupon. The answers can lead to better understanding the customers segments and to improving the sellers' decisions from the point of profit maximization and marketing costs minimisation. For this purpose, data mining offers various methods and techniques for processing, analysing and visualizing the results in simple understandable and interpretable form. Nowadays, a large volume of data processed in this domain creates requirements for suitable data storage, e.g. NoSQL databases [2].

1.1   Related Work

We present some selected existing studies devoted to the similar task, i.e. prediction of the future coupons use. If coupons will be delivered by email, it is important to avoid labelling as spam [20].

Recruit Ponpare is Japan's leading joint coupon site, offering huge discounts on everything from hot yoga, to gourmet sushi or a summer concert bonanza. The Recruit Coupon Purchase Prediction challenge on kaggle.com asked the community to predict which coupons a customer would buy in a given time period using past purchase and browsing behaviour. Cheung described in [8] his approach how to solve this task. At first, he transformed all categorical attributes to the binary, e.g. he changed an attribute describing a redemption location to a set of binary attributes: restaurant (0/1), hotel (0/1), spa (0/1), etc. In modelling phase, he tried several traditional classification methods such as logistic regression or neural networks to identify for each user which coupons she/he is interested in based on relevant purchase history. He failed with this approach, probably for relatively great diversity of the collected transactions. Next, he tried to quantify a similarity between any two coupons using a weighted version of cosine similarity. He aimed to find the most suitable weights assigned to each coupon feature. Finally, his best model ranked among the top 6% of all submissions to the competition.

Halla Yang attended this challenge too and finished second ahead of more than thousand other data scientists [17]. For each (user, coupon) pair, he calculated the probability of purchase during the test period using a gradient boosting classifier. He sorted the coupons for each user by probability and next he selected only top ten. For each pair he built a set of features including user-specific data (e.g. gender, days on site, and age), coupon-specific data (e.g. catalogue price, genre, and price rate), as well as user-coupon interaction data, e.g. how often has the user viewed coupons of the same genre. He tried logistic regression, random forest, SVM, deep neural network and gradient boosting. The last one generated the best single classifier. Authors in [9] applied similar approach on the same data. They focused on features selection, i.e. coupon-features, user-features and user-coupon-pair-features.

Nadj and Lazarevic analysed the datasets from Data Mining Cup 2015 in their work [12]. They created some dummy variables and new derived variables. They removed outliers and performed exploratory analysis in order to detect obvious relationships between the variables. They used linear models, random forests, boosted and decision trees with different combinations of predictors to build various models for all target attributes (coupon1Used, coupon2Used, coupon3Used). The lowest achieved error was 0.27 through the logistic binary model.

All presented works have some similar characteristics, i.e. it was necessary to realize many experiments to evaluate several possible approaches for finding the best prediction model. In addition, authors performed different preprocessing operations to extract possible useful metadata from initial datasets. Also, this type of data can be processed by the methods from the area of Formal Concept Analysis, especially generalized one-sided concept lattices, which can be applied to various data tables and attribute types and also computed in distributed environment for larger input datasets [6].

1.2   Methods

The CRISP-DM represents the most popular methodology for data mining and data science. This methodology defines six main phases [7, 18]:

- Business understanding deals with a specification of business goal followed with its transformation to specific analytical task(s). Based on this specification, we can select relevant mining methods and necessary resources.
- Data understanding starts with a collection of necessary data for specified task and ends with detailed description including some statistical characteristics.
- Data preparation is usually the most complex and most time-consuming phase usually taking 60 to 70% of the overall time. It contains data aggregation, cleaning, reduction or transformation. The result covers prepared data for modelling phase.
- Modelling deals with an application of suitable data mining algorithms on the pre-processed data. In addition, it is necessary to specify the correct metrics for results evaluation, e.g. accuracy, ROC, precision, recall, etc.
- Evaluation phase is oriented towards the evaluation of generated models and obtained results based on specified goals in business understanding.
- Deployment contains the exploitation of created mining models in real cases, their adaptation, maintenance and collection of acquired experiences and knowledge.

The decision tree is a flowchart-like tree structure, where each non-leaf node represents a test on an attribute, each branch represents an outcome of the test, and leaf nodes represent target classes or class distributions [11]. We decided to use this method, because we were able to visualise the tree or to extract the decision rules. The C4.5 algorithm used normalised information gain for splitting [16]. The C5.0 algorithm represents an improved version of the C4.5 that offers a faster generation of the model, less memory usage, smaller trees with similar information value, weighting and support for the boosting [13]. The CART (Classification and Regression trees) algorithm builds a model by recursively partitioning the data space and fitting a simple prediction model within each partition [3]. The result is a binary tree using a greedy algorithm to select a variable and related cut-off value for splitting with the aim to minimise a given cost function. Random forest (RF) is an ensemble classifier, which is using multiple decision tree models. The generalization error of a forest depends on the strength of the individual trees in the forest and the correlation between them [4]. Tree induction methods and linear models are popular techniques for supervised learning tasks. The logistic model tree (LMT) combines these two approaches into trees that contain logistic regression function at the leaves [5].

2   The Patterns Extraction for Coupon Marketing

This section summarizes the main points of our analytical process implemented in accordance to CRISP-DM methodology. We performed more than 150 experiments to generate the most fitting prediction model. In case of real task, we can use the extracted knowledge in deployment phase to improve the coupon marketing.

2.1   Business Understanding

The business objective was to create a prediction model based on the historical order data from an online shop with accompanying coupon generation. From data mining point of view, it was a binary classification with three target attributes: coupon1Used (0/1), coupon2Used (0/1) and coupon3Used (0/1). For this purpose, we decided to use R language and following algorithms for decision tress generation: C4.5, C5.0, RF, CART and LMT. We evaluated the generated models by traditional matrix (Table 1) representing ability of the relevant models to classify correctly both values of the target attribute.

Table 1. Evaluation matrix

True values	Predicted values	
	0	1
0	TN	FP
1	FN	TP

TP (true positive) contains all correctly classified cases of coupon usage. FP (false positive) covers those cases in which we predict the usage of the coupon but it does not happen. FN (false negative) represents the opposite case as FP, i.e. we do not expect any customer action based on received coupon, but he or she will use it. TN (true negative) represents a situation in which we expect (predict) that a customer will not use the coupon and it happens. We selected the FP as most important from the both errors.

2.2   Data Understanding

We had available three data samples: training (5 603 orders), testing (669) and validation with the real values for testing orders. Each order was characterized by thirty-one variables including three target attributes (Table 2).

We investigated the quality of all input variables and we found missing values only in the attributes *brand1*, *brand2* and *brand3*. We decided to replace these values with zero. Next, we investigated different combinations of coupons usage, i.e. the most orders did not contain any coupons redemption. The least popular combination was the redemption of coupons 2 and 3 without 1. It could be caused by the fact, that product1 represented more expensive goods. Next, we performed some statistical tests for

Table 2. Initial understanding of the available variables

Name	Description	Type
orderID	Unique identification of order	Numeric
orderTime	Time of order	Time stamp
userID	Unique identifier of user	String
couponsReceived	Time of coupon generation	Time stamp
price1	Current price of the 1st coupon product	Numeric <1.81, 87.99>
basePrice1	Original price of the 1st coupon product	Numeric <0, 3519.56>
reward1	Score value for the value-added of the product for the retailer	Numeric <0, 6.28>
premiumProduct1	Indicator whether the 1st coupon product is a premium product	Binary 0/1 0 - 4835 1 - 1218
brand1	Brand of the 1st coupon product	String
productGroup1	Product line of the 1st coupon product	String
categoryIDs1	Unique identifier of the categories of the 1st coupon product	List of strings
couponID1	Unique identifier of the 1st coupon product	String
coupon1Used	Indicator if 1st coupon redeemed	Binary 0/1 (target)
price2	Current price of the 2nd coupon product	Numeric <1.2, 74.05>
basePrice2	Original price of the 2nd coupon product	Numeric <0, 463.10>
reward2	Score value for the value-added of the product for the retailer	Numeric <0; 6.280>
premiumProduct2	Indicator whether the 2nd coupon product is a premium product	Binary 0/1 0 - 4714 1 - 1339
brand2	Brand of the 2nd coupon product	String
productGroup2	Product line of the 2nd coupon product	String
categoryIDs2	Unique identifier of the categories of the 2nd coupon product	List of strings
couponID2	Unique identifier of the 2nd coupon product	String
coupon2Used	Indicator if 2nd coupon redeemed	Binary 0/1 (target)
price3	Current price of the 3rd coupon product	Numeric <2.40, 56.67>
basePrice3	Original price of the 3rd coupon product	Numeric <0, 910.76>
reward3	Score value for the value-added of the product for the retailer	Numeric <0, 6.28>
premiumProduct3	Indicator whether the 3rd coupon product is a premium product	Binary 0/1 0 - 4529 1 - 1524
brand3	Brand of the 3rd coupon product	String
productGroup3	Product line of the 3rd coupon product	String
categoryIDs3	Unique identifier of the categories of the 3rd coupon product	List of strings
couponID3	Unique identifier of the 3rd coupon product	String
coupon3Used	Indicator if 3rd coupon redeemed	Binary 0/1 (target)

numerical variables to evaluate a possible relationship between input and output variables. We used Anderson-Darling normality test [1] (null hypothesis: the data follows the normal distribution) and non-parametric Mann-Whitney-Wilcoxon test (null hypothesis: the two populations are equal) [10]. The results confirmed the expected dependency for all investigated variables. For binary variables (premiumProduct$_i$) we performed Pearson chi-square independence test (null hypothesis: two categorical variables are independent) [14]. The calculated p-value was 0.0687 (1st combination), 0.4622 (2nd) and 0.01288 (3rd). Based on significance level 0.95 we were able to omit the premiumProduct2 from further experiments, but this operation did not improve the overall accuracy.

Figure 1 visualizes the unbalanced distribution of all three targets attributes, i.e. coupons redemption represents the minority class.

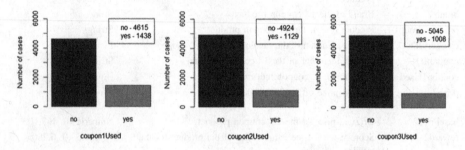

Fig. 1. Histograms for all target attributes (coupon1Used, coupon2Used, coupon3Used)

2.3 Data Preparation

We focused mainly on features selection and metadata extraction. At first, we selected only non-string variables because of their simpler interpretation (used for the first level of experiments). Next, we applied some sampling methods to solve the unbalanced distribution of three target variables (second level). We used both typical sampling methods, i.e. we replicated the minority class orders to balance the data (over-sampling) and we reduced the majority class orders to balance the data (under-sampling). We did it carefully to prevent loss of important information. These new datasets contained only twelve input variables and three target attributes. In parallel, we worked with the whole dataset to extract some new, possibly useful metadata about collected transactions:

- We created the three new variables from previous *couponsReceived: year_-couponsReceived, month_couponsReceived, day_couponsReceived, hour_-couponsReceived* and *minute_couponsReceived.*
- The same approach we used for variable *orderTime: year_orderTime, month_-orderTime, day_orderTime, hour_orderTime* and *minute_orderTime.*
- We calculated a time difference between couponsReceived and orderTime. This operation resulted in a range of values from 0.1 to 9218 min. Most values were less than 50 min, so in our future work, we will experiment with different discretization method to consider a speed of customer's reaction to the received coupons.

- We created three new variables focused on price differences: *price1_difference* (*price1* - *basePrice1*), *price2_difference* (*price2* - *basePrice2*) and *price3_difference* (price3 - *basePrice3*). Next, we discretized these variables based on our own structure, i.e. we created a scale (1 to 21) for the entire range of possible differences in prices. In addition, this step opens a space for possible future improvement based on a different scale like −1 (negative difference), 0 (the price has not changed) and 1 (positive difference).
- We transform the variables *brand1, brand2 and brand3* to nominal, i.e. we calculated multiplicity for each different brand and labelled them with new values. The new ranges were 0 to 26 for *brand1*, 0 to 22 for *brand2* and 0 to 24 for *brand3*. If some concrete brand was the same in the particular attributes, we labelled it with the same new value.
- The similar approach we applied on variables *productGroup1* (new range 1 to 174), *productGroup2* (1 to 180), *productGroup3* (1 to 207), *categoryIDs1* (1 to 15), *categoryIDs2* (1 to 14) and *categoryIDs3* (1 to 16).

These operations resulted in pre-processed dataset characterized by twenty-eight input variables and three targets attributes. We applied the both sampling methods again (level 3).

2.4   Modelling

For modelling we had available several pre-processed training sets, i.e. sample containing 12 numeric variables and 3 target attributes; sample 12/3 with under-sampling; sample 12/3 with over-sampling; sample 28/3, sample 28/3 with over-sampling and sample 28/3 with under-sampling. We performed more than 150 experiments divided into 3 levels. In each level, we tried several algorithms to generate the most suitable model for the training set and next we evaluated it through testing data. We examined various combinations of input variables and finally extract some interesting rules for this type of coupon marketing. We present only the best model for each level.

The first level focused on the initial experiments to decide which algorithms had the best potential for this data. We applied all selected algorithms C4.5, C5.0, RF, CART and LMT on the following training samples:

- All numeric variables with only one target variable (1st, 2nd, 3rd).
- Only numeric variables related to the relevant target variable (1st, 2nd, 3rd).

We generated around 30 classification models, the best ones for coupon1Used (85.35%) and coupon3Used (89.37%) were generated by C5.0, the coupon2Used model (83.56%) by RF. The low value of TN characterized all these models.

The second level covered the experiments only with good performance algorithms, i.e. C4.5, C5.0 and RF. We generated more than 50 classification models based on previous training samples with oversampling and undersampling. The best models were C4.5 for coupon1Used (83.86%), C5.0 for coupon2Used (88.49%) and C4.5 for coupon3Used (89.98%) again. The classification accuracy was higher with oversampling that with undersampling. The worst performance had the models based only on relevant attributes for particular coupon(i)Used, around 60%. This result supported our findings from data understanding phase.

The third level contained a similar number of experiments with the same algorithms but with different training data, i.e. sample 28/3, sample 28/3 with over-sampling and sample 28/3 with under-sampling. For each target attribute, we obtained the best performance: coupon1Used (92.53%), coupon2Used (91.63%) and coupon3Used (94.2%). The C5.0 algorithm was the most suitable for this type of data.

2.5   Evaluation

In this section, we present some interesting findings from previous phase. We tried various selections of input variables, e.g. based on our own cut-off values, but it did not result in any improvement in overall accuracy. We generated about 10% models with accuracy higher than 91% and more than 60% models between 81% and 90%. The most important variables in the partial results were $reward_i$ (score value for the value-added of the product for the retailer) and $basePrice^i$ (original price of the $coupon_i$ product). The best model we obtained through C5.0 algorithm applied on sample 28/3 with over-sampling (Table 3).

Table 3. Evaluation matrix for the best *coupon3Used* model

Predicted values	True values	
	0	1
0	577	6
1	33	53

For example, we extracted some interesting decision rules:

- **IF** the customer received the coupons in January **AND** he created the order before 27th day **AND** after 03:00 pm **THEN** the coupon for product no. 1 was redeemed.
- **IF** the product no. 2 belonged to the category with products occurrence in training data lower than 13 **AND** ID of this category was "1f26675d7c5cfea5899291 a241171282" **AND** this product was premium **THEN** the coupon for product no. 2 was redeemed.
- **IF** the customer received the coupons in February or March **AND** the reward for product no. 3 was less than 0.63 **AND** it belonged to the category with products occurrence in training data more than 31 **AND** the difference between its price and basePrice was negative **THEN** the coupon for product no. 3 was redeemed.

3   Conclusion

The presented work dealt with the extraction of the potentially useful patterns from transaction data representing the customers' behaviour after receiving three coupons. In our experiments we focused mainly on data preparation phase, e.g. how to improve the unbalanced distribution of all target attributes and if we are able to identify some metadata about performed orders. Next, we applied some machine learning algorithms such as C4.5, C5.0, Random forest, CART and LMT. We obtained the best performance within C4.5 and C5.0 classification models. Our results are plausible, but in our future work, we are going to test the gradient boosting method and investigate other possible hidden knowledge like time difference or in customer's ID.

Acknowledgments. The work presented in this paper was partially supported by the Slovak Grant Agency of the Ministry of Education and Academy of Science of the Slovak Republic under grant no. 1/0493/16, by the Cultural and Educational Grant Agency of the Ministry of Education and Academy of Science of the Slovak Republic under grants no. 025TUKE-4/2015 and no. 05TUKE-4/2017.

References

1. Anderson, T.W., Darling, D.A.: Asymptotic theory of certain "goodness-of-fit" criteria based on stochastic processes. Ann. Math. Stat. **23**, 193–212 (1952)
2. Bednár, P., Sarnovský, M., Demko, V.: RDF vs. NoSQL databases for the semantic web applications. In: SAMI 2014: IEEE 12th International Symposium on Applied Machine Intelligence and Informatics, Herľany, Slovakia, pp. 361–364 (2014)
3. Breiman, L., Friedman, J.H., Olshen, R.A., Stone, Ch.J.: Classification and Regression Trees. CRC Press (1999)
4. Breiman, L.: Random forests. Mach. Learn. **45**, 5–32 (2001)
5. Landwehr, N., Hall, M., Frank, E.: Logistic model trees. Mach. Learn. **59**, 161 (2005)
6. Butka, P., Pócs, J., Pócsová, J.: Distributed computation of generalized one-sided concept lattices on sparse data tables. Comput. Inform. **34**(1), 77–98 (2015)
7. Chapman, P., Clinton, J., Kerber, R., Khabaza, T., Reinartz, T., Shearer, C., Wirth, R.: CRISP-DM 1.0 Step-by-Step Data Mining Guide (2000)
8. Cheung, P.: Top 6% on Kaggle Project: Coupon Purchase Prediction. NYC Data Science Academy (2015)
9. Gupta, A.: Predicting Coupon Purchases on ポンパレ (Ponpare). Uhuru Data Lab (2015)
10. Mann, H.B., Whitney, D.R.: On a test of whether one of two random variables is stochastically larger than the other. Ann. Math. Stat. **18**(1), 50–60 (1947)
11. Murthy, K.S.: Automatic construction of decision tress from data: a multidisciplinary survey. Data Min. Knowl. Discov. **2**, 345–389 (1997)
12. Nadj, J., Lazarevic, J.: Influence of Coupons on Order Patterns Data Mining Course Project (2015)
13. Patil, N., Lathi, R., Chitre, V.: Comparison of C5.0 & CART classification algorithms using pruning technique. Int. J. Eng. Res. Technol. **1**(4), 1–5 (2012)
14. Pearson, K.: On the criterion that a given system of deviations from the probable in the case of a correlated system of variables is such that it can be reasonably supposed to have arisen from random sampling. Philos. Mag. **50**(302), 157–175 (1900). Series 5
15. PRRI-US 2017 Coupon and promo code use study. http://www.opportunityhealthcenter.org/spotlight/2017-coupon-promo-code-study/
16. Quinlan, J.R.: C4.5: Programs for Machine Learning. Morgan Kaufmann Publishers, Burlington (1993)
17. Recruit Coupon Purchase Winner's Interview: 2nd Place. http://blog.kaggle.com/2015/10/21/recruit-coupon-purchase-winners-interview-2nd-place-halla-yang/

18. Shearer, C.: The CRISP-DM model: the new blueprint for data mining. J. Data Ware-Housing **5**(4), 13–22 (2000)
19. The Shoppers Trend Report (2014). https://www.retailmenot.com/blog/2014-consumer-insights.html
20. Vokorokos, L., Hurtuk, J., Madoš, B., Obešter, P.: Security issues of email marketing service. Acta Electrotechnica et Informatica **15**(2), 9–14 (2015)

Identifying Lithuanian Native Speakers Using Voice Recognition

Laurynas Dovydaitis[(⊠)] and Vytautas Rudžionis

Kaunas Faculty, Vilnius University, Muitinės str. 8, Kaunas, Lithuania
{laurynas.dovydaitis,vytautas.rudzionis}@khf.vu.lt

Abstract. In this paper, we analyze speaker identification and present identification test results on Lithuanian native speakers' database LIEPA. Two approaches for speaker acoustic modeling are examined. We start by extracting MFCC features from audio samples, then we feed this data to create speaker acoustic model with hidden Markov models (1) and with deep neural networks (2). We compare both methods by nalyzing the subset of samples from LIEPA database. This helps to achieve more than 96% identification accuracy on sample dataset.

Keywords: Speaker identification · Deep neural networks · Hidden Markov models

1 Introduction

Continuing on previous work we presented in [1], our focus was towards implementation of speech recognition system. We proposed to use such system as gateway for security access control, or as authorization service, for phone, voice mail or voice access services. We are continuing our work on speaker recognition, with more focus on speaker identification by analyzing voice examples.

Previously we faced a challenge with our dataset size, as it was too small to have significant results. Just recently, with project LIEPA [2] completion, substantial set of speaker data became available for deep learning and analysis. This database contains approximately 100 h of samples, from more than 370 Lithuanian native speakers.

This paper shows the results of speaker recognition system for speaker identification, using acoustic modeling with Hidden Markov Models (HMM), as well as, acoustic modeling with Deep Neural Network (DNN) techniques.

1.1 Previous Work

In previous paper [1] we showed results of our experiments. We conducted proof of concept for speaker recognition system, that could be used for user authentication.

We also outlined, that the identification module performance, should be tested on larger dataset. During the experiments, we saw that best identification accuracy was achieved on voice signals without noise.

In [1] we concluded, that in order to increase accuracy, we need to split users' speech stream into smaller windows. We also considered to experiment with speech

© Springer International Publishing AG 2017
W. Abramowicz (Ed.): BIS 2017 Workshops, LNBIP 303, pp. 79–84, 2017.
https://doi.org/10.1007/978-3-319-69023-0_8

recognizers which are based on different speech features (LPC, MFCC etc.) and different machine learning techniques.

Speaker Dataset. For this identification, project LIEPA [2] Speaker dataset was used. This data set includes 376 unique speakers and provides around 100 h of spoken sentences and words. Initial wave format .wav, sampling rate - 22 kHz, quantization - 16 bit, number of channels 1 [2].

Validation Data and Test Data. Original data subset, was split into 70% of samples for training, 30% for testing created model. Splitting was done randomly.

2 Speaker Features

Feature Extraction. Mel-frequency cepstral coefficients (MFCC) were as extracted features. This choice was made because of MFCC feature robustness for speaker recognition [3].

All samples were split ušing 20 ms length window function, with the help of HTK toolkit software [4]. For each windowed sample, 39 total features were extracted - 13 MFCCs, 13 delta and 13 delta-delta coefficients.

The following parameters were set in HTK configuration files

```
SOURCEKIND=WAVEFORM
SOURCEFORMAT=WAVE
TARGETKIND=MFCC_D_A_E
SAVEWITHCRC=F
SOURCERATE=454.54
TARGETRATE=100000.0
WINDOWSIZE=250000.0
USEHAMMING=T
PREEMCOEF=0.96
NUMCEPS=12
NUMCHANS=20
```

To execute feature extraction, we used HCopy executable

```
HCopy.exe -C CONFIG -S visi_wav-mfc
```

This way we created a speaker feature set, that can be processed further, to create speaker acoustic model.

3 Speaker Acoustic Model

Acoustic model for each speaker was created using two methods. By using Hidden Markov models (HMM) [5] we experimented with various number of hidden states until we got best recognition accuracy. For the second experiment, we created differing deep neural networks architectures [6, 7].

3.1   HMM Model Creation

To train HMM model, the following command was executed from HTK application

```
HRest.exe -T 1 -S $train -i 100 -l $label -L $labeldir
$hmm
```

3.2   Neural Network

We experimented on number of different configurations in order to create best per-forming neural network architecture.

The network input layer was a vector of 999 × 39 dimensions, while output layer was had number of nodes, equal to number of unique speakers. Different architectures were used to choose number hidden layers. This was achieved by increasing number of nodes, as well as different depth of networks. Hidden layers consisted of recurrent neural network implementation of Long short-term memory (LSTM) cells [8, 9].

To create and train the network we Python Keras [10] module. One of the architectures that we used can be examined in code example below.

```
model = Sequential()
model.add(Masking(mask_value=0.,          input_shape=(999,
39)))
model.add(LSTM(1536,
               implementation=2))
model.add(Dense(67,
               activation='softmax'))

sgd    =    SGD(lr=0.1,    decay=1e-6,    momentum=0.9,
nesterov=True)

model.compile(optimizer='sgd',
              loss='sparse_categorical_crossentropy',
              metrics=['accuracy'])

model.fit(X_train, y_train,
          epochs=150,
          validation_data=(X_test, y_test),
          callbacks=[csv_logger])
```

4   Test Results

We tested and compared accuracy of the speaker models in two phases. 1st phase was conducted on pilot dataset. This dataset contained 9 unique speaker examples, with total of 540 sample data. In second testing phase, we took subset of LIEPA dataset with 66 unique speakers, with total of 4691 samples.

For DNN results, shown in Table 1, input had a 25 × 39 dimensional vector (Table 2).

Table 1. Pilot dataset accuracy results for 9 speaker voice examples.

Signal to noise ratio	HMM model accuracy	DNN model accuracy
1	1	0.9958
0.9	0.9631	0.9532
0.85	0.9315	0.9295
0.8	0.9105	0.8991

Table 2. Accuracy results with HMM model for experiment running on 66 speaker subset from LIEPA database.

Test sq. number	HMM states	Accuracy
1	8	0.9562

Training for DNN model was stopped at 75 to 150 epochs, depending on loss value, which had to be below 0,05 (Table 3, Figs. 1, 2, 3, and 4).

Table 3. Accuracy results with DNN model for experiment running on 66 speaker subset from LIEPA database.

Test sq. number	DNN architecture	Accuracy
1	1 × 1000 LSTM	0.9048
2	1 × 1500 LSTM	0.8807
3	1 × 2000 LSTM	0.8970
4	1 × 3000 LSTM	0.9097
5	3 × 1000 LSTM	0.9624
6	5 × 1000 LSTM	0.9261
7	7 × 1000 LSTM	0.7990

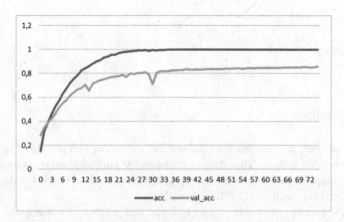

Fig. 1. Accuracy convergence through training epochs on 1st DNN Test sq.

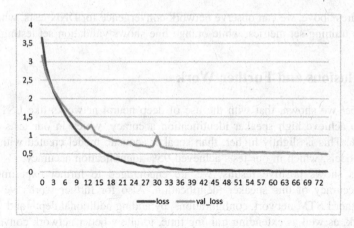

Fig. 2. Loss convergence through training epochs on 1st DNN Test sq.

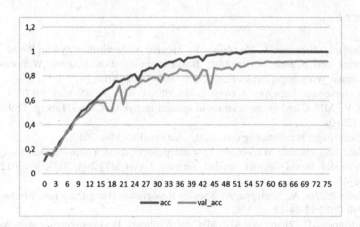

Fig. 3. Accuracy convergence through training epochs on 6th DNN Test sq.

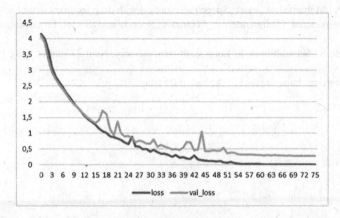

Fig. 4. Loss convergence through training epochs on 6th DNN Test sq.

In Figures above, we can observe network convergence for DNN tests, where blue line shows training set metrics, while orange line shows validation set testing.

5 Conclusions and Further Work

In this paper we shown, that with the use of deep neural networks like LSTM, it is possible to achieve high speaker identification accuracy, which in our tests reached above 96%. This is slightly higher, than speaker acoustic model created with hidden Markov models, which in our tests achieved 95% identification accuracy.

As this shows positive results, we are encouraged to further experiment and improve accuracy of this speaker identification. Also for further work, we plan to examine other LSTM network configurations, by adding additional depth and width to the network, as well as extending training time, to allow better network convergence.

References

1. Dovydaitis, L., Rasymas, T., Rudzionis, V.: Speaker Authentication System Based on Voice Biometrics and Speech Recognition, Business Information Systems Workshops, BIS International Workshops, Series Print ISSN 1865–1348 (2016)
2. LIEPA Homepage. https://www.xn-ratija-ckb.lt/liepa. Accessed 09 May 2017
3. Tiwari, V.: MFCC and its applications in speaker recognition. Int. J. Emerg. Technol. 1(1), 19–22 (2010)
4. HTK Homepage. http://htk.eng.cam.ac.uk/. Accessed 09 May 2017
5. Abdallah, J.S., Osman, M.I., et al.: Text-independent speaker identification using hidden markov model. World Comput. Sci. Inf. Technol. J. (WCSIT) 2(6), 203–208 (2012). ISSN: 2221–0741
6. Fandrianto A., Jin, A., Neelappa, A.: Speaker Recognition Using Deep Belief Networks [CS 229] Fall 2012:12-14-12
7. Garcia-Romero, D., Zhang, X., Alan McCree, A., Povey, D.: Improving speaker recognition performance in the domain adaptation challenge using deep neural networks. In: Spoken Language Technology Workshop (SLT), IEEE (2014)
8. Graves, A., Mohamed, A., et al.: Speech recognition with deep recurrent neural networks. In: IEEE International Conference on Acoustics, Speech and Signal Processing (ICASSP) (2013)
9. Hochreiter, S., Schmidhuber, J.: Long short-term memory. Neural Comput. 9(8), 1735–1780 (1997)
10. Keras hompage. https://keras.io/. Accessed 09 May 2017

Dereferencing Service for Navigating Enterprise Knowledge Structures from Diagrammatic Representations

Mihai Cinpoeru[✉]

Business Informatics Research Center, Babeş-Bolyai University,
Cluj-Napoca, Romania
mihai.cinpoeru@econ.ubbcluj.ro

Abstract. This paper aims to offer a straightforward solution to the need of cross-diagram semantic navigation in business diagrams while it also emphasizes the potential and importance of a core Linked Data concept which has yet to gain widespread recognition or implementation, the dereferencing. Business process models that are exported as queryable data in graph databases, using the Resource Description Framework (RDF) for enterprise data storage and retrieval, so that resources have HTTP identifiers which can be interpreted as Web locations (URLs) to gain direct access to a resource instead of querying it. The work at hand implements the URI dereferencing concept through RESTful services. A specific business example will be discussed to demonstrate the new way of accomplishing navigation between diagrammatic enterprise knowledge structures outside the modelling tool, thus making model elements queryable in an external environment.

Keywords: Enterprise resource identity · Linked data · RESTful services · Cross-diagram · URI dereferencing

1 Introduction

Diagrams play an increasingly important role in business applications development, as they are not only used to illustrate structures anymore, but are also able to store extensible and exportable pieces of information and connections to other diagrams, in order to access their items.

At the same time, Smart Data technologies are becoming more and more popular, being able to deliver solutions to problems that have existed for a long time in other types of storage such as relational databases. Considerable attention is being paid to graph databases and the possibility they offer for linking data, as there are constant developments in this field in making data more accessible than ever.

Linked Data follows four important principles proposed by Sir Berners Lee [1]:

1. Use URIs as names for things.
2. Use HTTP URIs so that people can look up those names.
3. When someone looks up a URI, provide useful information, using the standards (RDF, SPARQL)
4. Include links to other URIs, so that they can discover more things.

© Springer International Publishing AG 2017
W. Abramowicz (Ed.): BIS 2017 Workshops, LNBIP 303, pp. 85–96, 2017.
https://doi.org/10.1007/978-3-319-69023-0_9

Whilst the first two principles are used as rules in Linked Data, in this paper the focus is set on the last two, introducing the concept of dereferencing for rule number 3 by dynamically transforming the URI (Uniform Resource Identifier) into a URL (Uniform Resource Locator) through a RESTful Web Service designed to link the URIs to the data they represent when accessed via HTTP.

Furthermore, by respecting the fourth principle, everything needs to be linked in the application developed to enable movement from one resource to another or even from one diagram to another through the hyperlinks elements have, which, in Linked Data, are stored or, more specifically for this situation, exported as statements.

This paper further develops ideas briefly introduced in the author's prior work [2], in the context of the EnterKnow Project [3] (Enterprise-Aware Application Based on Hybrid and Formal Representation of Enterprise Knowledge), which aims to demonstrate the notion of "information system aware of enterprise semantics". This article aims to contribute to this project by enabling enterprise knowledge structures navigation in diagrammatic representations by using Semantic Web specifics.

The next section provides background on the problem described, followed by the goal statement of this paper, to prove that the solution proposed in this article can bring value to the field. Afterwards, there is an example of such a Web Service and a Web Client, that use URI dereferencing to navigate through diagrams, showing how this paper offers an up-to-date, straightforward method to respond to the need mentioned, that of navigating between diagrammatic representations that are exported in RDF and accessed through a dereferencing Web Service developed by the authors and adapted to the specific need of manipulating structures outside the modelling tools. At the same time, there will be details of the architecture and implementation of such a service and then there will be the conclusions to show how the techniques proposed in this paper suit and solve the problem described.

2 Background and Related Works

2.1 Background on Linked Data

Linked Data is a very efficient way for storing and connecting large amounts of data using graphs, benefiting from the unlimited and highly extensible number of connections they can offer and also from the good performance Graph Databases allow.

During the last decade, there has been considerable efforts made in the field of Linked Data, a type of NoSQL that is also referred to as Smart Data or Semantic Web and has been dubbed as Web 3.0 [4].

The model for these data interchange specifications is RDF (Resource Description Framework). In RDF, as mentioned in the Introduction, data is stored as triples of the following form:

```
@prefix : <http://example.org/> .
:John :WorksAt :UBB .
```

Linked Data enables the understanding of data semantics on Web and allows creating new RDF statements through inferences based on the existing ones. RDF Statements do not only give information about a resource, but can also store unlimited relationships between resources, known as metadata.

In a triple, the first resource is the Subject, the second one is the Predicate, and the third one the Object. The prefix sets a symbol that replaces an expression: in this case, when encountering the ":" symbol the machine will read it as http://example.org/ and form an URI such as http://example.org/John. In this example, there are no ontologies used, only terms created in the context presented. The format used is N-Triples, but there are more formats such as TriG or Turtle.

At the same time, there is another format, JSON-LD [5], which is the latest added and the most popular and promising, considering the fact that it is an adaptation of JSON, widely used by Web applications today, which means that client applications developers do not need to be familiar with RDF specific formats.

To ease this up even more, the dereferencing service proposed here can request data by simply calling the resource by its name, sparing the client from having to learn the RDF specific query language, SPARQL, which is included in the service we will describe later in this paper. The client only has to be able to manipulate JSON responses.

2.2 Background on RESTful Web Services

Considering the fact that the URIs from RDF have an HTTP form and that, for the purpose of dereferencing, there is a need for direct calls to URLs, it results that RESTful Web Services are the obvious response to this matter.

REST (Representational State Transfer) is a stateless communication architecture where HTTP protocol is used. RESTful Web Services require every resource to be accessible by HTTP requests such as GET, POST, PUT, DELETE. The RDF based systems include a RESTful API [6], which makes it possible to perform SPARQL queries on the repositories accessed. Though, they do not offer direct support for URI dereferencing. For the latter concept, REST is also the right architectural style, not only because RESTful services are widely used nowadays, but especially because the RESTful architecture relies on HTTP likewise URIs. To make the concept highly scalable, a distributed application is necessary, which involves cross-domain requests. This type of Web Services is also highly suitable for this need.

2.3 Related Works

In the last years, there has been a growing interest in the way that diagrams can contribute to the Web development process. While, years ago, the diagrams had the singular role of illustrating steps or structures, thanks to more recent studies it has come to the point where by designing a diagram the developer can actually develop a well-structured, maintainable model for an application.

Researches conducted by OMILAB, a collaborative research environment where an international community of conceptual modelling researchers contribute with knowledge and resources for modelling method engineering, have added much value to this field, as it is now possible to export diagrams as RDF, enriching Graph Databases with diagrammatic model information [7]. Another solution, referring to UML diagrams is described in [8], but the downsize of this is that is only refers to UML diagrams, while the previous reference allows any kind of diagrammatic representation to be exported.

For retrieving enterprise knowledge stored diagrammatic representations, prior studies have provided methods in the field of model queries such as GMQL (Generic Model Query Language) [9]. In most of the prior studies though, including the referenced one, the data gathering happens inside the modelling tools, whereas for this study it is necessary to access this type of knowledge outside the tools, at client level.

The start point for this work is BPMN (Business Process Model and Notation), a widely-used standard model for representing processes graphically. In BPMN, Business Process Diagrams (BPD) are based on events which have a Start point and an Ending point, between which there are Tasks and Gateways. The Tasks specify the action to be done, whilst the Gateways represent decision points where, depending on the condition and results, the event is going on one direction or another.

Along with the BPD, there is the Working Environment Model (WEM), which provides specifications for describing the business's organigram. The designer is able to create Organizational Units such as Departments, Task Performers such as Employees or Automated performers and assign them to specific roles, such as Manager or Sales Assistant. The BPM and the WEM can be linked through hyperlinks from the first one to the latter. At task level, it is possible to store various pieces of information, one of which is the task assignment to a Task Performer or a Role. In this project, hyperlinking relies on the Turtle format.

As dereferencing is concerned, to the author's best knowledge, very few publications can be found in the literature that address the issue of URI dereferencing. One paper that discuss it is [10], which though discusses the matter in a specific context which does not suit the purpose this paper aims to achieve.

3   Goal Statement

Based on the approach presented, the purpose of this paper is to establish a connection between the concept of URI dereferencing and navigation between diagrammatic representations used outside the modelling tools, by using HTTP to call the resources by their names through the dereferencing RESTful Web Service, get the data about the concept and show the other URIs that are linked to the concept, making them accessible for dereferencing.

By using diagrammatic representations outside the modelling environment, the diagram's role is enhanced, becoming a run-time level usable piece within an application. The authors aim to add extra value to this concept through the dereferencing Web service, which facilitates access between the models represented in the diagram, allowing easy navigation and complex access between represented structures.

Specifically, this paper aims to dereference a task's URI, then, having the information about that task, to dereference the roles it is linked to, and when the roles are accessed, they offer direct access to the persons responsible for accomplishing the task.

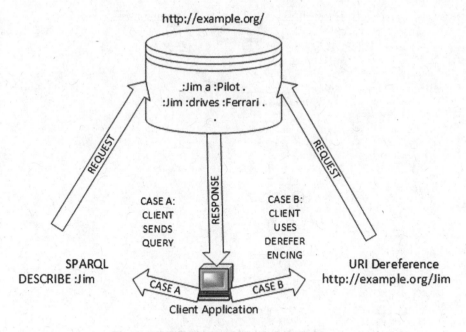

Fig. 1. URI dereference instead of SPARQL query

Figure 1 illustrates a graph database in the middle, which stores three statements in Turtle syntax. Now, in order to retrieve data from the database, the classic choice is to send a query to the RDF API, which would return a response in a format which depends on the header attached.

The option created and proposed within this paper is the URI dereferencing service, for which a second RESTful Web Service will be used. As it is shown in the figure, it is able to retrieve the same data as through the SPARQL query, by calling a resource by its unique identifier, the URI.

This succession of items dereference can show how this concept provides a very useful way to move between items, searching for concrete connections in order to perform the cross-diagram navigation.

The approach of this paper is to use a redesigned RESTful Web Service, which responds to the problem of URI dereference to provide an efficient, straight-forward solution enable navigation1 between diagrammatic representations in the process through Semantic Web and a specifically designed Web Service, contributing to the higher purpose of creating information systems aware of enterprise semantics, through the EnterKnow project.

4   Design Decisions

4.1   Requirements and Architecture

At first, in order to be able to develop a proof-of-concept application for the statement of this paper, it is required to formulate all the requirements and design the architecture.

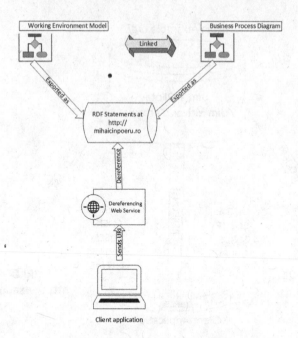

Fig. 2. Application architecture

As shown in Fig. 2, the Working Environment Model and the Business Process Diagram are exported as RDF to a graph database, where they are stored. Furthermore, all the metadata is also stored there, which will be helpful to the matter.

Separately from the storage site, there is the Client Application, which does not need to be aware of the diagrams or the graphs. It simply sends requests to the URI dereferencing Web Service, which is the main contribution enunciated within this paper, a concept developed within the author's recent researches, which requests data via the RDF API, requesting JSON-LD as the format, mainly because it is easy to manipulate even by clients who are not knowledgeable in Smart Data.

The client application, when receiving triples in JSON, can display the data as a table, but it is really important that it respects the fourth principle enunciated by Tim Berners Lee, that links to other URIs must be included in order to access any of the items in the purpose of dereference.

4.2 Business Scenario

In order to exemplify the concepts this paper previously enunciated, it is useful to give an example of a business scenario which could benefit from them.

In this case, to keep focusing on the most important parts, a small scenario would be enough, consisting in a TV store. It only has a Sales Department with one Sales Manager and one Assistant Salesman.

Also, the store only sales TVs, so the two employees are only responsible for selling these. This example could easily be expanded at a larger scale; the authors decided to keep it at this level to avoid the possibility of it becoming confusing.

5 Implementation Details

Diagrams and Graph Database. The separate elements will be implemented considering the order in which others depend on them. This means that at first, the diagrams are required, because the Graph Database depends on them (the diagrams will be exported as graph items).

The diagrams will be implemented through the Bee-Up Modelling Toolkit [11], a modelling toolkit developed at OMiLAB [12] that offers BPMN diagrams and contains the RDF export option, for building the Business Process Diagram, which will represent the succession of steps, and the Working Environment Model, representing the company's organigram.

At first, it is important to have to Working Environment Model, as the BPD will be the one holding references to the WEM. It will cover what was described in the business scenario.

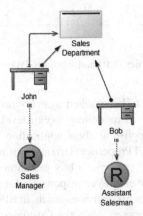

Fig. 3. Working Environment Model diagram

In Fig. 3 there is the small store's WEM, which only consists in the Sales Department. John is the Manager and is also a member of the Sales Department (the left arrow represents the "is Manager of" relationship, whilst the right one represents the "Belongs to" relationship). Bob, on the other hand, is an Assistant Salesman. He only has one relationship with the department, the "Belongs to" one. Further on, it is necessary to create a BPD with tasks and link them to the elements of it.

The RACI matrix [13] describes the participation of various roles in cross-functional or cross-departmental processes.

The acronym of RACI comes from:

- *Responsible.* The person or role that does the actual work in order to complete the task.
- *Accountable.* The one who is responsible for the task's achievement and deliverance. This person also delegates the work, assigning it to the ones responsible.

- *Consulted.* The experts on the matter. When necessary, their feedback or advice is requested. They have the capacity to complete the work.
- *Informed.* It is not necessary to consult them, but they need to be notified on the results.

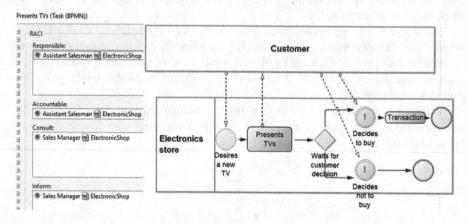

Fig. 4. RACI properties (left) and Business Process Diagram (right)

These four properties need to be attached to every task in the Business Processes Diagram, linking to the WEM. At modelling toolkit level, this enables cross-diagram access, which we aim to accomplish at client application level too.

As illustrated in Fig. 4. RACI Properties (left) and Business Process Diagram (right), this diagram's start event is the customer's buy intention ("Desires a new TV"). It is followed by a task, in which the employee responsible for its achievement presents the TV to the customer, then waits for his decision, which, in BPMN, is a gateway (exclusive, in this case). The actions go forward when the Customer makes a decision, which is communicated through Intermediate Events (Decides to buy/ Decides not to buy). If the customer decides to buy, this is followed by another task, the transaction, then the End Event point ("Deliver TV"). Else, it is followed by the "Customer Leaves Store" End Event.

The RACI properties for each task can be added in a special menu from Bee-Up, as it can be viewed in Fig. 4. RACI Properties (left) and Business Process Diagram (right). Here, is has been decided that while the Assistant Salesman is responsible and accountable for presenting the TV, the Sales Manager is to be consulted or informed (as the roles were explained in Sect. 2.2). The RACI properties were also assigned for the second task. The diagrams, along with the metadata must be exported now as RDF, for which purpose Bee-Up offers support. These are exported in a Turtle file.

In Fig. 5. A task exported in RDF, there is the "Presents TV" task, exported as RDF. This figure presents only the properties relevant to the matter this paper is describing, especially the RACI properties. This data needs to be uploaded to the Graph Database, using the platform offered by GraphDB [14], a Semantic Graph Server.

```
<http://mihaicinpoeru.ro/Task_BPMN-12453-Presents_TVs>
    a                        mm:o_Task_BPMN , cv:o_Modelling_object ;
    rdfs:label               "Presents TVs" ;
    mm:r_Accountable         <http://mihaicinpoeru.ro/Role-12637-Assistant_Salesman> ;
    mm:r_Consult             <http://mihaicinpoeru.ro/Role-12626-Sales_Manager> ;
    mm:r_Inform              <http://mihaicinpoeru.ro/Role-12626-Sales_Manager> ;
    mm:r_Is_inside           <http://mihaicinpoeru.ro/Pool_BPMN-12439-Electronics_store> ;
    mm:r_Responsible         <http://mihaicinpoeru.ro/Role-12637-Assistant_Salesman> ;
    cv:a_Name                "Presents TVs" ;
    cv:described_in          <http://mihaicinpoeru.ro/Working_Environment_Model-ElectronicShop> .
```

Fig. 5. A task exported in RDF

URI Dereferencing and Client. The other thing that needs to be done in order to prove the concept is to create a client application that uses URI dereferencing to get data, manipulates it by JavaScript and displays it in a table to be accessed further by user clicks.

The dereference service is developed through Java with the Spring framework, using Spring Boot to create an application with an embedded servlet container. It needs to be able to receive GET requests and forward them with a hardcoded SPARQL describe query. Also, as a distributed application is desirable, it needs to be able to receive cross-domain requests. For this, we need to enable CORS (Cross-Origin Resource Sharing); this can be done in Spring with the @CrossOrigin annotation.

```
@CrossOrigin
@RestController
public class Controller {
    public Controller() {
    }

    @RequestMapping({"/{uri}"})
    public ResponseEntity requester(@PathVariable String uri) {
        Caller call = new Caller(uri);
        return call.getJson();
    }
}
```

The service takes what is after http://mihaicinpoeru.ro/ (/{uri}) as a parameter and invokes an object that attaches it to a DESCRIBE query, sent forward to the RDF API with the Content-Type set as "application/ld+json" in the header. The service will return a JSON-LD response, returned to the one that makes the request to the Web Service. The results in JSON-LD returned when asking about the Presents TV task (http://mihaicinpoeru.ro/Task_BPMN-12453-Presents_TVs) look like this:

```
"http://austria.omilab.org/psm/content/bee-up/1_2#r_Accountable" : [ {
    "@id" : "http://mihaicinpoeru.ro/Role-12637-Assistant_Salesman"
} ],
//[…] two more similar results here for Consult and Inform Items
    "http://austria.omilab.org/psm/content/bee-up/1_2#r_Responsible" : [ {
    "@id" : "http://mihaicinpoeru.ro/Role-12637-Assistant_Salesman"
```

Table 1. Example of displayed results

Task_BPMN-12453- Presents_TVs	#r_Accountable	Role-12637- Assistant_Salesman
Task_BPMN-12453- Presents_TVs	r_Consult	Role-12626-Sales_Manager
Task_BPMN-12453- Presents_TVs	r_Inform	Role-12626-Sales_Manager
Task_BPMN-12453- Presents_TVs	r_Responsible	Role-12637- Assistant_Salesman

The tasks can be seen at the end of the url sent to the server, after the last ' / ' sign.

The client needs to be able to make cross-domain calls to the dereferencing service, receive JSON responses and manipulate them as a HTML table with clickable links in order to be able to dereference each item from it that belongs to the http://mihaicinpoeru.ro prefix (it only dereference resources created within the context – all the items created in the Bee-up modelling toolkit were exported with this prefix). The client application will practically establish a connection with the URI dereference service and will have a stateless communication with it; the client is responsible for displaying the properties of each item that is dynamically dereferenced. For this paper, the script will not sort out any properties, but in case of a more complex application, this would happen in the background, manipulating the items that are necessary.

In Table 1 there are just four of the statements displayed by the client application when accessing the item from the first column (the "Presents TV" task), the ones that were also shown in the JSON-LD example. All the prefixes have been filtered out, as they are added with JavaScript in the background. A click on the URI of the role item will retrieve and provide to the client an RDF description of the role responsible for the task. The dereference service will create an URL out of it and bring back data to the application in the same way as for the first task.

```
Performer-12634-Bob              @type      o_Performer
```

This is one of the statements retrieved when clicking on the Role-12637-Assistant_Salesman item. Following the former steps, an available Assistant Salesmen for the job requested was discovered. This statement was chosen because it is most important in this context; doing this, this paper's statement has been accomplished, showing how the URI dereference service contributed to accomplishing the cross-diagram navigation: starting from a task from the BPD diagram, the WEM diagram was accessed, retrieved data needed for the task from it.

6 Conclusions

Based on these results, it can be concluded that the method described has accomplished its purpose, the navigation between enterprise knowledge structures in diagrammatic representations at application level, outside the modelling tools. It has been exemplified on a toy example reduced to a minimum level in order to facilitate understanding, but this principle can be generalized to the numerous enterprise facets that can be modelled and connected through semantic links. Amongst these facets can document models, actors, products and many others. By dereferencing the URIs it is now possible to reach all the elements' machine-readable properties, and when some of these properties have hyperlinks to other diagrams, the latter are reachable through those links in any web application using the URI dereference.

This technique can be easily used by enterprise applications that use Graph Databases as their Model, offering easier access to the resources. As shown here, an organigram can be reached from a business process description, a fact that is useful to business applications.

Table 2 presents some performance results of the client application through the dereferencing service, taking into consideration the time it takes for the statements on an item to be shown to the client.

Table 2. Performance table

Item dereferenced	Time needed to dereference and display an item in client application	Number of statements
Task	19 ms	48
Role	16 ms	12
Performer	18 ms	15

To conclude, the main contribution of this study is proving how a URI dereferencing service can be used in the purpose of accomplishing cross-diagram navigation in applications based on Smart Data.

Acknowledgment. The work presented in this paper is supported by the Romanian National Research Authority through UEFISCDI, under grant agreement PN-III-P2-2.1-PED-2016-1140.

References

1. Berners-Lee, T.: Design Issues. W3 Homepage. https://www.w3.org/DesignIssues/LinkedData.html. Accessed 01 May 2017
2. Cinpoeru, M.: Design and implementation of a dereferencing service for enterprise resource identifiers. In: IE 2017 Conference Proceedings, pp. 501–506. Bucharest University of Economic Studies Press, Bucharest (2017)
3. EnterKnow Homepage. http://enterknow.granturi.ubbcluj.ro. Accessed 09 May 2017

4. Markoff, J.: Entrepreneurs see a web guided by common sense. New York Times. http://www.nytimes.com/2006/11/12/business/12web.html. Accessed 09 May 2017
5. JSON LD – the official website. http://json-ld.org/. Accessed 11 May 2017
6. RDF RESTful API Documentation – the official website. http://docs.rdf4j.org/rest-api/. Accessed 11 May 2017
7. Karagiannis, D., Buchmann, R.A.: Linked open models: extending linked open data with conceptual model information. Inf. Syst. **56**, 174–196 (2015)
8. Daniel, G., Sunyé, G., Cabot, J.: UMLtoGraphDB: mapping conceptual schemas to graph databases. In: Comyn-Wattiau, I., Tanaka, K., Song, I.-Y., Yamamoto, S., Saeki, M. (eds.) ER 2016. LNCS, vol. 9974, pp. 430–444. Springer, Cham (2016). doi:10.1007/978-3-319-46397-1_33
9. Delfmann, P., Steinhorst, M., Dietrich, H.-A., Becker, J.: The generic model query language GMQL – conceptual specification, implementation, and runtime evaluation. Inf. Syst. **47**, 129–177 (2015)
10. Colpaert, P., Verborgh, R., Mannens, E., Van de Walle, R.: Painless URI dereferencing using the DataTank. In: Presutti, V., Blomqvist, E., Troncy, R., Sack, H., Papadakis, I., Tordai, A. (eds.) ESWC 2014. LNCS, vol. 8798, pp. 304–309. Springer, Cham (2014). doi:10.1007/978-3-319-11955-7_39
11. OMILAB Bee-up – the official website. http://austria.omilab.org/psm/content/bee-up/info. OMILAB, Accessed 09 May 2017
12. Karagiannis, D., Buchmann, R.A., Burzynski, P., Reimer, U., Walch, M.: Fundamental conceptual modeling languages in OMiLAB. In: Karagiannis, D., Mayr, H., Mylopoulos, J. (eds.) Domain-Specific Conceptual Modeling, pp. 3–30. Springer, Cham (2016). doi:10.1007/978-3-319-39417-6_1
13. Jacka, M., Keller, P.: Business Process Mapping: Improving Customer Satisfaction, pp. 257–260. Wiley, Hoboken (2009)
14. GraphDB – the official website. http://graphdb.ontotext.com/. Ontotext, Accessed 09 May 2017

DEA Based Algorithm for EU Healthcare Efficiency Evaluation

Dalia Kriksciuniene and Virgilijus Sakalauskas[✉]

Department of Informatics, Vilnius University,
Universiteto str. 3, Vilnius, Lithuania
{dalia.kriksciuniene,virgilijus.
sakalauskas}@knf.vu.lt

Abstract. The problem of efficiency evaluation in healthcare is recently dealt from many perspectives, such as analysis of investment and cost containment, development of country ranking models or designing new indicators for characterizing healthcare status. The article explores the healthcare efficiency in EU countries by applying a DEA (Data Envelopment Analysis) method. The modification of DEA gives several advantages of the proposed model, as it not only computes healthcare efficiency of a country, but it enables to give quantitative characteristics of particular deficiencies which explain differences of efficiency levels; it also. The research results highlight different levels of efficiency of EU healthcare systems determined by hierarchical selection and grouping health-related input characteristics and by comparing them to the financial value of investment. The experimental analysis revealed that DEA-based model allows estimating the limits of increasing efficiency of country healthcare within same expenditure levels.

Keywords: Efficiency evaluation · Healthcare system · Data Envelopment Analysis (DEA) · EU countries

1 Introduction

The concept of efficiency in the healthcare is developed based on the overall goal to achieve maximum quality and effective utilization of the investments made in this sphere. The variety of options and decisions of where to use the expenditures for health care makes this task complicated. Although most EU countries spend similar share of 8–11% of their GDP for healthcare (OECD.org 2017), the financial value of investment and its target areas differ significantly. As a result the research literature and consulting companies propose analysis in the forms of the reports on country rankings according to their efficiency. However, the efficiency evaluation has no standard template; instead it presents vast variety of models used for country rankings. The models not only analyse different groups of countries, but use different data sets for input and output variables, which hinders possibility for validation of findings. The rankings proposed by Bloomberg (Lu and Du 2016) analyse only medium and large countries (over 5M population),

© Springer International Publishing AG 2017
W. Abramowicz (Ed.): BIS 2017 Workshops, LNBIP 303, pp. 97–109, 2017.
https://doi.org/10.1007/978-3-319-69023-0_10

EU reports focus on statistical data analysis of EU15 and EU28 country sets (Medeiros and Schwierz 2015).

The statistical data and criteria used for healthcare system ranking are defined in different ways. In the research of Bloomberg (Lu and Du 2016) it is based on data of life expectancy; cost of health care per capita (percentage of GDP per capita); and the absolute per capita cost of health care (including costs for preventive and curative services, family planning, nutrition and emergency aid). The report of World Health organization presents 100 indicators, categorized into four main groups of Health status, Risk factors, Service coverage, Health system for monitoring healthcare (World Health Statistics 2016).

The availability of statistical data determines wide usage of indicators, such as life duration at birth, expected life duration after 65 or expected duration of healthy life after 65 for measuring output of healthcare efficiency level. Some indicators denoting subjective patient-reported characteristics are not consistently collected by countries and have limited use in healthcare evaluation in the forms of survey reports, such as Patient safety and quality of care (2013).

The selection of indicators for analysis is partly determined by the methods used for efficiency evaluation. In order to explore efficiency of the healthcare in different EU countries, we proposed to apply DEA (Data Envelopment Analysis) method. This method is selected due to its ability to sort objects described by the set of factors or attributes. DEA is one of the prevailing methods used for efficiency evaluation in healthcare. As it can be observed in summary report (McGlynn 2008), the research literature on healthcare efficiency in USA during 1982–2006 is mainly based on DEA models, overcoming popularity of regression and ratio based methods. We have selected research of Medeiros and Schwierz (2015) for comparative evaluation of our findings. The authors of this report have applied DEA method for evaluation of healthcare in EU countries, however in different settings and with different indicators.

2 Efficiency Evaluation Indicators

Due to selection of the DEA based efficiency evaluation findings for validation of our research (Medeiros and Schwierz 2015) and the availability of statistical data we selected the indicators consistently reported by all EU countries. In general the statistical data of healthcare presents big variety of factors, which potentially have different impact to the efficiency of healthcare. However, there is lack of research works which explore interrelationships and importance of indicators of different origin. The necessity of grouping input variables is also implied by the DEA method selected for analysis, as it has a limitation for the number of included input variables (in respect to the number of research objects – 28 EU countries). As an advantage, grouping of variables is helpful in the cases of missing statistical data in particular countries, where some characteristics within the group can be defined by experts or replaced by aggregated influence of the group.

The other important difference of experimental approach is in application of financial data of healthcare expenditures. Most research works include it into input variable set. For our research we aimed to define healthcare status of the country without using this variable, and making further quality-cost analysis in the second stage of research.

We have divided the healthcare factors into 5 indicator groups (Fig. 1): Infrastructure, Life style, Country general statistics, Service consumption and Subjective healthcare measures.

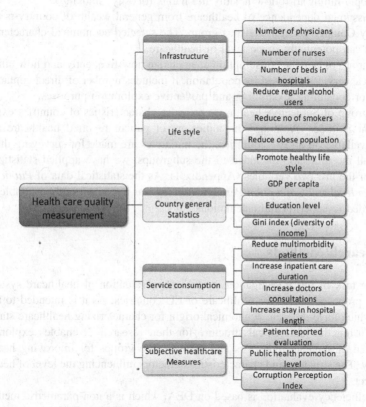

Fig. 1. Factors describing the healthcare quality

The hierarchical structure enables to include subgroups of factors which can affect efficiency of healthcare, and imply costs (as in Fig. 1). The number of indicators can be extended, but for each group we have limited to 3 or 4 factors per group, as the further applied research method is very sensitive to big number of input variables.

The Infrastructure group characterizes the expenditures of the country to the main infrastructural compounds of healthcare, such as hiring professional physicians and nurses, buying equipment for hospitals, increasing number of beds for patients. The medical reforms of EU countries revealed different strategies addressing financing of these indicators aiming to improving efficiency of the overall infrastructure.

The Life style group characterizes general culture of nurturing personal health by people, it also includes preventive measures and treatment priorities to risk groups. The group describes country investments into promoting healthy life style, access to healthy environment, food, and preventive activities to alcohol consumption, also concern about people failing to follow healthy life habits (obesity, smoking).

The assumed dependence of healthcare from general wealth of country is charac-terized by Country general statistics group. The selected economical characteristic of countries can potentially shape level of healthcare.

The group of Service consumption characterize how frequently and how efficiently the medical services are used by population. It includes number of direct contacts with doctors for consulting, examining and preventive exploration purposes.

The group of Subjective healthcare provides characteristics of countries expressed by patient attitudes. Although the indicators of patient reported healthcare are not readily available on all EU countries, the initiatives are made for surveying the data.

For all the indicators included to the subgroups, we have applied statistical data except for the last two variables (Appendix 1). As the statistical data of *Public health promotion level* and *Corruption Perception index* was not consistently available, it was not included to experimental calculations.

3   Research Methods

The main task of our investigation is efficiency evaluation of healthcare systems by applying proposed model for healthcare of EU countries. As it is intended to explore factors which have different economical origin for characterizing healthcare status, we propose using the hierarchical structure for their research. It enables exploring the importance of separate indicators and of the entire groups for improving healthcare efficiency. The structure and characteristics of factors influencing the level of healthcare are in Sect. 2.

The efficiency evaluation is based on DEA, which is a non-parametric method for efficiency evaluation of the set of decision making units (DMU). DMU is understood as sample set of objects or products for which we want to estimate efficiency. In our case the DMU set consists of 28 EU countries. The aim of experimental analysis is to estimate healthcare efficiency for each corresponding country included to DMU set.

We understand the efficiency in healthcare as an attribute of performance that is measured by examining the relationship between a specific product of the health care system (output) and the resources used to create that product (inputs). We define a country to have efficient healthcare system if it is able to maximize output for a given set of inputs or to minimize inputs used to produce a given output.

The principles of DEA method were introduced by Charnes et al. (1978). By using linear programming method DEA helps to construct a piece-wise surface (or frontier) enclosing the data. Efficiency then is calculated as the distance relative to this surface.

DEA assigns a score of efficiency to DMU equal to 1 only when comparisons with other DMU do not show the inefficiency for any input or output (DMU is placed on the frontier). For the inefficient DMU its efficiency score is less than one. It means that a linear combination of other units could produce the same vector of outputs by using a smaller vector of inputs.

The formal expression of the DEA is as follows (Trick 1998). Let $\{X_i\}$ and $\{Y_i\}$ be the vectors of inputs and outputs of the DMUi. Let $\{X_k\}$ be the inputs and $\{Y_k\}$ be the output vector of DMUk for which we want to determine its efficiency. The measure of efficiency for DMU k is estimated by the following linear program:

$$Find \quad MinQ:$$
$$s.t. \quad \sum \lambda_i X_i \leq QX_k$$
$$\sum \lambda_i Y_i \geq Y_k, \lambda \geq 0$$

where λ_i is the weight assigned to DMU i, $Q \leq 1$ is the efficiency of DMU k.

In case of $Q = 1$ we have the efficient DMU unit. The DMU with nonzero λ_i is non-efficient and can be compared with the others DMU units. The differences expressed by $X_k - \sum \lambda_i X_i$ show the inputs which exceed the 'necessary' level, therefore the causes of DMU inefficiency can be explained by over extensive use of corresponding inputs.

The computations of DEA method can be performed by using Solver procedure of MS Excel, but it is not convenient for solving tasks for big DMU sets and numerous input/output variables. We applied the open source software (OSDEA), suitable for different types of DEA problems (http://opensourcedea.org/).

4 Research Results

By applying definition of variables and main concepts of applying DEA principles in Sects. 2 and 3, the efficiency is understood as the ratio of outputs to inputs. The greater efficiency means more output produced per unit of input.

We evaluate the efficiency of healthcare of EU countries by using DEA algorithm as described in Sect. 3. In order to reduce the number of variables, the inputs are selected as groups of quality factors (Fig. 1). The output variable should reflect the level of healthcare system in the country. We applied recommendation of medical authorities to use the Life expectancy at birth/at age 65 or Healthy life expectancy at birth/at age 65, which are determined by high level of healthcare system. Although DEA method allows to use several output variables, we have selected only one - *Healthy life expectancy at age 65* illustrated by country data (Table 1).

Table 1. Healthy life expectancy at age 65 (http://ec.europa.eu/eurostat)

AT	15.3	FI	16.1	MT	16.3
BE	15.8	FR	17.1	NL	17.9
BG	10.4	HR	8.6	PL	10.0
CY	13.3	HU	9.6	PT	10.4
CZ	12.1	IE	18.1	RO	11.6
DE	16.2	IT	13.6	SE	18.1
DK	16.1	LT	7.9	SI	12.7
EE	11.1	LU	16.1	SK	9.0
EL	14.2	LV	9.1	UK	17.9
ES	16.2				

In general, it is recommended that number of items in DMU set is at least twice bigger than number of inputs+outputs. As we have only 28 DMU (EU countries), we estimated the efficiency separately for each input factor group from Level 1 (see Fig. 1): *Infrastructure, Life style, Country general Statistics, Service consumption, Subjective healthcare Measures*. The Fig. 2 shows the OSDEA software tool window for calculation EU countries efficiency for the input of *Subjective healthcare Measures*.

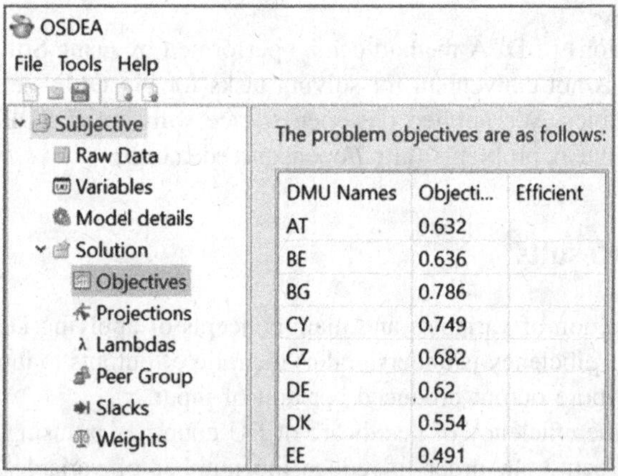

Fig. 2. Example of OSDEA program window

Using the OSDEA software we calculate the efficiency ratios for *Infrastructure, Life style, Country general Statistics, Service consumption, Subjective healthcare Measures* as input variables and *Healthy life expectancy at age 65* as output variable. In Table 2 we combine the efficiency ratios for all countries and all input factors of Level

Table 2. The efficiency ratios for EU countries

	Infrastructure	Life style	Country general	Service consumption	Subjective quality measures	Average all factors
AT	0.72	0.79	0.80	0.67	0.63	0,72
BE	0.81	0.87	0.88	0.91	0.64	0,82
BG	0.74	0.90	1.00	0.75	0.79	0,84
CY	1.00	0.85	0.75	0.76	0.75	0,82
CZ	0.62	0.69	0.82	0.59	0.68	0,68
DE	0.70	0.85	0.83	0.62	0.62	0,72
DK	0.73	0.82	0.87	1.00	0.55	0,79
EE	0.68	0.72	0.78	0.46	0,49	0,63
EL	1.00	1.00	0.89	0.88	1.00	0,95
ES	1.00	0.87	0.88	0.95	0.87	0,91
FI	0.92	0.82	0.92	0.63	0.56	0,77
FR	0.92	1.00	0.92	1.00	0.77	0,92
HR	0.61	0.50	0.70	0.43	0.54	0,56
HU	0.62	0.45	0.73	0.38	0.62	0,56
IE	1.00	0.95	0.88	1.00	0.77	0,92
IT	0.78	0.96	0.72	0.79	0.90	0,83
LT	0.44	0.58	0.57	0.36	0.41	0,47
LU	0.88	0.81	0.84	1.00	0.62	0,83
LV	0.69	0.53	0.73	0.39	0.49	0,57
MT	1.00	1.00	1.00	0.86	0.92	0,96
NL	1.00	1.00	0.99	0.78	0.67	0,89
PL	0.79	0.66	0.76	0.49	0.50	0,64
PT	0.70	0.73	0.73	0.48	0.52	0,63
RO	0.91	1.00	1.00	0.86	0.75	0,90
SE	1.00	1.00	1.00	1.00	0.64	0,93
SI	0.82	0.69	0.86	0.63	0.65	0,73
SK	0.59	0.55	0.65	0.44	0.55	0,56
UK	1.00	0.95	0.93	0.91	0.68	0,89

1. The input-oriented model is calculated, which shows how the inputs are used for achieving given level of output. In Table 2 the 7 most inefficient EU countries in healthcare under each input factor are highlighted.

The last column of Table 2 is average of all efficiency ratios under each input factor and indicate the overall level of healthcare system in selected country. From this point of view the most inefficient countries are Lithuania (LT), Latvia (LV), Slovakia (SK), Hungary (HU) and Croatia (HR).

This table also shows which input factors can be improved. As an example, Lithuania, Latvia, Slovakia, and Croatia should improve all the input factors, for Greece it is enough to change *Country general* and *Service consumption*. Similar findings can be done for other EU countries. The Appendix 2, discloses possible reduction of all income factors to fix output factor values to the present values.

As the second step, the Efficiency/Expenditure ratio for EU countries is explored. For this purpose we use the calculated healthcare efficiency estimate and the data of Expenditures (Appendix 1). The Fig. 3 presents scaterplots of efficiency vs. expenditures of EU countries.

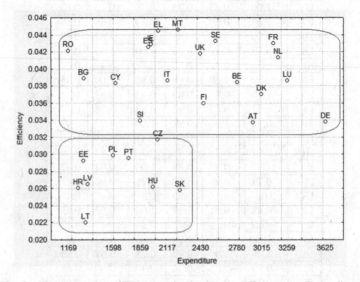

Fig. 3. The scatterplot of EU countries healthcare Efficiency vs Expenditure

On the Fig. 3 we have selected two groups of EU countries – with low and high efficiency. It is interesting to notice that low expenditure countries can be rather efficient in healthcare, but high level of expenditures can secure high efficiency.

The application of output-oriented DEA model enables us to estimate what is the optimal value of *Healthy life expectancy at age 65* in case the input factors are fixed to present value. It shows, how the output can be improved by efficiently using given inputs. The estimated optimal number of healthy years after 65, average value and current value of healthy years after 65 are calculated in Table 3.

In Table 3 we can notice that Lithuania (LT), Slovakia (SK) and Croatia (HR) can potentially double the expected healthy life after 65. They just need to optimally utilize the input factors.

Table 3. Optimal values of *Healthy life expectancy at age 65* in case of fixed input factors.

	Infrastructure	Life style	Country general	Service consumption	Subjective quality measures	Average	Today Situation
AT	21	21	38	25	24	26	15.3
BE	19	20	33	35	25	27	15.8
BG	14	10	10	10	13	12	10.4
CY	13	18	23	20	18	18	13.3
CZ	20	19	26	31	18	23	12.1
DE	23	25	35	23	26	26	16.2
DK	22	16	35	16	29	24	16.1
EE	16	19	21	11	23	18	11.1
EL	14	14	18	25	14	17	14.2
ES	16	18	16	20	19	18	16.2
FI	18	29	35	16	29	25	16.1
FR	19	17	31	17	22	21	17.1
HR	14	15	16	30	16	18	8.6
HU	16	10	18	27	15	17	9.6
IE	18	18	29	18	24	21	18.1
IT	17	19	21	35	15	21	13.6
LT	18	15	8	26	19	17	7.9
LU	18	16	40	38	26	28	16.1
LV	13	16	17	17	18	16	9.1
MT	16	16	16	31	18	20	16.3
NL	18	21	36	25	27	25	17.9
PL	13	18	20	20	20	18	10.0
PT	15	13	10	17	20	15	10.4
RO	13	12	12	37	15	18	11.6
SE	18	32	37	18	28	27	18.1
SI	16	22	26	22	20	21	12.7
SK	15	17	24	25	16	20	9.0
UK	18	18	28	20	26	22	17.9

In Appendix 2 we introduce the table calculated by using input-oriented DEA method. It shows the possible cutting level of input variables to keep the same *Healthy life expectancy at age 65*. From this table we can identify the factors which potential are insufficiently utilized.

5 Conclusions and Main Results

The efficiency testing procedures by using DEA method were applied for exploring efficiency of healthcare. The methodology includes proposed hierarchical grouping of the variable data by applying input- and output-oriented computation methodologies of DEA and comparing them to evaluation outcome (*Healthy life expectancy at age 65*). The experimental evaluation was applied for 28 countries of EU by using statistical data of 2013–2015.

The research revealed that the healthcare systems of EU countries are in very diverse positions by their efficiency. The 'old' EU countries allocate the considerable amount of GDP to this sector and manage to secure high level of healthcare efficiency. At the same time the healthcare quality outcomes (*Life expectancy, Healthy life expectancy*) are higher than in other EU countries.

The research also showed that number of countries with the low healthcare budget are capable to achieve high value of the long *Healthy life expectancy* factor, but this effect cannot be directly explained by the input variables applied for research. It can be assumed that the model should be amended by more variables characterizing other peculiarities of countries, such as good climate, healthy food, and no-stress living conditions.

The results obtained by our research can assist the healthcare authorities to identify the shortages in country healthcare system and invite for action for improving healthy life expectancy for all EU population.

Acknowledgement. This work was performed within the framework of the COST action "European Network for cost containment and improved quality of health care" http://www.cost.eu/COST_Actions/ca/CA15222.

Appendix 1. Data Set of Healthcare Quality Factors

	Infrastructure				Life style				Country general				Service consumption			Subjective quality measures		
	Total health expenditure per capita, in PPP	Physicians per 100000 population	Nurses per 100000 population	Beds per 1000 population	Alcohol consumption in litres per capita	Regular smokers, % of population aged 15+	Population with Body mass Index >=30, in %	People taking care on health-enhancing in %	GDP per capita, in PPP	Education Gini	Gini	Multimorbidity patients in %	Inpatient care duration	Doctors consultations (in all settings)	Average length of stay in hospitals	Corruption Perception Index	Patient reported evaluation	Public health promotion level
AT	2935	4,8	7,9	7,6	13,8	27,7	8,8	74,9	31588	77,1	27,2	35,8	8,2	6,8	9,8	75		
BE	2780	2,9	15,4	6,3	11	28,1	11,5	51,2	29520	68,1	26,2	24,9	8	6,4	8,4	77		
BG	1319	3,7	4,7	6,4	10	33,7	12,4	17,3	11259	76	37	20,5	8	6,4	5,4	41		
CY	1619	3	4,9	3,5	9,2	30,7	12,3	39,8	23133	71,7	33,6	32	8	6,4	5,8	55		
CZ	2025	3,6	8,5	6,8	11,7	25,4	12,9	52,6	20094	86,1	25	31,5	9,4	6,4	9,4	55		
DE	3625	3,8	11,6	8,2	11,2	24,5	12,2	71,2	30172	81,6	30,1	38,7	9	9,9	9	81		
DK	3015	3,5	15,7	3,5	12,2	35	8,6	81,3	31405	69,3	27,4	28	8	4,5	5,5	90		
EE	1315	3,3	6,5	5,3	7,3	31,6	13,3	47,7	17218	82,3	34,8	45,8	7,6	6,3	9,2	70		
EL	2032	6,1	3,3	4,9	10	38,2	10,7	25,9	20159	62,9	34,2	23,9	8	6,4	6,1	44		
ES	1937	4,1	5,5	3,1	11,9	31,8	11,3	49,0	23793	53	34,6	29,6	8	6,4	5,7	58		
FI	2461	2,7	10,7	5,5	8,8	24,1	10,1	77,0	28560	77,1	25,2	45,9	10,6	4,2	10,5	89		
FR	3127	3,1	9	6,4	14,8	28,1	7,3	51,0	27812	68,9	29,2	37	8	6,3	5,6	69		
HR	1266	2,8	5,7	5,8	12,9	27,4	11	41,4	14703	74,7	30,6	30,6	8	6,5	9,6	49		
HU	1978	3	6,4	7,2	12,8	34,9	18,5	56,6	16433	76,2	28,2	37	9,5	11,8	9,5	48		
IE	1962	2,7	12,6	2,9	12,6	29,3	13	51,2	31933	70,3	32	27,1	6	6,5	6,1	73		
IT	2117	4,1	6,6	3,4	9,5	25,2	8,4	35,0	25380	54,6	32,4	24,7	8	6,5	7,8	47		
LT	1395	3,7	7,2	7,4	7,1	28,6	16	36,3	16413	84,1	37,9	32,3	8	8,7	7,7	59		
LU	3259	2,8	11,6	5,4	14,9	26,3	16,5	63,5	63892	70,9	28,5	22,6	6,8	5,9	8,4	81		
LV	1352	2,9	4,9	5,9	8,7	32,3	15,5	48,6	14439	80,5	35,4	40,6	8,3	5,8	8,5	57		
MT	2218	3,1	6,8	4,5	6,4	25,2	23	52,7	21524	41,1	28,1	28,1	8	6,5	7,9	55		
NL	3172	3	8,6	4,7	9,9	34,1	7,8	51,2	31853	68,3	26,7	34,8	8	8	9	83		
PL	1598	2,2	5,8	6,5	8,4	34,9	11,4	41,2	16092	82,5	30,6	33,9	6,9	7,2	6,9	62		
PT	1748	3	6,3	3,4	13,7	22	12,2	37,2	19500	35,8	34	40,3	8,9	6,5	7,5	62		
RO	1169	2,4	5,4	6,1	10,8	21,7	8,6	15,6	12742	70,6	37,4	18,9	7,4	6,5	7,5	48		
SE	2578	3,9	11,1	2,7	6,3	21,3	8,9	75,4	30807	75,6	25,2	32,5	5,7	2,9	7,1	88		
SI	1859	2,5	8,4	4,6	11,8	25,8	12,3	61,0	20695	80,3	24,5	32,2	6,9	6,6	6,9	61		
SK	2232	3	6,3	6,1	10,5	23,3	16,8	52,3	18777	84,3	23,7	30,3	7,3	11,3	7,3	51		
UK	2430	2,8	10,3	2,9	10	27,4	18,3	59,8	26206	76,2	32,4	34,2	7,1	5,7	6,9	81		

Own calculations based on Eurostat, OECD, Heijink et al. (2015).

Appendix 2. Result Table of Possible Cutting Level of Input Variables to Keep the Same *Healthy Life Expectancy at Age 65*

	Infrastructure			Life style				Country general			Service consumption				Subjective quality measures		
	Physicians per 100000 population	Nurses per 100000 population	Beds per 1000 population	Alcohol consumption litres per capita	Regular smokers, % of population aged 15+	Population with Body mass index >=30, in %	People taking care on health-enhancing in %	GDP per capita, in PPP	Education-Gini	Multimorbidity patients, in %	Inpatient care duration	Doctors consultations (in all settings)	Average length of stay in hospitals	Corruption Perception Index	Patient reported evaluation	Public health promotion level
AT	28.4	28.4	47.0	27.7	27.7	27.7	27.7	59.4	59.4	59.4	38.9	38.9	38.9	36.8		
BE	18.7	28.6	59.8	21.6	33.5	21.6	21.6	52.5	52.5	52.5	55.2	55.2	55.2	36.4		
BG	26.2	26.2	67.5	0.0	0.0	0.0	0.0	0.0	0.0	0.0	0.0	0.0	0.0	21.4		
CY	0.0	0.0	0.0	24.6	48.0	24.6	24.6	42.4	42.4	42.4	34.8	34.8	34.8	25.1		
CZ	38.2	38.2	51.5	36.9	53.6	36.9	36.9	54.3	54.3	74.5	61.2	61.2	61.2	31.8		
DE	29.7	29.7	52.9	34.1	34.1	34.1	34.1	53.9	53.9	53.9	29.5	45.6	29.5	38.0		
DK	27.0	29.8	27.0	0.0	0.0	0.0	0.0	54.3	54.3	54.3	0.0	0.0	0.0	44.6		
EE	31.8	31.8	43.2	42.9	42.9	42.9	42.9	46.4	46.4	46.4	0.0	0.0	0.0	50.9		
EL	0.0	0.0	0.0	0.0	0.0	0.0	0.0	21.9	21.9	21.9	43.9	43.9	43.9	0.0		
ES	0.0	0.0	0.0	11.5	11.5	11.5	11.5	0.0	0.0	0.0	19.1	23.2	19.1	13.5		
FI	8.0	8.0	52.7	44.4	44.4	44.4	44.4	54.2	54.2	54.2	0.0	0.0	0.0	43.9		
FR	7.8	7.8	31.1	0.0	0.0	0.0	0.0	44.0	44.0	44.0	0.0	0.0	0.0	23.2		
HR	38.9	38.9	59.5	44.4	46.1	44.4	44.4	44.7	44.7	82.7	71.6	71.6	71.6	45.6		
HU	38.1	38.1	63.3	0.0	0.0	0.0	0.0	48.0	48.0	79.0	64.6	75.3	64.6	38.0		
IE	0.0	0.0	0.0	0.0	0.0	0.0	0.0	38.2	38.2	38.2	0.0	0.0	0.0	23.2		
IT	22.1	22.1	22.1	26.9	26.9	26.9	26.9	35.8	35.8	35.8	60.8	62.0	60.8	10.3		
LT	56.4	56.4	71.1	49.8	49.8	48.8	48.8	0.0	0.0	0.0	69.2	80.9	69.2	58.5		
LU	12.1	12.1	52.0	0.0	0.0	0.0	0.0	76.2	59.9	59.9	63.7	57.8	57.8	38.4		
LV	30.5	30.5	59.2	43.8	43.7	43.7	43.7	45.7	45.7	59.2	46.5	46.5	46.5	50.5		
MT	0.0	0.0	0.0	0.0	0.0	0.0	0.0	0.0	0.0	0.0	47.2	47.9	47.2	8.2		
NL	0.0	0.0	0.0	15.3	15.3	15.3	27.1	49.8	49.8	49.8	27.6	46.0	27.6	33.2		
PL	20.6	20.6	59.0	44.5	43.2	43.2	43.2	49.2	49.2	76.2	48.8	78.2	48.8	50.0		
PT	29.9	29.9	47.7	17.2	55.7	17.2	17.2	0.0	0.0	0.0	38.5	51.5	38.5	48.0		
RO	9.1	9.1	0.0	0.0	0.0	0.0	0.0	0.0	0.0	0.0	68.4	68.4	68.4	25.1		
SE	0.0	0.0	0.0	43.3	45.7	43.3	43.3	51.3	51.3	51.3	0.0	0.0	0.0	36.3		
SI	18.4	18.4	44.8	41.3	45.9	41.3	41.3	50.7	50.7	70.8	41.0	71.2	41.0	35.5		
SK	41.4	41.4	59.5	48.0	63.7	48.0	48.0	62.6	62.6	84.3	64.6	89.7	64.6	45.3		
UK	0.0	0.0	0.0	0.0	0.0	0.0	0.0	35.6	35.6	35.6	9.4	30.6	9.4	31.5		

References

Charnes, A., Cooper, W.W., Rhodes, E.: Measuring the efficiency of decision making units. Eur. J. Oper. Res. **2**, 429–444 (1978)

Heijink, R., et al.: Comparative efficiency of health systems, corrected for selected lifestyle factors. Funded by the European Commission and carried out by the Dutch National Institute for Public Health and the Environment (RIVM) (2015). http://ec.europa.eu/health/systems_performance_assessment/docs/2015_maceli_report_en.pdf

Medeiros, J., Schwierz, C.: Efficiency estimates of health care systems in the EU. European Commission, Directorate-General for Economic and Financial Affairs, Economic Papers 549, June 2015

Lu, W., Du, L.: U.S. health-care system ranks as one of the least-efficient (2016). https://www.bloomberg.com/news/articles/2016-09-29/u-s-health-care-system-ranks-as-one-of-the-least-efficient

McGlynn, E.A.: Identifying, categorizing, and evaluating health care efficiency measures. Final report (prepared by the Southern California Evidence-based Practice Center—RAND Corporation, Under Contract No. 282-00-0005-21). AHRQ Publication No. 08-0030. Agency for Healthcare Research and Quality, Rockville (2008)

Patient safety and quality of care: Special Eurobarometer 411 (2013). http://ec.europa.eu/commfrontoffice/publicopinion/archives/ebs/ebs_411_en.pdf

Trick, M.: Data envelopment analysis, 26 August 1998. Michael Trick's Operations Research Page: http://mat.gsia.cmu.edu/classes/QUANT/NOTES/chap12.pdf. Accessed 30 Sept 2012

World Health Statistics: Monitoring health for the SDGs (2016). http://www.who.int/gho/publications/world_health_statistics/2016/en/

OECD.org. Data for Measuring Health Care Quality and Outcomes (2017). http://www.oecd.org/els/health-systems/health-care-quality-indicators.htm

BITA Workshop

BITA 2017 Workshop Chairs' Message

Ulf Seigerroth, Kurt Sandkuhl, and Julia Kaidalova

A contemporary challenge for enterprises is to keep up with the pace of changing business demands imposed on them in different ways. Today there is an obvious demand for continuous improvement and alignment in enterprises, but unfortunately many organizations do not have proper instruments (methods, tools, patterns, best practices etc.) to achieve this. Enterprise modeling, enterprise architecture, and business process management are three areas belonging to traditions where the mission is to improve business practice and business and IT alignment (BITA). BITA is often manifested through the transition of taking an enterprise from one state (AS-IS) into another improved state (TO-BE), i.e., a transformation of the enterprise and its supporting IT into something that is regarded as better. A challenge with BITA is to move beyond a narrow focus on one tradition or technology. There is a need to be aware of and be able to deal with a number of dimensions of the enterprise architecture and their relations in order to create alignment. Examples of such dimensions are: organizational structures, strategies, business models, work practices, processes, and IS/IT structures. Among the concepts that deserve special attention in this context is enterprise architecture management (EAM). An effective EAM aligns IT investments with overall business priorities, determines who makes the IT decisions, and assigns accountability for the outcomes. IT governance is also a dimension that traditionally has had a strong impact on BITA. There are ordinarily three governance mechanisms that an enterprise needs to have in place: (1) decision-making structures, (2) alignment process, and (3) formal communications.

This workshop aimed to bring together people who have an interest in BITA. We invited researchers and practitioners from both industry and academia to submit original results of their completed or ongoing projects. We encouraged a broad understanding of the possible approaches and solutions for BITA, including EAM and IT governance subjects. A specific focus was placed on practices of business and IT alignment, i.e., we encouraged the submission of case study and experiences papers.

The workshop received ten submissions, of which the Program Committee selected five for presentation at the workshop.

We thank all members of the Program Committee, the authors, and the local organizers for their efforts and support.

Organization

Chair

Ulf Seigerroth   Jönköping University, Sweden

Co-chairs

Kurt Sandkuhl   Rostock University, Germany
Julia Kaidalova   Jönköping University, Germany

Program Committee

Jānis Grabis	Riga Technical University, Latvia
Birger Lantow	University of Rostock, Germany
Michael Fellmann	University of Rostock, Germany
Stijn Hoppenbrouwers	HAN University of Applied Sciences, The Netherlands
Nikolay Shilov	SPIIRAS, Russia
Alexander Smirnov	SPIIRAS, Russia
John Krogstie	IDI, NTNU, Norway
Janis Stirna	Stockholm University, Sweden
Andreas L. Opdahl	University of Bergen, Norway
Hasan Koç	Universität Rostock, Germany
Björn Johansson	Lund University, Sweden
Marite Kirikova	Riga Technical University, Latvia
Vladimir Tarasov	Jönkoping University, Sweden
Oscar Pastor Lopez	Universitat Politecnica de Valencia, Spain
Anne Persson	University of Skövde, Sweden

The Effect of Strategic Alignment of Complementary IT and Organizational Capabilities on Competitive Firm Performance

Rogier van de Wetering[1]([✉]) and Patrick Mikalef[2]

[1] Open University of the Netherlands,
Valkenburgerweg 177, 6419 AT Heerlen, The Netherlands
rogier.vandewetering@ou.nl
[2] Norwegian University of Science and Technology, Trondheim, Norway
patrick.mikalef@ntnu.no

Abstract. This study explores how firm performance can be explained from the strategic alignment of information technology (IT) and organizational capabilities, i.e., IT flexibility, dynamic capabilities, and absorptive capacity. We build upon dynamic capabilities theory and conceptualize our research model through the lens of strategic alignment methods. Then, we empirically test our main hypothesis using PLS-SEM analysis on a sample of 322 international firms. Outcomes show that measurements and indicators of all first-order and higher-order constructs are reliable and valid. Results also indicate that there is a positive relationship between strategic alignment and competitive firm performance. This study highlights the importance of alignment between IT and organizational capabilities. Strategic alignment can, therefore, be seen an important facilitator of competitive firm performance in constantly changing environments. We conclude with a discussion and conclusion, outline limitations of the current study and present some directions for future research.

Keywords: Strategic alignment · IT flexibility · Dynamic capabilities · Absorptive capacity · Third-order factor modeling · Structural Equation Modeling (SEM) · Firm performance

1 Introduction

During the past two decades, it has become apparent that firms that want to be more competitive need to align their business operations, information systems and information technology (IS/IT) resources and capabilities and take into account the dynamics of the changing environment [1–4]. Synthesizing from recognized sources on IS/IT development, effectiveness and IS/IT alignment [3, 5–8], we contend that a flexible IT infrastructure—as a key quality of IT capabilities [9, 10]—and other complementary organizational capabilities in harmony strengthen a firm's armory to drive a firm's competitive advantage [4, 11–14]. Organizational capabilities can be considered processes that facilitate the most efficient, effective and competitive use of firms' assets whether tangible or intangible [15]. Hence, capabilities, therefore, represent the potential of a firm to achieve certain objectives by means of focused

© Springer International Publishing AG 2017
W. Abramowicz (Ed.): BIS 2017 Workshops, LNBIP 303, pp. 115–126, 2017.
https://doi.org/10.1007/978-3-319-69023-0_11

deployment and are considered the building blocks on which they compete in the market. IT capabilities can be defined as firms' ability to mobilize and deploy IT-based resources in combination or co-present with other resources and capabilities in order to differentiate from competition [16].

Synergies between a firm's IT and organizational resources and capabilities are the foundation of what is called 'strategic alignment' [5, 17–19]. Recently, a growing body of literature has stressed the importance of adopting a dynamic methodological approach, in which scholars and practitioners are equipped with adequate assessment tools and mechanisms for examining the processes when IT adds value under rapidly changing conditions [4] and increases levels of competitiveness and innovativeness [14, 20–22]. However, there is currently very little published IS/IT and management scholarship that addresses this particular challenge of simultaneously leveraging and aligning current IS/IT, complementary organizational resources and IT capabilities to improve competitive firm performance (and hereinafter referred to as performance) [3, 8, 9, 11, 13, 23].

Given the above, our main objective is to investigate whether, and if so, to what extent strategic alignment of complementary IT and organizational dynamic capabilities influences performance. Strategic alignment, in this particular context, refers to the degree of equilibrium between different organizational dimensions [5, 6, 13, 24, 25]. Hence, we draw from theoretical developments of the dynamic capabilities theory (DCT) [2]. This is an influential theoretical perspective that is feasible to identify and prescribe organizational and strategic routines and explains how firms must co-evolve and reconfigure their IS/IT operations and IT architecture. Additionally, we build upon novel work done by Van de Wetering [24, 25] who developed a novel approach toward strategic alignment [2]. To this end, we conceptualize our research model through the lens of strategic alignment theories and methods.

The remainder of this paper is outlined as follows. First, we review theoretical aspects relevant to this study. Next, we outline our research model which is followed by the methods and results section. We end with main findings, discussions, inherent limitations of this study and we outline future research opportunities.

2   Theoretical Background

Emerging insights suggests that strategic alignment between IT and complementary organizational capabilities strengthen a firm's ability to generate IT business value and ultimately enhancing a firm's competitive advantage and innovativeness [11, 13, 14, 21]. Our current focus is on how firms can become more competitive by synchronizing their (a) ability to (re)use and reconfigure IS/IT strategically, (b) their capabilities to differentiate and compete in a turbulent environment, and (c) complementary IT-related capacities to learn and transform business operations. Thus, we now review the three core pillars of this research, i.e., (1) IT flexibility, (2) dynamic capabilities and (3) a firm's absorptive capacity.

2.1 Pillar I: IT Flexibility

IT flexibility can be defined as 'the degree of decomposition of an organization's IT portfolio into loosely coupled subsystems that communicate through standardized interfaces' [26]. Flexible and modular system design dates back to Simon's theory of near decomposability [27]. In essence, this theory argues that complex systems consisting of modular, or else nearly decomposable subunits, tend to evolve faster, increase the rate of adaptive response and tune towards stable, self-generating configurations [27]. Modularity is a characteristic which largely determines the effectiveness in implementing continuous change, and is suggested to be an antecedent of dynamic capabilities [23, 28], see next section. Abstracting these concepts to the IS domain, modularity has, e.g., been examined as the flexibility of the IT architecture and the decentralization of the IT governance structure [26]. It also emerged as a key competitive priority in many organizational activities and is considered as a critical component to efficaciously adapt and reconfigure IT architectures strategically [12, 29]. Moreover, flexible IT architectures have been labeled as a facilitator of IT-based competitive actions and recent work showed that characteristics of a firm's IT architecture facilitate and strengthen (IT-enabled) dynamic capabilities [23].

2.2 Pillar II: Dynamic Capabilities

DCT has emerged as an influential perspective in the study of strategic management over the past decade and attempts to explain the processes through which a firm evolves in changing environments and maintains a competitive edge [2, 30, 31]. Due to conditions of high environmental uncertainty, market volatility, and frequent change, scholars have raised questions regarding the rate to which traditional operational and existing 'resource-based' capabilities erode and cease to provide competitive gains [32, 33]. Literature has suggested that under these particular conditions the focus should be shifted toward strengthening 'dynamic' capacities of change and readjustment of operational capabilities [32]. Dynamic capabilities, therefore, constitute the firm's ability to use resources—specifically processes to integrate, reconfigure, gain and release resources—to match and even create market change [1, 2]. Studies have relied on baseline work by Teece et al. [2] in order to isolate main routines that underpin dynamic capabilities and empirically measure them. Most recent work suggests that dynamic capabilities comprise of the following routines: (1) sensing, (2) coordinating, (3) learning, (4) integrating, and (5) reconfiguring [23, 34, 35].

Synthesizing from the above, the DCT is therefore considered an appropriate 'framework' to explain how firms can differentiate and compete in a turbulent environment, taking into account that they must evolve and co-evolutionary reconfigure their (IS/IT) operations and IT architecture in order to remain competitive.

2.3 Pillar III: Absorptive Capacity

Strongly related to DCT is a firm's absorptive capacity (ACAP). This capacity refers to the ability to identify and recognize the value of new, external information, acquire, assimilate or transform this information (or knowledge) into the firm's knowledge base, and apply this new knowledge through innovation and competitive actions [36, 37]. This 'hard-to-copy' capacity does not simply depend on firms' direct interface with the external environment, but actually, also on the transfer of knowledge across and within the organization. ACAP is a multidimensional construct, through which a firm's long-term survival and success can be strengthened [36]. This particular concept has been studied in the context of many IS/IT domains, i.e., IT business value, knowledge management/transfer, IT assimilation and business-IT knowledge [11, 12, 38].

A key takeaway from a recent study [11] is that IT business value is a result of a synergetic and complementary relationship between an organization's IT capabilities and ACAP. Following the dominant perspective and approach that ACAP is an organizational capability and not an asset, we subsequently regard a firm's ACAP as the complementary IT-related capability (to dynamic capabilities and IT flexibility) rather than a firm's prior related knowledge [7] that affects its ability to reconfigure its existing substantive capabilities [11].

3 Research Model

Within our research model we statistically and appropriately capture strategic alignment by a pattern of covariation, which coincides with the concept of (co-) alignment as a statistical scheme within Structural Equation Modeling (SEM) [24, 39]. Thus, strategic alignment of IT and organizational dynamic capabilities can be modeled using a generalized representation using higher-order latent constructs with underlying measurable indicators. Subsequently, we designed our model combining the three central pillars: (1) IT flexibility, (2) dynamic capabilities, (3) ACAP and the final construct 'Competitive firm performance' as the model's explanandum using a balanced and multifactorial evaluation perspective [40, 41].

In interconnecting the latent constructs and all manifest variables within our research model, we propose a reflective construct model, through which the manifest variables are affected by the latent variables [42, 43]. Our higher-order reflective construct model is specified as an alternative to a mode in which latent constructs are modeled using patterns of correlations (covariance based SEM). This is subsequently done using repeated indicators [42]. Indicators now share a common theme and are manifestations of key constructs. In addition, any changes in constructs cause changes in the indicators. Hence, variance in each measure is explained by a construct common to all measures and error unique to each measure, and covariance among the measures is attributed to their common causes.

Our research model perceives strategic alignment as a third-order latent construct representing three underlying second-order factors, i.e., IT flexibility, dynamic capabilities, and ACAP. First-order constructs represent the underlying dimensions of these respective pillars. Strategic alignment governs and represents the underlying second-order pillars and can be considered an overall trait that influences performance. The second-order latent constructs basically explain and encompass the first-order constructs in a more parsimonious way.

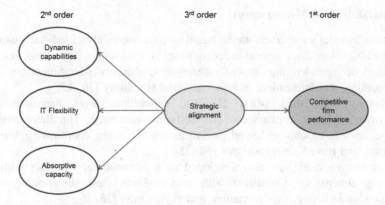

Fig. 1. Research model showing hypothesized interrelations between constructs.

Given the above, we define the following hypothesis: *"Strategic alignment of IT flexibility, dynamic capabilities, and firms' ACAP is positively associated with competitive firm performance"*.

Figure 1 portrays our research model and captures the theorized relationships.

4   Methods

4.1   Data and Sample Collection Procedure

A survey was administered to key informants (C-level managers and executives). Survey items used a Likert scale from 1 – strongly disagree to 7 – strongly agree and were pretested [23]. Also, non-response bias actions were taken into account. The final survey was sent to key informants within firms, including Chief Information Officers (CIO), IT managers, Chief Technology Officers (CTO), enterprise architects, and Chief Executive Officers (CEO). In total 1500 firms were randomly selected from the ICAP business directory, comprising of firms from almost all industries and sectors. To assure a collective response, the instructions asked executives to consult other members of their firm for information they were not highly knowledgeable about. The duration of the data gathering process was approximately nine months (January 2015–September 2015). In total, we incorporated 322 usable questionnaires yielding a valid response rate of 21.4%, which is consistent with comparable studies using key informant methodology [44]. In order to control *ex-ante* for common method bias, respondents were assured that data collected would remain anonymous, and would be used solely for research purposes at an aggregate level. The majority of responses were from consulting services (24%), high-tech (24%), financials (14%), consumer goods (10%), telecommunications (6%), industrials (6%), and consumer services (5%) industries. Less than 5% were obtained from the basic materials, healthcare, utilities, and oil & gas industries. The survey was in most cases completed by chief information officers (CIOs), chief executive officers (CEOs) and IT managers. In accordance with the EU commission size-class recommendation (2003/361/EC), firms were grouped into large (38%), medium (20%), small (26%), and micro (16%).

4.2   Variables and Measurement

Our research model's constructs are all based on past empirical and validated work. *IT flexibility* is developed as a second-order construct in SEM reflectively connecting them to the block of the underlying first-order dimensions, with first-order dimensions being, loose coupling, standardization, transparency, and scalability [26, 45].

Following established work, *Dynamic capabilities* were measured as a second-order construct, comprised of five first-order constructs. The dimensions that comprise dynamic capabilities are adapted measures of sensing, coordinating, learning, integrating, and reconfiguring routines [34, 35].

Absorptive capacity was also developed as a second-order construct with four underlying dimensions. Consistent with past research these dimensions include acquisition, assimilation, transformation, and exploitation [36, 46].

Finally, *Competitive performance* refers to the degree to which a firm performs better than its key competitors [47]. Specifically, respondents were asked to evaluate the relative performance of their firm in terms of profitability, market share, growth, innovativeness, cost leadership, and delivery cycle time [46, 47].

4.3   Model Validation

We use PLS (Partial least squares)-SEM in order to simultaneously assess our research model's measurement ('outer') and the structural ('inner') model [48]. We applied a multi-step analysis approach estimating parameters in the inner and outer models using SmartPLS version 3.2.6. [49], which is a SEM application using PLS. Also, we used the path weighing scheme available within SmartPLS in addition to centroid and factor schemes with the knowledge that the choice of each scheme has a minor impact on the final result [50]. Next, we employed a non-parametric bootstrapping procedure [50], to compute the level of the significance of the regression coefficients, with 500 replications to interpret their significance and to obtain stable results. The current study has a sample size of $N = 322$. Given the rationale above PLS-SEM is deemed particularly appropriate for this study since it also permits the simultaneous estimation of multiple causal relationships between one or more independent constructs and one or more dependent variables [51]. In terms of sample size requirements, the 322 responses received exceeds all minimum requirements concerning the measurement and structural model [51].

5   Results

5.1   Measurement Model (the 'Outer' Model)

In order to demonstrate the quality of the measurement model, we assessed the psychometric properties of the research model on satisfactory levels of validity and reliability. Thus, the measurement model was assessed for first-order constructs. To assess the convergent validity and reliability assessment of the indicators (i.e., manifest variables), composite reliabilities[1] (CR; [50]) and average variance extracted (AVE; [50])—i.e., the average variance of measures accounted by the latent construct—were computed. As a general rule of thumb, variables with a loading less than 0.6 should be removed from the sample. We also calculated and analyzed cross-loadings of all the reflective constructs. All cross-loadings and reliability measures (including the higher order constructs and associated loadings and reliability measures) exceeded the threshold, indicating sufficient convergent validity. Next, discriminant validity was assessed by verifying (1) whether indicators loaded more strongly on their corresponding (first-order) constructs than they did on other constructs and (2) that the square root of the AVEs is larger than the inter-construct correlations (see entries in bold in Table 1 along the matrix diagonal). The off-diagonal elements are correlations between latent variables as calculated by the PLS algorithm. As can be seen from Table 1, all square root scores of the AVEs are higher than the shared variances of the constructs with other constructs in the model.

Table 1. Assessment of convergent and discriminant validity of reflective first order constructs (Entries 1–4 concern dimensions of ACAP, 5–9 concerns dynamic capabilities and the entries 10–13 concern dimensions of IT flexibility).

	1	2	3	4	5	6	7	8	9	10	11	12	13	14
1. Acquisition	**0.901**													
2. Assimilation	0.665	**0.912**												
3. Exploitation	0.721	0.680	**0.874**											
4. Transformation	0.740	0.674	0.799	**0.888**										
5. Sensing	0.470	0.611	0.586	0.537	**0.844**									
6. Learning	0.493	0.543	0.631	0.583	0.708	**0.905**								
7. Integrating	0.430	0.545	0.537	0.514	0.738	0.645	**0.868**							
8. Coordinating	0.427	0.523	0.559	0.526	0.730	0.709	0.688	**0.830**						
9. Reconfiguring	0.434	0.519	0.593	0.525	0.737	0.732	0.695	0.700	**0.876**					
10. Loose Coupling	0.372	0.401	0.443	0.484	0.648	0.596	0.497	0.618	0.582	**0.820**				
11. Scalability	0.384	0.381	0.432	0.453	0.528	0.585	0.501	0.632	0.529	0.658	**0.896**			
12. Standardization	0.335	0.457	0.346	0.322	0.527	0.496	0.524	0.543	0.436	0.456	0.625	**0.811**		
13. Transparency	0.328	0.283	0.408	0.384	0.470	0.447	0.405	0.476	0.469	0.683	0.696	0.525	**0.811**	
14. Competitive Performance	0.423	0.466	0.428	0.367	0.506	0.386	0.382	0.459	0.497	0.493	0.319	0.399	0.389	**0.787**
AVE	0.812	0.833	0.764	0.789	0.712	0.820	0.754	0.689	0.767	0.672	0.804	0.658	0.657	0.620
Composite reliability	0.928	0.937	0.906	0.918	0.908	0.948	0.925	0.898	0.929	0.925	0.942	0.905	0.905	0.942

Thus, adequate convergent and discriminant validity was found for all constructs. Further evidence of discriminant validity was obtained using cross-loadings as quality criteria [42]. These findings indicate that the loadings for each indicator were greater than the cross-loading on other latent variables in the model.

In summary, the outcomes of the measurement model suggest that the constructed PLS model is valid and reliable. The relationships between the latent construct

---

[1] Composite reliability is similar to Cronbach's alpha without the assumption of the equal weighting of variables. Its mathematical formula (with the assumption that the factor variance = 1; standardized indicators) is $\rho = (\Sigma \lambda_i)^2 / ((\Sigma \lambda_i)^2 + \Sigma 1 - (\lambda_i)^2)$.

'Strategic alignment' and the underlying second-order factors are thereby confirmed. The same applies to the relationships between the second-order factors and their respective first-order constructs. The structural model can now be evaluated.

5.2 Structural Model (the 'Inner' Model)

Using SEM analysis we also estimated and validated the structural model and its relationship among (higher-order) latent constructs. We found support for our main hypothesis. There was a significant positive impact of Strategic alignment on performance ($\beta = .56$; $t = 10.77$; $p < .0001$). Although PLS modeling does not include a single proper single goodness-of-fit measure, the variance explained by the model (R^2) —the coefficient of determination—values of the endogenous constructs are commonly used to assess model fit. R^2 accounted for by Competitive firm performance was 0.31. This coefficient of determination, as model's predictive power, represent moderate to substantial predictive power and accuracy [48]. Our hypothesis that strategic alignment of IT flexibility, dynamic capabilities, and firms' ACAP is positively associated with competitive firm performance, was thereby confirmed.

Next to the explained variance of our model (R^2), we subsequently calculated the Q^2 of our endogenous constructs (i.e., using Stone–Geisser's test) to assess the quality of each structural equation measured by the cross-validated redundancy and community index (using the blindfolding procedure in SmartPLS v3.2.6) and to evaluate the predictive relevance for the model constructs [43]. Q^2 measures how well the observed values are reproduced by the model and its parameter estimates by using cross-validation [48]. Q^2 values > 0 imply the model's predictive relevance; values less than 0 suggest the model's lack of predictive relevance. In this study, all Q^2 values were above the threshold value of zero, thereby indicating the overall model's predictive relevance.

PLS-SEM studies rarely report critical heterogeneity issues concerning their data [52]. Traditional (sequential) clustering techniques (e.g., K-means, tree clustering) on manifest variables are ineffective to account for heterogeneity in path model estimates. We controlled for unobserved heterogeneity employing the finite mixture (FIMIX) PLS procedures. Doing so, we segmented the data sample into various segments (s2–s5) to identify whether there are factors that are not included in our analysis which might explain differences across various groups of firms [53]. Results indicate that higher levels of explained variance can be achieved for various homogeneous sub-groups. Currently, we did not provide a comprehensive *ex-post* FIMIX-PLS analysis.

6 Discussion and Conclusion

This research empirically supports the hypothesis that strategic alignment of IT and organizational dynamic capabilities is positively associated with performance. Results support the validity and reliability of our hierarchical higher-order model and the conceptualization and operationalization of strategic alignment using covariation as statistical scheme within SEM.

This study has some interesting findings that can be applied in practice as outcomes suggest that, to some extent, strengthening imperative pillars and firm investment cycles (or efforts) in isolation is not sufficient in order to enhance a firm's competitive edge. Rather, the complementarities, synergies and ongoing interactions among different capabilities are a key enabler of performance, which is consistent with the extant literature [5, 6], determining factors that facilitate a state of alignment [54], and capabilities and their ability to launch competitive actions [10, 23]. This is an important insight for business, IT managers and executives because they can look at strategic alignment, with the underlying pillars, i.e., IT flexibility, dynamic capabilities, and a firm's absorptive capacity, as a mean (and key toolbox) to drive firm performance and systematically enhance the evolutionary fitness of the firm.

Our research, thus, shows that decision makers should employ a value yielding strategy that is focused on synchronizing efforts, resources, and activities. This, consequently, raises the need for decision makers to form multi-disciplinary teams of employees on all levels within the organization, including experts from both IT and the rest of the business functions.

Despite its contributions, the present study is constrained by a number of limitations that future research should seek to address. First, we currently did not perform a comprehensive *ex-post* FIMIX-PLS analysis through which multiple group and (sub) segments comparisons are analyzed in detail. Also, we currently did not compare outcomes of the model with respect to moderately turbulent and highly turbulent environments [55]. Outcomes of this study could then also be refined and substantiated by using configurational methods like e.g., fuzzy-set Qualitative Comparative Analysis (fsQCA). FsQCA enables the examination of interplays between elements of a messy and nonlinear nature [56, 57]. More detailed mechanisms will be unfolded concerning the limits and conditions to which alignment of IT and organizational dynamic capabilities add value. This perspective complements our theoretical 'lens'. Also, comparing results across industries, countries and distinct groups might also contribute to the generalizability of our findings.

Finally, we currently did not go into detail how firms can actually synthesize and define improvement activities that best meets a firms' current and future needs. Future work could address how managers should deploy improvement projects done simultaneously and hence by an integrated alignment perspective taking into account a variety of facets, e.g., risks, investment costs, critical success factors, and benefits.

References

1. Eisenhardt, K.M., Martin, J.A.: Dynamic capabilities: what are they? Strateg. Manag. J. **21**(10–11), 1105–1121 (2000)
2. Teece, D.J., Pisano, G., Shuen, A.: Dynamic capabilities and strategic management. Strat. Manag. J. **18**(7), 509–533 (1997)
3. Melville, N., Kraemer, K., Gurbaxani, V.: Review: information technology and organizational performance: an integrative model of IT business value. MIS Q. **28**(2), 283–322 (2004)

4. Kohli, R., Grover, V.: Business value of IT: an essay on expanding research directions to keep up with the times. J. Assoc. Inf. Syst. 9(1), 23 (2008)
5. Henderson, J.C., Venkatraman, N.: Strategic alignment: leveraging information technology for transforming organisations. IBM Syst. J. 32(1), 4–16 (1993)
6. Chan, Y.E., Reich, B.H.: IT alignment: an annotated bibliography. J. Inf. Technol. 22, 316–396 (2008)
7. Van den Bosch, F.A., Volberda, H.W., de Boer, M.: Coevolution of firm absorptive capacity and knowledge environment: organizational forms and combinative capabilities. Organ. Sci. 10(5), 551–568 (1999)
8. Wade, M., Hulland, J.: Review: the resource-based view and information systems research: review, extension, and suggestions for future research. MIS Q. 28(1), 107–142 (2004)
9. Kim, G., et al.: IT capabilities, process-oriented dynamic capabilities, and firm financial performance. J. Assoc. Inf. Syst. 12(7), 487 (2011)
10. Sambamurthy, V., Bharadwaj, A., Grover, V.: Shaping agility through digital options: reconceptualizing the role of information technology in contemporary firms. MIS Q. 27(2), 237–263 (2003)
11. Roberts, N., et al.: Absorptive capacity and information systems research: review, synthesis, and directions for future research. MIS Q. 36(2), 625–648 (2012)
12. Bhatt, G.D., Grover, V.: Types of information technology capabilities and their role in competitive advantage: an empirical study. J. Manag. Inf. Syst. 22(2), 253–277 (2005)
13. Van de Wetering, R., Mikalef, P., Pateli, A.: A strategic alignment model for IT flexibility and dynamic capabilities: toward an assessment tool. In: Proceedings of the 25th European Conference on Information Systems (ECIS), Guimarães, Portugal, 5–10 June 2017, pp. 1468–1485 (2017)
14. Van de Wetering, R., Mikalef, P., Pateli, A.: Managing firms' innovation capabilities through strategically aligning combinative IT and dynamic capabilities. In: Proceedings of the Twenty-Third Americas Conference on Information Systems (AMCIS), Boston, United States, 10–12 August 2017
15. Sharma, S., Vredenburg, H.: Proactive corporate environmental strategy and the development of competitively valuable organizational capabilities. Strateg. Manag. J. 19, 729–753 (1998)
16. Bharadwaj, A.S.: A resource-based perspective on information technology capability and firm performance: an empirical investigation. MIS Q. 24(1), 169–196 (2000)
17. Ward, J., Peppard, J.: Strategic Planning for Information Systems, 3rd edn. Wiley, Chichester (2002)
18. Coleman, P., Papp, R.: Strategic alignment: analysis of perspectives. In: Proceedings of the 2006 Southern Association for Information Systems Conference, Jacksonville, Florida USA, pp. 241–250 (2006)
19. Van de Wetering, R., et al.: A situational alignment framework for PACS. J. Digit. Imaging 24(6), 979–992 (2011)
20. Agarwal, R., Selen, W.: Dynamic capability building in service value networks for achieving service innovation. Decis. Sci. 40(3), 431–475 (2009)
21. Pavlou, P.A., El Sawy, O.A.: From IT leveraging competence to competitive advantage in turbulent environments: the case of new product development. Inf. Syst. Res. 17(3), 198–227 (2006)
22. Wu, L., Chen, J.-L.: A stage-based diffusion of IT innovation and the BSC performance impact: a moderator of technology–organization–environment. Technol. Forecast. Soc. Change 88, 76–90 (2014)

23. Mikalef, P., Pateli, A., van de Wetering, R.: IT flexibility and competitive performance: the mediating role of IT-enabled dynamic capabilities. In: Proceedings of the 24th European Conference on Information Systems (ECIS), Istanbul, Turkey, 12–15 June 2016
24. Van de Wetering, R., Batenburg, R.: Towards a theory of PACS deployment: an integrative PACS maturity framework. J. Digit. Imaging 27(3), 337–350 (2014)
25. Wetering, R.: Modeling alignment as a higher order nomological framework. In: Abramowicz, W., Alt, R., Franczyk, B. (eds.) BIS 2016. LNBIP, vol. 263, pp. 111–122. Springer, Cham (2017). doi:10.1007/978-3-319-52464-1_11
26. Byrd, T.A., Turner, D.E.: Measuring the flexibility of information technology infrastructure: exploratory analysis of a construct. J. Manag. Inf. Syst. 17(1), 167–208 (2000)
27. Simon, H.A.: The architecture of complexity. Gen. Syst. 1965(10), 63–76 (1965)
28. Pil, F.K., Cohen, S.K.: Modularity: Implications for imitation, innovation, and sustained advantage. Acad. Manag. Rev. 31(4), 995–1011 (2006)
29. van de Wetering, R., Bos, R.: A meta-framework for efficacious adaptive enterprise architectures. In: Abramowicz, W., Alt, R., Franczyk, B. (eds.) BIS 2016. LNBIP, vol. 263, pp. 273–288. Springer, Cham (2017). doi:10.1007/978-3-319-52464-1_25
30. Priem, R.L., Butler, J.E.: Is the resource-based "view" a useful perspective for strategic management research? Acad. Manag. Rev. 26(1), 22–40 (2001)
31. Schilke, O.: On the contingent value of dynamic capabilities for competitive advantage: the nonlinear moderating effect of environmental dynamism. Strateg. Manag. J. 35(2), 179–203 (2014)
32. Drnevich, P.L., Kriauciunas, A.P.: Clarifying the conditions and limits of the contributions of ordinary and dynamic capabilities to relative firm performance. Strateg. Manag. J. 32(3), 254–279 (2011)
33. Helfat, C.E., Peteraf, M.A.: The dynamic resource-based view: capability lifecycles. Strateg. Manag. J. 24(10), 997–1010 (2003)
34. Pavlou, P.A., El Sawy, O.A.: Understanding the elusive black box of dynamic capabilities. Decis. Sci. 42(1), 239–273 (2011)
35. Protogerou, A., Caloghirou, Y., Lioukas, S.: Dynamic capabilities and their indirect impact on firm performance. Ind. Corp. Change 21(3), 615–647 (2012)
36. Zahra, S.A., George, G.: Absorptive capacity: a review, reconceptualization, and extension. Acad. Manag. Rev. 27(2), 185–203 (2002)
37. Cohen, W.M., Levinthal, D.A.: Absorptive capacity: a new perspective on learning and innovation. Adm. Sci. Q. 35(1), 128–152 (1990)
38. Sambamurthy, V., Zmud, R.W.: Arrangements for information technology governance: a theory of multiple contingencies. MIS Q. 23(2), 261–290 (1999)
39. Venkatraman, N.: The concept of fit in strategy research: towards verbal and statistical correspondence. Acad. Manag. Rev. 14(3), 423–444 (1989)
40. Kaplan, R.S., Norton, D.P.: Alignment: Using the Balanced Scorecard to Create Corporate Synergies. Harvard Business Press, Brighton (2006)
41. Van de Wetering, R., Batenburg, R.: Defining and formalizing: a synthesized review on the multifactorial nature of PACS performance. Int. J. Comput. Assist. Radiol. Surg. 5(Suppl. 1), 170 (2010)
42. Wetzels, M., Odekerken-Schröder, G., Van Oppen, C.: Using PLS path modeling for assessing hierarchical construct models: guidelines and empirical illustration. MIS Q. 33(1), 177–195 (2009)
43. Chin, W.: The partial least squares approach to structural equation modeling. In: Marcoulides, G.A. (ed.) Modern Methods for Business Research, pp. 295–336. Lawrence Erlbaum Associates, Mahwah (1998)

44. Capron, L., Mitchell, W.: Selection capability: how capability gaps and internal social frictions affect internal and external strategic renewal. Organ. Sci. **20**(2), 294–312 (2009)
45. Tafti, A., Mithas, S., Krishnan, M.S.: The effect of information technology-enabled flexibility on formation and market value of alliances. Manag. Sci. **59**(1), 207–225 (2013)
46. Liu, H., et al.: The impact of IT capabilities on firm performance: the mediating roles of absorptive capacity and supply chain agility. Decis. Support Syst. **54**(3), 1452–1462 (2013)
47. Rai, A., Tang, X.: Leveraging IT capabilities and competitive process capabilities for the management of interorganizational relationship portfolios. Inf. Syst. Res. **21**(3), 516–542 (2010)
48. Hair Jr., J.F., et al.: A Primer on Partial Least Squares Structural Equation Modeling (PLS-SEM). Sage Publications, Thousand Oaks (2016)
49. Ringle, C.M., Wende, S., Becker, J.-M.: SmartPLS 3. SmartPLS GmbH, Boenningstedt (2015). http://www.smartpls.com
50. Tenenhaus, M., et al.: PLS path modeling. Comput. Stat. Data Anal. **48**(1), 159–205 (2005)
51. Hair, J.F., Ringle, C.M., Sarstedt, M.: PLS-SEM: indeed a silver bullet. J. Market. Theory Pract. **19**(2), 139–152 (2011)
52. Esposito Vinzi, V., et al.: Capturing and treating unobserved heterogeneity by response based segmentation in PLS path modeling. A comparison of alternative methods by computational experiments. ESSEC Working Papers (2007)
53. Sarstedt, M., Ringle, C.: Treating unobserved heterogeneity in PLS path modeling: a comparison of FIMIX-PLS with different data analysis strategies. J. Appl. Stat. **37**(8), 1299–1318 (2010)
54. Mikalef, P., et al.: Investigating the impact of procurement alignment on supply chain management performance. Procedia Technol. **9**, 310–319 (2013)
55. Pavlou, P.A., El Sawy, O.A.: The "third hand": IT-enabled competitive advantage in turbulence through improvisational capabilities. Inf. Syst. Res. **21**(3), 443–471 (2010)
56. Fiss, P.C.: A set-theoretic approach to organizational configurations. Acad. Manag. Rev. **32**(4), 1180–1198 (2007)
57. Mikalef, P., et al.: Purchasing alignment under multiple contingencies: a configuration theory approach. Ind. Manag. Data Syst. **115**(4), 625–645 (2015)

Two Stage Business and IT-Alignment: Initial Experiences from Portal Implementation for Non-traditional Study Formats of a University

Kurt Sandkuhl[(✉)] and Holger Lehmann

Chair of Business Information Systems, University of Rostock,
18051 Rostock, Germany
{kurt.sandkuhl, holger.lehmann}@uni-rostock.de

Abstract. Business and IT-alignment (BITA) is a continuous process aiming at aligning strategic and operational objectives and ways to implement them between the business divisions of an organization and its information technology. The work presented in this paper focuses on a specific aspect of BITA: the process of creating an alignment between stakeholders in an organization and the IT. In a project aiming at the implementation of lifelong learning services, experiences were collected supporting a two stage BITA process. The organizational objective of the project was to offer tailor-made learning possibilities at university level to new, non-traditional target groups. New study formats allow to start studying at any stage of life and offer appropriate IT support for new target groups and study formats. The central technological idea consists in a context-oriented, information technology portal for e-learning, the MyKOSMOS portal, with an individualized and demand-based supply of information for the learners.

1 Introduction

Business and IT-alignment (BITA) in general is a continuous process aiming at aligning strategic and operational objectives and ways to implement them between the business divisions of an organization and the organization's information technology division. BITA is not limited to commercial enterprises but also required in public authorities and non-profit organizations. Many challenges are linked to BITA since the business environment continuously changes and so does the IT in an enterprise, but the pace of change and the time frame needed to implement changes are different. The reasons for changes are quite diverse [20] and include, e.g., changes legal aspects and regulations, new business requirements, or economic developments. Technological trends such as business as a service, virtualization, cloud computing or digital enterprise architectures are influencing the way in which IT-functionality can be provided [21]. Model-based approaches and IT governance are potential candidates to support capturing of business context, organizational needs and required IT support [22].

One of the challenges in business and IT-alignment frequently experienced is how to integrate different organisational stakeholders and their demands into the alignment

W. Abramowicz (Ed.): BIS 2017 Workshops, LNBIP 303, pp. 127–136, 2017.
https://doi.org/10.1007/978-3-319-69023-0_12

process. In this context, this paper will focus on a two stage alignment approach observed in a case from higher education (cf. Sect. 2). In this case, a university made a number of strategic changes which also affected the traditional education programs and aimed at a more prominent support of life-long learning services. When analysing requirements for the support of the new university strategy in life-long learning (cf. Sect. 3), we realized that an IT-support aligned to the changed organisational needs would not only have to support strategic aspects, but also the demands on operational level, e.g. of the different study format managers and even of individual teachers. We also realized that the adjustment demand is not a mere configuration of functionality but a composition of different functional modules to reflect teaching models and distribution strategies beyond the university level.

From a business and IT-alignment perspective, we consider this as an alignment process divided into several phases:

- The strategic alignment on university level: starting from a decision to invite new target groups and to create new study formats, the IT support and functionality had to be designed for the need
- The operational alignment, upper level: for every specific study format, the second alignment stage addressed organisational and didactic needs, based on various factors, like, e.g., the geographical distribution of participants, their distribution in different time zones, and required software bundles and combinations of IT
- The organisational alignment, refined level, addresses the needs of module teachers for individual classes or cohorts and mostly can be implemented by configuration of functionality.

The purpose of this paper primarily is to describe the different alignment stages based on a case from higher education and to share experiences about the alignment process. A clear limitation of the work is that we only have one case to report on, i.e. our findings are meant to inspire future research work and kick-off further activities into the direction of "staged alignment processes" but are not generalizable.

The core instrument from a method perspective is the definition of guidelines packaged in a 6-step process for performing the upper level of operational alignment (cf. Sect. 4). These guidelines were a result of the prior alignment on strategic level.

2 Background

This section provides background information on the works presented in this paper including the project in which the results were achieved (Sect. 2.1.), the field of teaching and learning systems (Sect. 2.2) and IT-supported portals (Sect. 2.3).

2.1 Project Context: KOSMOS

The work presented in this paper was realized in the project "Konstruktion und Organisation eines Studiums in offenen Systemen (construction and organization of studies in open systems) KOSMOS[1]", funded by the BMBF and the EU at the University of Rostock. The University of Rostock is aiming to implement a concept of Life Long Learning (LLL) offering tailor-made possibilities to study at University level to traditional and non-traditional target groups. New study formats allow to start studying at any stage of life. They offer follow-up opportunities after vocational training and professional activity. However, the integration of Life Long Learning cannot be achieved unless the University as institution is reorganized. Accordingly, organization development is part of the project and connected with the objective of implementing a content-related, structural and organizational framework for Life Long Learning.

The implementation of the above-mentioned objectives does not only require new study models and study formats, it is also necessary to take into account the technical and organizational preconditions and tools provided for the learners and the teachers. That is why, in the KOSMOS project, one work package focuses especially on the "medial infrastructure", since new target groups, study formats and learning culture can also imply new challenges for the supporting IT systems (e.g., so-called learning management systems or learning systems) and for the relevant contents. This paper presents results from this work package.

2.2 Learning Management Systems and Infrastructures

Technical, organisational and didactic support for life-long learning has been subject of research since many years with a lot of focus on how to bridge the dimensions time and space, i.e. to support co-located and distributed e-learning scenarios as well as synchronous and asynchronous settings. Many different systems, services and standard proposals were developed. Integration of different functionalities and services into a single user interface is a feature of contemporary learning management systems [5] (e.g. Ilias, Stud.IP, Moodle, Sakai, OLAT, Clix etc.) which provide a platform for co-located and distributed teaching.

New teaching and learning styles [4], for example with alternating co-located and distributed phases (for example based on content recorded with Lecturnity, Opencast Matterhorn or synchronous communication with Adobe Connect or Open Meeting) and completely digital and virtualized study modules are more and more common practice in universities. This leads to a high demand regarding service quality and availability of IT infrastructures. Already in 2003, the Atkins-report of the US National Science Foundation (NSF) [6] developed a vision of a reliable cyber-infrastructure for this purpose. Many development in Europe (e.g. e-science in UK or d-grid in Germany) extend this idea towards implementing a middleware also suitable for scientific demands.

2.3 Portals

Information technology portals generally unify the access to different applications and information sources under one single interface [16] adapted to the actual user and

---

[1] http://www.kosmos.uni-rostock.de/.

concealing different applications behind it [15]. Portals are a technology used in enterprise IT and especially in knowledge management [3]. For its usage in a University context, it is crucial to think of a portal in the sense of a "Single Point of Entry" [1] for all applications to be used online for continuing education or to support them.

A market analysis of portals and portal platforms [2] showed a prevalence of Liferay[2]. It is characteristic for Liferay to function on the basis of the model-view-controller principle allowing to separate the presentation of the contents from the processing logic. Thus, it is possible to shape the processing logic in software modules and to present it to the user in an aggregated form without any clashes with existing functionalities. Extensions in Liferay can be integrated in two different ways. First, they can be simply embedded without any further adaptation as additional pages. The second option is to work with portlets which is more complicated in technical terms but they alone enable the presentation adapted to the user. Among other things, they allow for data exchange with other application.

3   Alignment on Strategic Level

In the KOSMOS project (see Sect. 2.1), the first stage of business and IT alignment consisted of defining new strategic requirements for lifelong-learning and implementing an IT support aligned to these requirements. Section 3.1 will discuss the strategic context, Sect. 3.2 the MyKosmos portal as implementation of the IT support for the strategic aspects.

3.1   Strategic Direction and Requirements

Care staff, landscape architects, physicians and psychologists in one and the same course of study? Kindergarten teachers, school teachers and special education teachers with common study interests? – These situations are rather unusual for traditional courses of study at Universities. However, in the new strategic objectives at Rostock University such situations are seen as commonplace. The goal is to open up the University to non-traditional target groups by offering new study formats, such as "horticultural therapy" or "gifted education", and to support the overall process of teaching and studying in a lifelong learning context.

The central infrastructure idea to support the above strategic aim consists in a context-oriented, information technology portal for e-learning with an individualized and demand-based supply of information for the students. Within the frame of the portal design, a central aspect had to be the context orientation, i.e., the testing and evaluation of context-based learning systems and teaching contents for the university continuing education. Many investigations from the field of knowledge management and information logistics point to the fact that understanding and support of the user context has a significant influence on the acceptance and the quality of IT systems and contents as perceived by the user.

---

[2] Siehe http://www.liferay.com.

3.2   Requirements to IT Support

With the background of the strategic aspects (see Sect. 3.1) aiming at opening up for new target groups and study formats in the frame of university education, a stronger individualization for the single learner and their actual context was identified as a core requirement to the IT support. In this respect, the "context" implies all information describing the situation of the learner and which should thus be taken into account for the individualization. The focus on a stronger individualization is explained by the following background:

- Learning is a process which any person needs to integrate individually in their routines and backgrounds. Learning occurs in different speeds, with different associations and with different previous experiences.
- The specific teaching-learning experiences in different university disciplines (engineering, social sciences, humanities, natural sciences) vary significantly. Therefore, we can speak of a culture of disciplines which has to be taken into account in the teaching-learning process of the continuing education.
- The learners in the new study formats differ in their age, their background knowledge, their learning objectives, their time availability, their sex etc. Thus, they claim a much stronger individualization of the learning process, the study offers and the teaching-learning organization compared to the common university practice.

Work in the area of knowledge management [17] emphasizes that understanding and support of the user context has a significant influence on the acceptance of learning systems and teaching contents as perceived by the user. In this regard, the user context comprises not only the actual role or task of a user, but also his educational background, experiences and personal preferences. Therefore, the objective is to guide the learners with their different prior knowledge more individually and to offer them further electronic support possibilities.

3.3   IT Support for the Requirements

In order to support new study formats and target groups, the portal system MyKosmos was designed and developed. Portal design followed the requirements identified and outlined in Sect. 3.2 by translating them into appropriate functionality. The current implementation of the MyKosmos portal integrates different functionalities and applications into a single user interface. Examples are:

- Meta-search engine: one element of the integration is to provide a single user interface to searching several literature database and research information systems. Based on the student profile (i.e. the study format, current integration into working groups and personal background), the meta-search is configured to search with priority in those databases assumed to be the most important ones for the task at hand.
- Integration of learning management systems: Rostock University has a learning management system for supporting teaching in different courses (Stud.ip), for interactive content and learning objects (ILIAS) and for scheduling education and

providing individual information (LSF). These systems are integrated into the MyKosmos portal provided a joint view on relevant data.

- Collaborative work of distributed student groups is supported by integrating synchronous (Skype) and asynchronous communication, document sharing, joint editing of documents and awareness functions for group work. This functionality is required, as group work is considered increasingly important in education in general [11] and considered as valuable support by the learners [7, 12].
- Program managers and course responsible persons (teachers) may integrate additional functionality into the portal by using the "portlet" concept of the Liferay platform which forms the basis for MyKosmos.

The above summary shows that MyKosmos is contributing to the integration of various applications. Furthermore, the portal also contributed to more synchronized work flows as the portal development was accompanied by business process integration activities. More concrete, we modelled all future usage scenarios for the portal and derived integration needs on process and application level from the scenario models. For this purpose we used an approach from enterprise modelling based on Troux Architect as a tool and Troux Semantics as notation. We modelled the different planned ways how myKOSMOS would be used by the future users.

This resulted in process model-like scenarios, as depicted in Fig. 1 showing the example "distributed study formats: assignment work". The scenario starts with the student logging in. According to his profile he is provided with an individually configured entry page, making offers for his learning process. Following his course of study, completing different modules within the study format, the student choses to open or proceed with his assignment work for a certain module, which is loaded presenting the recent state of his work in progress. Once having caught up with his recent results, the student is confronted with different tasks to be fulfilled in order to fulfil the

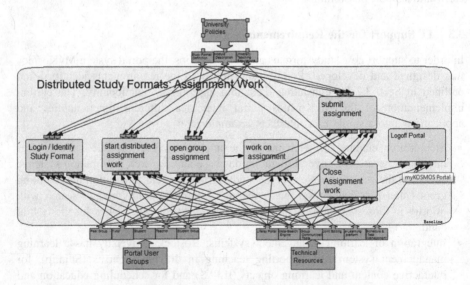

Fig. 1. Process model (excerpt) for new study format

assignment, however her or she is free to choose which task to pick. A regular assignment the designed study formats includes information research the portal supports providing the appropriate sources for the study format. In addition, many assignments also involve the communication with fellow students since they are assigned group work. In the process the work should be documented to be handed in, where the kind of documentation being determined in the assignment description.

4   Alignment on Operational Level

While the previous section addressed the strategic alignment on university level, this section focuses on operational alignment. This alignment stage takes place when a new study format is in the process of implementation and the IT infrastructure created for supporting the strategic decision, i.e. the MyKosmos portal, has to be put in operation. For such a study format, the organisational and didactic needs have to be taken into account. Here, the alignment demand is created by the stakeholder group of study program managers and includes various factors, like, e.g., the geographical distribution of participants, their distribution in different time zones, and required software bundles and combinations of IT.

How the alignment on operational has to be performed is defined in a methodical guideline. The aim of this guideline [8] is to describe a systematic approach on how to decide whether the MyKOSMOS portal is suitable for a study format and how to adapt the portal for this study format. The guide has been prepared with a view to the professional responsibilities for a study format. Thus, no special knowledge is required in the field of information technology. The guideline consists of 6 steps described in the following.

Step 1:   *Evaluate the suitability of the portal*

The use of the portal does not make sense if the content and didactic concept of the study format does not provide or even explicitly excludes the use of IT-supported media or teaching and learning platforms. The use of the portal is particularly useful when there is an added value compared to the "standard" e-learning platform Stud.IP. Stud.IP is integrated into MyKOSMOS, so its functions are already available. In order to facilitate the evaluation, a questionnaire was developed as an aid. If a clear picture does not arise by answering the questions, a discussion with the professional responsibilities for the portal is recommended for a joint decision-making.

Step 2:   *Specify the scope of the portal use*

Since, in principle, it is not possible to provide a portal usage for the entire course of the study format, but only for selected content, the scope of portal use must be determined in this step. The scope is most easily defined by the modules of the study format, which are to be supported in the portal. On the basis of the module list, the relevant teachers and students can be specified (in the case that not all participants in the study format have to participate in the modules).

Step 3: *Analyze the need for information*

One of the main goals of portals is to provide students with access to information that is important to the organization of tasks or topics within their study format. On the one hand, this ease is achieved by the fact that, in the search for information or literature, it is already preset which sources of information have the highest relevance for the study format. If the student does not change this default, the search functionality built into the portal will first search in these sources. On the other hand, applications can also be integrated into the portal interface that provide the required information. These could be special information services or systems that are not accessible with general search.

In order to determine the information requirements, a method for analyzing the need for information is available, which investigates the information requirements in detail from tasks and responsibilities. This method is documented in [19]. Since the full execution of such an analysis can be quite complex, it is recommended to use a "simplified" method. On the basis of the study format and the tasks performed in the individual modules, this method determines which information sources are relevant, the importance of the information from these sources for the task, and the consequences of the lack of information. Based on this assessment of the information sources, priority information sources are identified, which are included in the profile of the study format and are used in step 6 to configure the meta-search.

Step 4: *Determine the need for portal functionality*

This step defines how the initial or "default" configuration of the portal should be set. This includes, among other things, which portlets to integrate and which layout is to be realized. Furthermore, it is determined whether there should be adjustments for individual subgroups of the students in order to support e.g. collaborative learning. For each developed portal functionality (see Sect. 3), it will be determined whether this is needed and how the basic configuration should be.

Step 5: *Compile the required portal customization*

Since the determination of the information requirements and the determination of the required functionality of the portal may be carried out with the cooperation of different parties and at different times, this work step was integrated into the sequence in order to compile a total view from the partial results. In the simplest case, this step consists only of combining the results documents of the previous activities into one overall document. The consistency of the overall picture should be examined. In a few cases, it will become clear that there is a need for additional information or additional portal functions, which can only be seen in the overall view. In this case it is recommended to resume the work in the corresponding step.

Step 6: *Launch portal customization*

The central goal of this activity is to initiate the implementation of the required portal adaptations in order to ensure a soon provision of the portal. Part of this work step is also to examine the feasibility of all requirements and, if necessary, to specify them. In many cases, the actual portal customization will not require any programming tasks, but will only include the configuration of the portal and therefore be performed quickly.

This usually involves setting up a so-called "profile" for the study format in the portal search function, whereby the relevant information sources with priority are searched for the system. In rare cases, the technical access interface to the information sources must also be set up, which may require a programming interface. Furthermore, to configure the portal, you must make the basic settings for the functions that should be available in the study format. If functional extensions are required, such as the integration of additional applications or portlets, the procedure must also be clarified.

5 Summary and Outlook

In the context of strategic changes within a university regarding lifelong learning services, the paper investigated the process of business and IT alignment. When analysing requirements for the support of the new university strategy in life-long learning we realized that the alignment process should be divided into several phases. The paper reports on the strategic alignment stage on university level and the operational alignment (upper level) for every specific study format. A clear limitation of the work is that we only have one case to report on, i.e. our findings are meant to inspire future research work and kick-off further activities into the direction of "staged alignment processes" but are not generalizable.

Furthermore, the paper presents, in the context of the KOSMOS project, the basic idea, the concept and experiences of the realization of the MyKOSMOS portal with its central approach of a demand-based information supply and user-specific provision of functionality in e-learning. The future extension of the portal will be to set up, record and maintain the portfolios of the learners which is partly a compilation of systemic data, but which will be extended by personal data. Thus, it would be conceivable to retain the training level in relation to the basic subjects (e.g., mathematics) or the professional status in order to provide additional material. This information would have to be uploaded by the participants themselves. According to the data provided, additional material can be identified and recommendations can be formulated and represented.

Acknowledgement. The work within the frame of the KOSMOS project presented in this contribution was funded by the BMBF and the ESF Programme of the EU.

References

1. Hepper, S., Hesmer, S.: Introducing the Portlet specification. Java World Journal (2003)
2. Jastram, S.: Analyse und Vergleich von Portal-Entwicklungstools am Beispiel des E-Learning. Bachelorarbeit im Studiengang Wirtschaftsinformatik. Universität Rostock (2013)
3. Sandkuhl, K.: Wissensportale. Informatik-Spektrum **28**(3), 193–201 (2005)
4. Coates, H., James, R., Baldwin, G.: A critical examination of the effects of learning management systems on university teaching and learning. Tert. Educ. Manag. **11**, 19–36 (2005)

5. Watson, W.R., Watson, S.L.: What are learning management systems, what are they not, and what should they become? TechTrends **51**(2), 29 (2007)
6. Atkins, D.: Revolutionizing science and engineering through cyberinfrastructure: Report of the National Science Foundation blue-ribbon advisory panel on cyberinfrastructure (2003)
7. Borchardt, U., Sandkuhl, K.: Wahrnehmung der Online-Unterstützung in der wissenschaftlichen Weiterbildung. In: KOSMOS (Hrsg.). Die Wahrnehmung der wissenschaftlichen Weiterbildung an der Universität Rostock. Eine qualitative Untersuchung der Studienformate Gartentherapie und Inklusive Hochbegabtenförderung (2014)
8. Sandkuhl, K., Stamer, D., Borchardt, U.: Portaleinsatz in der wissenschaftlichen Weiterbildung: Erfahrungen und Leitfaden. Universität Rostock, März (2015)
9. Ackermann, S.: Bildung von Nutzerprofilen aus dynamischen Nutzungsdaten im Lernportal des Kosmos Projektes. Masterarbeit im Studiengang Wirtschaftsinformatik. Universität Rostock (2014)
10. Weigel, T.: Joint editing support in academic further education – cloud linkage for myKosmos. Masterarbeit im Studiengang Wirtschaftsinformatik. Universität Rostock (2014)
11. Dillenbourg, P.: What do you mean by collaborative learning? Collaborative-learning: Cognitive and Computational Approaches, pp. 1–19 (1999)
12. Laal, M., Ghodsi, S.: Benefits of collaborative learning. Procedia – Soc. Behav. Sci. **31**(2012), 486–490 (2012)
13. Wilson, J., Goodman, P., Cronin, M.: Group learning. Acad. Manag. Rev. **32**(4), 1041–1059 (2007)
14. Weigel, T.: Analyse und Konzeption des Identity Managements für Cloud Services am Beispiel iSM. Universität Rostock, Bachelorarbeit im Studiengang Wirtschaftsinformatik (2013)
15. Bellas, F.: Standards for second-generation portals. IEEE Internet Comput. **8**, 54–60 (2004)
16. Schelp, J., Winter, R.: Enterprise portals und enterprise application integration. HMD **225**, 6–20 (2002)
17. Sandkuhl, K.: Information logistics in networked organizations: selected concepts and applications. In: Filipe, J., Cordeiro, J., Cardoso, J. (eds.) ICEIS 2007. LNBIP, vol. 12, pp. 43–54. Springer, Heidelberg (2008). https://doi.org/10.1007/978-3-540-88710-2_4
18. Goldkuhl, G., Lind, M., Seigerroth, U.: Method integration: the need for a learning perspective. IEEE Softw. **145**(4), 113–118 (1998)
19. Lundqvist, M., Sandkuhl, K., Seigerroth, U., Holmquist, E.: IDA User Guide - Handbook for Information Demand Analysis. Version 2.0. InfoFLOW project deliverable. Technical report. Jönköping University, Sweden (2010)
20. Seigerroth, U.: Enterprise modeling and enterprise architecture: the constituents of transformation and alignment of business and IT. IJITBAG **2**(1), 16–34 (2011)
21. Woitsch, R., Karagiannis, D., Plexousakis, D., Hinkelmann, K.: "Business and IT alignment: the IT-Socket", e & i. Elektrotechnik und Informationstechnik **126**(7–8), 308–321 (2009)
22. Krogstie, J.: Model-Based Development and Evolution of Information Systems - A Quality Approach. Springer, London (2012)

The Impact of Digitization on Information System Design - An Explorative Case Study of Digitization in the Insurance Business

Rainer Schmidt[1](✉), Michael Möhring[1], Florian Bär[1], and Alfred Zimmermann[2]

[1] Munich University of Applied Sciences,
Lothstrasse 64, 80335 Munich, Germany
Rainer.Schmidt@hm.edu
[2] Reutlingen University, Reutlingen, Germany

Abstract. Digitization transforms business process models and processes in many enterprises. However, many of them need guidance, how digitization is impacting the design of their information systems. Therefore, this paper investigates the influence of digitization on information system design. We apply a two-phase research method applying a literature review and an exploratory case study. The case study took place in the IT service provider of a large insurance enterprise. The study's results suggest that a number of areas of information system design are affected, such as architecture, processes, data and services.

Keywords: Digitization · Digital transformation · Information systems

1 Introduction

Digitization [1] has a huge impact on economy and society and is questioning fundamental structures in the economy and society [2]. The business perspective of digitization is illustrated by the fact that a number of new companies in the market appear [3], at the same time established businesses have to fight for their existence [4]. Digitization is discussed also from a technological view. From a technological view, digitization is be described as the cooperation of several technologies [5]. However, the question how digitization impacts the design of information systems beyond technological considerations remains unanswered. On the other hand, information technology departments are eager to know which changes are necessary to fully exploit the potential of digitization.

Overall, the question driving our research is: *How does digitization impact the design of information systems in the insurance business?* Answering this question, we apply a two-phase research method comprising a literature review and an exploratory single-case study. While the former allows to identify digitization patterns and impact factors, latter is used to validate them and identify aspects that have not discussed in prior research yet. The case study addresses digitization in the insurance business. Digitization has an increasing importance in the insurance business. According to a study of Deloitte LLC [6], the percentage of Canadian consumers obtaining insurance

W. Abramowicz (Ed.): BIS 2017 Workshops, LNBIP 303, pp. 137–149, 2017.
https://doi.org/10.1007/978-3-319-69023-0_13

quotes online went from 23% to 40% from 2008 to 2013. The key to understanding the upcoming changes is a fundamental change in the value creation model of insurance. The prevention of damage and the continuous monitoring of customers is at the center of customer interest and no longer the settlement of claims. In [6] this thought is summarized as "Consumers are expecting insurers to provide products, services and advice".

This article is structured as follows. In the next section we give a more detailed description of our research method. In the Sect. 3 the results of the literature review regarding digitization impact factors on information system design are discussed respectively. In Sect. 4 we provide a detailed description of the selected case including the examined sources of evidence and present insights on the case. Section 5 concludes the article and discusses the study's limitations.

2 Research Methods and Data Collection

To answer our research question, we implement a two-step research approach with well-known and applied research methods in computer science as well as information systems. Our research methodology comprises two separate phases with: First, we implemented a literature review to get insights of current research about digitization according to general literature review guidelines [7, 8]. As recommended by Kitchenham [8], we identified the need for this research already in the introductory section. Following the approach of [9] we identified primary research papers by selecting articles of leading computer science and information systems as well as management journals and leading conferences. To ensure a high quality, we only looked at research papers with a good ranking according to the CORE conference Ranking (we selected only A*, A, B publication) and the leading German management publication ranking VHB Jourqual version 3 (we selected only A*, A, B, C) [7, 10, 11]. Using this ranking for IS research is common practice (e.g. [12, 13]). Furthermore, we used key words like "digitization", "digital transformation" "information system" in research databases like AISNet, SpringerLink, Science Direct, IEEExplore, ACM Digital Library. We included research that appeared after 1999 (until mid 2016). The collected papers were than analyzed according to the relevance to the research topic (digitization) with respect to quality (e.g. trough quality assessment via e.g. external/internal validity, study design, bias) [7]. We excluded papers using other interpretations of the term digitization, e.g. the digitization of pictures. From an analysis of the literature, relevant patterns and impact factors to answer the research question are derived. Finally, we extracted the following research papers related to their digitization concept (Table 1):

To evaluate the extracted patterns, we used a single case study method according to [14]. Single case studies are often used in research (e.g. [15–17]) and generate interesting and deep insights and understandings [18]. Furthermore, single case studies are generizable and generate "empirical circumstances" [18]. Data are collected from a leading European enterprise in the insurance sector, that is selected based on a quasi-convenience approach to case selection. The enterprise has a dominant role in the German as well as European insurance business. Thus the enterprise has sufficient resources to implement even ambitious digital initiatives. On the other hand, there is an enormous amount of legacy systems and applications. To cope with these special

Table 1. Reviewed literature

Year	Authors
2015	Goes [55]
2015	Piccinini et al. [58]
2003	Boland et al. [59]
2012	Lee and Berente [31]
2015	Matt et al. [36]
2015	Babar and Yu [34]
2014	Porter and Heppelmann [29]
2015	Westerman and Bonnet [20]
2013	Grover and Kohli [35]
2014	Henningsson and Hedman [54]

challenges the pragmatic solutions introduced in [18] can be applied. The project providing the input for the case study had the objective to identify the changes on IT systems of insurance enterprises triggered by digitization. It started in April 2015 and ended December 2015. Five workshops took place with several employees from the strategy department including the chief operating officer. During the workshops presentations were given, internal documents were reviewed and key aspects were discussed as part of open-ended interviews. Hence, as recommended in [25], we collected multiple sources of evidence and thereby strengthening our internal validity. For each workshop a protocol was created serving as our field notes. We created memo-files containing our explanations and comments on the obtained insights. As the explanations and comments are linked to the overall research question, this approach allows for the establishment of a chain of evidence [25].

3   Impact of Digitization on Information Systems

Based on the literature review described above, the influence of three domains of digitization [1] on information systems shall be investigated. They are: the relationship with the customer, the design of products and the value creation model. In each of these areas, we will develop hypotheses how these domains impact information systems. We will consider four areas of impact in information systems: architecture, processes, data and services.

3.1   Customer

Deep Integration with the Customer
Digitization fosters the deep integration with the customer [19, 20]. Thus it breaks with tayloristic [21] and fordistic [22] thinking that implied the separation of producer and consumer. Today, transaction oriented models are replaced with relationship oriented ones. Digitization enables the creation of a huge number of touchpoints with the customer on three classes of devices. Interfaces are available on mobile phones, tablets,

convertibles, notebooks or desktop PCs. The interaction may take place with intelligent gadgets such as smart watches, fitness bands etc. Third, the customer may interact using sensors such as cameras, microphones etc. Thus, the deep integration with the customer and the intensive use of self-service require additional meta-model elements for process modelling leads us to the following hypothesis:

Hypothesis 1: Digitization requires the extension of standard process-meta-model to represent processes appropriately.

Self-Service
An increasing number of customers prefers to use a web-based interface instead of a human counterpart. In the beginning the research on this topic was primarily focused on examining and explaining the role of the individual customers participating in self-service based service encounters [23–25]. With regards to this research, the customers of self-service offers should be viewed as partial employees or co-developers by the service organizations [23, 26]. This is because, in a self-service context the customers perform a significant set of activities regarding the production and delivery of services by themselves. Current studies suggest that the service organizations have to ensure a high level of customer satisfaction in order to reach an acceptable rate of customer adoption and usage rate [27, 28]. According to the studies, this is a basic requirement for the service organizations to leverage the advantages of the self-service concept [24]. To realize self-service in information systems domain-knowledge has to be created from a multitude of data sources. To represent their differences in quality, reliability etc., an extension of standard data-modelling is required. This leads us to:

Hypothesis 2: Digitization requires an extension of the standard data-modelling.
Furthermore, it is necessary to appropriately model flexible decisions. Therefore, we created the following hypothesis:

Hypothesis 3: Digitization requires flexible decision mechanisms.

3.2   Products

Dynamic and Personalized Products
Dynamic products are products whose functionality is not fixed during production but extensible in the field. Digitization achieves this by integrating the physical product with hardware, software and connectivity that enable the device to connect to the internet and use services in the cloud [29–31]. Dynamic products are the basis for mass customization [32] of products. Dynamic products can be easily configured and extended according to the individual customer requirements.

Life-Time Integration of Products
Digitization enables products to stay in contact with the producer during their whole lifecycle [29]. Products in the field can easily exchange data with their producers. Data send to the producer may contain information about the functionality used or not used, the status of the device, usage frequency and duration etc. The product can also inform the customer about interruptions and terminations of its usage.

Transformation to Hybrid Products

The possibility to increase and decrease the functionality of dynamic products and the tight integration of physical products during their whole lifecycle enables their transformation to services [33]. That means, the physical product is no longer sold to the customer but offered as a service [33]. In order to transform a physical product to hybrid, its functionality is split up into a set of services. Furthermore, service lifecycle management has to enable that the set of services can be tailored to the customer's requirements and to evolve the functionality seamlessly. Information systems that shall support dynamic products have to show the same level of flexibility [34]. It is important to flexibly reconfigure digital capabilities [35]. We therefore create the hypothesis 4:

Hypothesis 4: Information systems have to support service lifecycle management and in particular the tailoring service sets.

3.3   Value Creation

In [36] value creation is identified as one of four dimensions of digital transformation. Two ways of value creation shall be investigated: network effects and bidirectional value creation.

Network and Lock-in Effects

Digitization enables the creation of platforms [37]. In former times, establishing a physical product platform required a huge effort. Only huge enterprises had the necessary engineering capacities [38]. Now, digitization facilitates the creation of new digital platform significantly. On these platforms network and lock-in effects are activated. Thus digitization transforms value chains to value networks [33]. The value-in-use of products that are part of the platform is increased by the possibility of cooperation with user users. The tight integration of process into the platform creates lock-in effects that reduce the inclination of the customer to churn.

Bidirectional Value Creation in Value Networks

Changes in value-creation have been identified as one important element of digital transformation strategies [36]. Up to digitization, value creation had been influenced strongly by tayloristic [21] ideas. That means, value creation takes place separately from the customers, in the production site. Digitization enables a bidirectional networked model of value creation. Smart, connected products [29] and social software [39] provide a permanent feedback on the usage and perception of the product by the customer. Combined with the capability to configure and extend dynamic products a close feedback loop of product improvements using the customer feedback can be established. An information system that shall be able to support bidirectional value creation, therefore we create the following hypothesis.

Hypothesis 5: Digitization fosters bidirectional value creation by network and lock-in effects on platforms.

4 Evaluation via Case Study

In this chapter the hypotheses developed in Sect. 3 shall by evaluated in a case study in the insurance business, according to the research methodology described in Sect. 2. The following table (Table 2) defines an overview of the analysis done so far.

Table 2. Digitization domains, impact areas and hypotheses

Digitization domains	Impact areas	Hypotheses
Customer product value-creation	Architecture	Hypothesis 5: Digitization fosters bidirectional value creation by net-work and lock-in effect on platforms
	Processes	Hypothesis 1: Digitization requires the extension of standard process-meta-model to represent processes appropriately
	Data	Hypothesis 2: Digitization requires an extension of the standard data-modelling
	Services	Hypothesis 3: Digitization requires flexible decision mechanisms
		Hypothesis 4: Information systems have to support service lifecycle management and in particular the tailoring service sets

4.1 Case Description and Insights

The need for information systems in the insurance business can be described by the typical value chain, consisting of product development, sales and contract management including claims processing. Digitization influences nearly the whole Insurance life cycle. By digitization high quality data are available that can be used to determine risks and to develop new products. Accumulation risks [40] can be identified and the risk of infection can be determined. E.g. by the analysis of social networks new trends, behaviors, etc. can be identified that influence the risks. By using data from the Internet of Things [41] and of social software [39] cross- and upselling opportunities can be identified. In addition, complaints can be evaluated by customers on social platforms. The digitization can develop a range of useful services in the area of claims settlement. Thus, the occurrence of the damage can be detected by cross-linked products in many areas. Examples are cars that possess a crash detection or home automation systems detect the fire or water damage. This may already be able to help the loss amount to reduce by as soon as possible emergency measures are initiated. Simultaneously, the later claims can be prepared by an intensive data collection. The data collected can also be used to detect possible fraud. In claims management, the data can be used to accelerate the process of claims settling as much as possible. In addition, it is also possible any spurious damage seen by more accurate detection of the accident is used.

4.2 Results

Hypothesis 1: Digitization requires the extension of standard process-meta-model to represent processes appropriately

To capture systematically the influence of digitization on process design, perspectives [42] shall be used to categorize the points of impact digitization has on process design. Perspectives are disjoint sets of meta-model elements representing orthogonal domains of the business process. At the beginning [42], four perspectives had been identified, the functional, organizational, informational and behavioral perspective. Perspectives have been used to systematically describe flexibility [43].

Functional Perspective

The functional perspective describes how the overall goal of the process shall be achieved by decomposing it into tasks and subtasks. The functional perspective mirrors the operational perspective. While the functional perspective specifies what is to do, the operational perspective describes how it is be done. New functional elements are necessary to support the bidirectional creation of value in digitization enabled by a multitude of touchpoints [44]. Older process modelling approaches such as ARIS [45] did not provide explicit points of communication with the environment of processes. Later approaches such as BPMN [46] introduced modelling elements to represent the communication with the outside world. These elements have to be refined to represent the diversity of communication points created by digitization. The customer does interact with processes not only by sending explicit messages as conceptualized in BPMN but also be interactions with digitized products. An example is the Amazon Dash Button [47]. Pressing it initiates the delivery of the specified product.

Operational Perspective

The operational perspective describes the operations to fulfill the tasks specified in the functional perspective. From the operational perspective, digitized processes differ by replacing human operations with automated operations. Automation covers two main areas, decision making and customer interaction. Decisions making in digitized processes is based on Big Data [2] and Advanced Analytics [48]. It supplements descriptive analytics with predictive and prescriptive analytics [30]. Domain knowledge is embedded into software and replaces human decision making. To achieve this progress in analytical capabilities it is necessary to appropriately represent the data sources, the decision rules and their foundation as in Decision Modeling Notation Standard [49]. Here, the rule tasks of BPMN are augmented by a detailed modelling of decisions. Self-service is the automation of the customer interaction. Digital means to enable the customer to interact directly with a business process. Thus there are no intermediating employees.

Behavioral Perspective

The behavioral perspective [42] represents existence relationships between tasks. There are synchronous and asynchronous relationships. The synchronous relationship may be either temporal or rule-based. Temporal relationships express the sequence and simultaneity of tasks. Rule-base relationships select one or several other tasks to be executed after the completion of a task. Digitization requires more asynchronous relationships. They are dependent on the existence of an event or the fulfillment of a condition. Such events may stem from smart, connected things, social media etc.

Informational Perspective

The informational perspective [42] defines the data in the process that is imported, created, exchanged, transferred and changed. Before digitization nearly all data was either structured [50] or handled as an opaque binary large object. Digitization introduced further kinds of data such as semi- and unstructured data. Semi-structured data [50] is data that has an implicit structure. Its schema information is not explicitly available but can be recovered by analysis. An important example are log files [51]. Unstructured data [50] has no recoverable schema. Extensions to several perspectives of process models are necessary. Therefore, hypothesis 1 can be confirmed.

Hypothesis 2: Digitization requires an extension of the standard data-modelling

Schema information is the most widely used type of meta-data in enterprises and organizations. In digitized enterprises, the use of data increases evidently. New types of data such as semi- and unstructured data are part of processes. The automation of tasks and decision is based on data. Much more than in the past, data originates from external sources. Not only the schema-information but also further meta-data has to be defined. Thus hypothesis 2 can be confirmed. These additional meta data cover security, quality and reliability. Data is used to create decisions either directly or indirectly. Data is directly used as variable in decision models. Indirectly data is used to capture domain knowledge. By forging data a malicious attacker could be able to influence decisions of the enterprise according to his interest. External data may contain errors of course. Therefore, it is necessary to know about the reliability of external data sources. Finally, external data sources differ in their technical reliability. There are reliable and less reliable ones, showing disruptions in the data provisioning.

Hypothesis 3: Digitization requires flexible decision mechanisms

In many processes, decision logic is embedded directly into the business process models or applications [52]. However, this method is unfavorable because process and decision logic evolve at different speeds. Therefore, the decision logic should be modelled separated in the form of decision models [52]. In this way, decisions can be managed and dealt with separately. In particular, the re-use of decision models in different contexts is possible. A further reason to separate decision logic and processes are their different characteristics [52]. Decisions are declarative, hierarchical and stateless. Processes, on the other hand, are imperative, sequential and stateful. The progress of process instances is represented by the positioning of tokens in the process graph. Due to the different evolution speeds business processes and decision-making a separate modeling of the two domains is advisable. Defining decision models separate the base for decision making processes and the data to be used. Decision models are implemented as decision services that use as decisions foundations, procedures, and data encapsulated as a service. Since these services can also be external, ensuring a reputation model that safety and quality requirements are met and are the provided meta-services.

Otherwise, a new attack vector would be opened for fraudulent activities. An attacker could influence by manipulating the output data, procedures or bases the decisions of the attacked company in his favor. These considerations confirm hypothesis 3.

Hypothesis 4: Information systems have to support service lifecycle management and in particular the tailoring service sets

The transformation of physical products to services implies that these services can be appropriately adapted to the customer's requirements. They should allow him to enlarge or decrease the set of services booked (and billed). Therefore, hypothesis 4 can be confirmed. To avoid any misunderstandings, both service provider and service user should have a common definition to which extent the set of services can be changed and how much services can be tailored to individual needs. To do so, operations on the services provided have to be offered to the customer. To the customer it is important to not only know about the kind of changes but also about their quality. That means they want to know how fast these changes can be accomplished, when are these changes available and how reliable are the changes executed. Such a combination of functionality provided together with a description of its quality is nothing else than a service. Because these services act upon other services, they shall be called meta-services [53].

Hypothesis 5: Digitization fosters bidirectional value creation by net-work and lock-in effect on platforms

An architecture supporting bidirectional value creation is illustrated in the following figure (Fig. 1). Thus hypothesis 5 can be confirmed. The architecture has an integration layer to open up and consolidate data in particular from the Internet of Things, Social Media and Open Data. The integrated information will be used in two ways. In order to implement the co-creation oriented value creation model, it is necessary to constantly interact with the customers. Therefore, in the IT architecture an event processing mechanism is provided which detects relevant events in the incoming data. These events may be, to externally triggered events such as loss events, or other, also by the customers themselves, triggered events. In addition, a new decision function is necessary, which is able to process semi- and unstructured data from external sources. Furthermore, this architecture should be a continuous process. Both events and analysis results are then included in the process support, which controls the interaction with the customer. Since there may be incidents that are relevant to analysis, there is a connection from process support to the event detection and analysis.

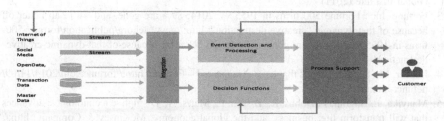

Fig. 1. Generic information system architecture for digitized insurances

5 Conclusions and Limitations

As the research at hand is based on only one case selected not on a random, but subjective basis, we are not able to make general assumptions about its representativeness. Nevertheless, we provide detailed descriptions and insights on the case, allowing the reader to transfer the study's results to its own similar and contextual settings of interest. We showed, that digitization has impact on several areas of information system design. The modelling of processes and data has to be extended. Service definitions have to be supplemented by meta-service in order to define their lifecycle. Decisions have to be separated from processes in order to achieve flexibility. In all, a stream- and event-oriented architecture is necessary in order to support bidirectional value creation.

Research can benefit in different ways from our research. First, we extent the current IS literature by exploring new effects of digitization of information systems via a literature review and case study. Second, industry specific insights in the use and adoption of information through digitization in the financial industry is presented. Furthermore, our research can help to get a better understanding of further impacts of digitation in practice. There are also practical implications. Managers can use the results to evaluate their current state of digitization and can further develop their enterprise architecture. Decisions related to digitization in the financial industry can be supported by our work.

Limitations of our work can be found in the used research methods as well as samples. We looked at a sample of the literature according to the literature method. Furthermore, we validate our findings in one case study. Furthermore, the case study was implemented in the financial industry in a European country. Therefore, future research should evaluate our findings via different case studies in different industry sectors as well as countries. There should be great opportunities for future research according to the different adoption of digitization via information systems in different countries (e.g. EU vs. South Africa).

References

1. Schmidt, R., Zimmermann, A., Nurcan, S., Möhring, M., Bär, F., Keller, B.: Digitization – perspectives for conceptualization. In: Taormina, Italy (2015, to appear)
2. Manyika, J., Chui, M., Brown, B., Bughin, J., Dobbs, R., Roxburgh, C., Byers, A.H.: Big data: the next frontier for innovation, competition, and productivity, pp. 1–137. McKinsey Global Institute (2011)
3. Fortune, Inc.: Fortune 500 firms in 1955 vs. 2014; 89% are gone, and we're all better off because of that dynamic "creative destruction". http://www.aei.org/publication/fortune-500-firms-in-1955-vs-2014-89-are-gone-and-were-all-better-off-because-of-that-dynamic-creative-destruction/
4. Locker, M.: 8 iconic brands that have disappeared – Fortune. http://fortune.com/2014/11/09/defunct-brands/
5. Manyika, J., Bughin, J., Dobbs, R., Bisson, P., Marrs, A.: Disruptive technologies: advances that will transform life, business, and the global economy. McKinsey & Company. http://www.mckinsey.com/insights/business_technology/disruptive_technologies

6. Deloitte LLP and affiliated entities: Property and Casualty Insurance Re-imagined: 2025, Canada (2015)
7. Cooper, H.M.: Synthesizing Research: A Guide for Literature Reviews. Sage, Thousand Oaks (1998)
8. Kitchenham, B.: Procedures for performing systematic reviews. Keele, UK, Keele University. 33, 1–26 (2004)
9. Webster, J., Watson, R.T.: Analyzing the past to prepare for the future: writing A. MIS Q. 26, xiii–xxiii (2002)
10. Computing Research and Education Association of Australasia: CORE JOURNAL RANKING. http://portal.core.edu.au/conf-ranks/
11. VHB-JOURQUAL: Verband der Hochschullehrer für Betriebswirtschaft e.V. http://vhbonline.org/service/jourqual/
12. Kossahl, J., Busse, S., Kolbe, L.M.: The evolvement of energy informatics in the information systems community-a literature analysis and research agenda. In: ECIS, p. 172 (2012)
13. Montagud, S., Abrahão, S., Insfran, E.: A systematic review of quality attributes and measures for software product lines. Softw. Qual. J. 20, 425–486 (2012)
14. Yin, R.: Case Study Research: Design and Methods. Sage Publishing, Beverly Hills (1994)
15. Warrington, E.K.: The fractionation of arithmetical skills: a single case study. Q. J. Exp. Psychol. 34, 31–51 (1982)
16. Walsham, G., Waema, T.: Information systems strategy and implementation: a case study of a building society. ACM Trans. Inf. Syst. (TOIS) 12, 150–173 (1994)
17. Laumer, S., Maier, C., Eckhardt, A.: The impact of human resources information systems and business process management implementations on recruiting process performance: a case study (2014)
18. Darke, P., Shanks, G., Broadbent, M.: Successfully completing case study research: combining rigour, relevance and pragmatism. Inf. Syst. J. 8, 273–289 (1998)
19. Piccinini, E., Gregory, R.W., Kolbe, L.M.: Changes in the producer-consumer relationship-towards digital transformation. Changes 3 (2015)
20. Westermann, G., Bonnet, D.: Revamping Your Business Through Digital Transformation. http://sloanreview.mit.edu/article/revamping-your-business-through-digital-transformation/
21. Taylor, F.W.: The principles of scientific management, New York, p. 202 (1911)
22. Henry, F.: My Life and Work. Cosimo Inc., New York City (2005)
23. Mills, P.K., Morris, J.H.: Clients as "partial" employees of service organizations: role development in client participation. Acad. Manag. Rev. 11, 726–735 (1986)
24. Lovelock, C.H., Young, R.F.: Look to consumers to increase productivity. Harvard Bus. Rev. 57, 168–178 (1979)
25. Chase, R.B.: Where does the customer fit in a service operation? Harvard Bus. Rev. 56, 137–142 (1977)
26. Prahalad, C.K., Ramaswamy, V.: Co-opting customer competence. Harvard Bus. Rev. 78, 79–90 (2000)
27. Chen, S.-C., Chen, H.-H., Chen, M.-F.: Determinants of satisfaction and continuance intention towards self-service technologies. Ind. Manag. Data Syst. 109, 1248–1263 (2009)
28. Shamdasani, P., Mukherjee, A., Malhotra, N.: Antecedents and consequences of service quality in consumer evaluation of self-service internet technologies. Serv. Ind. J. 28, 117–138 (2008)
29. Porter, M.E., Heppelmann, J.E.: How smart, connected products are transforming competition. Harvard Bus. Rev. 92, 11–64 (2014)
30. Porter, M.E., Heppelmann, J.E.: How smart, connected products are transforming Companies. Harvard Bus. Rev. 93, 96–114 (2015)

31. Lee, J., Berente, N.: Digital innovation and the division of innovative labor: digital controls in the automotive industry. Organ. Sci. **23**, 1428–1447 (2012)
32. Gilmore, J.H., Pine 2nd, B.J.: The four faces of mass customization. Harvard Bus. Rev. **75**, 91–101 (1996)
33. Sinfield, J., Calder, N., Geheb, B.: How industrial systems are turning into digital services. https://hbr.org/2015/06/how-industrial-systems-are-turning-into-digital-services
34. Babar, Z., Yu, E.: Enterprise architecture in the age of digital transformation. In: Persson, A., Stirna, J. (eds.) Advanced Information Systems Engineering Workshops, pp. 438–443. Springer, Cham (2015). doi:10.1007/978-3-319-19243-7_40
35. Grover, V., Kohli, R.: Revealing your hand: caveats in implementing digital business strategy. MIS Q. **37**, 655–662 (2013)
36. Matt, C., Hess, T., Benlian, A.: Digital transformation strategies. Bus. Inf. Syst Eng. **57**, 339–343 (2015)
37. Eisenmann, T., Parker, G., Van Alstyne, M.W.: Strategies for two-sided markets. Harvard Bus. Rev. **84**, 92 (2006)
38. West, J.: How open is open enough? Melding proprietary and open source platform strategies. Res. Policy **32**, 1259–1285 (2003)
39. Schmidt, R., Nurcan, S.: BPM and Social Software. In: Ardagna, D., Mecella, M., Yang, J., Aalst, W., Mylopoulos, J., Rosemann, M., Shaw, M.J., Szyperski, C. (eds.) Business Process Management Workshops, pp. 649–658. Springer, Heidelberg (2009). doi:10.1007/978-3-642-00328-8_65
40. Principles of Risk Management and Insurance. Prentice Hall, Boston (2013)
41. Atzori, L., Iera, A., Morabito, G.: The internet of things: a survey. Comput. Netw. **54**, 2787–2805 (2010)
42. Curtis, B., Kellner, M.I., Over, J.: Process modeling. Commun. ACM **35**, 75–90 (1992)
43. Regev, G., Soffer, P., Schmidt, R.: Taxonomy of flexibility in business processes. In: Proceedings Seventh Workshop on Business Process Modeling, Development, and Support (BPMDS 2006). Requirements for flexibility and the ways to achieve it, Luxemburg, pp. S.90–S.93 (2006)
44. Edelman, D.C.: Branding in the Digital Age: You're Spending Your Money in All the Wrong Places. https://hbr.org/2010/12/branding-in-the-digital-age-youre-spending-your-money-in-all-the-wrong-places
45. Scheer, A.W.: ARIS-Business Process Modeling. Springer, Heidelberg (2000)
46. White, S.A.: Introduction to BPMN. IBM Cooperation, pp. 2008–2029 (2004)
47. Amazon.com: Dash Button. https://www.amazon.com/b/?node=10667898011&sort=date-desc-rank&lo=digital-text
48. Barton, D.: Making advanced analytics work for you. Harvard Bus. Rev. **90**, 78–83 (2012)
49. OMG: DMN 1.0. http://www.omg.org/spec/DMN/1.0/Beta1/
50. White, T.: Hadoop: The Definitive Guide. O'Reilly & Associates, Sebastopol (2015)
51. Unified Log Processing. https://www.manning.com/books/unified-log-processing
52. Hof, H.-J., Schmidt, R., Brehm, L.: Enabling digital transformation using secure decisions as a service. In: Celesti, A., Leitner, P. (eds.) ESOCC Workshops 2015. CCIS, vol. 567, pp. 289–298. Springer, Cham (2016). doi:10.1007/978-3-319-33313-7_22
53. Schmidt, R.: Meta-services as third dimension of service-oriented enterprise architecture. In: 2010 14th IEEE International Presented at the Enterprise Distributed Object Computing Conference Workshops (EDOCW) (2010)
54. Henningsson, S., Hedman, J.: Transformation of digital ecosystems: the case of digital payments. In: Linawati, M.M.S., Neuhold, E.J., Tjoa, A.M., You, I. (eds.) Information and Communication Technology, pp. 46–55. Springer, Heidelberg (2014). doi:10.1007/978-3-642-55032-4_5

55. Goes, P.: Big data - analytics engine for digital transformation: where is IS? In: AMCIS 2015 Proceedings (2015)
56. Zimmermann, A., Schmidt, R., Jugel, D., Möhring, M.: Adaptive enterprise architecture for digital transformation. In: Celesti, A., Leitner, P. (eds.) ESOCC Workshops 2015. CCIS, vol. 567, pp. 308–319. Springer, Cham (2016). doi:10.1007/978-3-319-33313-7_24
57. Zimmermann, A., Schmidt, R., Sandkuhl, K., Wissotzki, M., Jugel, D., Möhring, M.: Digital enterprise architecture - transformation for the internet of things. In: IEEE International Enterprise Distributed Object Computing Conference (EDOC 2015), Workshop Proceedings. IEEE Computer Society, Adelaide 2015 (2015)
58. Piccinini, E., Hanelt, A., Gregory, R., Kolbe, L.: Transforming industrial business: the impact of digital transformation on automotive organizations. In: ICIS 2015 Proceedings (2015)
59. Boland, R., Glymph, J., Zahner, B., King, J., Lyytinen, K.: Computing on the scaffolds: the coming transformation of architecture and construction with digital technologies. In: ICIS 2003 Proceedings (2003)

Evaluation of Application Architecture Change Cases: Building Blocks Reusability Assessment Method

Rūta Pirta[✉] and Jānis Grabis

Department of Management Information Technology, Riga Technical University,
Kalku 1, Riga LV-1658, Latvia
{ruta.pirta, grabis}@rtu.lv

Abstract. The reuse of IT solutions plays an important role, as it enables organizations to develop services more quickly and at reduced cost, and promotes greater interoperability, standardization and cooperation. Organizations increasingly include the reuse principle in their Enterprise architecture (EA) development vision. However, they often lack methods for comprehensive evaluation of changes in Application Architecture (AA) including assessment of reuse of AA components. In this paper, we outline a method for AA change evaluation. The objective of the proposed method is to provide support for establishing a controlled environment for AA change implementation planning to meet defined EA principles. In this paper, we focus on the reuse principle, however the approach can be also adapted for change assessment with regards to other principles such as centralization and standardization.

Keywords: Enterprise architecture · Application Architecture · Architecture principles · IS changes · Reuse

1 Introduction

Enterprise architecture (EA) is a commonly accepted instrument to guide enterprise transformations. Its main goal is to enhance and maintain the mutual alignment of business and IT [2, 3]. EA vision is frequently led by architecture principles that support decision making across enterprise [4]. Nowadays large-scale organizations and public administration bodies more frequently include reusability principle in their EA development vision [5–7]. The reuse is not a goal by itself but is mainly motivates by such business goals as increase of productivity, reduction of development effort, time and cost, improvement of quality and increase of interoperability [8]. Thus, the principle supports enterprises in information technology (IT) related decisions making that can add value to the business and improve business and IT alignment.

However, the strategic level pursuit is often neglected as the operational level and individual units tend to prefer to build their own IT solution rather than reuse existing solutions. In many cases, that means greater autonomy but can also contribute to an expensive and fragmented EA, which often duplicates IT solutions and impedes the sharing and reuse of software and IS services [1]. The organizations with decentralized

W. Abramowicz (Ed.): BIS 2017 Workshops, LNBIP 303, pp. 150–162, 2017.
https://doi.org/10.1007/978-3-319-69023-0_14

IT governance often faces "Not-invented-here syndrome" - software engineers prefer to re-write components as they believe that they can improve the reusable component and writing original software is seen as more challenging than reusing existing one [8]. Not all Application Architecture (AA) components are reusable. Solutions might have dependencies or reuse constraints. These dependencies can either be of a technical nature (e.g. reliance on a specific third party product) or relative to specific legislation or business domain [6].

Empirical observations show that enterprises lack a comprehensive approach for evaluation of proposed changes in AA with regards to facilitating reusability. Decisions about changes in AA often are subjective and require extensive manual work (IT solutions technical documentation analysis, solutions audits etc.) [6].

In this paper we propose a method for evaluation of changes in AA according to EA development principles. This method generates recommendations for implementing changes in AA in a way to attain the best alignment with defined EA principles. In the paper we focus on the reuse principle, however the approach also can be adapted for assessment of compliance with other principles, for example, adoption of centralized IT management and preference for standardized solutions.

The proposed method is envisioned as a middle-ground between isolated evaluation of the IS change requests and comprehensive strategic level planning of EA evolution. It provides a tactical level tool helping organizations to understand implications of their IS change requests. The method is intended for large-scale organizations, including international corporations, concerns with several legal entities, as well as for public administration bodies. It focuses on significant changes in the AA that can be classified as incremental changes and re-architecting changes according to the TOGAF classification in [9].

The rest of the paper is organized as follows. Section 2 states the background and briefly outlines the related works. In the Sect. 3 the approach's outline is given. Section 4 describes an illustrative example. The paper closes in Sect. 5 with the conclusions.

2 Foundations

2.1 Problem Statement

Given EA, architecture principles and change case (CC) raised by user of enterprise information systems, the objective is to find the most suitable solution for implementing the requested architecturally significant changes without starting a new architecture development cycle. The most suitable solution is provided as a set of recommendations indicating which elements of the EA should be altered.

The EA consists of at least three views [9], namely, AA, information architecture (IA) and business architecture (BA). Each view consists of specific elements (Fig. 1). Logical application components represent application functionality independent of implementation. In this paper, logical application components are referred as Information Systems (IS). IS services represent automated elements of business service and are implemented using application components. Data entities encapsulate data that is recognized by a business domain expert as a discrete concept. They are processed by logical application components, are accessed and updated by business services and supported or consumed by actors. Business services support business capabilities through an explicitly defined interface and is explicitly governed by an organization. They are realized through business processes and consumed by actors.

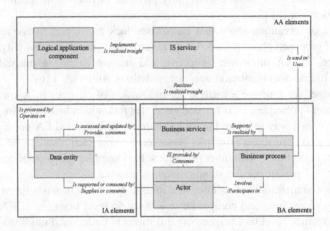

Fig. 1. Views and elements of EA used in evalaution of change cases

A CC defines a need for adjustments in enterprise business processes or information technologies in a semi-structured manner. It is assumed that the CC contains information allowing to identify IS used by an actor raising the CC as well as requested new or existing IS service can be implied by an expert from the description provided.

EA principles are statements of intent or purpose that support business needs and changing customer desires, they guide business & IT decisions and investments [10]. The principles in enterprises are chosen so as to ensure alignment of IT strategies with business strategies and visions [9], and well-formulated principles are measurable [7]. This paper focuses on the reuse principle and reuse efficiency is measured as total amount of reused EA components.

Evaluation of changes could be aided by consulting a domain specific reference architecture. The reference architecture encompasses domain specific knowledge and provides a template for accelerating and improving the EA development process [13].

2.2   Related Work

The need for more standardized products promotes an explicit (reusable) architecture and reuse of components [14]. Software reuse is: "the process whereby an organization defines a set of systematic operating procedures to specify, produce, classify, retrieve, and adapt software artefacts for the purpose of using them in its development activities." [15].

The reuse principle is currently widely used in public administration bodies and large enterprises. The reuse enables organizations to develop services more quickly and at a reduced cost, and promotes greater interoperability, standardization and cooperation [1]. Two distinctive directions of research are exploration of reusability benefits [14–17] and software reusability assessment [6, 20, 21].

For example, a case study at a large telecom company provides evidence of quality benefits of large-scale reuse programs [14]. Other key benefits of software reuse are increased productivity, lower fault/defect-density, lower number of changes per module or per LOC, reduced development and maintenance effort, reduced complexity, and consistency of applications and the software architecture [16, 17]. These articles investigate benefits of reuse but they do not address planning for reusability.

A dependency model is used to evaluate reusability of open source components from both static and dynamic perspectives [21]; and three metrics based on the model to measure interaction behavior complexity between component and its context. For performance evaluation, the authors suggest using performance measurement model. [21] specifically addresses software source code reuse topic. The paper presents extraction and analysis methods for developers' source code reuse behavior. In [22], a method for aspect oriented software reusability assessment using inheritance metrics is proposed. The authors state that it is not possible directly measure reusability from the design of software, and propose to develop a quality model to quantitatively assess the reuse of components. These papers mainly focus on software elements (source code and others) technical characteristics evaluation and do not include architectural considerations.

A reuse reference grid is proposed as an assessment framework to help categorize and assess the cost/benefit of the current level of reuse as a prelude to considering future reuse opportunities [23]. It facilitates reuse assessment in three ways: (1) categorizing existing reuse, (2) assessing current reuse levels, and 3) considering future reuse strategy.

European Commission [6] proposed a template for a factsheet that would facilitate the assessment of solutions reuse by providing useful and detailed information that should be considered when evaluating reuse of a solution in a specific context. The template focuses on reusability of technical solutions both as a software component and as a service. However, the template does not support enterprise architects in the evaluation process. Template's usage requires architects to have a good understanding of the solution that would benefit from reuse.

3   Change Evaluation Method

The proposed method (Fig. 2) supports assessment of reuse potential of existing AA components, namely, architecture building blocks (ABB) and solutions building blocks (SBB) in the case of implementing architecturally significant change requests. A research method to be taken to address research method and practical challenges follows the nested design science problem solving approach [24].

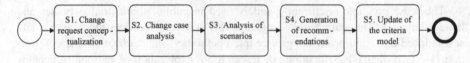

Fig. 2. Phases of the change evaluation method

The reuse principle is enshrined in the organization's EA vision. The method focuses on significant changes, which can be classified as incremental changes and re-architecting changes according to the TOGAF classification in [9]. Simplification changes are outside the scope, as they do not have a significant impact on EA and they can normally be handled via change management techniques. The types of reuse [11] considered in this paper are function reuse, component reuse and full model reuse.

3.1 Change Case Analysis (S1)

The evaluation process is initiated by receiving a CC containing information as defined in Sect. 2. The CC contains both structured and unstructured data and implies what IS services are pertinent to the request. These IS services are identified by an enterprise architect. The requested IS services can be delivered by introducing new or reusing existing EA components. The enterprise architect also links IS services to supported Business services (BS) and Business processes (BP), what facilitates identification of IS services in the reference model. The result of the CC analysis is a list with requested IS services and related BS and BP, which are referred as elements mentioned in the change request and are denoted as ISS*, BS* and BP*, respectively.

3.2 Development of Change Implementation Architectural Scenarios (S2)

A change implementation scenario defines one of alternatives for updating EA in response to the change request. It specifies ABB and SBB to be considered to implement the change. In this case, ABB are IS and SBB are IS services.

Change implementation scenarios are dependent of changes implementation type and level of components reuse (Table 1). Possible implementation types are new IS implementation or existing IS modification. Possible levels of IS services reuse are:

- The functionality provided by new IS services;
- The functionality provides new and reused IS services;
- The functionality provides reused IS services.

Table 1. Levels of reuse

Implementation type	Level of reuse		
	New IS services	New & reused IS services	Reused IS services
Existing IS modification	X	X	X
New IS implementation	X	X	

Combining implementation alternatives in ABB level and different levels of components reuse in SBB level are defined change implementation scenarios.

Change implementation scenarios are defined in two successive steps – initially ABB alternatives are set, then SBB alternatives are identified and combined with defined ABB, jointly creating change implementation architecture scenarios.

Identification of ABB

Analysis the change request, existing EA model and reference model is performed to identify ABB. Firstly, IS to be modified and/or IS to be implemented are inferred by analyzing the change request and existing EA model. The inference rules are aimed at narrowing a set of potential modification and implementation alternatives. Given ISS*, BS* and BP*, the inference rules analyze relationships in the EA model and selects candidate IS services for modification/implementation. The selection rules are: (1) select all IS mentioned in the change request; (2) select all IS supporting BP*; (3) select all IS supporting BS*; (4) select all IS maintaining data that is accessed or modified by BS*; and (5) select all IS maintaining data linked to the actor requesting changes. The selected IS are collectively denoted as IS'.

Secondly, existing EA and reference model gap analysis is performed. During the analysis common IS supporting BP* and BS* are identified and selected as potentially modifiable AA components. As well as gaps are identified (IS that exists in reference models but does not exists in existing EA model) and selected as potentially new AA components.

The analysis yields candidate ABB for implementation of each ISS*. The architect manually accepts or rejects each candidate ABB.

Identification of SBB

Analysis of the existing EA model and reference model is performed to identify candidate SBB what are linked to the candidate ABB. ISS* are mapped to the existing EA model and reference model as shown in Fig. 3. If an appropriate service is available its reuse is recommended. Otherwise mapping to the reference model is performed resulting in recommendations to implement a new IS service, to use a similar service and to review the service. The service review is recommended if similar services are not available in the reference architecture what suggests a need reconsider architecture design.

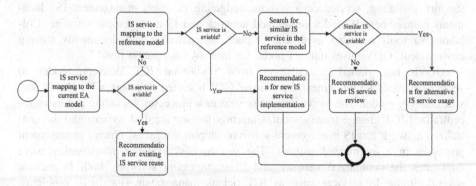

Fig. 3. SBB analysis process

3.3 Scenarios Analysis (S3)

Scenarios analysis consists of: (1) assessment of ABB alternatives; (2) assessment of SBB alternatives and (3) evaluation of ABB and SBB interoperability.

Technical criteria are used for assessment of candidate SBB and ABB, as well as for evaluation of ABB and SBB interoperability. These criteria are directly related to defined EA principles. They include specific ABB and SBB reusability evaluation criteria as proposed in [6]. The examples of ABB and SBB interoperability criteria are use of standards and availability of well-defined application programming interfaces. The standards used by a solution could either make it a good reuse candidate for a specific solution or exclude it due to conflicting choices already made.

The technical criteria are calculated from the EA model to analyze scenarios.

3.4 Recommendations Generation (S4) and Criteria Model Update (S5)

During the recommendation phase, the most appropriate implementation scenario is selected. Values of the selected technical criteria are calculated for every scenario. The tentative landscape having the best values of criteria is selected. It is recommended as the most appropriate way of implementing the change request.

To allocate resources efficiently, after the existing components evaluation, financial calculations must be performed (Total Cost of Ownership vs Total Cost of Reuse) to compare existing components reuse vs new components implementation alternatives.

The process ends with criteria model update. After several rounds of change implementation in the EA model, the enterprise architect updates the criteria model with empirical knowledges about changes implementation practice.

4 Illustrative Example

An example is based on the real-life case in a government body (further referred as GOVb). The organization runs centralized IT service that serves more than 13 partly autonomous departments. The organization has complex AA architecture that consists of more than 30 partly integrated IS supporting delivery of public services as well as internal administrative processes. Several IS are used for IT services management support, including, service desk system, budgeting IS, users management IS, documents management IS and a centralized network and IS management software. Collaborative tools are also used, e.g., e-mail, internal chat and documents sharing environment. GOVb uses intranet portal for internal information flow.

GOVb has started a transition from traditional ICT delivery model to service-oriented. To implement the change, GOVb started to design a "to-be" IT service delivery model. The model defines several new processes, including processes for centralized ICT change management. Currently the service desk system and the centralized network and IS management software support the "as-is" change management processes in a fragmented manner. The service desk system's functionality party duplicates the centralized network and IS management software, both IS include several similar IS services such as ICT tickets management (incidents, problems, changes). The service desk system manages user tickets, while the centralized network and IS management software are used to report work performed by ICT personnel and ICT items configuration management.

Several AA CC were identified during implementation of the centralized and standardized ICT change management process. The enterprise architect reviews the CC and identifies included IS services and links them to supported BS and BP (Table 2) as defined in Sect. 3.

Table 2. Identified IS services and linked BP (all BP are associated with ICT change management BS)

ID	IS service	BP
1.	ICT change request data automatic processing and importing	ICT change request registration
2.	ICT change request data fill	ICT change request registration
3.	ICT change request workflow management	ICT change request registration; ICT change request approval; ICT changes planning; ICT changes approval; ICT changes control; ICT changes review and closing
4.	ICT change request status changes management (registered, approved, closed etc.)	ICT change request registration; ICT change request approval; ICT changes planning; ICT changes approval; ICT changes control; ICT changes review and closing
5.	ICT change request classification	ICT change request approval
6.	Notifications management (notifications about status changes etc.)	ICT change request registration; ICT change request approval; ICT changes planning; ICT changes approval; ICT changes control; ICT changes review and closing
7.	ICT change project documentation management	ICT changes planning; ICT changes approval; ICT changes control; ICT changes review and closing
8.	ICT items data update	ICT changes review and closing

IS to be modified are identified by analyzing the existing EA model and reference model. The inference rules suggest that the change might relate to the following existing IS: (1) Intranet portal (because IS currently supports related BS); (2) Service desk system (because IS currently supports related BS); (3) Users management IS (IS maintaining data accessed or modified by BS); (4) Documents management IS (IS maintaining data accessed or modified by BS); (5) Centralized network and IS management software (IS that currently is used to support BS); and (6) Documents sharing environment (IS maintaining data that is accessed or modified by BS).

IS to be implemented are identified by performing gap analysis between the existing EA and reference model. For the change evaluation, the ITIL ARIS domain-specific reference model is chosen. IS that exist in the reference model but do not exist in the EA model are identified: (1) ICT asset management system (IS that currently is used to support BS); (2) ICT services catalogue (IS maintaining data that is accessed or modified by BS); (3) Configuration database (IS maintaining data that is accessed or modified by BS).

Table 3. Selected candidate ABB (a fragment)

ID	IS service	Candidate ABB	
		Existing IS modification	New IS implementation
1	ICT change request data automatic processing and importing to the change request	Intranet portal	–
		Service desk system	–
		Centralized network and IS management software	–
		Documents management system	–
2	ICT change request data fill	Intranet portal	–
		Service desk system	–
		Centralized network and IS management software	–
		Documents management system	–
3	ICT change request workflow management	Documents management system	–
		Service desk system	–
		Centralized network and IS management software	–
7	ICT change project documentation management	Documents management system	–
		Documents sharing environment	–
8	ICT items data update	Centralized network and IS management software	–
		–	ICT asset management system
		–	Configuration database

The enterprise architect reviews and accepts or rejects candidate ABB. The accepted candidate ABB are listed in Table 3.

Candidate SBB are identified by mapping the candidate IS services to existing EA. Candidate SBB for implementation of new IS services are identified by mapping of the candidate IS services to the ITIL ARIS reference model. They are ICT change request classification, ICT change project documentation management and ICT items data update.

The SBB level alternatives are combined with the ABB level alternatives and several changes implementation scenarios are proposed. These scenarios are evaluated according to GOVb's architecture principles, which include reusability and interoperability. For each scenario its rating is calculated, using measures appropriate for the candidate ABB and SBB. Examples of the criteria used to evaluate the candidate ABB are given Table 4. The criteria evaluation metrics is in the range between 0 and 5 with boundary values defined in the table.

Table 4. Criteria for evaluation of candidate ABB

#	Criteria	Criteria description [6]	Criteria evaluation metrics
1	Interfaces (interoperability principle)	Information on the architecture of the component and any expectations that the component would have of the overall solution (e.g., configurability, API)	0 – ABB is a stand-alone system 5 – well-defined open interfaces
2	Actual reuse (reuse principle)	Cases where the solution has already been reused, either as a service or as a software component. The extent to which a solution is already reused is a good indication of its maturity and reusability, both in technical terms but also potentially in terms of policy domains.	0 – ABB has not been reused 5 – maximum level of reuse across all ABB
3	Modularity (reuse principle)	Measures taken to ensure that this solution has been built as reusable from the ground up (e.g., non-proprietary technologies, modular software architecture, SOA)	0 – homogeneous ABB 5 – fully modularized ABB
4	Maturity (reuse principle)	The status of the solution in terms of maturity, to indicate its ongoing development and design stability. The solution's development status is expressed using the following values: (1) Plan, (2) Design, (3) Development, (4) Integration and testing, (5) Deployment, (6) Operation, (7) Disposal.	0 – disposed ABB 5 – implemented and used in BS and BP
5	Extensibility (reuse principle)	Information regarding the possibility to extend of modify the component to suit a specific solution's needs.	0 – ABB has not been extended 5 – maximum level of extension across all ABB
6	Use of standards (interoperability principle)	The standards that the solution uses and conforms to ranging from business and data standards to technical and communication standards.	0 – only proprietary solutions are used 5 – only standard solutions are used

Selected criteria are measured by analyzing the EA model. For example, for ABB actual reuse criteria links between ABB logical application components and different BS are analyzed – if ABB supports at least 2 unlinked BS that processes separate data entities, it is assumed that the component is reused. Based on the analysis results for each candidate ABB and scenario their ratings are calculate according to each criterion. An example of ratings for candidate ABB is shown in the Fig. 4.

As the result, one scenario (Table 5) is recommended for implementation in alignment with the AA evolution vison. The recommended scenario has the best overall rating, which is based on ratings in several measurement positions.

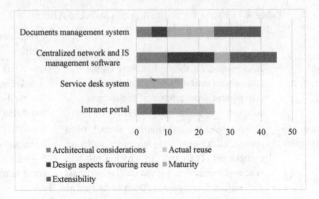

Fig. 4. Rating of candidate ABB

The implementation scenario suggests that the IS service for ICT change request data automatic processing and importing can be developed by modifying the existing Centralized network and IS management software (ABB level) where existing IS service can be reused (SBB level). The ICT change request classification IS service also can be implemented by modifying the same existing IS through development of a new IS service is required at the SBB level. The former case exemplifies high level of reuse while the latter case has a moderate level of reuse. There is no reuse in the case of IS service for ICT items data update that requires implementation of a completely new IS.

Table 5. Recommended change implementation scenario

ID	IS service	ABB		SBB	
		Existing IS modification	New IS implementation	Reused IS service	New IS service
1	ICT change request data automatic processing and importing to the change request	Centralized network and IS management software		X	
2	ICT change request data fill	Centralized network and IS management software		X	
3	ICT change request workflow management	Centralized network and IS management software		X	
7	ICT change project documentation management	Documents sharing environment			X
8	ICT items data update		ICT asset management system		X

5 Conclusions

This paper outlines a method for identification and evaluation of scenarios for modifying AA to accommodate CC raised by users of enterprise IS. The method focuses on promoting reuse of existing architectural and solution level building blocks. It combines expert judgment with quantitative and network analysis of EA models. It uses network analysis to identify candidate building blocks for implementing the change and multi-criteria quantitative analysis to evaluate the candidates. The paper presents preliminary rules for network analysis and measurable criteria for evaluation of the candidates. These set of rules and criteria are indented as extensible and are subject of further refinement and validation.

The main benefits of the method are the following: (1) the method helps aligning IS changes with the EA evolution strategy, thus facilitating business and IT alignment as well; (2) more transparent decision-taking process and (3) reduced need of expert involvment.

There are several limitations to be addressed on the future research: ensuring completeness of CCs; accounting for differences in the level of details in EA and reference models; and extending the analysis beyond evaluation of the AA components.

References

1. European Commission: The Sharing and Reuse IT Solutions Framework, Fostering collaboration among Public Administrations (2015). https://joinup.ec.europa.eu/sites/default/files/sharing_and_reuse_of_it_solutions_framework_final.pdf
2. Henderson, J.C., Venkatraman, N.: Strategic alignment: leveraging information technology for transforming organizations. IBM Syst. J. **32**(1), 472–484 (1993)
3. Luftman, J.N., Lewis, P.R., Oldach, S.H.: Transforming the enterprise: the alignment of business and information technology strategies. IBM Syst. J. **32**(1), 198–221 (1993)
4. Urbaczewski, L., Mrdalj, S.: A comparison of enterprise architecture frameworks. Issues Inf. Syst. **7**(2), 18–23 (2006)
5. Guimarães, Th.S.M.: 21 principles of enterprise architecture for the financial sector (2012). http://www.ibm.com/developerworks/rational/library/enterprise-architecture-financial-sector/index.html?ca=drs
6. European Commission: Reusability Factsheet Template (2015). https://joinup.ec.europa.eu/sites/default/files/sc73_d02.03_reusability_factsheet_v4.00.pdf
7. Greefhorst, D., Proper, E.: Architecture Principles: The Cornerstones of Enterprise Architecture. Springer, Heidelberg (2011). doi:10.1007/978-3-642-20279-7
8. Sommerville, I.: Software Engineering, 9th edn. Addison-Wesley, Boston (2011). pp. 429–452
9. The Open Group: TOGAF, Version 9, Personal PDF Edition (2012). http://www.kingdee.com/news/subject/10togaf/pdf/TOGAF_Manual_G091.pdf
10. PricewaterhouseCoopers: Enterprise Architecture Training materials (2009)
11. Reese, R., Wyatt, D.L.: Software reuse and simulation. In: Proceedings of the 19th Conference on Winter Simulation. ACM, Atlanta, Georgia, United States, pp. 185–192 (1987)
12. Op't Land, M., Proper, H.A.: Impact of Principles on Enterprise Engineering, In: ECIS 2007 Proceedings, p. 113 (2007)

13. Noran, O.: Using reference models in enterprise architecture: an example. In: Fettke, P., Loos, P. (eds), Reference Modeling for Business Systems Analysis, Idea Group, Hershey, USA, pp. 141–165 (2006)
14. Mohagheghi, P., Conradi, R.: An empirical investigation of software reuse benefits in a large telecom product. ACM Trans. Softw. Eng. Methodol. (TOSEM), 17(3), Article no. 13 (2008)
15. Mili, H., Mili, A., Yacoub, S., Addy, E.: Reuse Based Software Engineering Techniques Organizations and Measurement. Wiley, Hoboken (2001)
16. Selby, W.: Enabling reuse-based software development of large-scale systems. IEEE Trans. Softw. Eng. 31(6), 495–510 (2005)
17. Mili, A., Chmiel, S.F., Gottumkkala, R., Zhang, L.: An integrated cost model for software reuse. In: Proceedings of the 22nd International Conference on Software Engineering (ICSE 2000), pp. 157–166 (2000)
18. Pirta, R., Grabis, J.: Integrated methodology for information systems (IS) change control based on enterprise architecture (EA) models. Inf. Technol. Manag. Sci. 18(1), 103–108 (2015)
19. Zhang, W., Jarzabek, S.: Reuse without compromising performance: industrial experience from RPG software product line for mobile devices. In: Obbink, H., Pohl, K. (eds.) SPLC 2005. LNCS, vol. 3714, pp. 57–69. Springer, Heidelberg (2005). doi:10.1007/11554844_7
20. Wu, J., Liu, Y.P., Jia, X.X., Liu, C.: Mining open source component behavior and performance for reuse evaluation. In: The 9th International Conference for Young Computer Scientists, Hunan, pp. 1241–1247 (2008)
21. Ohta, T., Murakami, H., Igaki, H., Higo, Y., Kusumoto, S.: Source code reuse evaluation by using real/potential copy and paste. In: 2015 IEEE 9th International Workshop on Software Clones (IWSC), Montreal, QC, pp. 33–39 (2015)
22. Vinobha, A., Senthil Velan, S., Babu, C.: Evaluation of reusability in aspect oriented software using inheritance metrics. In: IEEE International Conference on Advanced Communications, Control and Computing Technologies, Ramanathapuram, pp. 1715–1722 (2014)
23. Waguespack, L.J., Schiano, W.T.: A reuse reference grid for strategic reuse goals assessment. In: Proceedings of the 39th Annual Hawaii International Conference on System Sciences (HICSS 2006), pp. 228a (2006)
24. Wieringa, R.: Design science as nested problem solving. In: Proceedings of the 4th International Conference on Design Science Research in Information Systems and Technology. Pennsylvania (2009)

Triple-Agile: A Paradigm for Cloud Based SME Process Support

Ligita Businska[1], Maris Dargis[1], Marite Kirikova[1(✉)],
and Edgars Salna[2]

[1] Department of Artifical Intelligence and Systems Engineering,
Riga Technical University, Riga, Latvia
{Ligita.Businska,Maris.Dargis,Marite.Kirikova}@rtu.lv
[2] Datorzinibu centrs, SIA, Lacpleša iela 41, Riga LV-1011, Latvia
Edgars.Salna@dzc.lv

Abstract. Considering cloud based solutions in business and IT alignment, an ecosystem perspective is here taken. If small and medium enterprises are willing to act agilely and developers of cloud IT solutions are willing to support these enterprises, then it is necessary to ensure rapid and flexible delivery/acquisition/ migration regarding new IT solutions and new features thereof. When looking at enterprises and cloud solution providers as constituents of a business ecosystem, a Triple-Agile paradigm emerges, that considers agility from the following three perspectives: the perspective of SME processes, the perspective of adopting of and/or migrating to cloud solutions, and the perspective of cloud service development and management. While there is considerable theoretical and practical experience in each of the perspectives of agility mentioned, their Triple-Agile combination has not yet been properly researched. This paper investigates the possibility of the application of the Triple-Agile paradigm in the context of SMEs and cloud services.

Keywords: Agile enterprise · Cloud services · Agile information systems · SaaS · PaaS · SME

1 Introduction

Since the time of publishing the agile manifesto for agile software development [1], the term "agile" is used in different contexts such as business agility, information systems agility, and many others. Following [2], agility is a capability that companies can possess to a varying extent – the capability of acting agilely. Agility is closely related to flexibility. However the following has to be taken into consideration: without flexibility there cannot be any agility, while with excessive flexibility which invokes excessive complexity, agility will decline due to the problematic use of the flexibility [2].

In theory and practice the usage of cloud-based IT solutions has been recognized as the key means for SMEs in improving their business process flexibility and effectiveness. Thus agility implies a proper level of flexibility. Consequently in this paper we assume that, in SME and cloud service provider ecosystems, the SME's agility can be achieved if the following three conditions are met. First, the business processes of

W. Abramowicz (Ed.): BIS 2017 Workshops, LNBIP 303, pp. 163–174, 2017.
https://doi.org/10.1007/978-3-319-69023-0_15

the SME must be flexible, i.e. they must adjust to the ever-changing environment. Second, the IT solutions that enterprises are using must support the changing business processes by high modularity and high configurability, so that enterprises can use the proper functionality at the proper time. This implies also a rapid (agile) development of new functionality based on needs of the enterprises. Third, it is necessary to ensure rapid and flexible delivery/acquisition/migration regarding new IT solutions and their new features. Thus the Triple-Agile paradigm emerges and this considers agility from three related perspectives, the perspective of SME processes, the perspective of adopting of/migrating to cloud solutions, and the perspective of cloud service development and management.

While there is considerable theoretical and practical experience in each of the aforementioned perspectives of agility, their Triple-Agile combination has not yet been properly researched. This paper uses the Triple-Agile paradigm in the context of SME business processes; focusing on so called non-core or support processes that do not involve core competences of SMEs. The cloud service support for these processes differs from SME core process support, which is usually in the form of ERP cloud services or manufacturing cloud services which are outside the scope of this paper.

The paper is structured as follows. Section 2 briefly presents the background information on cloud services and agility. In Sect. 3 we discuss the Triple-Agile paradigm. In Sect. 4 we discuss the candidate non-core SME processes for cloud based support in the context of the Triple-Agile paradigm. Conclusions are presented in Sect. 5.

2 Background

Agile software development was formally introduced to the software engineering community in 2001 through a set of four core values and twelve principles, laid out in the "Agile Manifesto" [3]. The Agile Manifesto focuses on the delivery of valuable software. Quite often agile approaches are related to Lean [4] where every activity that does not add value is seen as waste [5]. Since the publication of the Agile Manifesto, the interest in agile approaches has continued to grow (see Fig. 1).

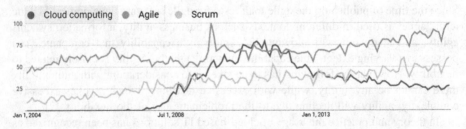

Fig. 1. Google trends on Cloud computing, Agile, and Srum

As was mentioned in the introduction, flexibility is a precondition of agility; however, with the growth of flexibility, agility may decline. In agile software development, the emphasis on delivering functionality often quickly lessens the focus on aspects such as design, good programming practices, and test coverage: with conse-quences leading to the rise of technical debt, which then needs to be addressed in later phases of the development process [6] and can seriously hinder the overall flexibility.

In some cases plan-driven approaches seem to work better than the agile ones. One example would be from a Multi-Tenant architecture based cloud environment [7]. Application-level multi-tenancy is an architectural approach for Software-as-a-Service (SaaS) applications which enable high operational cost efficiency by sharing one application instance among multiple customer organizations (the so-called tenants). One of the specific aspects of this architecture is that change (delivery) affects multiple, if not all, users at once. As quick delivery is generally manifested by more errors (bugs) – the cumulative effect of quick bug-fixes, or introduction of a new feature for one customer, might have an adverse effect resulting in implementation problems, – as multiple customers are affected. Another example would be related to the agile prin-ciple "Individuals and interactions over processes and tools" [3]. In a Multi-Tenant architecture based system one platform and service might be shared between hundreds, thousands, or even millions of customers. An individual-focused approach might just not be feasible; rather, well defined processes are required to enforce systemic order. Concerning the principle "Working software over comprehensive documentation" [3], with thousands of tenants it is close to impossible to run an effective service without comprehensive and elaborate documentation. If a customer must be addressed on an individual basis then the whole concept of relatively low cost efficiency is lost. It is not difficult to come up with many more cases where the plan driven approach seems to be more efficient than the agile one.

In literature, when analyzing agile approaches, such concepts as "challenge", "risks", and "success factors" are common. The word "failure" is almost never used. However, more and more, the voices pointing to the problems are appearing in prac-titioner blogs. The superficial adherence to agile values and principles is one of the reported problems [8].

The above mentioned concerns mainly refer to the service delivery and mainte-nance perspective of the Triple-Agile paradigm. The related work shows that when developing and maintaining the services, the scope and methods of agile software development approaches (e.g. Scrum – see Fig. 1) have to be carefully controlled so as not to reach the level of flexibility which starts to hinder the agility of the delivery and maintenance of the services.

In this paper only cloud services are considered with respect to the Triple-Agile paradigm. The birth of cloud services can be dated back to 2006 – the first launch of a general purpose public cloud service by the current most prominent public cloud service provider: Amazon Web Services (AWS) [8]. As we can see from Google trends, cloud services have a stable level of attention according to public sources (Fig. 1).

There are challenges associated with cloud services. In this paper we will mainly address the challenge of requested variability. Based on the users' needs, various types of services can be delivered that must often be composed differently to meet individual user requests [9]. On the other hand, the variety of services combines with the variety of ways that SMEs are discovering and adopting these services.

From the above, it can be seen that there is a potential for agile development in the cloud context, on the one hand, and for agile delivery and acquisition of cloud services, on the other. However, it is also necessary to consider the challenges. For instance Cisco's experience shows "that companies need to take a holistic, systematic approach to handling the transition to the agile development method". It sheds light on the challenges of adopting agile development practices by small to medium-size companies. Study illustrates that the agile approach demands close and intense coordination with customers and requires organizational units and engineering teams to be self-contained and autonomous [10].

Taking into account that not only agility of software development, but also the ability to manage the services developed, as well as service delivery and adoption (which depend on individual characteristics of SMEs as users of services), matter in the SME and service provider ecosystem; and taking into consideration the necessity to apply a systemic approach with respect to agility, we can see that a distinct set of concepts is needed to apply the capability to act agilely so that the balance of flexibility and complexity would be maintained. This could help to obtain the gains that the agile approach and cloud solutions can give to the SME agile business process and IT solution alignment. The Triple-Agile paradigm, discussed in the next section, tries to tie together relevant aspects of agility to create an understanding and, possibly, control over the complexity in achieving the desired level of agility.

3   Triple-Agile Paradigm

The Triple-Agile paradigm is designed with the purpose of enabling IT companies to agilely support SMEs (that themselves aim to act agilely) with appropriate IT services. Its main concepts are introduced in [11]. The paradigm addresses the following aspects of agility:

- Agility of SME processes (specifically, in this research, only non-core business processes are considered).
- Agility of cloud service production processes.
- Agility of putting the services produced into use.

According to [2] we consider the following three levels of agility (from the highest to the lowest):

- Versatility, which implies that the existing business and/or software system, as it is currently set up, is flexible enough to cope with changing conditions.
- Reconfiguration, by using different configuration, when the existing scope of functionality is sufficient.
- Reconstruction, when new functionality has to be developed from scratch.

The goal here, in the context of the Triple-Agile paradigm, is to find the right mix of approaches that will ensure the agility of cloud based solutions provided and the SME business processes. When looking at the three levels of agility with respect to the three above-mentioned aspects, several options of cooperation in the SME and service provider ecosystem can be recognized. We propose considering these options as the conceptual basis for choosing and developing IT solutions ensuring the desired level of agility of the business ecosystem's actors. Traditionally, it would be possible to distinguish between three types of actors: Service user (in our case – SME), service broker and service developer/maintainer. However, brokering and development activities can be performed by one and the same company. Thus we will illustrate the cooperation options, not by actors, but by processes: SME business processes; IT services (performing activities that are or will be used by SME business processes) and their brokering processes; and service development processes. Table 1 amalgamates 10 different options for three levels (versatile, configurable and reconstruction) of SME process and service agility. It is also true that the processes or their activities can be performed at three different automation levels, namely: automatically, semi-automatically, and manually.

The table shows that there are a number of alternative ways to ensure that the current needs of SMEs are met, depending on the level of agility of their processes. The difference between situations where services are already in use in SMEs and where they are still to be adopted is seen in the first column of the table, where the concepts "supporting" and "initiation" are used accordingly. Table 1 shows that, for most options, the cloud based solutions must be easily accessible and versatile or configurable. With respect to development processes, attention is paid to the mode of service development. It can be reactive, which corresponds to traditional agile software development (i.e. there is a user on site who can advice on requirements to be fulfilled). However, in most cases proactive service development is needed. It is essential to understand here that being proactive neither contradicts nor implies an agile software development process. The reconstruction, and in some cases also the reconfiguration, can be done on either a reactive or proactive basis.

In mainstream IT development there are a number of approaches that define the processes of the maintenance of IT solutions, bug fixes, handling change requests and new products. And the developer has the right to choose the more familiar or more suitable approach in the particular situation. Yet, considering that SMEs are highly sensitive to long development processes, and the sensitive nature of cloud based solutions for rapid development processes, there is a need for proper management processes that can guide developers in order to ensure high development flexibility, yet also ensuring high quality of the development process. Detailed discussion on service development and maintenance management processes is outside the scope of this paper.

Table 1 shows only basic cooperation options between SMEs and service providers. Over time enterprises using one cooperation option can switch to the different ones.

The variability of cloud service development options and possible ways of putting them into use expose quite a high level of complexity that, when there is striving for flexibility, can actually hinder agility. Nevertheless, clear mapping of options at hand can help to maintain agile values and principles in the business ecosystem. Figure 2 illustrates how the options of cooperation can change with time. Each node number in Fig. 2 corresponds to the cooperation option number in Table 1.

Table 1. Cooperation options according to the Triple-Agile paradigm

N	Cooperation option	MVU processes	Service and brokering processes	Development processes
1	Preventive initiation of cooperation	Any level of agility	Service advertising/marketing	Proactive service development
2	Automatic initiation of cooperation	Any level of agility	Service can be acquired without direct communication between actors	Proactive service development
3	Manual initiation of cooperation	Any level of agility	Manual initiation of service usage (e.g. manual initiation of migration process)	Proactive service development
4	Initiation of the cooperation via service development project	Any level of agility	Service development	Reactive service development
5	Supporting versatile BP with the versatile service	Versatile	Versatile service, no specific brokering needed	Proactive service development
6	Supporting configurable BP with the versatile service	Configurable	Versatile service, no specific brokering needed	Proactive service development
7	Supporting configurable BP with configurable service automatically	Configurable	Configurable service, automatic brokering process (or service)	Proactive service development
8	Supporting configurable BP with configurable service manually	Configurable	Configurable service, manual brokering	Proactive service development
9	Supporting configurable BP with configurable service semi-automatically	Configurable	Configurable service, brokering by manual service configuration using the configuration service	Proactive service development
10	Reconstructing the business process with service reconstruction	Reconstruction	Reconstruction	Reactive service development

As we can see, the ten cooperation nodes yield 20 basic change options. In general, all cooperation possibilities can be chosen in each node, however, it is assumed here, that the cooperation options do not move from the higher level of agility to the lower level of agility. There are no links shown from Nodes 5, 6, and 9. There is no higher level of agility possible after Node 5 is reached; there are no more agile alternatives for Node 6 unless the level of agility of SME processes changes. Node 9 is a specific case that combines the functionality of Nodes 7 and 8, so possible switching to other alternatives is already described through these two nodes. The service provider actually has to be ready for all of these changes (and possibly other alternatives depending on the cooperation context). Nevertheless, when cooperation options and change options are well conceptualized, companies can choose a set of options they are going to maintain in an agile manner.

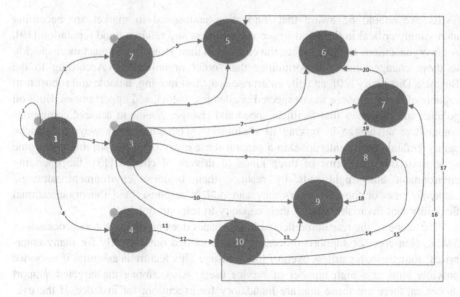

Fig. 2. Changes in cooperation options

Table 1 shows that the Triple-Agile paradigm accommodates both – the traditional agile IT solution development (reactive development – that follows user stated requirements) and proactive service development. It is obvious that in the Triple-Agile paradigm, the proactive service development dominates over the reactive service development. Therefore there should be methods and approaches available that support proactive service development.

In the next section of the paper we will discuss some best practice based possibilities for supporting proactive service development. Namely, the section will discuss how target SME processes (in our case – non-core processes) for proactive service development can be selected on the basis of business process frameworks and actual information on the spectrum of IT services available in the market.

4   Selecting Services for Proactive Development

According to the European Commission [12], SMEs can be defined as companies with less than 250 employees and an annual turnover below 50 million Euros or an annual balance sheet total not exceeding 43 million Euros. While much has been researched about agility in the context of large companies, SMEs are also supposed to be well served by embracing the agile concept and especially through the use of cloud services [13–18].

An essential issue in developing services proactively is identification of target SME business processes for which the services are to be developed. The approach discussed in this section is based on the selection of target SME business processes from process classification frameworks with the set of considerations that can help to decide upon the necessity of developing particular services. When selecting target processes of agile

SMEs, we should be aware that innovation and speed to market are becoming increasingly critical in the effort to serve consumers and retain a good reputation [19]. Agile organizations are able to face the changes in their industry and react more quickly to those changes and/or opportunities than other organizations. According to the Business Dictionary [20], an agile enterprise is a, "fast moving, flexible and robust firm capable of rapid response to unexpected challenges, events, and opportunities. Built on policies and processes that facilitate speed and change, it aims to achieve continuous competitive advantage in serving its customers". There are many ways to achieve agility throughout the enterprise. In a general sense every company striving to become agile must think in terms of three kinds of drivers of change [13]: the operating environment that might radically reshape their business environment; strategic responsiveness or the soft levers they can pull in response; and the organizational flexibility that invariably affects their capacity to respond quickly.

The scope of the research reflected in this paper does not include core processes of SMEs. Non-core (or support) processes can be carried out similarly for many enterprises; sometimes regardless even of the industry. This feature is essential if a service provider aims at a high number of service users. Also, among the targeted support processes, there are those that are mandatory for execution; for instance, if the execution of the process is required by the law. Additionally, it is quite possible to define the support processes that are most often performed in SMEs. This could be defined by analyzing surveys and statistics published in scientific papers and journals. In related works, it is also possible to identify which SMEs business processes are supported by different IT solutions, including cloud services. Summarizing the above mentioned issues, we can distinguish the following considerations for the selection of candidate non-core business processes for the development of cloud services for SMEs:

- The business process supports or coordinates the day-to-day primary operations of an organization, and does not provide value to customers directly.
- The business process is carried out in accordance with the rules, which are established by legislation.
- The business process is absolutely essential for an SME (this means that in the daily activities of the enterprise the significance of this process is so high that the automation of it would, indirectly, bring economic value to the enterprise).
- Presently there are only non-cloud IT solutions in the market for the support of the process (so room for cloud services exists).
- There is a principal opportunity to support the execution of a process with cloud services, i.e., IT services are applicable from a practical point of view.

To have a set of processes for the choice at hand, process classification frameworks can be used, e.g. Cross Industry Process Classification Framework (PCF) [21]. Further in this paper we will show how one specific process category of this framework, namely category No. 11.0 – "Manage Enterprise Risk, Compliance, Remediation, and Resiliency" is used for selecting the target non-core processes for potential IT service development. The sub-processes of process category No. 11 are reflected in Table 2 with their original sequence numbers showing that these are the fourth level processes in the process classification tree.

Table 2. Risk management in SMEs

APQC PCF processes	SMEs processes	IT support [26–29]
11.1.1 Establish the enterprise risk framework and policies		
11.1.1.1 Determine risk tolerance for organization	Develop risk management plan - *provide consistency with the organization's strategic objectives and determine the context of analysis*	–
11.1.1.2 Develop and maintain enterprise risk policies and procedures		
11.1.1.3 Identify and implement enterprise risk management tool		
11.1.1.4 Coordinate the sharing of risk knowledge across the organization		
11.1.1.5 Prepare and report enterprise risk to executive management and board		
11.1.2 Oversee and coordinate enterprise risk management activities		
11.1.2.1 Identify enterprise level risks	Identify risks - *specify all possible risks that could threaten the enterprise*	- Practical Threat Analysis[a] - ORICO[a] - STREAM[a] - GRC Cloud[b]
11.1.2.2 Assess risks to determine which to mitigate	Risk assessment and analysis - *evaluate, analyze and prioritize risks. The goal is to identify probability and extent of damage*	ProcessGene GRC Software Suite[b] - A1 Tracker[b c] - RiskGap[b c] - EMEX EHS Solution [b c]
11.1.2.3 Develop risk mitigation and management strategy and integrate with existing performance management processes	Treatment - *identify unacceptable risks and determine what action should be taken to reduce it*	- GRC Cloud[b] Optial SmartStart Tracker - OneSoft Connect etc.
11.1.2.4 Verify business unit and functional risk mitigation plans are implemented	Monitor risks - *periodically monitor risks to reflect changing circumstances*	GRC Cloud[b] ProcessGene - GRC Cloud[b] Optial SmartStart GRC Software Suite[b] Simbiant Tracker [b c] - RiskGap[b] Active Risk Manager
11.1.2.5 Ensure risks and risk mitigation actions are monitored		
11.1.2.6 Report on enterprise risk activities		
11.1.2.7 Coordinate business unit and functional risk management activities		
11.1.2.8 Ensure that each business unit/function follows the enterprise risk management process		
11.1.2.9 Ensure that each business unit/function follows the enterprise risk reporting process		
11.1.3.7 Report on risk activities		

[a]free tools, [b]cloud service, [c]tool for SME

When a particular set of processes is chosen (see the first column of Table 2), the process selection considerations can be applied to evaluate whether they are suitable as target business processes for developing new cloud services. For this, scientific studies can be consulted, which, in this case (regarding the process category No. 11 of PCF), revealed that risk management has a weak reputation within SMEs [22, 23]. Only recently business management literatures started to show an interest in applying risk management in SMEs; for this reason, many areas are still understudied. Due to the fact that risk management is inevitable but does not provide value directly, SMEs usually perform it in an ad-hoc style – less formally and less structured compared to large enterprises. Table 2 (the second column) summarizes SME risk management information gathered from sources [22–25].

Comparing processes in the first column with reported SME risk management processes (the second column of Table 2), we can conclude that mostly it is only the basic risk management activities that are performed in SMEs. SMEs do perform risk identification and assessment processes. The minimum amount of resources is spent on planning and monitoring tasks. As risk management activities are not mandatory, SMEs consequently need to motivate themselves to allocate resources for such activities. Regarding IT support (the third column of Table 2) a number of risk management tools are available in the market; some of the tools are available for free and there are also commercial tools appropriate for SMEs. Also cloud services are available among the existing IT solutions. The proposed tools and services are mainly developed for the identification and assessment of risk.

Looking at commonalities and differences between the APQC PCF processes and reported SME processes and also the supporting technologies in Table 1, it is possible to decide whether the particular process should (or should not) be considered for proactive IT service development. Besides the aforementioned considerations regarding the suitability of the non-core SME processes to be targeted by new cloud services, the variability of processes, with respect to the types of SMEs perceived as potential customers of these services, has to be taken into consideration.

5 Conclusions

In this paper the Triple-Agile paradigm was applied and its use with respect to cloud services and agile approaches was discussed. The discussion was done in the context of non-core business processes of SMEs. Currently the following conclusions can be made:

- The Triple-Agile paradigm has potential with respect to balancing flexibility and complexity so as to achieve the desired level of agility in the business ecosystem and in business and IT alignment.
- It is possible to use generic business process analysis to support proactive service development for supporting SME processes.
- Three aspects of agility and three levels of agility are important and relevant for aligning SME processes with supporting IT services.

The concept of Triple-Agile paradigm so far has been tested on 10 SME and service provider cooperation scenarios which combine 16 different attributes of the business ecosystem. At the abstraction level used in this paper, the paradigm was able to accommodate all of these scenarios. Future work will be concerned with the technical implementation of the Triple-Agile paradigm, and the design of flexibility control mechanisms that help prevent agility losses caused by levels of complexity that are too high.

Acknowledgment. The research has been supported in part by the funding from the research project "Competence Centre of Information and Communication Technologies" of EU Structural funds, contract No. 1.2.1.1/16/A/007 signed between IT Competence Centre and Central Finance and Contracting Agency, project No. 1.13.

References

1. Manifesto for Agile Software Development. http://agilemanifesto.org/
2. Martenson, A.: Produsing and consuming agility. In: Desouza, K.C. (ed) Agile Information Systems, pp. 41–51 (2007)
3. Hoda, R., Salleh, N., Grundy, J., Tee, H.M.: Systematic literature reviews in agile software development: a tertiary study. Inf. Softw. Technol. **85**, 60–70 (2017)
4. Nurdiani, I., Börstler, J., Fricker, S.A.: The impacts of agile and lean practices on project constraints: a tertiary study. J. Syst. Softw. **119**, 162–183 (2016)
5. Alahyari, H., Berntsson Svensson, R., Gorschek, T.: A study of value in agile software development organizations. J. Syst. Softw. **125**, 271–288 (2017)
6. Behutiye, W.N., Rodríguez, P., Oivo, M., Tosun, A.: Analyzing the concept of technical debt in the context of agile software development: a systematic literature review. Inf. Softw. Technol. **82**, 139–158 (2017)
7. Walraven, S., Van Landuyt, D., Truyen, E., Handekyn, K., Joosen, W.: Efficient customization of multi-tenant Software-as-a-Service applications with service lines. J. Syst. Softw. **91**, 48–62 (2014)
8. Kratzke, N., Quint, P.-C.: Understanding cloud-native applications after 10 years of cloud computing - a systematic mapping study. J. Syst. Softw. **126**, 1–16 (2017)
9. Vakili, A., Navimipour, N.J.: Comprehensive and systematic review of the service composition mechanisms in the cloud environments. J. Netw. Comput. Appl. **81**, 24–36 (2017)
10. Chen, R.R., Ravichandar, R., Proctor, D.: Managing the transition to the new agile business and product development model: lessons from cisco systems. Business Horizons. **59**, 635–644 (2016)
11. Kirikova, M., Salna, E.: Triple-Agile: cloud solutions for SMEs. In: Johansson, B., Møller, C., Chaudhuri, A., Sudzina, F. (eds.) BIR 2017. LNBIP, vol. 295, pp. 260–267. Springer, Cham (2017). doi:10.1007/978-3-319-64930-6_19
12. EUR-Lex - 32004R0364 - EN - EUR-Lex. http://eur-lex.europa.eu/legal-content/LV/TXT/?uri=CELEX%3A32004R0364
13. Cisco: Cornerstones of Agile Business. http://www.cisco.com/c/dam/en/us/solutions/collateral/collaboration/white-paper-c11-737626.pdf
14. The European Cloud Initiative|Digital Single Market. https://ec.europa.eu/digital-single-market/european-cloud-initiative/
15. Salleh, S.M., Teoh, S.Y., Chan, C.: Cloud enterprise systems: a review of literature and its adoption. In: PACIS 2012 Proceedings (2012)

16. Eurostat: Cloud computing services used by one out of every five enterprises in the EU28. http://ec.europa.eu/eurostat/documents/2995521/6208098/4-09122014-AP-EN.pdf

17. Yeboah-Boateng, E.O., Essandoh, K.A.: Cloud computing: the level of awareness amongst small & medium-sized enterprises (SMEs) in developing economies. J. Emerg. Trends Comput. Inf. Sci. **4**, 832–839 (2013)

18. Vasiljeva, T., Shaikhulina, S., Kreslins, K.: Cloud computing: business perspectives, benefits and challenges for small and medium enterprises (case of Latvia). Procedia Eng. **178**, 443–451 (2017)

19. Technology Institute: Building Enterprise Agility. http://www.pwc.com/us/en/technology/publications/assets/enterprise-agility.pdf

20. Business Dictionary. http://www.businessdictionary.com/definition/agile-enterprise.html

21. Process Classification Framework|APQC. https://www.apqc.org/pcf

22. Rostami, A.: Tools and techniques in risk identification: a research within SMEs in the UK construction industry. Univ. J. Manag. **4**, 203–210 (2016)

23. Ekwere, N.: Framework of effective risk management in small and medium enterprises (SMESs): a literature review. Bina Ekonomi. **20**, 23–44 (2016)

24. Verbano, C., Venturini, K.: Managing risks in SMEs: a literature review and research agenda. J. Technol. Manag. Innov. **8**, 186–197 (2013)

25. Boubala, H.G.O.: Risk management of SMMEs (2010)

26. 5 free tools for governance, risk management and compliance. http://www.polecat.com/blog/free-grc-tools/

27. Top 20 Risk Management Software 2017 - Compare Reviews. http://www.capterra.com/risk-management-software/

28. Best Risk Management Software For Small Business (2017). https://cloudsmall businessservice.com/small-business/best-risk-management-software-for-small-business.html

29. Central Statistical Databases. http://data.csb.gov.lv/pxweb/en/?rxid=cdcb978c-22b0-416a-aacc-aa650d3e2ce0

SESSISE Workshop

SESSISE 2017 Workshop Chairs' Message

Rainer Unland, Lars Mönch, and Ryszard Kowalczyk

Climate change, the Fukushima disaster, the recent biggest blackout in history in India due to an overloaded electricity grid, or the dwindling oil reserves world-wide are some of the manifold different reasons why countries massively increase their efforts in shaping their future energy generation, distribution, transportation, and consumption, i.e., in future smart sustainable energy systems, smart infrastructures, and smart environments. They are expected to be the enablers of a high penetration of renewable energy, facilitate the wide adoption of electrical vehicles, increase the awareness and the involvement of the end-user in the energy scene, and altogether contribute to create a sustainable lifestyle for the eco-aware twenty-first-century citizen. Although much is still in a state of flux, it is nevertheless commonly accepted that existing energy systems, infrastructures, environments, and business opportunities cannot simply be adapted or extended to address the requirements of the next generation of energy supply and consumption. Instead, a fundamental re-engineering is required. Thus, all these prospective transformations also bring with them numerous challenges and opportunities.

Regardless of whether and how the energy supply will be designed and operated in the near future, it is obvious that the key enabler for a successful transformation of the energy supply will be a meaningful and purposefully used ICT infrastructure. New solutions will consolidate and represent the combined knowledge and experience of different disciplines as engineering, business management, and economics, and computer science and, thus, contribute significantly to the stabilization of the energy supply and to the success of the companies involved. The IT backbone for such solutions will be distributed, collaborative, autonomous, and intelligent software packages for simulation, monitoring, control, and optimization as well as appropriate data and business models, reporting systems, and perhaps also mobile solutions.

Besides the topic of future energy grids, the recent and past was also dominated by the discussion about so-called smart cities and smart homes. A smart city uses information and communication technologies (ICT) to enhance the quality, performance, and interactivity of urban services. This especially means that the contact between citizens and government is eased and improved substantially with the aim of equipping inhabitants with more power and responsibility and easing their life substantially from bureaucratic and useless tasks. Another highly relevant goal is to reduce costs and resource consumption. Smart cities will connect, utilize, and optimize a number of sectors including transport and traffic management, energy consumption, and management or water and waste issues. However, they also need to rely on the next lower level of abstraction, namely, smart buildings and homes. This, however, implies that smart grids, smart cities, smart buildings and homes, and smart infrastructures need to be deeply integrated in order to shape the smart overall energy environment of the future. And that looks more like a revolution than an evolution.

Based on these topics, the SESSISE workshop provided an interdisciplinary forum for presenting and discussing recent advances and experiences in building and using new IT-based solutions for Sustainable Energy Systems, Smart Infrastructures, and Smart Environments.

Organization

Chairs

Rainer Unland · University of Duisburg-Essen, Germany
Lars Mönch · Fernuniversität Hagen, Germany
Ryszard Kowalczyk · Swinburne University of Technology, Melbourne, Australia

Program Committee

Alexander Fay · Helmut Schmidt Universität Hamburg, Germany
Anke Weidlich · Hochschule Offenburg, Germany
Christian Derksen · Universität Duisburg-Essen, Germany
Costin Badica · University of Craiova, Romania
Fabrice Saffre · British Telecom, EBTIC, UK, UAE
Fernando Gomide · University of Campinas, Brasil
Giancarlo Fortino · University of Calabria, Italy
Hangseng Che · University of Malaya, Malaysia
Hanno Hildmann · Khalifa University, UAE
Hartmut Schmeck · Karlsruher Institut für Technologie, Germany
Huaglory Tianfield · Glasgow Caledonian University, UK
Ingo J. Timm · University of Trier, Germany
Jingxin Zhang · Swinburne University of Technology, Australia
John Collins · University of Minnesota, USA
Krzysztof Chmielowiec · AGH University of Science and Technology, Poland
Liana Cipcigan · Institute of Energy at Cardiff University, UK
Matthias Klusch · DFKI GmbH, Germany
Michael Sonnenschein · Carl von Ossietzky Universität Oldenburg, Germany
Peter Palensky · AIT Austrian Institute of Technology, Austria
Sajjad Siddiqi · Jubail University College, Saudi Arabia
Sascha Ossowski · Universidad Rey Juan Carlos, Spain
Stamatis Karnouskos · SAP, Germany
Zbigniew Nahorski · Polish Academy of Sciences, Poland

Human-Computer Cloud for Smart Cities: Tourist Itinerary Planning Case Study

Alexander Smirnov, Andrew Ponomarev, Nikolay Teslya[✉],
and Nikolay Shilov

SPIIRAS, St. Petersburg, Russia
{smir,ponomarev,teslya,nick}@iias.spb.su

Abstract. The development of smart cities provides a lot of data and services that can be utilized to improve the tourists' experience during the trip. Information technologies affect directly the development of tourism industry. Tourists and cities' inhabitants take an active part in the production of tourism products, as well as in sharing their knowledge and experience. To help them in this activity and provide an interface to communicate with other people and computer resources the human-computer cloud concept has been viewed. The paper proposes a workflow that uses computer and human processing units for tourist's itinerary planning. The workflow integrates data analysis from various sources with computer and human-based calculation of itineraries in the cloud system. The case is implemented based on the smart destination services of St. Petersburg, Russia.

Keywords: Cloud · Human · Computer · GIS · Smartness · Itinerary · Big data

1 Introduction

Currently the development of ICT has a direct impact on a city infrastructure management. A lot of sensors and information sources are used to gather information about the current state of the city that helps to make management decisions about all aspects of the city life, like transportation planning, ecology control, environment consumption, etc. The development of smart cities also gives certain benefits to their inhabitants. For instance, information services for transportation, traffic control, emergency support, automated inquiry service, government services make life safer and more comfortable.

Tourism can be viewed as one of the largest and fastest growing economic sector in the world. The last report of the United Nations world tourism organization (UNWTO) confirms this and shows that international tourists' arrivals doubled in the last two decades [1]. Development of the smart cities has a direct impact on the development of tourism industry. The involvement of information and communication technologies in tourism has entailed an appearance of e-tourism concept at the beginning of the XXI century. This concept assumes business organizations to use electronic channels such as Internet, TV, etc. that allows to automate the functions of tourism industry and to organize interactive communication between business partners [2].

© Springer International Publishing AG 2017
W. Abramowicz (Ed.): BIS 2017 Workshops, LNBIP 303, pp. 179–190, 2017.
https://doi.org/10.1007/978-3-319-69023-0_16

The automation has led to the emergence of the concept of an intelligent environment, at that, the focus has been transited from e-tourism to the intelligent tourism. Intelligent tourism or "i-tourism" is defined as tourism supported by an integrated effort at the site of the tourist destination to find innovative ways of accumulation and aggregation or use big data extracted from the infrastructure, social relations, public or institutional sources as well as people. "I-tourism" is viewed in conjunction with the use of information technology for the extension of tourism opportunities and increasing the business attractiveness with a clear focus on the efficiency, sustainability and enriching the tourist experience during the trip [3]. The principal component of intelligent tourism is the presence of the intelligent environment at the tourist destination. This environment also corresponds to the concept of smart city [4].

Service interaction in smart tourism destinations is based on the use of cloud technologies. Services represent sensors, program units, information storages, and processors. Information from the smart destination can be used to provide information assistance to tourist during the trip. Modern tourists started to take an active part in the production of tourism products, being no longer satisfied with standardized products. Smart destination concept allows the tourists to take part in creation of destination image through leaving their reviews, rating and discussions about it. In addition, a tourist can be involved in assistance to other tourists by creating itineraries, recommending attractions, etc.

The paper proposes a workflow that implements itinerary recommendation based on the human-computer cloud approach. The novelty of the approach is in using human and computer resources in a common workflow [5] to provide for flexibility of human task solving at a computer speed. Workflow activities related to information querying, and sorting as well as calculation of simple routes are better to be solved by computer units, however, complex tasks like itinerary composition between selected attractions, choosing the best itinerary based on non-numeric parameters (like degree of the interest) are better to be solved by humans.

2   State-of-the-Art

The concept of joint task solving by computer and human is being actively developed and viewed as a distributed system that involve mobile resources (computers and people) [6]. The concept of human-machine cooperation is at the heart of the decision support systems (DSS) for the prevention of the earthquake consequences [7], the development of an unmanned aerial route planning strategy [8], and other.

Approaches to the application of cloud principles for managing smart city resources to a wider range of resources than in classical cloud technologies can be divided into two groups: (1) cloud environments for sensor networks and actuators (Internet of Things); (2) cloud management of human resources.

Systems of the first group are mainly focused on the integration of sensors/actuators into the cloud architecture. For example, in [9], a sensor (or rather, the ability to receive data from a specific sensor) is treated as a service, that can be accessed in some unified way. Human resources are considered only because a person, being the owner of the smart phone, can give an access to it and, possibly, perform some operations (e.g., taking a picture of an object) requested by the application working over the infrastructure layer of the cloud. An example is the cloud architecture for mobile crowdsensing, MCSaaS (mobile crowdsensing as a service) [10]. It defines a unified interface that allows the smartphone owner to become a part of the cloud computing environment and to use some sensors of his/her smartphone in exchange for cash consideration or even for free. Another example is the ClouT project [11]. It is aimed at building the "smart city" infrastructure by integrating the principles of cloud computing and the Internet of Things. Within this project, a tiered cloud architecture is proposed, where the lower layer (the infrastructure layer) manages both the computing resources and the sensors/actuators of the smart city. At the same time, a person can be not only an information provider (as a sensor), but also a participant of information processing, and this possibility is not considered in the framework of the mentioned projects.

The work of the second group is aimed at incorporating a person into cloud computing, which implies flexible management of skills and competences of the system participants [12, 13]. For instance, the article [12] proposes the concept of a cloud environment consisting of services provided by people (human-based services, HBS) and software services (software-based services, SBS). At the infrastructure level, the authors of the article consider human-based computing units (HCUs) providing relevant services. Moreover, the concept of social computing units (SCUs) is a composition of several HCUs and also possesses the ability to provide services. Computing units that include a person are described by a set of skills.

Intermediate position between the two groups is presented in a series of articles [14–16]. In these works, the concept of the cloud environment consisting of people and robots (human-robot cloud, HRC) is proposed. The authors offer an extension of the classical cloud technology in two ways: first, by the resources include sensors and actuators, and second, the medium is supplemented with human physical and cognitive "components". There are two ways to create end-applications: automatic configuration of the service network based on the information flow specification or (more "high-level") application of planning and restriction mechanisms.

The approach proposed in this paper is partly based on the ideas of sensor virtualization and the convergence of cloud computing and the Internet of Things proposed in [14, 15], but extends and complements these ideas by treating human resources as one of the types of resources directly controlled by the infrastructure layer (similar to [12]). Closest to this project is the concept of HRC, however, in a series of articles Mavridis and other do not offer ways to implement this concept, the main emphasis is made on identifying and analyzing problems that need to be addressed.

3   Human-Computer Cloud Approach

The idea of human-computer cloud (HCC) is in the use of human and computer units to create a content, process it, and provide decision support [17]. It applies the distinctive features of the cloud computing (resource virtualization, abstraction, and elasticity) to the construction of information processing systems containing hardware, software, and humans [12–14]. The cloud-managed human resource environments are aimed at

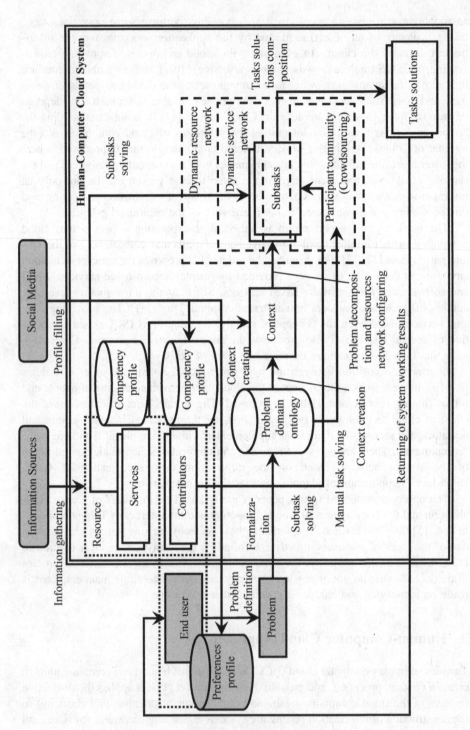

Fig. 1. Human-computer cloud approach

managing member's skills and competencies in a standardized flexible way (e.g. [12, 13]), regarding human as a specific resource that can be allocated from a pool for performing some tasks.

The common approach to the task solving system configuration based on HCC is presented in the Fig. 1. In accordance with the approach humans implement two roles: end user (a decision maker) or contributor (a computing resource for manual solving of certain tasks type). Contributors can join HCC and define the resources they can provide, time and load restrictions, a type of tasks they want to participate in. A contributor may also define the expected compensation for his/her efforts. There exist multiple possible schemes of incentivization [18]. Three of them are the most appropriate: monetary reward, artificial reward measured in some cloud-based "contribution points", allowing, say, for the use of resources of the cloud in the future; and voluntary participation. Resources can also be presented by program services that support autonomous task solving. Each resource is described by the competency profile defined in terms of problem domain ontology. This profile is used for resource search at the stage of task solving. The profile can be filled by the service developer, by contributor/end user him/herself, or in an autonomous way by gathering information from social media. Complex tasks can be decomposed into subtasks based on their context. Each subtask is solved by appropriate resources of HCC. According to the NIST recommendation, this function is laid on services at the platform layer. This layer may provide, for example, an Iterative-Improvement (see, e.g., [19]) of human computation pattern implemented as an allocation of several human members (meeting some requirements), and redirecting a task to them in a sequence. Solutions are composed into the common solution and are returned to the end user.

4   Itinerary Planning Workflow

The tourism destination is an intelligent environment based on the smart city infrastructure, where the administration and tourists constantly interact with each other with the aim of gathering and accumulation of data from various sources about the activities in this place. Gathered information is used in the analysis in order to develop actions to improve the destination (increase its attractiveness, reliability, adaptability to the purposes and tastes of tourists) and increase tourist satisfaction. "Intelligence" of the destination is ensured by the implementation of information and communication technologies in the physical facilities available at this location [20].

Tourism is an area where people usually like to contribute (by leaving comments, posting pictures and reports), partially that roots to the traditions of hospitality, partially in actualizing joyful moments of vacations [21–23]. People usually have key competences that are relevant to tourism, e.g., languages' skills, local knowledge and knowledge of already visited destinations [17]. At the same time, there are many services for tourists that provide context-aware information about current destination based on the facilities of smart cities, like services for searching the nearby attractions, routing information, weather, etc. It allows applying HCC approach to tourism for creating an itinerary for smart tourism destination.

4.1   Task Description

Creating an itinerary is one of the typical tasks performed by the tourist or by the travel agency. Usually, it is performed either at the trip planning phase, or at the trip execution phase (when environment changes and original plan, if any, turns out to be invalid).

The task of the itinerary planning is in searching for a plan for attraction visiting by the tourist that will satisfy his/her preferences and restrictions. Restrictions from the tourist side can include trip length, duration, and maximal/minimal number of visited attractions. Input for the itinerary planning task includes:

- tourist location, from which the itinerary is to be built;
- time restrictions, specified as absolute timestamps with time zone of the period that should contain the itinerary. Absolute time stamps may be useful to consider an inclusion in the itinerary of some unique events that might occur in the destination;
- tourist preferences (shared portions of the information contained in tourist information profile and additional requirements) including places a tourist would like to see, those he/she has already seen, general interests etc. Tourists transfer their preferences themselves;
- attractions. List of nearby attractions that has been queried and ranged by tourist preferences helps to calculate a personalized itinerary;
- existing itineraries. During the planning process, the tourist can be proposed to select one of the existing itineraries, extracted from internal service database or from external itinerary sources. These sources are usually created by destination management organizations or by volunteers (see Sect. 2.3).
- environmental context. The context provides information from smart tourism destination that allows for adjusting an itinerary to the current situation. The examples of environmental context from smart destination are attractions' opening hours, weather conditions, available transportation with schedule, routes, cost, etc.

This task can be solved using the HCC platform. As itinerary planning is the end user functionality, it can be implemented as a service in the SaaS layer. Moreover, it could be concurrent implementations of itinerary planning services, provided by various vendors, with different characteristics (price of solving, time, etc.).

4.2   Services for the Tourist Itinerary Planning Workflow

To perform the itinerary planning the following services should be developed for HCC. The first is the itinerary searching service that provides for some existing tourist itineraries from various sources in the Internet. These sources can be provided by tourism destination management organizations as well as by volunteers. Most of them have API that can be utilized to get access to officially approved or user-generated itineraries. *Attraction searching service* is used to search for places of interest nearby the tourist location or selected location. *Itinerary planning service* builds an itinerary based on the provided attractions. Attractions should be searched with due account for tourist preferences to provide for a personalized plan. Therefore, it is proposed to use a *recommendation service* that implements recommendation techniques based on the rating from other tourists to calculate the rating of the selected attractions and then to sort attractions by their rating. To provide for navigation between attractions *the navigation service* is proposed. The service uses region road map and available public transport routes to calculate the route. It should account for the *local context* (like weather, traffic intensity, public transport timetable) to provide for fast, safe and economically justified routes. The *itinerary planning service* is constructed using the storage service and *workflow control services* provided by the cloud platform. The *database service* is used to store accepted (and probably high quality) itineraries made for different users in the past. The workflow control service is used to define an Iterative-Improvement scheme for itineraries being composed. Besides, the itinerary planning service uses some of the core application services, e.g., *local context service* (providing current and predicted information about weather, traffic situation etc.). Itinerary service, at first, enriches the incoming request with local context, supplied by local context service, then looks up in the storage for the past accepted itineraries for users with similar preferences and contexts, and, finally, allocates several contributors (among computer units, past tourists, and local citizens) via workflow control service to review and possibly improve the candidate itineraries. *Itineraries comparing service* is used to compare the planned itineraries with each other ones based on the tourist preferences. Comparing process forms Pareto optimal set of provided itineraries that is presented as the workflow result.

All services interoperate in the cloud system in the order defined by selected workflow. Interoperation between services is provided by using ontologies. Service ontology contains service description (service type, competences, input/output structure) and data description. Each service works with its own problem domain; therefore, the used ontologies can be different. In this case, the ontology matching technique is used at the platform level of human-computer cloud to provide for service interoperability [24].

The workflow for itinerary planning is described in the next section. A set of itineraries from existing sources and calculated itineraries are formed during the workflow processing. According to the tourist preferences this set is filtered and only a subset of Pareto optimal itineraries is returned to the tourist.

4.3 Workflow

Task solving workflow organized over HHC allows taking advantages of computer resources at computation speed and accuracy together with advantages of human resources to resolve a wide spectrum of problems. Infrastructure level of HCC wipes borders between computer and human resources. Each resource provides a set of competences that allows for allocating resource that is the best in meeting the task requirements. The itinerary planning task is divided into the following activities:

1. Search for existing itineraries in internal and external sources (e.g., WikiLoc [21]).
2. Prepare data for itinerary planning: (a) Search attractions (Wikipedia Nearby, GeoNames, etc.); (b) Estimate transportations between pairs of attractions.
3. Check tourist preferences and sort attractions.
4. Assemble itinerary. Assemble whole plan from parts and evaluate each route.
5. Plan itinerary. Solve the travelling salesman problem.
6. Compare itineraries and create set of Pareto optimal solutions.

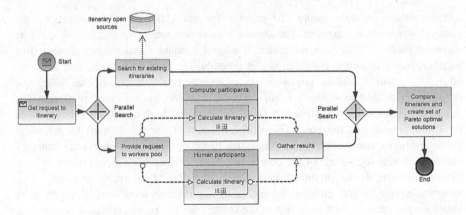

Fig. 2. Itinerary planning workflow

The itinerary planning workflow is presented in the Fig. 2. There are two types of workflow decomposition used for itinerary planning: iterative and parallel. Figure 3 describes tasks sequence for parallel solving of the planning task. It uses only computer resources and is applied in case of strong time restrictions (e.g., when plan should be formed in real time) or in works like data analysis from information sources for activities 1 and 2. Workers create several alternative plans with different characteristics during the parallel solving. All plans are estimated by time, difficulty, duration and cost characteristics. The solution composing is based on the tourist preferences. If only one "best" itinerary should be selected, then all solutions are compared based on the Pareto optimality with all characteristics. In the other case, the tourist gets a list of all itineraries sorted by a defined characteristic. Figure 3 describes the iterative process of task solving.

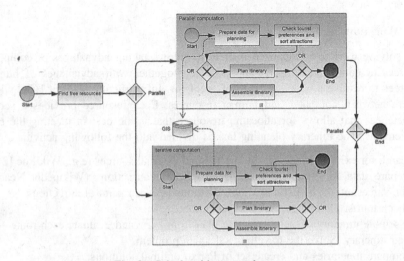

Fig. 3. Calculate itinerary subprocess

During the iterative process, the workers iteratively improve plan based on the tourist preferences. Several independent workers can perform each activity. For example, the number of workers equal to the number of available itinerary sources can perform itineraries search. Activities have their own workflows that describe functional scheme of solving activity tasks by available resources in HCC.

5   St. Petersburg' Case Study

Tourism in St. Petersburg is one of the leading economic sectors. In 2016 St. Petersburg became a winner of the 23rd World Travel Awards in nomination of "World's Leading Cultural City Destination" [25]. In addition, the development of intelligent transportation system (St. Petersburg public transport portal [26], traffic counters, etc.) allows for implementing the presented workflow in the area of St. Petersburg. Smart tourism destination requirements are also satisfied due to the development of integrated museum information systems, electronic catalogues, and mobile networks.

The workflow is proposed to be implemented based on the existing service, developed by the authors: "Tourist Assistant—TAIS" [27]. The goal of the service is to improve the tourist experience while visiting any place in the world, including St. Petersburg. TAIS is a mobile application for cloud-based service related to the category of intelligent tourist guide applications. It recommends nearby attractions to the tourist, considering, at that, the tourist's preferences and context situation in destination (Fig. 4). Various accessible Internet services are used in big data information sources for TAIS, e.g., Wikipedia (869 thousand of geocoded articles only in English),

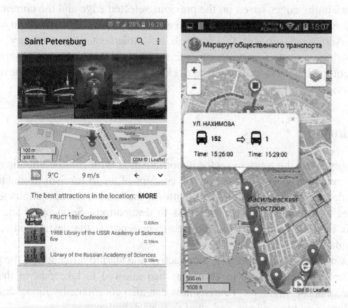

Fig. 4. TAIS screenshots. Left – main interface with context information. Right – multimodal route

Wikivoyage (over 27.5 thousand destinations), OpenStreetMap (1.3 mln. objects with tag "tourism"), Flickr, WorldWeatherOnline, to provide the actual and comprehensive text as well as multimedia information about different places of interests and user's context [27].

The TAIS architecture is based on the use of cloud services to process information from various sources. The cloud is based on the Smart Space concept. Each service is presented as a single Knowledge Processor (KP) and processes one and only one source. The results of processing are shared through the Smart Space and then obtained by the TAIS client on the tourist's mobile device [27]. The list of available attractions is obtained by the recommender service to rank attractions based on ratings from other users [28].

The multimodal routing service has been developed for tourist support while moving between attractions [29]. It provides the routing for pedestrians, cars, and public transport in various combinations of these transportation types. For pedestrian and car routes it uses a map obtained from the OpenStreetMap project (406666 edges in road graph for St. Petersburg). It takes into account the local context like road types, traffic jams, average allowable speed, and turn restrictions. For the multimodal routes on public transport in St. Petersburg the service uses public transport routes in GTFS [30] format from the city portal of public transport of St. Petersburg [26]. In addition to the timetable the portal provides current position of the vehicles, which can be used to predict the time of arrival to a selected stop (Fig. 3). Raw data from GTFS are presented by weighted multigraph, where stops and routes correspond to nodes and edges accordingly (6962 stops and over 2.1 million edges for public transport—19773 edges for routes with 108 of 10-min intervals for each route in schedule). To find a path in the multigraph the modified Dijkstra shortest path algorithm is used. The modification allows for scanning edges based on the previous selected edge and the current context.

TAIS already includes most of the services needed for the tourist itinerary planning workflow. Additional services that have to be implemented are itinerary searching service, workflow control service, storage service, itinerary planning service; and itineraries comparing service. The future work will be concentrated on the development of these services.

6 Conclusion

The development of the tourism sector in combination with cloud computing and IoT allows to implement systems based on the concept of smart tourism destination. This concept is described as a technological platform that unites the ubiquitous and cloud technologies to provide for some smartness to destinations. Services of smart tourist destinations increase quality of the tourist's experience at the destination as well as resident's quality of life.

At the same time tourists become more active and start to influence on the proposed services. Development of web-technologies had allowed to take part in the content creation for smart destinations. Tourists now can also contribute by rating destinations and attractions, leaving reviews and sharing their experience.

The proposed workflow is aimed at the tourist itinerary planning. The workflow is based on the human-computer cloud concept. It involves human resources into the data processing activities. Human resources provide a higher flexibility and creativity in task solving than computer units. In case of itineraries the workflow allows to provide planning concentrated on human vision of the plan: it should be interesting and easy to follow. Computer units of the workflow have been implemented in the Tourist Assistant – TAIS to verify its correctness. System scaling is available by the usage of simple services for all local data sources as well as by usage of worldwide services.

The future work is focused on the proposed workflow improvement and implementation. The workflow can be created by the human or processed automatically based on the available services descriptions. Task decomposition is also expected to be automated. The monetization of HCC as also an open task. Currently, the possibility of using monetization techniques similar to crowdsourcing is being considered.

Acknowledgements. The research is funded by the Russian Science Foundation (Project # 16-11-10253).

References

1. UNWTO: Tourism highlights. http://www.e-unwto.org/doi/pdf/10.18111/9789284418145
2. Buhalis, D.: ETourism: Information Technology for Strategic Tourism Management. Financial Times Prentice Hall, Harlow (2003)
3. Gretzel, U., Reino, S., Kopera, S., Koo, C.: Smart tourism challenges. J. Tour. **16**, 41–47 (2015)
4. Khan, Z., Anjum, A., Soomro, K., Tahir, M.A.: Towards cloud based big data analytics for smart future cities. J. Cloud Comput. **4**, 1–11 (2015)
5. Smirnov, A., Ponomarev, A.: Crowd computing framework for geoinformation tasks. In: Popovich, V., Claramunt, C., Schrenk, M., Korolenko, K., Gensel, J. (eds.) Information Fusion and Geographic Information Systems (IF&GIS' 2015). LNGC. Springer, Cham (2015). doi:10.1007/978-3-319-16667-4_7
6. Adla, A., Nachet, B., Ould-Mahraz, A.: Multi-agents model for web-based collaborative decision support systems. In: CEUR Workshop Proceedings, pp. 294–299 (2012)
7. Gowri, S., Vigneshwari, S., Sathiyavathi, R., Kalai Lakshmi, T.R.: A framework for group decision support system using cloud database for broadcasting earthquake occurrences. In: Proceedings of the International Congress on Information and Communication Technology, pp. 611–615 (2016)
8. Sun, X., Cai, C., Shen, X.: A new cloud model based human-machine cooperative path planning method. J. Intell. Robot. Syst. **79**, 3–19 (2015)
9. Distefano, S., Merlino, G., Puliafito, A.: SAaaS: a framework for volunteer-based sensing clouds. Parallel Cloud Comput. **1**(2), 21–33 (2012). http://mdslab.unime.it/node/134
10. Merlino, G., Arkoulis, S., Distefano, S., Papagianni, C., Puliafito, A., Papavassiliou, S.: Mobile crowdsensing as a service: a platform for applications on top of sensing Clouds. Future Gener. Comput. Syst. **56**, 623–639 (2016)
11. Formisano, C., Pavia, D., Gurgen, L., Yonezawa, T., Galache, J.A., Doguchi, K., Matranga, I.: The advantages of IoT and cloud applied to smart cities. In: 2015 3rd International Conference on Future Internet of Things and Cloud, pp. 325–332. IEEE (2015)

12. Dustdar, S., Bhattacharya, K.: The social compute unit. IEEE Internet Comput. **15**, 64–69 (2011)
13. Sengupta, B., Jain, A., Bhattacharya, K., Truong, H.-L., Dustar, S.: Collective problem solving using social compute units. Int. J. Coop. Inf. Syst. **22**, 1–21 (2013)
14. Mavridis, N., Bourlai, T., Ognibene, D.: The human-robot cloud: situated collective intelligence on demand. In: 2012 IEEE International Conference on Cyber Technology in Automation, Control, and Intelligent Systems (CYBER), pp. 360–365. IEEE (2012)
15. Mavridis, N., Konstantopoulos, S., Vetsikas, I., Heldal, I., Karampiperis, P., Mathiason, G., Thill, S., Stathis, K., Karkaletsis, V.: CLIC: A Framework for Distributed, On-Demand, Human-Machine Cognitive Systems. arXiv:1312.2242 (2013)
16. Mavridis, N., Pierris, G., Benabdelkader, C., Krstikj, A., Karaiskos, C.: Smart buildings and the human-machine cloud. In: 2015 IEEE 8th GCC Conference and Exhibition, GCCCE 2015, pp. 1–6. IEEE (2015)
17. Smirnov, A., Ponomarev, A., Levashova, T., Teslya, N.: Human-computer cloud for decision support in tourism: approach and architecture. In: Balandin, S., Tyutina, T. (eds.) Proceedings of the FRUCT 19. pp. 226–235, Jyvaskyla, Finland (2016)
18. Scekic, O., Truong, H.-L., Dustdar, S.: Incentives and rewarding in social computing. Commun. ACM **56**, 72 (2013)
19. Little, G., Chilton, L.B., Goldman, M., Miller, R.C.: Exploring iterative and parallel human computation processes. In: Proceedings of the ACM SIGKDD Workshop on Human Computation - HCOMP 2010, p. 68. ACM Press, New York (2010)
20. Gretzel, U., Werthner, H., Koo, C., Lamsfus, C.: Conceptual foundations for understanding smart tourism ecosystems. Comput. Hum. Behav. **50**, 558–563 (2015)
21. Castelein, W., Grus, L., Crompvoe, J., Bregt, A.: A characterization of volunteered geographic information. In: 13th AGILE International Conference on Geographic Information Science, pp. 1–10 (2010)
22. Mashhadi, A., Quattrone, G., Capra, L.: The impact of society on volunteered geographic information: the case of OpenStreetMap. In: Jokar Arsanjani, J., Zipf, A., Mooney, P., Helbich, M. (eds.) OpenStreetMap in GIScience. LNGC, pp. 125–141. Springer International Publishing, Cham (2015). doi:10.1007/978-3-319-14280-7_7
23. Coleman, D.J., Georgiadou, Y., Labonte, J., Observation, E., Canada, N.R.: Volunteered geographic information: the nature and motivation of produsers. Int. J. Spat. Data Infrastruct. Res. **4**, 332–358 (2009)
24. Seigerroth, U., Kaidalova, J., Shilov, N., Kaczmarek, T.: Semantic web technologies in business and IT alignment: multi-model algorithm of ontology matching. In: Fifth International Conference on Advances in Future Internet, pp. 50–56 (2013)
25. World's Leading Cultural City Destination 2016 – World Travel Awards. https://www.worldtravelawards.com/award-worlds-leading-cultural-city-destination-2016
26. St. Petersburg Public Transport Portal. http://transport.orgp.spb.ru/Portal/transport/main?lang=en
27. Smirnov, A., Kashevnik, A., Shilov, N., Teslya, N., Shabaev, A.: Mobile application for guiding tourist activities: tourist assistant - TAIS. In: Conference of Open Innovation Association, FRUCT, pp. 95–100. IEEE Computer Society (2014)
28. Smirnov, A., Kashevnik, A., Ponomarev, A., Shilov, N., Teslya, N.: Proactive recommendation system for m-tourism application. In: Johansson, B., Andersson, B., Holmberg, N. (eds.) BIR 2014. LNBIP, vol. 194, pp. 113–127. Springer, Cham (2014). doi:10.1007/978-3-319-11370-8_9
29. Smirnov, A., Teslya, N., Shilov, N., Kashevnik, A.: Context-based trip planning in infomobility system for public transport. In: Abraham, A., Kovalev, S., Tarassov, V., Snášel, V. (eds.) IITI 2016. AISC, vol. 450, pp. 361–371. Springer, Cham (2016). doi:10.1007/978-3-319-33609-1_33
30. Google: GTFS Static Overview. https://developers.google.com/transit/gtfs/

On Battery Management Strategies in Multi-agent Microgrid Management

Roozbeh Morsali[1(✉)], Sajad Ghorbani[2], Ryszard Kowalczyk[1,3], and Rainer Unland[2,4]

[1] Swinburne University of Technology, Melbourne, Australia
{rmorsali,rkowalczyk}@swin.edu.au
[2] Institute of Computer Science and Business Information Systems, University of Duisburg-Essen, Essen, Germany
{sajad.ghorbani,rainer.unland}@icb.uni-due.de
[3] Systems Research Institute, Polish Academy of Sciences, Warsaw, Poland
[4] Department of Information Systems, Poznan University of Economics, Poznan, Poland

Abstract. Multi Agent Systems (MAS) have been incorporated in numerous engineering applications including power systems. In recent years, with the advancement in Information and Communication Technology (ICT), Internet of Things (IoT) and smarter devices, this concept has become more and more applicable to grid management. Microgrids, as part of distribution grid are subject to continuous variation in demand, generation and grid conditions. Also, due to private ownership of some or all part of the microgrid (at least in the demand side), and privacy concerns of data transmitted, intelligent and independent agents could be used in management process by representing each component of the grid as an agent. As the importance of storage systems (especially batteries) is increasing with the higher penetration of the renewable energy into the electricity grid, proper battery management becomes vital in efficient microgrid management. In this paper, we focus on battery agent and propose three strategies for battery management in the multi agent based microgrid management framework. We also investigate the effect of each strategy on the total costs as well as the battery itself. In this system, the agents of different components are independent and they collaboratively communicate with each other to fulfil a global objective which is set to be minimising the total costs.

Keywords: Multi-agent systems · Microgrid management · Battery · Management strategy

1 Introduction

Multi Agent Systems (MAS)s have been around since 80's and they have been regarded as a "societies of agents" which interact with each other to coordinate their behaviours and possibly achieve a common goal [1]. Nevertheless, the concept of agent is rather ambiguous among researchers, and it ranges from a simple

© Springer International Publishing AG 2017
W. Abramowicz (Ed.): BIS 2017 Workshops, LNBIP 303, pp. 191–202, 2017.
https://doi.org/10.1007/978-3-319-69023-0_17

entity which only can communicate to the one with proactiveness ability showing a goal-oriented behaviour to satisfy general optima in collaboration with other entities. The application of MAS in autonomous power management are widely accepted and studied in recent years. Grid control, electricity market modelling, fault restoration, and grid protection are some examples the MAS utilization in power management systems. More localized energy production and consumption have emphasized the need to have autonomous system structures to control the increasing emergence of distributed energy resources (DERs). Wider implementations of so-called Microgrids, as groups of interconnected DERs (mainly in the form of renewable energy resources), loads, and storage facilities, are changing the traditional grid control, shifting it toward more decentralized and autonomous control.

In this paper we proposed three strategies for battery management in a multi agent based microgrid management system. The paper is organised as follows: in Sect. 2 we briefly review the applications of multi agent systems in power engineering, next, we describe the structure of the microgrid under investigation. In Sect. 4, we explain the multi agent micro grid management and define the role of each agent in this system, we also propose three strategies for battery management to be implemented by its agent. Simulation results and comparisons are presented in Sect. 5 and the paper is concluded in Sect. 6.

2   Related Work

There are important issues in microgrid control which makes the application of MAS very prospective. For instance, adding new distributed sources without considerable modification in the current equipment, and isolating an area from the main grid in case of any failure in either side or connecting it again to the grid in a timely manner, are among the Microgrid key functionalities that can be solved using the MAS [2]. Kantamneni et al. [3] reviewed the applications of MAS in microgrid, from Microgrid market operations, to protection of microgrid and service restorations. *Distributed architecture*, *flexibility*, and *resiliency* are three advantages of MAS architecture which makes it appropriate choice to model the newly shaped grid particularly incorporating the expansion of distributed renewable energy sources [3].

One of the challenges of Microgrid systems which rely on several renewable energy resources (RES) is the fluctuating nature of these energy sources. The power output of RES is rather intermittent, making the reliability issues bolder in Microgrid energy managements. Also, the generation time of DERs are not sync with the high demand time. Hence, to have a reliable power delivery with the acceptable power quality and more economic energy management, incorporating Battery Energy Storage Systems (BESSs) is inevitable when implementing a microgrid. There have been studies trying to address various aspects of Microgrids storage management. In [4] a proof of concept for load-curve smoothing was presented using a BESS. A fuzzy logic based approach was proposed in [5] for a better utilization of microgrids storage systems, and in [6] the impact of storage system in the operational cost of a typical microgrid was investigated.

Utilizing the benefits of MASs was of a paramount interest in the energy storage management of microgrids. In [7] an agent-based control of battery energy storage was proposed using multiple agents to control the output of DERs. Also in [8] a multi agent fuzzy-logic-based energy management of a DC hybrid microgrid was proposed. The system consists of Photo Voltaic (PV) and fuel cell for generation and battery storage management to preserve the smooth overall generation of microgrid.

Uncertainty of microgrid's load and generation units, especially renewable ones, have always been the major concern of microgrid designer and operator. Although myriad of methods have been proposed to implement an accurate prediction of the grid, but still they embody errors and can not be fully trusted. Moreover, forecasting and communicating the results require much more advanced and expensive technologies as well as accessing lots of data which make it out of reach for most of the microgrids. One way to tackle this problem is to limit the prediction to very limited time, e.g. one hour only and make the decisions based on the current state of the grid.

In this paper, we focus on a battery agent (and its battery management strategies) that operates within a MAS based microgrid management framework using minimal data communicated among the components (agents) of the grid and without using long term prediction.

3 Microgrid Model

In this paper, the main goal in all proposed strategies is to effectively manage the battery and energy providers in a MAS framework with independent agents such that the cost for end users are as low as possible. In this framework, the agents do not share private data and they control their own actions while keeping the power balanced and stable in the microgrid. To make the model closer to real world, we assumed that agents do not have future knowledge or prediction of future state of other agents. The agents act on current (for next hour) and limited past data.

To have a comprehensive model of microgrid, we assume that in this microgrid, there are renewable generation unit, conventional fuel based diesel generation unit, battery storage system and it is connected to the main grid. In our MAS-based management system, each of these components are represented by their intelligent agents.

Before each time slot, the agents communicate and interact with each other to decide how much energy is going to be consumed and where should it come from. The objective in this microgrid is to maintain power balance with minimum total cost. The decision variables are the output power of battery ($r(t)$), power from Diesel Generator ($DG(t)$) and the power supplied from Main Grid ($MG(t)$). It is assumed that all the Renewable Generation ($RG(t)$) is consumed inside the microgrid.

The main decision making agents in this configuration are first the battery agent and then the procurement agents (diesel generation and main grid). Other agents are passive agents which only estimate their own state and communicate it with other agents.

For the consumption side of the microgrid, we assume that there are $\mathcal{N}$ households, each having $\mathcal{A}_n$ number of appliances. Each household i has a Home Intelligent Agent (HIA) which monitors the ON/OFF state and consumption of each appliance j in that house. Using Eq. (1), HIA collects all the data and based on current state, estimates the total consumption of the house for next time slot t and send it to the load aggregator/utility company.

$$P_i(t) = \sum_{j \in \mathcal{A}_n} p_{i,j}(t) \tag{1}$$

The Load aggregator agent, aggregates the consumption of all houses and therefore the total demand at time t is as follows:

$$P_D(t) = \sum_{i \in \mathcal{N}} P_i(t) \tag{2}$$

The diesel generator output depends on its fuel consumption which implies costs. But, the fuel consumption of generator is mostly not linear to the generated power, and the relationship between the fuel consumed and the output power for single generator is usually described as a cost function such as (3).

$$Cost_{DG}(P(t)) = a\,P(t)^2 + b\,P(t) + c \tag{3}$$

And the power balance at each time slot could be represented as Eq. (4).

$$P_D(t) = RG(t) + DG(t) + MG(t) - r(t) \tag{4}$$

With the quadratic cost function, minimum total cost could be obtained when the demanded load is the same (flat load profile) for all times. Therefore, to minimize the generation cost, the battery should absorb the fluctuations of the net demand as much as possible.

On the other hand, the usage of the battery and charging/discharging pattern effects its lifespan and effectiveness. This effect has been captured by a cost function as shown in (5) [9].

$$Cost_{bat} = \eta_1 \sum_{t=1}^{24}(r(t))^2 - \eta_2 \sum_{t=1}^{23} r(t+1)r(t) + \eta_2 \sum_{t=1}^{24}(\min(SoC(t), \delta Cap))^2 \tag{5}$$

In this equation, the first part represents the fast charging burden on the battery. Alternating between charging and discharging also damages the battery which is captured in second term of (5). The third part, indicates that draining the battery below a certain point (δCap) is also damaging the battery. The η_1, η_2, η_3 which are all positive values represent the characteristic of the battery.

4   Proposed Microgrid Management Model

The first decision is made by battery's agent on how much to charge or discharge. Based on Eq. (4), if $r(t) \leq 0$ it means that battery is discharging and act as a producer and vice versa. We also assume that maximum charging and discharging rates are the same and it is shown by $rate$. In our proposed microgrid each agent has specific role which is described in Table 1.

Table 1. Agents in proposed microgrid and their assigned roles

Agent	Role
Home intelligent agent	Estimate the consumption of the house and send it to load aggregator agent
Load aggregator agent	Aggregate the consumption of all consumers
Renewable generation agent	Estimate and announce the renewable generation amount
Utility company agent	Coordinate communication among agents
Main grid agent	Calculate the cost of requested amount of energy
Battery agent	Decide on battery dis/charging rate based on predefined strategy
Diesel generator agent	calculate diesel generation based on requested amount and communication with main grid agent

4.1   Management Strategies for Battery Agent

Strategy I: In first approach, the battery agent gets the total demand $P_D(t)$ and renewable generation $RG(t)$ and also estimates its current charge $SoC(t)$ and based on these informations follows the algorithm shown in flowchart Fig. 1a.

First, the agent calculate the Net Demand ($ND(t) = P_D(t) - RG(t)$). Here, the $RG(t)$ is treated as a negative load to the microgrid. Next, the agent assesses the $ND(t)$, and if it is negative it means the renewable generation is more than the total demand and this excess energy should go to the battery($ND(t) \leq 0 \implies P_D(t) \leq RG(t)$). But there might not be enough capacity in the battery which should be checked by comparing the $(-ND(t))$ and $(capacity - SoC(t))$. If remaining capacity in battery is less than excess generation, battery is charged only that amount. Also, charging $rate$ should be considered as well, the charging rate $r(t)$ should not exceed the battery's maximum dis/charging limit (shown by $rate$). In this case, no energy should come from generation units (MG and DG).

If $ND(t) \geq 0$, it should be provided by the generation units. The battery agent evaluate its $SoC(t)$ and if it is less than 30% of the battery's capacity, it starts charging the battery with full rate and continues in coming hours until the $SoC \geq 80\%$. Likewise, if $SoC \geq 80\%$, battery starts discharging to meet $ND(t)$ up to its full capacity until it reaches back to the 30% of capacity. Equivalently, if $30\% \leq SoC \leq 80\%$, the agent looks at previous hour's charging flow and if it was charging, it keeps charging and vice versa. This charging rate $r(t)$ is signalled to generation agents (DG and MG).

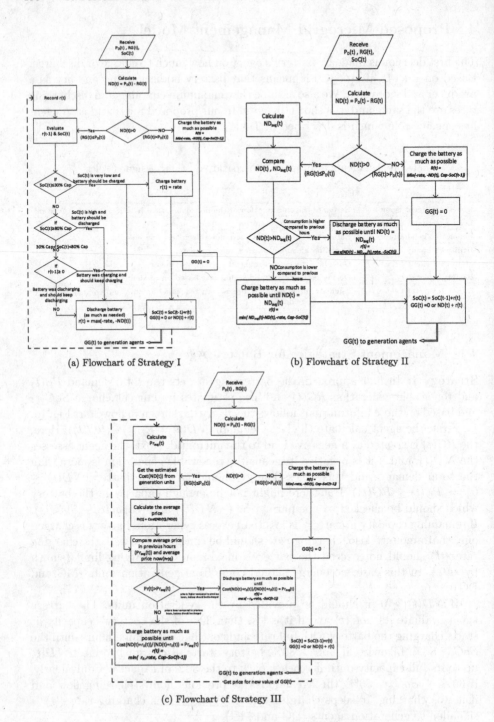

(a) Flowchart of Strategy I

(b) Flowchart of Strategy II

(c) Flowchart of Strategy III

Fig. 1. Proposed strategies for battery agent

Strategy II: In previous strategy, the decision is made based on battery's state $(SoC(t))$ and the net demand at that hour $(ND(t))$; but in the second approach, the average consumption of the scheduling hour (t) and the previous hours $(1, 2, \ldots, t-1)$ are compared. In this strategy, the main goal is to keep the consumption as close as possible to the average of previous hours.

The algorithm shown in Fig. 1b, starts like previous strategy by evaluating $ND(t)$ and if it is negative, like previous strategy, the excess energy goes to battery as much as possible.

But when $ND(t) \geq 0$ and the renewable energy can not provide enough energy to meet the demand, other sources be used. In this case, battery agent compare the requested net demand $ND(t)$ and the average net demands of previous hours shown by $ND_{avg}(t)$. This average is obtained by (6).

$$ND_{avg}(t) = \frac{\left(\sum_{\tau=1}^{\tau=t-1} ND(\tau) \right)}{t-1} \tag{6}$$

If $ND(t) \geq ND_{avg}(t)$ it means that the consumption at this hour is greater than previous hours and the battery should be discharged as much as possible to elevate that extra demand and bring the net demand close to total average. On the flip side, the battery should be charged if consumption is less than average to keep the average at steady value. Again, the remaining capacity and *rate* should be checked and the $r(t)$ should not exceed these values.

Strategy III: In third proposed approach, at each time slot t, the battery agent acts based on the price of electricity at that time and average price up to that hour. This approach is like the previous one, but instead of comparing current consumption and average consumption, price of electricity is assessed and compared. In this approach, the goal of battery agent is to maintain the price stable during the day.

Similar to former approaches, first $ND(t)$ is checked and if it is negative, the excess energy goes to the battery.

If not (and $ND(t) \geq 0$), the battery agent asks the generation agents (MG and DG), what is the cost of generation without battery $(Cost(ND(t)))$. This cost is used to calculate the price for that time using (7).

$$\overline{Pr}(t) = \frac{Cost(ND(t))}{ND(t)} \tag{7}$$

This value is then compared to average price among previous hours obtained by (8).

$$\overline{Pr}_{avg}(t) = \frac{\left(\sum_{\tau=1}^{\tau=t-1} \overline{Pr}(\tau) \right)}{t-1} \tag{8}$$

and if current price is more than average during previous hours, the battery tries to compensate the difference by discharging until the price of current hour is equal to historic average prices. If we call the compensation charge from battery as r_0, its value can be expressed as Eq. 9.

To get the r_0 value, either the battery agent can suggest different values to the generation agents and in iterative way find it or it can send desired price and let the MG and DG agents iterate between themselves and find the appropriate generation value which r_0 could be obtained from.

$$r_0 = Arg(\overline{Pr}(ND(t) + r_0) = \overline{Pr}_{avg}(t))$$
$$= Arg(\frac{cost(ND(t) + r_0)}{ND + r_0} = Avg(\frac{cost(P(1))}{P(1)}, \ldots, \frac{cost(P(t-1))}{P(t-1)}) \quad (9)$$

Again, the acceptable $rate$ and remaining charge or capacity limit in the battery should be evaluated against the compensating value r_0. After finding the acceptable charging rate, $GG(t)$ and its corresponding cost are sent to be recorded for future hours. The whole process is described in Fig. 1c.

4.2 Management Strategy for Generation Agents

In this framework, the DG agent gets and accumulates the net demand and battery dis/charging rate to calculate how much energy should be provided by the main grid and the diesel generator which we call General Generation ($GG(t)$). From (4) we can formulate it as follows:

$$GG(t) = DG(t) + MG(t) = ND(t) + r(t) \quad (10)$$

If the DG and MG agents do not share their cost functions, they start iterating values until their incremental costs are equal. This can be presented as (11a and 11b).

$$\begin{cases} \dfrac{\partial Cost_{DG}(DG(t))}{\partial DG(t)} = \dfrac{\partial Cost_{MG}(MG(t))}{\partial MG(t)} & (11a) \\ GG(t) = MG(t) + DG(t) & (11b) \end{cases}$$

It is also assumed that the cost from main grid and from diesel generation unit are both quadratic functions and main grid follows dynamic pricing scheme and cost function could be different at each hour.

5   Numeric Results and Comparison

To evaluate the effect of each strategy on the microgrid management and related costs, we simulate the proposed microgrid with different scenarios.

Simulated Microgrid Configurations: In our simulations, consumers are considered to be 10 households with two typical synthesised load profile showed in Fig. 2a. Aggregated load of consumers and renewable generation which here is assumed to be PV panels are also presented in Fig. 2b. The cost function from main grid is assumed to be the same quadratic function for all hours. Battery capacity is assumed to be 20 KWh and maximum dis/charging rate ($rate$) is considered to be 3 KW per hour.

Case Study Without PV: First, we evaluate each method when there is no renewable generation. The results from each strategy is presented in figure 3. As can be seen in Fig. 3a, with first strategy, the battery charges until it reaches

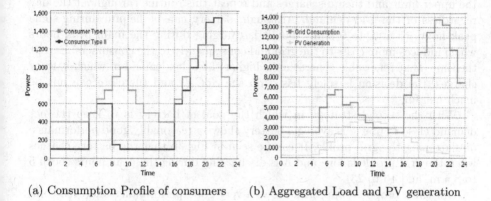

(a) Consumption Profile of consumers   (b) Aggregated Load and PV generation

Fig. 2. Consumption pattern of consumers type I and II (left) and total grid consumption and PV generation (right)

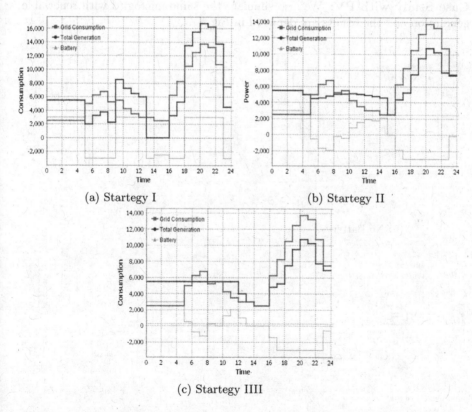

(a) Startegy I   (b) Startegy II

(c) Startegy IIII

Fig. 3. Grid consumption and battery dis/charging profile obtained by strategy I (up-left), strategy II (up-right) and strategy III (down)

the upper limit and then discharges and repeat this routine throughout the day regardless of the grid demand. Although, battery can be helpful during some peak hours (5 a.m. to 9 a.m.), but it is charging during the main peak hours which induces more costs to the grid and consequently to the consumers. Except the times that renewable generation is higher than the demand in which battery charges, the decision is solely based on the $SoC(t)$ and therefore can not be much helpful.

With the second strategy in which the goal of battery is to keep the net demand close to previous average, battery shows a reasonably good performance on flattening the grid profile. It can be seen in Fig. 3b that the battery charges when the grid profile is low, and it is discharging during the peak hours (both 5 to 8 a.m. and 16 to 23).

Our third proposed approach shows a very good performance and even completely flattens the load profile before 12. The battery charges during low consumption hours (before 5 a.m. and between 10 to 13) and discharge when consumption is high both in morning peak and night peak.

Case Study with PV: We also simulate the same microgrid with renewable generation and the results are depicted in Fig. 4.

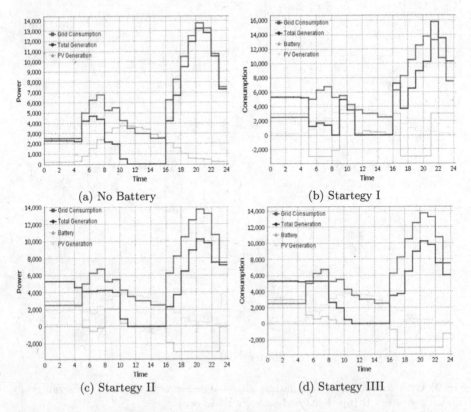

(a) No Battery   (b) Startegy I

(c) Startegy II   (d) Startegy IIII

Fig. 4. Grid consumption and battery charging/discharging profile obtained by no battery, strategy I, strategy II and strategy III with renewable generation

Table 2. Comparing costs and prices with different strategies

Strategy	Total generation costs ($)	Average daily price($\frac{\$}{kWh}$)	Net battery consumption (kWh)	Net battery consumption cost($)	Battery degradation costs($)	Reduction in costs($)
No battery	337	2.36	0	0	0	0
Strategy I	383	2.68	11.5	−31	4.6	−19.6
Strategy II	310	2.17	−2	4.3	2.6	20.1
Strategy III	308	2.15	−2	4.3	2.6	22.1

Like previous case, with the first strategy, because the charging pattern does not follow the grid consumption, again it is not helping the grid.

The second and third strategies with the simulated microgrid with renewable generation show similar pattern as previous case. Again, the third strategy with the price as the decision criteria delivers better results in comparison.

By comparing the two graphs in Fig. 4c and d, we can see that price is a better mean for representing the state of the network and can yield better results (lower costs). Although we used same price function for all hours, but if the cost functions for different hours are not identical, the difference between strategy II and strategy III could be more significant. Also, it can be seen that the excess energy from renewable is not fully absorbed just because battery was full during those hours (11 to 16).

Comparison and Evaluation: Detailed results of different scenarios have been listed in Table 2. Due to similarities, we only showed the results of the scenarios with renewable generation. In our simulations, total demand of consumers is 143 Kwh and total PV generation is 39 kWh.

In this table, *average daily price* is obtained by dividing total daily cost by total daily grid consumption. *Net battery consumption* is the difference between initial charge of the battery and its final SoC at the end of the day. The corresponding cost of this difference is calculated by multiplying this value by average daily cost. In strategy I, the positive sign of this value means that a portion of the 383 kWh consumption is saved in the battery and its cost should be reduced from total cost (−31$).

It can be seen that with first strategy and without incorporating the microgrid's state in decision making process, it is possible that in some cases the battery impose more costs to the grid instead of reducing it. Although, the charging direction is more stable in first strategy, and therefore second part of the (5) is comparatively smaller, but because *net battery consumption* stored in the battery is significantly higher compared to other two strategies (11.5 kWh), the degradation costs is also higher. The negative reduction of strategy I shows that actually, in this scenario the battery increased the total cost of the grid.

The two other strategies which the battery charging rate is based on the microgrid's state, the reduction in total costs are significantly higher and it shows the price in the grid is the best signal to be used to decide on battery charging profile.

6   Conclusion

In this paper, we proposed different strategies for storage management in a multi agent based microgrid management system in which the agents independently make decisions based on their local states and information from other agents. In our proposed strategies for storage system, the agents collaborate with each other to meet a global objective which is reducing the cost in the microgrid. In this management system, the agents do a *rolling horizon* scheduling and do not have access to long term data of the grid. By simulating multiple scenarios, we demonstrated that by selecting right decision making criteria for battery agent, more economically efficient MAS-based microgrid management could be obtained. The more information of the microgrid the battery agent have, the more efficient management could be implemented. Also, we showed that for reducing the costs, the price is the best signal among the agents. We are also working on the interaction between local generation units and main grid agents and also more advanced strategies for battery and other agents.

Acknowledgements. This research was partially supported by the Australia-Germany Joint Research Cooperation Scheme.

References

1. Ferber, J., Gutknecht, O., Michel, F.: From agents to organizations: an organizational view of multi-agent systems. In: Giorgini, P., Müller, J.P., Odell, J. (eds.) AOSE 2003. LNCS, vol. 2935, pp. 214–230. Springer, Heidelberg (2004). doi:10.1007/978-3-540-24620-6_15
2. Davis, G.: Integration of distributed energy resources the CERTS microgrid concept (2003)
3. Kantamneni, A., Brown, L.E., Parker, G., Weaver, W.W.: Survey of multi-agent systems for microgrid control. Eng. Appl. Artif. Intell. **45**, 192–203 (2015)
4. Baun, M., Awadallah, M.A., Venkatesh, B.: Implementation of load-curve smoothing algorithm based on battery energy storage system. In: 2016 IEEE Canadian Conference on Electrical and Computer Engineering (CCECE), pp. 1–5. IEEE (2016)
5. Mahmoud, T.S., Habibi, D., Bass, O.: Fuzzy logic for smart utilisation of storage devices in a typical microgrid. In: 2012 International Conference on Renewable Energy Research and Applications (ICRERA), pp. 1–6. IEEE (2012)
6. Alqunun, K., Crossley, P.A.: Rated energy impact of BESS on total operation cost in a microgrid. In: 2016 IEEE Smart Energy Grid Engineering (SEGE), pp. 292–300. IEEE (2016)
7. Yoo, C.H., Chung, I.Y., Lee, H.J., Hong, S.S.: Intelligent control of battery energy storage for multi-agent based microgrid energy management. Energies **6**(10), 4956–4979 (2013)
8. Lagorse, J., Simoes, M.G., Miraoui, A.: A multiagent fuzzy-logic-based energy management of hybrid systems. IEEE Trans. Ind. Appl. **45**(6), 2123–2129 (2009)
9. Li, N., Chen, L., Low, S.H.: Optimal demand response based on utility maximization in power networks. In: 2011 IEEE Power and Energy Society General Meeting, pp. 1–8, July 2011

Doctoral Consortium

Doctoral Consortium Chair's Message

Agnieszka Figiel

The Doctoral Consortium was held in conjunction with the BIS 2017 conference, a well-respected event bringing together international researchers to discuss the development, implementation, application, and improvement of business applications and systems. The consortium provided doctoral students with the chance to present and receive comments on their research, to hear about the work of their peers at other universities, and to interact with today's leading researchers from different universities and countries. It was also an opportunity to meet interesting people and make new friendships. We invited students at different career stages: advanced students who have a clear topic and research approach as well as less experienced students who are starting their PhD track.

The consortium was divided into two parts: plenary sessions and mentoring session. During the plenary session each student presented his or her work (research ideas, the current progress, future plans) and then received constructive criticism and insights relating to his or her paper. Five sessions were organized and 15 PhD students from four countries were invited to attend the conference. Our guests had a chance to see 12 presentations and to attend very good and inspiring discussions. The mentoring session took place after the plenary sessions. Consortium mentors were assigned to each student to provide individual feedback and advice on the paper, the focus of the work, and further developments.

After the reviewing process, five papers were accepted for publication in the proceedings at hand. Although every proposal is related to the topic of big data the scope of the proposals is wide-ranging. We hope it will be an interesting reading and a great inspiration for further analysis and research.

Organization

Chair

Agnieszka Figiel   Poznan University of Economics and Business, Poland

Program Committee

Agata Filipowska	Poznan University of Economics and Business, Poland
Ralf-Christian Härting	Aalen University, Germany
Tahir Emre Kalayci	Research Centre for Knowledge and Data (KRDB), Free University of Bozen-Bolzano, Italy
Nina Khairova	National Technical University Kharkiv Polytechnic Institute, Ukraine
Gary Klein	University of Colorado, USA
Jun-Lin Lin	Yuan Ze University, Taiwan
Julie Yu-Chih Liu	Yuan Ze University, Taiwan
Kurt Sandkuhl	The University of Rostock, Germany
Krzysztof Węcel	Poznan University of Economics and Business, Poland

Continuous Requirements Engineering
Support Environment Model
in Methodologically Heterogeneous Projects

Anita Finke[✉]

Riga Technical University, Daugavgrīvas iela 2, Riga, Latvia
anita.finke@rtu.lv

Abstract. In the result of scientific and technological evolution in Software and Requirements Engineering fields many techniques, methods and tools have been developed to support our daily work. Most of them are more suited for big organizations and companies. Of course this is a positive development that brings value to engineering. But not always these innovations bring value to small or medium companies working on Information Systems development and support projects. A good example is the issues with requirements management in long term use of requirements and system. If we use agile methods, in most cases in practice, the documentation is very poor or limited. Another example is the waterfall method where the documentation is developed in the beginning of the project, but at the end of the project the requirements can be changed (in practice). This all can bring us to certain problems in future work. For example, how will we know the build of a certain system, how it must work etc. This work is focusing on requirements inheritance and availability issue in small and medium companies with heterogeneous projects.

Keywords: Requirements engineering · Requirements distribution · Continuous requirement engineering

1 Introduction

The role of digital world, information and knowledge in organizations has become increasingly important. Fast changing information systems (IS) and requirements ask for fast reactions and rich knowledge about existing solutions.

Evolution of science and technologies in Software and Requirements Engineering fields has provided many techniques, methods and tools in order to support our daily work. Most of them are more suitable to big organizations and companies. Of course it is a positive development that brings value to engineering. But not always the innovations bring value to small or medium companies working on Information Systems development and support projects. And one of the reasons is costs of these technologies.

In most cases small and medium companies do not use costly and extensive tools to perform Software Engineering (SE) and Requirements Engineering (RE) activities. A part of these companies uses systems and tools like MS Word, MS Excel, open source tools or some small free of cost tools.

© Springer International Publishing AG 2017
W. Abramowicz (Ed.): BIS 2017 Workshops, LNBIP 303, pp. 207–215, 2017.
https://doi.org/10.1007/978-3-319-69023-0_18

The basal problem is that we do not have even poorly documented or up to date requirements, knowledge and related information as an output from RE (Requirements Engineering) activities. As a hypothetical reason, the author wants to mention organizations' willingness to save resources. For example, by 'skipping' such important activities output as documentation.

As the second hypothetical reason the author wants to point out an issue which arises when we realize that in practice we do not use one single tool. In most situations during the IS (Information Systems) development projects or during any other type of project, we use more than one tool, for example: e-mail, MS Word and/or Excel documents, file systems, some special tools like JIRA [9] or SharePoint and others. Situation becomes more complex in a case when more than one project team is involved during a certain project. For example: client's project team and developer's project team. This means that each project team can potentially use different tools and technologies.

Also companies and organizations are interested in resource (like human resources) savings. And one of the ways to save resources is to minimize the time we spend on documentation. If we are saving time on documentation, this means that the documentation is pure or is not updated. It is an acceptable scenario if we have one time solution (a short-term solution, for example a year). But what happens when we have a solution expected to be used for many years, and it will be in need for support, changes etc.?

This all can result in problems related to multi tool use and work with requirements in future. For example multi tool and technology use during one project brings problems and challenges as:

- requirements and information tracking and traceability;
- unsynchronized versions of documents and requirements;
- a lot of resources spent on manual work for version management and traceability;
- other problems and challenges.

During this research the author will analyze existing methods in RE to predict how much do these methods support the idea of continuous work on solutions and on requirements. What kind of support do we need to provide a possibility to work continuously with solutions and requirements? And is there a possibility to create a support model with technological support that can provide requirements inheritance with minimized manual work for small and medium organizations? In this case the author uses the term Continuous Requirements Engineering and Requirements Inheritance.

During the paper and research the author will use the following CRE definition: requirements engineering activities (for example requirements identification, analysis, design and modeling, traceability, management, communication, validation) continual execution during all IS lifecycle. This means that during the IS lifecycle we are working continually on these IS requirements. It can mean that we reuse these requirements in similar projects or we work on specific system requirements during all IS lifecycle. For example during the IS life there are certain change requests and support projects, and in each of them we use existing requirements, improve or change them and work on new ones.

In the previous papers the author describes [8, 17] the information inheritance problem and importance of information availability as well as hypothetical solutions for these problems. Also the author described ideas about the socialization aspect which can support requirement management process and improve knowledge availability, for example, the requirements realization process and the use of requirements results.

This paper contains 5 sections: Sect. 1 – introduction, Sect. 2 – related work about CRE, Sect. 3 – research methodology, Sect. 4 – research questions, Sect. 5 – solution design proposal and work progress.

2 Related Work

Requirements engineering (RE) concerns IS life cycle activities like requirements elicitation, requirements analysis, requirements management and other requirements management activities [1, 2] and tools for requirements documentation. These are the classic RE activities and they are widely described in scope of a project. The author noticed that these methods and guidelines are mostly focused on activities during the project and do not discuss the effect of these activities in the future.

In previous papers [17] the author describes certain ideas about communication, socialization, and the role of knowledge in RE. The reason for it was the fact that requirement engineering includes communication too, but it does not describe socialization tools and their use to gather knowledge about requirements process, requirements gathering, the process of approval, requirements realization specifics and use of development results.

Knowledge creation, capturing and diffusion have become important aspects in organizations [12]. Knowledge in all aspects, including requirements management and solution development, is the most valuable asset in organizations [13]. Success of many organizations depends on availability of knowledge, particularly the amount and quality of explicit knowledge. Even the success in RE process depends on the available knowledge. Moreover in knowledge elicitation and requirements elicitation process we can use the same techniques: like interviews, shadowing etc. [2, 10]. It gives us a reason to think about possibilities to adapt KM practices and tools in CRE.

Aziza and Wong [4] talk about the relationship between requirements and knowledge. They describe the importance of the relationship between requirements and knowledge, because "...managing these incremental changes in software development is very challenging. The knowledge and management of requirements changes is crucial in the management of software changes". Ebert and De Man [5] state that knowledge about techniques, project portfolio and processes and information is important in continuous systems and requirement improvements.

We can talk about knowledge only if we have gathered some knowledge. Last year there was some research done on usage of today's social messaging (SM) tools in enterprises [14] in context of knowledge elicitation and management. It can be one of the possible ways to support knowledge elicitation and transformation into written form in a natural way. The only aspect worth considering is how structured and analyzable this information is.

Social messaging [14], Internet of Thing and Cloud technologies [12] and socialization tools are the latest trends in KM solutions. Solutions as Facebook and WhatsApp and others bring new possibilities and ideas about the ways of knowledge elicitation and management in organizations. Today the business decisions have to be made on the move. And such applications as WhatsApp and others support this style of work.

In [13] authors talk about KM role in risk management. Matti Mäntymäki and Kai Riemer talk about enterprise social networking [15] and the role of it. Researches [15] reveal that social networking in enterprise for professional purposes can improve everyday communication and is positively associated with employee performance.

There are some studies about challenges in Requirement Engineering: Besrour et al. Dominic describe such challenges as poor communication during requirement elicitation, undocumented relations among requirements and stakeholders, requirements inconsistency and others [16].

Requirements engineering is strongly related to communication and knowledge. Today's tools for RE and software development support include an option for socialization (online communication, discussions, sharing etc.).

Information, data and knowledge is most useful only in situations when it is put to use. CRE concept concerns continuous work on requirements and solutions. Continuous work means reuse of existing requirements and improvement of them in the context of IS changes. The term of CRE [6, 11] is not widely described in research. But some concepts of continuity are already described, for example in SWEBOK (Software Engineering Body of Knowledge) [3] it is pointed out that requirements process is "... initiated at the beginning of a project that continues to be refined throughout the life cycle." In practice the requirements appear before the information technology project is started, before the official start of the project.

BABOK (Business Analysis Body of Knowledge) 3 [2] points out the necessity to plan business analysis information management (requirements capture, storage and integration with other information) in a way that provides long term use. And long term use means continuous work on requirements and the solution as well.

There are some more specific topics too, e.g. model (Model Federation) for CRE to support and propose an approach of model federation that allows information sharing by maintaining dynamic links between different models [13].

3   Research Methodology

During this research the author uses the Design Science Methodology [18]. This method provides guidelines for doing scientific research in information systems and software engineering. The main object of study is an artifact in a context. And by artifact we understand, for example, methods, techniques, and algorithms. And by context we understand design, development, maintenance, use of software etc.

The cycle of this method is shown in Fig. 1.

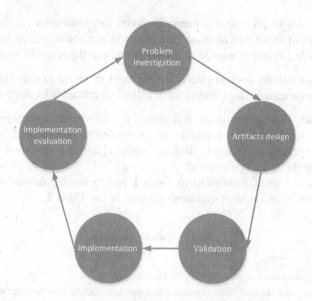

Fig. 1. The engineering cycle [18]

The engineering cycle is a rational problem-solving process with the structure shown in Fig. 1. It consists of the following tasks:

- Problem investigation: What is the problem, what phenomena must be improved and why? The author will focus mostly on the question why.
- Artifact design: Designing one or more artifacts that could treat the problem.
- Artifact validation: Would these artifacts solve the problem?
- Artifact implementation: Treat the problem with one of the designed artifacts.
- Implementation evaluation: How successful has the designed artifact been? This may be the start of a new iteration through the engineering cycle.

In this research the artifact in context is: Continuous requirement engineering model for support of continual work on requirements in small and medium organizations. The context is continuous requirements engineering in methodologically heterogeneous projects in small and medium enterprises.

The author made the following research goals, shown in Table 1.

Table 1. Research goals

Nr.	Research goals
1.	Designed CRE support model that allows to work continuously with requirements during all IS lifecycle in SME
2.	Defined CRE definition
3.	Identified criteria and designed guidelines for CRE process support
4.	Designed CRE support model evaluation criteria, to evaluate CRE support model efficiency

4 Research Questions

The research aims to provide a conceptual model for continuous requirement engineering support in small and medium enterprises in methodologically heterogeneous projects. To define research questions, author points out the research problem:

- RE activities outputs contain poorly documented or no up to date (final) requirements documentation, documented knowledge and related information.

Consequently that mostly means that in next RE activity or next project or next IS life cycle we have partially available or incompletely documented requirements, knowledge and related information. And this leads to gaps in information that we need to fill in before the work is continued.

To achieve the goals mentioned in Table 1 and to resolve defined problem, the author has defined the research questions showed in the Table 2.

Table 2. Research questions

Nr.	Research question
1.	Why organizations save resources on documentation?
2.	How can we minimize used resources and provide documented requirements, knowledge and related information?
3.	Do these problems affect CRE and how do they affect CRE?
4.	Can CRE support model improve existing situation in RE and prevent or reduce RE problems?
5.	Can we predict the "minimum program" that needs to be performed to provide continuous work on requirements?

5 Solution Design Proposal and Work Progress

This section of the paper describes the concept idea of requirement management approach. Nowadays the biggest focus in IS projects is mostly put on fast product delivery but there are no assumptions on future work with requirements. If we lack an effective approach for requirements management and distribution, this can result in incomplete requirements, outdated requirement versions and missing information and knowledge.

Many approaches and possibilities in knowledge management and distribution are described in literature. There are some assumptions about recommendation tools and their effort in requirement engineering and distribution [7] but this requires high requirement quality. For example, lack of requirement quality can contribute to bad practice in RE.

Author proposes a concept of an approach describing the key principle or blocks that we need to consider. These blocks can help make requirements distribution more effective and even make requirements management simpler. An early stage of his approach has been adopted in a real company. The validation of results will be shown in next research papers.

The basic idea of the approach is:

- **By reducing the number of requirements management tools** and channels we can save resources (time resources) for requirement management and simplify communication management (communication mostly is organized trough the tool and all communication is documented). It can be done by implementing one or more than one requirements repository and tool instances in which communication (data interchange) is fully or partially automated. This includes the knowledge elicitation and management activities by using tool support for communication and socialization.
- **Providing access** to these requirements' repository to all stakeholders involved in RE process (client, developers, third party representatives). This means that all stakeholders and project team members use one tool or repository for RE. And use all available functionality for RE support, like comments, sharing etc.
- **Providing technological support** for quality and process control. To minimize resources we spend on RE documentation, we need to consider the possibilities to provide technological support for automated or partly automated process support.
- Ensuring that all stakeholders, including analysts and developers **use concrete and preferably single standard or best practice for RE** and **adhere to quality requirements**.

This simple idea can be shown as a model of requirement management approach (see Fig. 2).

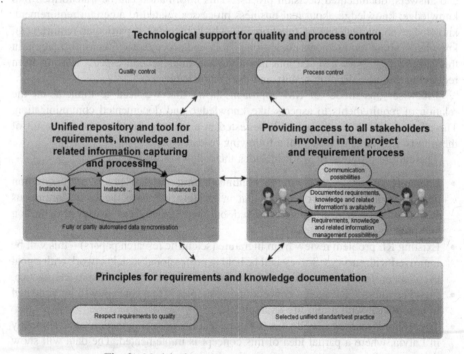

Fig. 2. Model of requirements management approach

The model of requirements management approach presented in Fig. 2 illustrates the key concept: less tools, multi-functional options for communication and socialization, traceability, search, accessibility possibilities, versioning and traceability support, development process support and other functionality.

If we make a mathematical comparison, for example, 2 organizations each have 2 tools for requirement input. We can assume that the requirement input in each tool requires the same time – X. Then the cumulative time = number of tools * 2 * X. When the number of tools is minimized, it reduces the total time spent on requirement input. It can save 1 h per day or even more.

The next aspect is time the involved persons spend on search in documented communication process and linking to requirements. If we assume that most of communication and socialization activities are fixed among requirements, it can save us time for searching in different sources and linking them. Of course, the effectiveness depends on quality of the written communication.

This model of RM approach brings restrictions or rules such as the need to ensure the use of the tool by all involved persons and the need to provide the availability of tools to all involved persons.

Requirements usually are stored in "requirements register or repository" – it can be stored in MS Word, MS Excel or other type of system. And usually it contains requirements and their attributes like author, priority, number, date of requirements capture, status etc. Socialization possibilities can bring a new way of requirements management.

Socialization means that requirements have a new attribute – comments, questions and answers, documented decision process. This information can be transformed into knowledge; knowledge about real business processes related to a certain requirement, knowledge about real use of functionality which includes a particular requirement, knowledge about requirements elicitation history and process, and other information. In this case in Fig. 2 we can see that this approach links several aspects starting from requirement to socialization results and even knowledge.

Likewise, this model of RM approach shows that we need to think about the relation of requirements to aspects like knowledge and documented communication. The efficiency of this approach will be tested in a real organization and the result of these tests will be described in the following research papers.

The current progress of work includes the following results:

- Literature review – this will be continued until the last phase of dissertation development. The author realizes that in existing literature the term Continuous Requirements Engineering is mentioned, but there are no clear visions of definition and process concept.
- Existing RE problem review from literature (scientific research papers) – this will be improved with surveys. Survey will be held in professional social network with a goal to collect professionals' opinion and data/facts about existing situation in RE practice.
- First version of CRE model concept and principles – this concept will be validated in accordance with a real life example.
- The author is starting to collect data from a real life project in medium size company in Latvia, where a partial idea of this concept is implemented. The data will show the pros and cons of the concept.

References

1. Young, R.R.: The Requirements Engineering Handbook. Artech House, Norwood (2004)
2. International Institute of Business Analysis: A Guide to the Business Analysis Body of Knowledge v3 (2015)
3. Bourque, P., Fairley, R.E.: Guide to the Software Engineering - Body of Knowledge. IEEE Computer Society, Washington, D.C. (2014)
4. Aziz, R.A., Wong, B.: The interplay between requirements relationships knowledge and requirements change towards software project success: an assessment using partial least square (PLS). Procedia Comput. Sci. **46**, 732–741 (2015)
5. Ebert, C., De Man, J.: Requirements uncertainty: influencing factors and concrete improvements. In: Proceedings of the 27th International Conference on Software Engineering, ICSE 2005, pp. 553–560 (2005)
6. Kirikova, M.: Enterprise Architecture and Knowledge Perspectives on Continuous Requirements Engineering (2015). http://ceur-ws.org/Vol-1342/05-CRE.pdf. Accessed 10 Jan 2016
7. Maalej, W., Kumar Thurimella, A.: Towards a research agenda for recommendation systems in requirements engineering. In: 2009 Second International Workshop on Managing Requirements Knowledge (MaRK 2009) (2010)
8. Finke, A.: Requirements Inheritance in continuous requirements engineering: a position paper, CRE 2017 (2016)
9. Atlassian: JIRA Products. https://www.atlassian.com/software/jira. Accessed 02 Jan 2017
10. Sandkuhl, K., Stirna, J., Persson, A., Wißotzki, M.: Elicitation approaches in enterprise modeling. In: Sandkuhl, K., Stirna, J., Persson, A., Wißotzki, M. (eds.) Enterprise Modeling: Tackling Business Challenges with the 4EM Method. TEES, pp. 39–51. Springer, Heidelberg (2014). doi:10.1007/978-3-662-43725-4_4
11. Finance, J.-P. (ed.): Fundamental Approaches to Software Engineering, vol. 1577. Springer, Heidelberg (1999)
12. Balco, P., Drahošova, M.: Knowledge management as a service (KMaaS). In: 2016 4th International Conference on Future Internet of Things and Cloud Workshops (2016)
13. Mercier-Laurent, E.: Knowledge management and risk management. In: Proceeding of the Federated Conference on Computer Science and Information Systems, pp. 1369–1373 (2016)
14. Pilat, L., Kaindl, H.: A knowledge management perspective of requirements engineering. In: 2011 Fifth International Conference on Research Challenges in Information Science (RCIS) (2011)
15. Mäntymäki, M., Riemer, K.: Enterprise social networking: a knowledge management perspective. Int. J. Inf. Manag. **36**(2016), 1042–1052 (2016)
16. Besrour, S., Bin, L., Rahim, A.B., Dominic, P.D.D.: A quantitative study to identify critical requirement engineering challenges in the context of small and medium software enterprises. In: 2016 3rd International Conference on Computer and Information Sciences (ICCOINS) (2016)
17. Finke, A.: Socialization aspect in requirements engineering. In: REFSQ 2017 Joint Proceedings of the Co-located Events (2017)
18. Wieringa, R.J.: Design Science Methodology for Information Systems and Software Engineering. Springer, Heidelberg (2014)

Enrichment of Information in Multilingual Wikipedia Based on Quality Analysis

Włodzimierz Lewoniewski[✉]

Poznań University of Economics and Business,
Al. Niepodległości 10, 61-875 Poznań, Poland
wlodzimierz.lewoniewski@ue.poznan.pl

Abstract. Despite the fact that Wikipedia is one of the most popular sources of information in the world, it is often criticized for the poor quality of content. In this online encyclopaedia articles on the same topic can be created and edited independently in different languages. Some of this language versions can provide valuable information on a specific topics. Wikipedia articles may include infobox, which used to collect and present a subset of important information about its subject. This study presents method for quality assessment of Wikipedia articles and information contained in their infoboxes. Choosing the best language versions of a particular article will allow for enrichment of information in less developed version editions of particular articles.

Keywords: Wikipedia · Article quality · Infobox · DBpedia

1 Introduction

Knowledge exchange is one of the key factors for success. Internet allows to interact and share global information. According to the Internet World Stats in March 2017, about half the world's population are Internet users[1]. Web 2.0 technologies allows users became producers of the online-content through collaborative platforms. Collaborative editing can be defined by its attributes: writing in a shared document, collaborative processes, data lineage, distributed teams, placeless document philosophy, flexible handling of content and layout [1]. At present everyone can contribute to common human knowledge on the Internet. One of the best examples of such online repositories are wiki websites where content can be created and changed from a web browser. The most popular wiki website is Wikipedia.

More than 15 years, Wikipedia exists as a general available encyclopaedia, where everyone can contribute to contributing content. Wikipedia also is one of the most successful examples of mass collaboration [2]. However, this free online-encyclopaedia does not fulfil all the attributes of a classical collaborative tool. For example, Wikipedia users do not work with separate documents, but with articles, which are integrated in a searchable knowledge base [3].

---

[1] http://www.internetworldstats.com/stats.htm.

© Springer International Publishing AG 2017
W. Abramowicz (Ed.): BIS 2017 Workshops, LNBIP 303, pp. 216–227, 2017.
https://doi.org/10.1007/978-3-319-69023-0_19

According to the latest statistics, Wikipedia is fifth most popular website in the Internet[2]. For more than 15 years this free online encyclopedia as become more and more popular and important sources of knowledge throughout the world. Wikipedia contains over 44 million articles in about 300 language editions[3]. The biggest language version is English with over 5.4 million articles.

Despite the fact that an article in Wikipedia on the same topic can be presented in different languages, each of these versions can be created and edited by users separately. Consequently, this can often be observed differences between information quality in various languages of the same article. Naturally, to compare such versions it is often necessary for users to have knowledge in these languages.

Wikipedia pages about famous people, firms, products often appear as first in search results of Google, Bing, Yandex and other search engines. It is expected that visitors of Wikipedia and its editors are interested in the high quality of content contained in this online knowledge base. So presentation of information in different languages is particularly important for users who use search engines in their native (non-English) language. Also, some topics may be more popular in some countries and therefore more likely to find more information on same topic in relevant language versions (other than English). In addition, there are topics that are not described in English Wikipedia, despite the fact that the less developed language versions of Wikipedia have these informations [4, 5].

Wikipedia has a quality grading system for articles, but a specific language version may use its own standards and grades [6]. That means that each language community of Wikipedia can create own standards for the quality evaluation of articles.

Articles in Wikipedia can consist special tables which present shortly important information about subject. This table is usually placed at the top of the right side of the article, and has name "infobox". Information from these infoboxes also used to automatically enrich various public databases (such as DBpedia[4]). Just as in the case of articles, these infoboxes are often created and edited by users in each language separately.

This work try to answer the following main questions:

1. How to determine the quality of a Wikipedia articles?
2. How automatically enrich wiki pages with information (elements of the infoboxes) coming from the counterparts of this Wikipedia article in other languages?

In addition, auxiliary questions were formulated:

1. How to determine quality measures of a Wikipedia article?
2. How automatically evaluate the quality of a Wikipedia articles based on the selected quality measures related to timeliness, validity and completeness?

---

[2] http://www.alexa.com/siteinfo/wikipedia.org.

[3] https://meta.wikimedia.org/wiki/List_of_Wikipedias.

[4] http://dbpedia.org.

3. Can the quality of Wikipedia article help to evaluate the quality of infobox contained in it?
4. Is the quality of the infobox in particular language version of article dependent on the demand for the related content?
5. How to choose a better quality infobox parameters from different language versions?

2 Quality of Wikipedia Articles

In each Wikipedia language editions there is system of grades for articles quality. Practical every language version has special mark for articles are considered to be the best. In English Wikipedia they are called "Featured Articles" (FA), in polish Wikipedia - "Artykuły na Medal". Such best articles should meet the specified quality criteria related to accuracy, neutrality, completeness and style. For example, FA articles content must be written with professional standard, neglects no major facts or details and places the subject in context, consist high-quality reliable sources, have lead section that summarizes the topic and prepares the reader for the detail in the subsequent sections and others[5]. There is also a mark for high-quality decent articles, not have met the criteria for FA - "Good articles" (GA)[6]. English Wikipedia have other marks for lower quality articles: B-class, C-class, Start, Stub. One of the important difference between high-quality grades (FA and GA) and lower ones is evaluation procedure. Articles can get or lose FA or GA grade after discussion and voting by Wikipedia users, which can be carried out within about one month from the date of nomination. In case of lower grades it is enough initiative of an individual user. It should be noted, there is also high-quality grade A-class, which can also be given without special voting procedure. However, A-class articles usually at the same time have FA or GA grade.

Other language versions of Wikipedia may have own grading scheme. For German Wikipedia, which have over 2 million articles, there are only 2 higher-quality grades "Exzellente Artikel" and "Lesenswerte Artikel", which are equivalents for FA in GA in English Wikipedia. Russian Wikipedia have more developed grading scheme with 7 grades, but not all of them are equivalent for English grades. Figure 1 shows the differences between quality grades in particular Wikipedia language: English (EN), German (DE), French (FR), Russian (RU), Polish (PL), Ukrainian (UK), Belarussian (BE).

The great challenge is the large number of articles that do not have quality grade. Some language versions (such as BE, DE, PL) have over 99% unassessed articles.

Nowadays, there exist quite a lot of the studies that describes different methods for automatic quality prediction of Wikipedia articles. One of the first researches in this direction proposes to analyse volume of articles content [7]. Such simple metric as word count can help to assess quality of the Wikipedia

---

[5] https://en.wikipedia.org/wiki/Wikipedia:Featured_article_criteria.
[6] https://en.wikipedia.org/wiki/Wikipedia:Good_article_criteria.

Grade / Language	BE 143,712	DE 2,066,144	EN 5,414,400	FR 1,874,309	PL 1,224,639	RU 1,396,925	UK 699,052
Featured Article (FA)	X	X	X	X	X	X	X
Good Article (GA)	X	X	X	X	X	X	X
Solid Article						X	
A-class			X	X			
Four					X		
Full						X	X
B-class			X	X			
Developed						X	X
C-class			X				
In develpment						X	X
Start			X	X	X		
Stub	X		X	X	X	X	X
Unassessed	99,34%	99,68%	10,16%	39,30%	99,50%	85,01%	97,04%

Colors   are marked grades that have similar characteristics

Fig. 1. Quality grading schemes in different language versions of Wikipedia. Source: own calculations.

articles [8]. The best articles use also more references and consits more sections [6,9]. In addition it can be taken into account special templates which describes quality gaps such as credibility, writing style, structure, and other issues [10].

There are studies that use lungusitics features extracted from the articles texts to analyse the articles quality. Lipka [11] exploit an articles character trigram distribution for the automatic assessment of information quality. Another studies proposed to use the number of facts and the factual density as features to identify high quality articles in Wikipedia [12,13], wherein Fact can have the form of a triplet with two entities and a relationship between them [14].

Assesment of the quality of Wikipedia articles can be based not only on content metrics. Other studies shows how characteristics related to contributors' reputations and edit network, article status, external factual support and other features can help in determining the quality of the article [15,16].

Many of these studies solve the problem of evaluating articles as a classification task - all grades are divided into two groups: Complete and Incomplete [6,9,13,14,17]. Complete group consist FA and GA grades. The remaining lower-quality grades are included in Incomplete group. So, various measures that describes the Wikipedia articles are independent variables, quality group - binary dependent variable [6,9,17,18]. Studies have shown that there differences between quality models of particular language versions of Wikipedia using same set of independent variables [6,17,18]. Most commonly for these tasks researches used data mining algorithms, and in particular Random Forest, which showed the highest precision in the classification [6,9,17,18].

Using a binary measure for quality assessment of the articles typically give a high precision in classification models (over 95% in different versions of Wikipedia), but this approach has some disadvantages and limitations. If articles belong to the same group (e.g. Incomplete), then it is not possible to compare their quality between each other.

In some works quality in quality models is also considered a categorial variable [6,9,19]. However, the precision in such models is much lower than with the use of a stochastic dependent variable - about 60%. In addition, in this approach, the comparison of the quality of the articles in different languages will be challenging task due to the differences in grade systems in different language versions of Wikipedia.

It may be more useful to use articles quality grade as continuous measure. For example, online service WikiRank[7] used some quality metrics of articles (such as text length, number of images, references, headers, etc.) to calculate the so-called relative quality of the same article in different language versions of Wikipedia on a scale from 0 to 100 [6].

Metrics of wiki pages analysis are extracted in different ways. One of the most important elements of wiki pages are references. Most research usually focuses on counting number of references used in Wikipedia articles and uses that number to create other (derivative) indicators (e.g. ref./length). Promising is the direction to study the similarity of references between different language versions of a wiki page on a specific topic.

Like in other websites with user-generated content, quality of Wikipedia articles can be determined through an evaluation of the following measures: Completeness, Validity, Timeliness and others [20]. Quality measure - appropriately selected set of metrics. Metric - quantitative value, calculated on the basis of the certain rules. For example completeness consist number of headers, test length, number of images and other.

3   Quality of Infoboxes

In fact, the infobox is a template that contains list of items "parameter = value". Depending on the topic, the infobox can contain a certain set of possible parameters. Data from the infoboxes can be used not only for receiving main facts about the subject by the reader of Wikipedia, but also to enrich other popular databases such as DBpedia. For this reason, it is particularly important to verify these informations, which are provided by users.

Quality of infoboxes is much less developed topic than articles quality in researches. Existing studies often explore the quality of databases created from infoboxes. Good example of such databases is DBpedia, which additionaly contains many links to other datasets in the LOD cloud such as Freebase, OpenCy- cand others [21]. Using comprehensive set of generic Data Quality Test Patterns it is possible to reveal a substantial amount of data quality issues [22]. Using

---

[7] http://wikirank.net.

special methods it is possible to analyze, the consistency, syntactic validity, conciseness and semantic accuracy of data contained in DBpedia [23]. Analysis of data quality in this semantic knowledge base is also possible without using of ontology [24]. There are also studies related to data fusion from different language versions of DBpedia [25]. However, most of the works does not take into account the various aspects of the quality of the infoboxes and the wiki pages from which the data was extracted.

One of the approaches propose to define relevant metrics and respective scoring functions for specific data quality assessment task [26]. In Linked Open Data (LOD) there are more than 50 quality metrics related to accessibility, intrinsic, trust, dynamicity and contextual dimension coategories [27]. For example, contextual category includes: completeness, amount-of-data, relevancy. Due to the fact that DBpedia is one of the biggest representatives of the LOD, quality of Wikipedia infoboxes can be determined through an evaluation of the following measures: completeness, validity, timeliness and others. The completeness can be connected with the analysis of the filled parameters in infobox [27]. Validity of infoboxes may include an analysis of references, including their similarity between different language versions of Wikipedia [28]. Preliminary analyzes have shown that articles that have been assessed by Wikipedia users for high quality do not always have the best quality information in the infobox in a given language version. Further experiments have shown a correlation between some quality metrics of articles and infoboxes. Figure 2 shows correlation matrix of quality measures of infoboxes and articles in selected language.

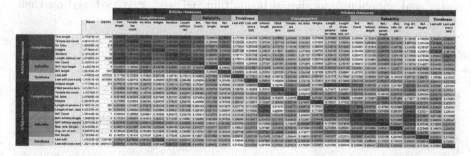

Fig. 2. Correlation matrix of articles and infoboxes quality measures in selected language topic. Source: own calculations.

An assessment of the quality of the infoboxes for each topic will allow you to select those language versions where the data has the best quality. In consequence that can help to improve the quality and enrich other Wikipedia language versions.

4   Comparing and Enrichment of Information in Wikipedia

An analysis of current approaches in assessing the quality of information in wiki sites shows that further research to develop new methods are required. The results obtained by using such methods may allow to more accurate assessment of the quality of information in wiki sites in different languages and thus help to improve their quality.

One of the good examples of such researches is Sieve framework, which is used to increase completeness, conciseness and consistency of Linked Oped Data [26]. However, in case of Wikipedia infoboxes it is necessary to take into account additional quality dimensions for more objective analysis [27].

In situations where none of the considered language versions have an infobox, special tools can be used to extract the necessary facts from the text of the article [29] with the best quality. In addition, other approaches for gathering knowledge from semi- and unstructured content can be used [30].

It is also possible that the described subject in Wikipedia has different infoboxes in the examined language versions. This is connected to the fact that Wikipedia communities tend to structure the articles and infoboxes in different ways. In this case cross-language can be exploited cross-language links to represent each infobox with parameters extracted from the corresponding articles [31].

The future researches will address the issue of evaluating the quality of information contained in wiki pages by developing an authoritative method for comparing and enriching information in multilingual wiki services based on their quality analysis.

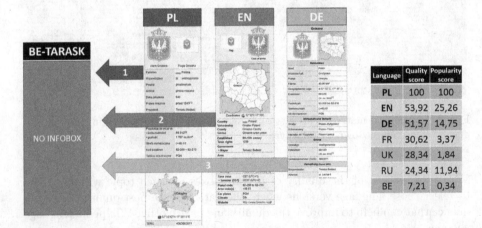

Fig. 3. Scheme of information enrichment of Wikipedia infobox based on quality and popularity assessment of other language versions on an example of a Gniezno city. Source: own calculations.

The developed method will then be evaluated on the basis of actual data from seven language versions of Wikipedia: English (EN), German (DE), French (FR), Russian (RU), Polish (PL), Ukrainian (UK), Belarusian (BE). One of the important metrics, which will be taken to the account is popularity of article, which contain the analyzed infobox. We can expect more relevant and verified information in articles, where the infobox is regularly reviewed by the bigger number of users. Figure 3 shows the general scheme of enrichment of information of infoboxes from the most popular language versions with the best quality score to Belarusian Wikipedia with classical orthography (BE-Tarask). In case when the information from the best language version is insufficient, other parameters will be transferred from other versions with high quality and popularity score. Before transferring values of particular parameters, information will be compared to other language versions, but versions with higher quality will have higher influence (weight) on decision making process on selecting the right value.

Table 1. Number of overlapping articles across language versions of Wikipedia. Source: own calculations in May, 2017.

	BE	DE	EN	FR	PL	RU	UK
BE	**143 105**	66 673	74 765	67 097	73 012	95 871	79 536
DE	66 673	**2 058 152**	1 045 390	704 217	489 443	492 078	275 593
EN	74 765	1 045 390	**5 405 997**	1 186 508	756 724	723 090	380 539
FR	67 097	704 217	1 186 508	**1 867 289**	550 315	519 651	313 706
PL	73 012	489 443	756 724	550 315	**1 220 272**	429 944	297 109
RU	95 871	492 078	723 090	519 651	429 944	**1 392 818**	401 051
UK	79 536	275 593	380 539	313 706	297 109	401 051	**694 670**

Volume for creating new Wikipedia articles based on other language versions can be assessed from the Table 1, which presents the numbers of overlapping articles across language versions of Wikipedia. Despite the fact that the English

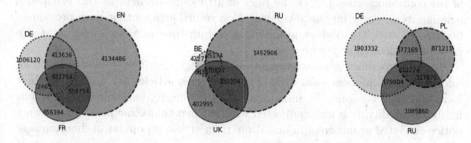

Fig. 4. Overlaps of articles between selected language versions of Wikipedia. Source: own calculations in May, 2017.

version of Wikipedia is the largest, it can also be enriched by other language versions.

While the Table 1 contains information on the coverage of articles between pairs of languages, the Fig. 4 shows the coverage between the triples of selected Wikipedia language versions using a Venn diagram.

5 Discussion and Future Works

The purpose of the proposed research is to develop a method of comparing and enriching information in multilingual wiki services based on their quality analysis on the example of Wikipedia. The proposed method differs from the approaches used so far in several respects. Firstly, in the past work, quality analysis was carried out mainly in one language version - mostly for English Wikipedia. Some metrics that can be considered when building article quality models are dependent on the language in which these articles are written. This includes also linguistic measures. Secondly, there is no study that would automatically assess the quality of the Wikipedia article selected in various language versions. It is related also on differences in evaluation systems used in each language version of Wikipedia. Thirdly, the current works focused mainly on the quality of the whole article, not on the particular elements of it - such as infobox. Preliminary studies show that not always the article with the highest grade among other languages also has infobox with the best data quality in a given language version.

In addition, most research uses a set of metrics to build quality models of Wikipedia articles. The selection of some of these metrics depends on the language, some on the data source, some on the extraction method. An additional factor is the development of wiki technology, which gives you the ability to extract new metrics. This means that extracting and combining multiple metrics based on literature and own experiments may allow a more objective and comprehensive approach to the analysis of the quality of Wikipedia articles in different languages.

Another issue is the constant updating and creating of new wiki pages, on the basis of which Wikipedia article quality models are built. The time factor is important not only because of the varying number of articles, but also because of the continuous changing of the rules of articles assessment by the Wikipedia community in every language version. As a result, articles that have previously been rated with the highest grade for a certain time may no longer meet the criteria and lose their featured status.

Initial experiments showed, that in language sensitive topics, quality of information in infoboxes are high. Typically, such articles are popular in their local language versions. So, measurement of popularity can help in assessment infoboxes quality. It is also connected with the fact that some part of users may notice outdated or incorrect information. If an article is popular in this language - then this corrects can happen faster.

In addition, auxiliary targets are defined that contribute to the main objective:

1. Develop a method for automatically evaluating wiki pages in different languages using appropriate metrics
2. Developing a method for comparing the quality of infobox and wiki page quality
3. Developing a method for identifying high quality infobox elements from wiki pages in different language versions
4. Developing a method of enriching infoboxes between wiki language versions using semantic representation of elements of these infoboxes.
5. Developing a method for creating a new page in a specific language with selected high-quality infobox elements from other language versions of the wiki.

References

1. Hodel-Widmer, T.B., Dittrich, K.R.: Concept and prototype of a collaborative business process environment for document processing. Data Knowl. Eng. **52**(1), 61–120 (2005)
2. Oeberst, A., Cress, U., Back, M., Nestler, S.: Individual versus collaborative information processing: the case of biases in Wikipedia. In: Cress, U., Moskaliuk, J., Jeong, H. (eds.) Mass Collaboration and Education. CCLS, vol. 16, pp. 165–185. Springer, Cham (2016). doi:10.1007/978-3-319-13536-6_9
3. Staub, T., Hodel, T.: Wikipedia vs. academia: an investigation into the role of the internet in education, with a special focus on Wikipedia. Univ. J. Educ. Res. **4**(2), 349–354 (2016)
4. Callahan, E.S., Herring, S.C.: Cultural bias in wikipedia content on famous persons. J. Am. Soc. Inform. Sci. Technol. **62**(10), 1899–1915 (2011)
5. Bao, P., Hecht, B., Carton, S., Quaderi, M., Horn, M., Gergle, D.: Omnipedia: bridging the Wikipedia language gap. In: Proceedings of the SIGCHI Conference on Human Factors in Computing Systems, pp. 1075–1084. ACM (2012)
6. Węcel, K., Lewoniewski, W.: Modelling the quality of attributes in Wikipedia infoboxes. In: Abramowicz, W. (ed.) BIS 2015. LNBIP, vol. 228, pp. 308–320. Springer, Cham (2015). doi:10.1007/978-3-319-26762-3_27
7. Stvilia, B., Twidale, M.B., Smith, L.C., Gasser, L.: Assessing information quality of a community-based encyclopedia. In: Proceedings of the ICIQ, pp. 442–454 (2005)
8. Blumenstock, J.E.: Size matters: word count as a measure of quality on Wikipedia. In: WWW, pp. 1095–1096 (2008)
9. Warncke-Wang, M., Cosley, D., Riedl, J.: Tell me more: an actionable quality model for Wikipedia. In: WikiSym 2013, pp. 1–10 (2013)
10. Anderka, M.: Analyzing and predicting quality flaws in user-generated content: the case of Wikipedia. Ph.D., Bauhaus-Universitaet Weimar Germany(2013)
11. Lipka, N., Stein, B.: Identifying featured articles in Wikipedia: writing style matters. In: Proceedings of the 19th International Conference on World Wide Web, pp. 1147–1148 (2010)

12. Horn, C., Zhila, A., Gelbukh, A., Kern, R., Lex, E.: Using factual density to measure informativeness of web documents. In: Proceedings of the 19th Nordic Conference of Computational Linguistics (NODALIDA 2013), 22–24 May 2013, Oslo University, Norway. NEALT Proceedings Series 16, vol. 085, pp. 227–238. Linköping University Electronic Press (2013)

13. Khairova, N., Lewoniewski, W., Węcel, K.: Estimating the quality of articles in russian wikipedia using the logical-linguistic model of fact extraction. In: Abramowicz, W. (ed.) BIS 2017. LNBIP, vol. 288, pp. 28–40. Springer, Cham (2017). doi:10.1007/978-3-319-59336-4_3

14. Lex, E., Voelske, M., Errecalde, M., Ferretti, E., Cagnina, L., Horn, C., Stein, B., Granitzer, M.: Measuring the quality of web content using factual information. In: Proceedings of the 2nd Joint WICOW/AIRWeb Workshop on Web Quality - WebQuality 2012, p. 7 (2012)

15. Wu, G., Harrigan, M., Cunningham, P.: Characterizing Wikipedia pages using edit network motif profiles. In: Proceedings of the 3rd International Workshop on Search and Mining User-Generated Contents, pp. 45–52. ACM (2011)

16. Velázquez, C.G., Cagnina, L.C., Errecalde, M.L.: On the feasibility of external factual support as wikipedia's quality metric. Procesamiento del Lenguaje Natural **58**, 93–100 (2017)

17. Lewoniewski, W., Węcel, K., Abramowicz, W.: Quality and importance of Wikipedia articles in different languages. In: Dregvaite, G., Damasevicius, R. (eds.) ICIST 2016. CCIS, vol. 639, pp. 613–624. Springer, Cham (2016). doi:10.1007/978-3-319-46254-7_50

18. Lewoniewski, W., Węcel, K., Abramowicz, W.: Analiza porównawcza modeli jakości informacji w narodowych wersjach Wikipedii. In: Porębska-Miąc, T. (eds.) Systemy Wspomagania Organizacji SWO 2015. Wydawnictwo Uniwersytetu Ekonomicznego w Katowicach, pp. 133–154 (2015)

19. Dang, Q.V., Ignat, C.L.: Quality assessment of Wikipedia articles without feature engineering. In: 2016 IEEE/ACM Joint Conference on Digital Libraries (JCDL), pp. 27–30. IEEE (2016)

20. Dalip, D.H., Gonçalves, M.A., Cristo, M., Calado, P.: A general multiview framework for assessing the quality of collaboratively created content on web 2.0. J. Assoc. Inf. Sci. Technol. **68**(2), 286–308 (2017)

21. Färber, M., Bartscherer, F., Menne, C., Rettinger, A.: Linked data quality of DBpedia, Freebase, OpenCyc, Wikidata, and YAGO. Semant. Web J., 3813–3842 (2016)

22. Kontokostas, D., Westphal, P., Auer, S., Hellmann, S., Lehmann, J., Cornelissen, R., Zaveri, A.: Test-driven evaluation of linked data quality. In: Proceedings of the 23rd International Conference on World Wide Web, pp. 747–758. ACM (2014)

23. Mihindukulasooriya, N., Rico, M., García-Castro, R., Gómez-Pérez, A.: An analysis of the quality issues of the properties available in the Spanish DBpedia. In: Puerta, J.M., Gámez, J.A., Dorronsoro, B., Barrenechea, E., Troncoso, A., Baruque, B., Galar, M. (eds.) CAEPIA 2015. LNCS, vol. 9422, pp. 198–209. Springer, Cham (2015). doi:10.1007/978-3-319-24598-0_18

24. Jang, S., Megawati, M., Choi, J., Yi, M.: Semi-automatic quality assessment of linked data without requiring ontology. In: NLP-DBPEDIA@ ISWC, pp. 45–55 (2015)

25. Tacchini, E., Schultz, A., Bizer, C.: Experiments with Wikipedia cross-language data fusion. In: Workshop on Scripting and Development (2009)

26. Mendes, P.N., Mühleisen, H., Bizer, C.: Sieve: linked data quality assessment and fusion. In: Proceedings of the 2012 Joint EDBT/ICDT Workshops, EDBT-ICDT 2012, pp. 116–123. ACM, New York (2012)

27. Zaveri, A., Rula, A., Maurino, A., Pietrobon, R., Lehmann, J., Auer, S.: Quality assessment for linked data: a survey. Semant. Web **7**(1), 63–93 (2016)
28. Lewoniewski, W., Węcel, K., Abramowicz, W.: Analysis of references across Wikipedia languages. In: Proceedings of the Information and Software Technologies: 23rd International Conference, ICIST 2017, Druskininkai, Lithuania, 12–14 October 2017 (2017). doi:10.1007/978-3-319-67642-5_47
29. Lange, D., Böhm, C., Naumann, F.: Extracting structured information from Wikipedia articles to populate infoboxes. In: Proceedings of the 19th ACM International Conference on Information and Knowledge Management, CIKM 2010, pp. 1661–1664. ACM, New York (2010)
30. Schmidt, R., Möhring, M., Härting, R.-C., Zimmermann, A., Heitmann, J., Blum, F.: Leveraging textual information for improving decision-making in the business process lifecycle. In: Neves-Silva, R., Jain, L.C., Howlett, R.J. (eds.) Intelligent Decision Technologies. SIST, vol. 39, pp. 563–574. Springer, Cham (2015). doi:10. 1007/978-3-319-19857-6_48
31. Palmero Aprosio, A., Giuliano, C., Lavelli, A.: Automatic expansion of DBpedia exploiting Wikipedia cross-language information. In: Cimiano, P., Corcho, O., Presutti, V., Hollink, L., Rudolph, S. (eds.) ESWC 2013. LNCS, vol. 7882, pp. 397–411. Springer, Heidelberg (2013). doi:10.1007/978-3-642-38288-8_27

Hazard Index for Assessment of Reliability of Supply and Risk in Maritime Domain

Milena Stróżyna[✉]

Poznań University of Economics and Business, Poznań, Poland
milena.strozyna@ue.poznan.pl

Abstract. The paper presents a method that concerns the problem of determining a hazard level for various maritime areas based on selected risk factors. These factors reflect hazards that may happen on the route of a given ship and thus may potentially influence on reliability of supply and level of maritime risk for the ship. The results of the method can be helpful in a process of planning a ship's voyage as well as when the transport service is already being realized in order to assess its reliability.

The aim of the article is to propose hazards which may be taken into account while assessing the reliability and risk of maritime transport, and present how they can be included in the process of risk assessment in a form of hazard index. The paper presents results for the proposed method, showing how the hazard index is calculated for different maritime areas and its evaluation based on examples of ship's routes.

1 Introduction

In the last years a dynamic development of international supply chains and logistic services has been observed. Along with that, a seaborne trade has started to play a key role in transporting goods, being the backbone of the international trade and the leader in terms of transport economics, safety and reliability of supply.

Another important aspect of realizing maritime transport services is ensuring supply security and risk management. With the growing seaborne trade increases the usage of maritime areas, which in turn leads to the rising number of maritime threats. As a result there emerge challenges and issues such as countering illegal activities at sea like piracy or terrorism, dealing with maritime accidents or a trend to register merchant vessels under the so-called "flag of convenience", which do not assure compliance with international safety and security standards [1].

These maritime threats result in the need to provide security of ships and transported cargo, and to assure appropriate level of supply reliability. This requires assessment of risk based on various risk factors while planning the voyage as well as at the time of transport realization.

Having these challenges in mind, the author proposes a method that concerns the problem of determining a hazard level for various maritime areas based on selected risk factors. These factors reflect hazards that may happen on the route

© Springer International Publishing AG 2017
W. Abramowicz (Ed.): BIS 2017 Workshops, LNBIP 303, pp. 228–241, 2017.
https://doi.org/10.1007/978-3-319-69023-0_20

of a given ship and thus may potentially influence on reliability of supply and level of maritime risk for the ship and its voyage. The obtained results can be helpful in a process of planning a ship's voyage as well as when the transport service is already being realized in order to assess its reliability and risk. Thus, the proposed method is addressed to different users from the maritime domain, since it can indicate potentially hazardous routes and may raise an alarm in case of sailing through dangerous areas.

The aim of the article is to propose hazards which may be taken into account while assessing the reliability and risk of maritime transport, and to present how they can be included in the process of risk assessment in a form of hazard index. The paper presents assumptions for the method, obtained results of the hazard index calculation for different maritime areas based on real data as well as evaluation from the point of view of method's usefulness in supporting a user in decision making and its compliance with maritime threats observed in the reality.

The structure of the paper is as follows: Sect. 2 presents related work. In Sect. 3 a concept of the hazard index is presented, followed by the obtained results (Sect. 4) and evaluation (Sect. 5). The article concludes with a summary.

2 Related Work

In the process of risk assessment of a given maritime route various risk factors can be taken into account. A group of factors, on which we focus in this paper, is geopolitical issues that may influence on security and safety of maritime traffic. The geopolitical factors which were taken into account in other research include inter alia political conflicts/unrest, piracy, hijacking, armed robbery, terrorism, crimes, corruption, civil disorders.

Lam [2] proposed a rough-set approach to marine cargo risk analyses and identified influential risk factors affecting shipping operations. He classified and judged the safety attributes related to marine cargo and vessel. In his research he considered the geopolitical factor that involves the relationships among politics and geography, demography and economies. In particular two sub-factors were included here: (1) Piracy, calculated based on analysis of piracy hijacking incidents, and (2) Political conflicts, such as war and terrorist attacks, including analysis of location of major terrorist hubs. These hazards are also stressed by [3] as one of the potential threats for transported cargo.

Another research, where geopolitical factors were taken into account, is model for assessment of operational reliability of maritime transport system proposed by [4]. In their approach, apart from factors like congestion and weather condition on the route, ships characteristics (age, crew, technological advancement, maintenance and past operational history) and probability of unforeseen events on the route were taken into account. The authors analysed whether a ship is sailing through areas which are prone to danger events such as ship hijacking or capturing, looting, pirate attacks, armed robbery. Also [5] indicate that areas of sailing is an important factor influencing the safety of ship's exploitation, especially areas threatened by piracy. The problem of piracy was addressed also by other research, for example [6–8] and European project PROMERC [9]. The PROMERC project developed a solution for route planning that allows to reduce piracy threat. They analyzed the historical piracy attacks and identified key parameters (ship's and environmental characteristics) which influence on the probability of an attack. These parameters are used to calculate risk of being successfully attacked.

[5] indicates that one of important hazard is phenomenon of registering ships under so-called flags of convenience (FOC). This issue is a danger stressed also by others, e.g. [10]. Nowadays, the majority of merchant vessels are from FOC. FOC refers to countries that offer shipowners competitive costs of registration and ship's service. They mostly don't assure compliance with international safety and security standards [1]. This trend creates a serious issue when it comes to providing protection and security at sea because the FOC ships pose environmental threats and often are engaged in illegal or criminal activities. It results from ineffective or lack of control by the flag states with the open registries. Moreover, their technical failure as well as involvement in maritime accidents is much higher than for ships from OECD countries [5].

3   Hazard Index

Having in mind challenges indicated in previous sections, the author would like to propose its own approach for incorporation of geopolitical factors in the process of maritime risk assessment. In this section, a concept of *Hazard* index is presented that aims at determination of hazard (risk) level for different maritime areas taking into account various geopolitical factors. The proposed *Hazard* index includes 3 types of factors:

1. Maritime Accidents, that takes into account number of maritime accidents which have happened in a given area in the past.
2. Piracy, that takes into account reported accidents of piracy and armed robbery which have happened in a given area in the past.
3. Country Risk, that analyses risk of departure and destination country of a given ship as well as countries the ships is/plans to sailing through during its voyage[1].

3.1   Data Sources

In order to calculate the *Hazard* index various open data sources can be used. In this research data about maritime accidents and piracy attacks has been collected from GISIS database[2]. In the analysis data from the period 2005–2016 were used.

When it comes to calculation of country risk index, the last reports published by three institutions were used: (1) Inter-Agency Standing Committee (IASC)

---

[1] A country means in this case Exclusive Economic Zone belonging to a given country.
[2] https://gisis.imo.org.

and the European Commission [11], (2) the Basel Institute on Governance [12] and 3) The United Nations University (UNU) [13]. Besides, information about the last published classification of flags was acquired from databases of Tokyo MoU Tokyo[3] and Paris MoU[4].

3.2 Maritime Accidents

The first variable, which may influence on the level of risk in a given maritime area, is number of maritime accidents (*Accidents* in short), which have happened there in the past. Although statistics show that number of accidents in the recent years have decreased, the total of accidents in each year is still quite high. In the last 5 years number of accidents amounted to: 436 (2012), 426 (2013), 354 (2014), 297 (2015), 161 (2016) Therefore, the author decided to check, how the accidents were spread out in space, whether it is possible to identify maritime areas which are significantly more prone to accidents, and whether the seasonality in number of accidents can be observed.

In order to calculate *Accidents* measure, the globe has been divided into 7200 sectors (by default sector of $3° \times 3°$[5]). Then, for each sector statistic on number of accidents in a given time period has been calculated.

Moreover, it was tested whether there is a trend or seasonality in occurrence of maritime accidents. For this end, at first a variance analysis has been conducted which has showed that there is a trend in occurrence of maritime accidents (p-value $2.2e-16$) Then, the trend has been eliminated in order to see whether there exists seasonality in particular months of the year. The received results confirm the seasonality of accidents (p-value $= 0.003372$). The results of anova tests are presented in Listing 1

Listing 1. Results of anova test for Accidents

```
## Analysis of Trend for Accidents
## Response: accidents_ts
##             Df Sum Sq Mean Sq F value
Pr(>F)
## r
7 7868.8 1124.12 29.9980 < 2.2e-16 ***
## s        11 1425.9   129.62
3.4591 0.0007138 ***
## Residuals 69 2585.6    37.47
## ---
## Signif. codes:
0 '***' 0.001 '**' 0.01 '*' 0.05 '.' 0.1 ' ' 1

## Analysis of Seasonality
## Response: diff(accidents_ts)
##             Df Sum Sq Mean Sq F value
Pr(>F)
## r[-1]       7   39.0   5.571
0.0691 0.999449
## s[-1]      11 2581.0 234.633
2.9097 0.003372 **
## Residuals 68 5483.3  80.637
## ---
## Signif. codes:
0 '***' 0.001 '**' 0.01 '*' 0.05 '.' 0.1 ' ' 1
```

---

[3] http://www.tokyo-mou.org/.

[4] https://www.parismou.org.

[5] In the presented approach the default value for the size of a sector can be adjusted. It means that all measures can be calculated for both smaller or bigger sectors/areas.

The results of anova were then proved using autocorrelation function (ACF), which also confirmed both trend and monthly seasonality of accidents. Taking into account the results of both analyzes, it is valid to include seasonality in the *Accident* measure. As a result, for each maritime sector a monthly *Accident* measure has been calculated. The measure relates number of accidents in a given month in a given sector to the total number of accidents reported between 2014–2016.

3.3 Piracy

Another important factor which influence on security and safety of shipping is piracy and acts of armed robbery (*Piracy* in short). Its significance can result from statistics on this phenomenon. According to [14] between 2010–2016 there were about 2527 incidents of piracy and robbery worldwide, of which most have occurred in South China Sea, East and West Africa. In these incidents over 170 ships were hijacked, 2504 crew members were held hostage, 127 people assaulted, 87 people were wounded and 22 people lost their lives (more data is presented in Table 1.

Table 1. Regional analysis of cts of piracy and armed robbery in 2010–2016

Location of incidents	South China Sea	Malacca Strait	Indian Ocean	Arabian Sea	East Africa	West Africa	Other	Total
Total number of incidents reported	717	303	262	146	517	375	207	252
Ship hijacked	26	7	14	13	76	40	1	177
Lives lost	3	0	4	4	3	8	0	22
Wounded crew	29	10	3	0	14	25	6	87
Crew hostage	187	46	257	223	1358	426	7	2504
Crew assaulted	36	10	6	0	25	48	2	127

Source: Own work based on data available on [14].

Similarly to *Accidents*, also for *Piracy* maritime areas with high density of this phenomenon were identified including a spread of *Piracy* over time. Firstly, it was tested whether there are trend and seasonality in occurrence of piracy incidents. The conducted anova analysis confirms existence of the trend in the data (p-value $= 3.858e-10$). However, after elimination of the trend it turned out that there is no seasonality in the data (p-value $= 0.4031$). The results of both tests are presented in Listing 2. As a consequence, for each maritime sector, *Piracy* measure has been calculated without differentiation on time periods (seasonality). The *Piracy* measure takes number of piracy attacks in a given sector to the total number of reported attacks in 2010–2016.

Listing 2. Results of anova test for Piracy

```
## Analysis of Trend for Accidents
## Response: piracy_ts
##              Df Sum Sq Mean Sq F value
Pr(>F)
## R
7 8429.4 1204.20 12.3625 3.858e-10 ***
## S           11 1355.0  123.18  1.2646
0.2635
## Residuals 69 6721.1   97.41
## ----
## Signif. codes:
0 '***' 0.001 '**' 0.01 '*' 0.05 '.' 0.1 ' ' 1

## Analysis of Seasonality
## Response: diff(piracy_ts)
##              Df  Sum Sq Mean Sq F value Pr(>F)
## R[-1]         7    95.7  13.671  0.0699 0.9994
## S[.-1]       11  2288.0 208.004  1.0637 0.4031
## Residuals   68 13297.0 195.544
## ----
## Signif. codes:
0 '***' 0.001 '**' 0.01 '*' 0.05 '.' 0.1 ' ' 1
```

3.4 Country Risk

In order to calculate a risk of a country that a ship is sailing through, various aspects can be taken into account, starting from government issues (e.g. regime type, corruption, public transparency), through security of the country (e.g. current and historical conflicts), social aspects (e.g. education) up to economical issues (income level, poverty, unemployment, money laundering) and natural hazards exposure. All these factors compose an overall assessment of a country from the point of view of safety and security. This, in turn, influence on a certainty that shipping through an Exclusive Economy Zone of a country or calling a port located in this country is safe for the ship, its crew and transported cargo.

Determination of country risk is subject of research of various international institutions. They publish their results on regular basis and include a wide scope of information for each analyzed country. In the research presented in this paper, three risk indicators created by different organizations have been selected as a basis for further calculation of *Country Risk* measure. These three indicators include:

- **INFORM** [11] - a risk assessment for humanitarian crises and disasters. It is a transparent tool for understanding the risk and how it affects sustainable development. This measure is a global index, calculated for 191 countries, which takes into account open data published by international organizations. INFORM takes under consideration a wide range of indicators (approximately 50) to measure hazards and people's exposures to them. It creates a risk profile for each country and rates them between 0 (low risk) to 10 (high risk).
- **Basel AML Index** [12] - a risk index regarding money laundering and terrorism financing that takes into account also other related factors such as financial and public transparency, judicial strength. It is published by the Basel Institute, affiliated with the University of Basel.
  Basel index is calculated for 149 countries and the overall score is aggregated from 14 indicators divided intro 5 weighted categories (Money laundering/Terrorist Financial Risk 65%, Financial Transparency & Standards 15%,

Corruption Risk 10%, Public Transparency & Accountability 5%, Political & Legal Risk 5%) and rated between 0 (low risk) to 10 (high risk).
- **World Risk Index** [13] - an index that measures the risk of disaster as a consequence of extreme natural events. It is created by United Nations University's Institute for Environment and Human Security and is calculated for 171 countries.
  It consists of four components: exposure to natural hazards, susceptibility, coping capacities and adaptive capacities, which further include 28 indicators. The results are presented as percentage.

For each of the above-described indicator last published data have been collected. In order to calculate a single *Country Risk* measure, the data had to be transformed. Firstly, the acquired country indexes have been unified to the values between 0 and 1. Then, for each country an average risk index based on the transformed values has been calculated.

Having the average country risk index, additionally information about type of flag for a given country has been included. The type of flag is an important maritime risk factor, but none of the selected indicators takes it into account. The flags are generally divided into three colors: black, grey and white. Classification to each group is based on number of inspections and detentions of ships under a given flag and performance of classification society the ship is affiliated with. The low risk flags are classified as white, while the high risk flags as black.

In order to include the information about type of flag, data published by two well-known Memorandum of Understandings - Paris MoU and Tokyo MoU - have been collected. Figure 1 presents a map with indication of flags' colors, including area of Exclusive Economic Zone (EEZ) of the country.

Information about the flag is included in the *Country Risk* by application of an increasing factor. If a given flag is on black list, the *Country Risk* measure is

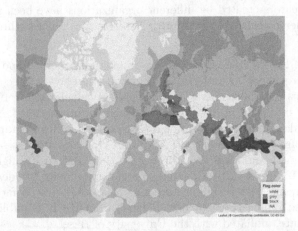

Fig. 1. Colors of flags (Color figure online)

increased by 20%, while for grey list by 10%[6]. As a result, the overall *Country Risk* index is calculated that takes value between 0 (low risk) and 1 (high risk). Figure 2 presents a map with values of the *Country Risk* value for different countries, including EEZ.

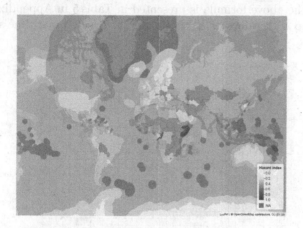

Fig. 2. Country risk map

3.5   Final Hazard Index

In the final step, the overall *Hazard* index for each maritime sector is determined. The value is calculated based on three factors: *Accidents*, *Piracy* and *Country Risk*, and each factor is additionally weighted according to its importance. The weights are subjectively assigned and their value can be adjusted if needed.

$$Hazard(S)_i = \alpha * A(S)_i + \beta * P(S) + \gamma * CR(S)$$
$$where \, \alpha = 0.3, \beta = 0.5, \gamma = 0.2$$
$$A - Accident, P - Piracy, CR - Country \, risk, S - sector, i - month$$

Due to the seasonality of the *Accident* measure, the *Hazard* index is calculated for each time period (months in this case) and for each defined maritime area (sector). Having the value and knowing the route of a given ship (set of sectors a ship plans to sail through), it is possible to estimate the risk for a given ship's route taking into account hazards defined in the index.

4   Results

In this section the results of the *Hazard* index calculation based on the proposed method is presented. As indicated in the previous section, the *Hazard* index

---

[6] Both increasing factors can be changed and adjusted if needed.

has been calculated based on 3 factors: *Accidents*, *Piracy* and *Country risk*. The index was calculated for a given time period (month) as well as for a sector. Table 4 in Appendix A presents values of particular factors, for selected maritime areas and time slots.

The final *Hazard* index calculated for the selected areas and time slots, according to the above formula is presented in Table 5 in Appendix A. Figure 3 presents a map with values of *Hazard* index for selected maritime sectors.

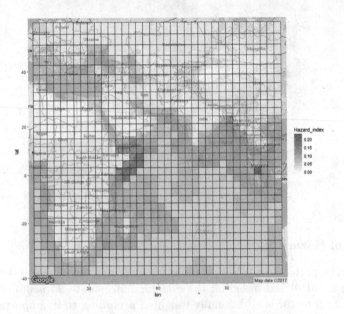

Fig. 3. Hazard index for selected maritime regions.

Having *Hazard* index for particular sectors, we can further obtain the *Hazard* index for a given ship's route/voyage, by calculating an average *Hazard* index for all sectors the ships is sailing through. Moreover, to see the dispersion of *Hazard* level between maritime areas also a standard deviation can be calculated.

5   Evaluation

The *Hazard* index calculation method was evaluated using the FEDS framework, proposed by [15]. For this end, an artificial summative evaluation was conducted. It means that the evaluation has been conducted at end of the development process, without real users/real system in real organizational situations, but included laboratory experiments (using the real data described in Sect. 3.1) and criteria-based analysis. This type of evaluation provide an appropriate rigor in the evaluation, and hence efficacy and reliability of the developed artifact (method) [15].

The criteria which were taken into account in conducting the evaluation include: (1) usefulness of the method in supporting a potential user in decision-making regarding which route to choose for a given voyage, and indicating potential hazardous areas that require a special attention; (2) compliance of the results with what is observed in reality regarding maritime threats.

In order to perform the evaluation, the method was implemented so that, based on the input data on a ship, its planned route and accepted risk threshold, *Hazard* index for a given voyage is calculated. Then, two types of experiments were conducted. First experiment assumes calculation of the *Hazard* index related to the maritime areas a ship plans to sail through in a given time. As a result, the total *Hazard* index for the voyage is calculated and information whether a risk threshold defined as an input is exceeded. The planned route is presented on a map with indication of hazard levels.

In the second experiment, for a given ship two alternative routes to a given destination were planned and using the method a less hazardous route for a given voyage is recommended.

Experiment 1. Below we present results of first type of experiment based on some illustrative example for two selected ships. For each ship, a planned route and travel period were simulated and a risk threshold was defined. In Table 2 and Fig. 4a and b we present the results obtained from the input parameters. Having this information, a user can foreseen potential hazards on the planned route as well as see whether a defined risk threshold is exceeded.

The results were additionally checked by the author for compliance with what has been observed in the reality. In case of ship 1, the method correctly assigned a higher *Hazard* index for regions near Netherlands, what is connected with relatively high number of recorded accidents and higher *Country risk* in comparison to areas near Denmark or Sweden. In case of ship 2, the high *Hazard* index near the coast of Somalia is related to high number of *Piracy* attacks and *Country risk* index.

Table 2. Experiment 1 - results

Ship	Ship 1	Ship 2
Planned route	Rotterdam - Goteborg	Mumbay-Pireneus
Voyage month	April	January
Risk threshold	0.1	0.15
Hazard index for route - average	0.06258315	0.07169936
Hazard index for route - standard deviation	0.0399446	0.03347267
Threshold exceeded	No	Yes (6 sectors)

Source: Own work.

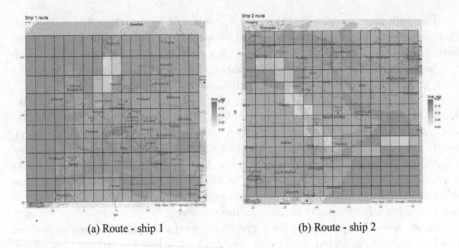

(a) Route - ship 1   (b) Route - ship 2

Fig. 4. Hazard indexes for maritime areas ships are sailing through.

Table 3. Experiment 2 - results

Route	Coega (RSA) - Dubai (UEA)	
Voyage month	June	
Risk threshold	0.1	
	Route 1	**Route 2**
Planned route	Through east coast of Madagascar	Through west coast of Madagascar
Hazard index for route - average	0.04742662	0.05519928
Hazard index for route - standard deviation	0.03269759	0.03121311
Threshold exceeded	Yes (1 sector)	Yes (3 sectors)

Source: Own work.

Experiment 2. The second experiment was conducted based on example for a single ship that plans its voyage and considers two alternative routes. In Table 3 and Fig. 5 we present the results obtained. They show that although both routes go through potentially dangerous maritime areas, the first route, going through the east coast of Madagascar, is less hazardous and requires sailing through less number of dangerous sectors. Having this information, a user that plans the voyage can select a safer route.

The analysis of the results confirms also what is observed in the real world, where countries like Mozambique and Tanzania are noted as more risky than Madagascar. Tanzania is additionally listed as a black flag. There were also cases of piracy attacks.

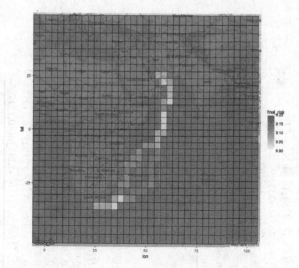

Fig. 5. Hazard indexes for alternative routes from Coega (RSA) to Dubai (UEA).

To sum up, we can conclude that the proposed method for determining *Hazard* index based on three hazard factors has been successfully evaluated, confirming its usefulness and conformance with real observations.

6   Conclusion

Planning and monitoring of a ship's voyage from the point of view of potential maritime threats is nowadays an important topic. However, it requires appropriate methods and tools allowing to quickly perform the risk assessment, also dynamically when a ship is already under way. Information about potential risk and hazardous routes affects various maritime stakeholders, who require such information for decision making.

In the article we propose an approach for determining the hazard index (risk level) for different maritime areas. The presented method takes into account three factors that jointly indicate the hazard level: (1) Maritime accidents noted in a given area, (2) Reported piracy attacks in a given area, and (3) Country risk that reflects the risk of a country the ship is sailing through.

The result of the method is the *Hazard* index that can be further taken into account while assessing the reliability and risk of maritime transport. Thus, it can be used for planning purposes, by supporting maritime users in making a decision which route should be followed by a ship in a given voyage to minimize the potential risk and ensure high transport reliability. The method can also be helpful in the process of monitoring routes being followed by different ships in order to assess whether there is a potential hazard for the voyage and reliability of the transport service being realized.

A   Appendix

Table 4. Accident, piracy and country risk values for selected maritime sectors (areas)

S	$A(S)_1$	$A(S)_2$	$A(S)_3$	$A(S)_4$	$A(S)_5$	$A(S)_6$	$A(S)_7$	$A(S)_8$	$A(S)_9$	$A(S)_{10}$	$A(S)_{11}$	$A(S)_{12}$	P	CR
1502	0,083333	0,166667	0,083333	0,25	0	0,083333	0,166667	0	0	0,083333	0,083333	0	0	0,229789
2731	0,083333	0,083333	0,083333	0	0,333333	0,083333	0	0,083333	0,083333	0	0	0	0,043905	0,579859
3101	0	0,083333	0	0	0	0,083333	0,083333	0,083333	0,166667	0	0,25	0	0,014066	0,608937
3195	0	0	0,083333	0	0	0	0,083333	0	0	0	0	0	0,001279	1
3575	0,25	0,166667	0	0	0	0,333333	0,25	0,25	0,083333	0,083333	0,166667	0,166667	0,174766	0,373646
4317	0	0	0	0,083333	0	0	0,083333	0	0	0	0	0	0	0,70883

Source: Own work.

Table 5. Hazard index for selected maritime sectors (areas)

S	$H(S)_1$	$H(S)_2$	$H(S)_3$	$H(S)_4$	$H(S)_5$	$H(S)_6$	$H(S)_7$	$H(S)_8$	$H(S)_9$	$H(S)_{10}$	$H(S)_{11}$	$H(S)_{12}$
1502	0,070958	0,095958	0,070958	0,120958	0,045958	0,070958	0,095958	0,045958	0,045958	0,070958	0,070958	0,045958
2731	0,162924	0,162924	0,162924	0,137924	0,237924	0,162924	0,137924	0,162924	0,162924	0,137924	0,137924	0,137924
3101	0,128821	0,153821	0,128821	0,128821	0,128821	0,153821	0,153821	0,153821	0,178821	0,128821	0,203821	0,128821
3195	0,200639	0,200639	0,225639	0,200639	0,200639	0,200639	0,225639	0,200639	0,200639	0,200639	0,200639	0,200639
3575	0,237112	0,212112	0,162112	0,162112	0,162112	0,162112	0,237112	0,237112	0,187112	0,187112	0,212112	0,212112
4317	0,141766	0,141766	0,141766	0,166766	0,141766	0,141766	0,166766	0,141766	0,141766	0,141766	0,141766	0,141766

Source: Own work.

References

1. Krzysztof, F., Sokołowski, W.: Środki transportu morskiego w zapewnieniu bezpieczeństwa dostaw gazu ziemnego. Logistyka (5), 401–411 (2012)
2. Lam, J.: Rough set approach to marine cargo risk analysis. In: International Forum on Shipping, Ports and Airports (IFSPA) 2012: Transport Logistics for Sustainable Growth at a New Level, pp. 1–12 (2012)
3. Jarysz-Kamińska, E.: Ocena ryzyka w transporcie morskim. Logistyka (6), 238–246 (2013)
4. Gaonkar, R.S.P., Xie, M., Ng, K.M., Habibullah, M.S.: Subjective operational reliability assessment of maritime transportation system. Expert Syst. Appl. **38**(11), 13835–13846 (2011)
5. Abramowicz-Gerigk, T., Burciu, Z., Kamiński, P.: Kryteria akceptowalności ryzyka w żegludze morskiej. Prace Naukowe Politechniki Warszawskiej. Transport (96), 7–17 (2013)
6. Andler, S.F., Fredin, M., Gustavsson, P.M., van Laere, J., Nilsson, M., Svenson, P.: SMARTracIn: a concept for spoof resistant tracking of vessels and detection of adverse intentions, vol. 7305, pp. 73050G–73050G-9 (2009)
7. Bouejla, A., Chaze, X., Guarnieri, F., Napoli, A.: A Bayesian network to manage risks of maritime piracy against offshore oil fields. Saf. Sci. **68**, 222–230 (2014)
8. Balmat, J.F., Lafont, F., Maifret, R., Pessel, N.: MAritime RISk Assessment (MARISA), a fuzzy approach to define an individual ship risk factor. Ocean Eng. **36**(15–16), 1278–1286 (2009)
9. Patrick, G., Davies, H., Baldacci, A., den Breejen, E.: The Addition of Near Real Time data and Forecast data. Deliverable of ProMerc project (2015). http://www.promerc.eu
10. el Pozo, F., Dymock, A., Feldt, L., Hebrard, P., di Monteforte, F.S.: Maritime surveillance in support of CSDP. Technical report, European Defence Agency (2010)
11. INFORM - Index for risk management. http://www.inform-index.org/
12. The Basel AML Index. https://index.baselgovernance.org
13. World Risk Index. http://collections.unu.edu/view/UNU:5763
14. International Maritime Organization: Global Integrated Shipping Information System. Regional analysis of reports on acts of piracy and armed robbery, On-line database (2014)
15. Venable, J., Pries-Heje, J., Baskerville, R.: FEDS: a framework for evaluation in design science research. Eur. J. Inf. Syst. **25**(1), 77–89 (2016)

Behavioural Profiling Authentication Based on Trajectory Based Anomaly Detection Model of User's Mobility

Piotr Kałużny[✉]

Poznań University of Economics and Business,
Al. Niepodległości 10, 61-875 Poznań, Poland
p.kaluzny.comedian@gmail.com

Abstract. Behavioural profiling and biometry are an interesting concept connected with authentication that have appeared in scientific literature and business world. Those methods indisputably offer new possibilities such as constant authentication and multi-user classification, but their taxonomy and definitions are not as clarified as it is for traditional authentication factors. The approach presented provides in this work provides an example of behavioural authentication model tested on a large dataset, focusing on one aspect of user behaviour - mobility, which can be adjusted to include other aspects in user behavioural authentication model. Also possible applications and extensions to the model are proposed.

Keywords: Behavioural biometry · Behavioural profiling · User profile · Authentication · CDR · Mobility · Trajectory extraction · Stay-time · Anomaly detection

1 Introduction

Due to the ubiquitous nature of the mobile phones, with the current mobile cellular subscription penetration rates achieving more than 97% worldwide [1], phones have became so common that they are considered a basic tool for everyday use. Users everyday patterns are closely resembled in the data their devices produce [2]. Value of this data have risen significantly over the years and the devices indisputably contain a wealth of valuable data [3] including important private information belonging to their owners. Regardless of user perceived value of his/her data, mobile devices need proper protection against unwanted access in cases of theft (of both the device or user identity) and unindented use. Proper authentication techniques and automatic systems are needed to ensure the safety of those devices. Currently used methods work mainly as a point of entry mechanism and do not allow setting privileges for multiple users of the device [4]. They are troublesome to use [5]. Extensive study conducted by Muslukhov et al. in 2013 [6] found, that most users consider the insider threat as important as the stranger threat when considering access to the phone data. It also shows that

© Springer International Publishing AG 2017
W. Abramowicz (Ed.): BIS 2017 Workshops, LNBIP 303, pp. 242–254, 2017.
https://doi.org/10.1007/978-3-319-69023-0_21

more than 12% of the users experienced situations where somebody accessed their data or application on a smartphone without them wanting to. Current authentication methods are limited in dressing those issues, which may be solved by a new family of behaviour based methods.

2   Behavioural Biometry and Profiling in Authentication

The traditional user associating factors consisting of: knowledge, possession and inherence are based on a commonly known model [7] originating from access control systems. Those examples cover methods that are well known, such as: PIN/Password for knowledge factor, fingerprint or face scans representing inherence and token devices used as a possession factor. Unfortunately, regardless of the popularity and availability of those methods about 40% of the phones are still not secured by any means [8].

Reasons for that are multiple, as e.g. biometrical sensors (for fingerprint scanning) are available in only about 28% of the global base of smartphones used [9]. Also, observed user "negligence" in securing their devices can be explained by the usability barrier of the current methods, as frustration connected with passwords is brought as one of the main factors brought in recent surveys. A **recent report** carried out by TeleSign, where **a total of 600** security, risk, and fraud **professionals who are responsible for user authentication in companies with 100 or more employees** expressed their opinions in the questionnaire. The respondents came from many-sectors connected with the IT industry and keen on authentication processes (Computer hardware and software, banking, business services, e-commerce, hospitality, telecoms, social networking and similar services). The results clearly confirm, that the influence of usability reducing factors may be a significant factor in building new methods shown in the Fig. 1.

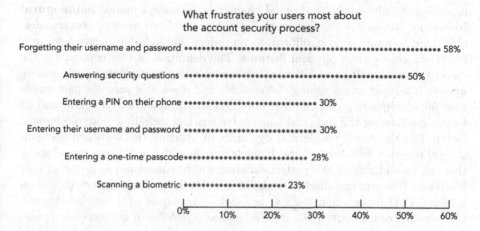

Fig. 1. Findings of TeleSign sponsored report on the causes of frustration during the authorization process. Source: [5]

2.1   Benefits of Using Behavioral Biometry and Profiling

An answer to those traditional means of authentication can be provided by the means of behavioural biometry and profiling. The use of behaviour as a factor in authentication model is a rather new approach. This field covers **what the user does (e.g. patterns, behaviour, contacts)** and is also often mentioned together with time, location or signature aspects. The concept, although not defined clearly, is present in business solutions and scientific literature [5, 10–13].

The use of those methods can provide an **additional layer of security** on top of existing methods **without diminishing the usability**, which can also be confirmed by the above mentioned survey findings [5], especially when they can be used in **multi-factor authentication**. The authentication process utilizing two or more factors is a widely accepted standard in large companies and the adoption of said methods is predicted to achieve nearly 90% [5]. That way, the traditional methods can still be used to e.g. provide PIN, but only when the behaviour analysis system is not sure user about user identity. Adding the behavioural aspect also enables contextual work of many applications based on the profile built, which can improve the overall usability of the device and applications. Usage of those methods, beyond the **constant authentication** process, also allows for **the recognition of multiple users**. With the use of pattern recognition along with the non-binary score/probability based authentication defining different access privileges for different users is possible. This can also be used to **tag data with different sensitivity levels** and allow access based on the method output.

2.2   Definitions

Regarding the above mentioned behavioural factors, a family of concepts can be described. Similar to the traditional biometrics, a concept named **behavioural biometry** [10] covers the factors that can be considered unique, non transferable, hard to forget or lose, difficult to reproduce and hide but derive from user behaviour rather than physical features. The definition of this concept for the use of this work will be as follows: *Any readable and processable representation of user behaviour which exhibits identifiable and repeatable patterns that can be used for identification and authentication.* As an example the stylometry and all factors considering the style and language of writing, including more mechanical factors like the touch profile and dynamics of utilizing the keyboard are considered together as a behavioural biometrics example. Each distinctive element that can be understood as a pattern-creating will be considered an aspect of user behaviour (like e.g. mobility). The definition of a **behaviour aspect** (based on a recent PhD dissertation [14]) is as follows: *An aspect of a user's behaviour is a smaller component of the user behaviour which has a capture-able (quantifiable) regularity, and where deviations from this regularity are indicators of anomalous behaviour.* Taxonomy of methods connected with this concept vary, whether placing it as a part of traditional biometry [10, 11] or something inbetween knowledge and inherence factors [12]. Nonetheless, most of the researchers

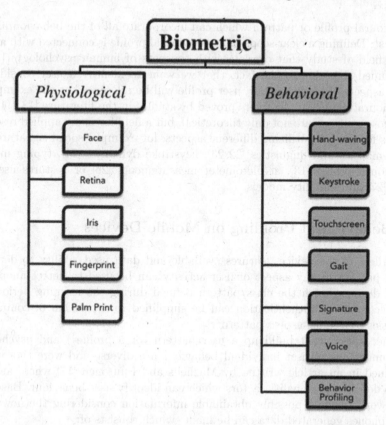

Fig. 2. Simple description of concepts used in user authentication with focus on the taxonomy of behavioural profiling. Source: [11]

agree on a similar model [11,15]. The basic biometry as we understand it, can be divided into two: physiological and behavioural. The former incorporates concepts which cover traditional biometrical features and methods e.g. fingerprint or iris recognition. The latter describes all of the concepts that can include user specific content, besides the traditional biological user specific features. That field incorporates methods studying: Gait and Signature recognition, Voice verification, Keystroke dynamics and behavioural or linguistic profiling. A simple representation of proposed taxonomy of methods is shown in the Fig. 2.

Within those methods exists a subgroup, referred to as **behavioural profiling**, which: *identifies people based upon the way in which they interact with the services of their mobile device* [16] and the user's identity is determined based upon the comparison of activity sample with their profile. If the sample matches, the user will be granted access, otherwise they will be refused [15] or an additional proof of identity need to be brought (e.g. PIN). This taxonomy leaves the name of the aggregated profile quite ambiguous: as the features derived from user specific way of interaction with the phone can be aggregated to a user behavioural profile or pattern which can incorporate all of the behavioural biometrics[1]. Defining a clear scope of a behavioural profile is connected with a very broad field of study that overlaps with concepts of human psychology [17]. It is assumed that due to the fact, that we want to identify a user considering many aspects of his behaviour, user profile will be referenced as the example of behavioural biometry identifier (proved by studies in the literature [18,19]).

Those concepts are not only theoretical, but a field for many applied research studies focusing on utilizing different aspects, for example: social signature [20, 21], semantics and linguistics [22,23], keystroke dynamics [24], typing motion [25], touch profile [13], accelerometer measurements [26] or gestures used by users [27] and mobility models.

3   Behavioural Profiling on Mobile Devices

Regardless of the device, features available and data used, ability to detect a stable pattern in any aspect of user activity can be used to detect anomalies which do not match the class/pattern defined during the learning period. As an effect of this, authentication can be simplified to a problem of comparing activities to a multi-aspect pattern[2].

The aspects that build up a user pattern (or a profile[3]) and psychological foundations of user individual behaviour are diverse and were thoroughly explained in an article written by Mazhelis and Puuronen [17] where authors try to describe personality factors which can identify user behaviour. Based on their work a list of possibly obtainable information considering the nowadays smartphones generated data can be made, which consists of:

- Usage of services and its characteristics (e.g. number of SMS sent, time spent online),
- Users way of communication with their contacts (including time required for user to respond to an action e.g. SMS from a friend),
- Movement, locations and routes,
- Time devoted to work/entertainment,
- Way of performing tasks including sequence of actions performed on the device itself (typing, using menus and applications, touch trace),
- Messages content (stylometry, voice characteristics, visited web pages),
- Stability of actions and changes in his behaviour[4].

---

[1] This work focuses on implementing only the behavioural profiling methods based on mobility into a practical authentication framework.
[2] Meaning both the pattern and each activity can be analyzed in multiple dimensions considering eg. geography, time, sequence of actions or semantics of the content.
[3] Those two concepts will be used interchangeably in this work.
[4] This aspect importance is twofold, defining the stability of a given user and his behaviour and enabling the updating of a profile (its evolution) considering the fact that user behaviour tends to change in a long period.

Each of the proposed methods in applied behavioural authentication scenario can be based on some sort of a sensor installed on the device. By utilizing multiple sensors and methods there is a possibility of creating a flexible framework that can be added to traditional authentication methods:

- **Increasing the performance of methods without hindering the usability** due to the addition of a new layer of security.
- **Increasing the usability** due to constant authentication and no user interaction required besides questionable cases.
- Allowing for building solutions that **enable multiple user profiles/presets** and multi-user access.
- Enabling the introduction of **different security levels, based on the applications sensitivity and the value of the data stored**.

3.1 Results of Current Authentication Approaches

Utilizing simple statistical methods [28] based on probability of features occurrences (phone calls, sms) showcased results not worse than complicated machine learning approaches in this field. Simple mathematical formula was able to address most of the issues and consider fast event-based detection achieving user authentication EER of 5.4%, 2.2% for the telephony and text messaging activities. These results were provided by using a 14 days dynamic time window [19] for profile creation which even solved the problem of profile evolution and updating. Another example, showcasing the influence of data sampling frequency on method results can be seen in a recent model [8]. Researchers collected the data from 200 of android devices over the period of 30 days (sharing the common geographical features being students and employees of Drexel University). It included: text typed, apps used, websites visited and location. Then a binary classifier was constructed for all four of the modalities trained on all data available (1 user data against 199 not valid datasets). What is important to note, is that the time period of provided data required to perform the classification was addressed. The results have shown that regularly sampled geographical data contributed the most to the overall model. The model achieved EER of 5% after one minute and 1% after 30 min for binary activity-user classification. They proved that classification on a single GPS coordinate is sufficient to correctly verify the user with an FAR of under 0.1 and an FRR of under 0.05. This proves, that the granularity and frequency of data gathering is the main factor influencing the methods results.

3.2 Mobility as a Behavioural Authentication Method

Mobility and its models are an interesting field of study for many researchers, especially considering telecom mobile phone deriving data which have proven to give insight on the characteristics of human movement [29]. When using logs for the analysis of user mobility only very brief moments of his whereabouts are known connected to the calls or other services performed that were handled by

BTS (Base transceiver station). This estimation of location is not ideal, but its accuracy can be measured based on the density of the towers. However it has been proven to be sufficient to perform analysis of human mobility on a small scale focusing on estimating user's visited locations temporal patterns and building his mobility profile [30,31]. The concept of mobility can be used as an aspect for providing an anomaly detection framework. In the literature, approaches deriving from domain specific algorithms are used for this task, including:

- 2006 [32] - Where researchers proposed a theoretical approach tested on self generated data. This approach, based on the list of cells (BTS locations), builds a Markov model utilizing EWMA (Exponentially Weighted Moving Average) mobility tries which are then used to populate a user pattern. Then test cases probability is predicted by the EWMA-based mobility trie. When the probability is less than a threshold Pthr (a design parameter, which the authors tune using entropy), the current activity is identified as anomalous. The drawback of this method is that every location not visited before results in probability equaling zero, regardless if it its close to the user normal are or not.
- 2009 [33] - The comparison of naive Bayesian probability based classifier with Markov Chain approach is used to consider the sequential characteristics of mobility traces. The researchers proposed a similar model for mobility anomaly detection when considering the geo-spatial trace of WLAN devices that considered various interesting areas concerning: the potential oscillations (hand-offs) between locations and possibilities of clustering similar days in the weekly mobility pattern.

Few interesting approaches were identified working on real life datasets which can be seen in Table 1. The results provided may look interesting, but they all work on regularly sampled and small datasets, the use of those models on sparse activity based datasets (like CDR) is not tested - which may prove valuable in evaluating their capabilities. What is also important, is that there are three parameters that greatly influence the results of the model which may differ between approaches:

- Sampling frequency and characteristics of data,
- Time spent for learning the pattern (or create a profile),
- Anomaly detection delay.

The characteristics of mobility data require specific methods due to the spatial, temporal and sequential characteristics of movement. Calculating similarity and distance metrics on trajectories along with the definition of standard area user moves through (done utilizing e.g. SVM) and sequential aspects (which can be covered by MC models) together remains a challenge in current literature. All of the above mentioned methods also consider the 0 probability rule for visiting new locations and do not clear the BTS deriving data of possible hand-off errors. Those conclusions prove that some of the more specific domain based methods considering those characteristics may be more suitable for the analysis of mobility.

Table 1. Table depicting the results of chosen approaches to user pattern differentiation, anomaly detection and authorization. Source: Own elaboration based on sources listed

Title and year	Dataset	Method used	Accuracy
Mobility - based anomaly detection in cellular mobile networks [34]	Own simulated dataset showcasing the graph resembling the cellular mobile network. Call durations are the same for all calls and exponentially distributed with mean value of 3 min. Given fixed call duration, the higher the mobility level, the more the cells traversed in given speed - set between 20 and 60 miles/h for testing purposes	High order Markov model exponentially weighted moving average for updating the profile. Design parameter Δ based on entropy of current trace used for changing the detection threshold. Anomaly detection based on calculating the distance between the current trace and the EWMA-based mobility trie	89% accuracy with 13% FRR
Mobi watchdog: you can steal, but you can't run! [35]	Reality mining dataset - BTS cell id labeled activities from 100 users sampled here every 30 min to showcase CDR granularity level. 30 days used to train the model and 30 for testing the performance	HHMM (hierarchical hidden Markov model). Decision is made after τ (design parameter) consecutive activities have been found anomalous (parameter in the model). Working authentication software raising alerts by requesting the device holder to re authenticate himself when an observed mobility trace significantly deviates from the trained model	Accuracy above 90%, for similar users between 50% and 70%. FRR about 13% for one anomalous activity window and 9% when using 3 activities
Efficient location aware intrusion detection to protect mobile devices [36]	Geo life dataset - GPS trajectories from 178 users with about 5 s sampling. Reality mining dataset - 68 users chosen with an average 2.5 min sampling. 100 sample batches of x (5, 15, 30, 60 min) used for testing	Trajectory based mobility model on frequently visited locations with 30 min stay time and confidence interval of 90% for anomaly detection (accepting 90% of the user's normal behaviour based on the trace samples). Zero probabilities for visiting new locations	94% Accuracy in anomaly detection with FRR <= 10% within 15 min - about 6 activities
Active authentication for mobile devices utilising behaviour profiling [16]	Reality mining dataset - 76 users chosen. RBF tested on 20 users with the dataset length divided on two halves	Differentiating between user patterns (is this user who he appears to be based on all of the others data). 7/10/14 used for learning, smoothing function applied to the tested activities for anomaly detection - up to 6	Best results - 9.8% EER with 10 days learning period and 6 activities smoothing. RBF neural network achieved 10,5% EER. Rule based approach - statistical occurrences 11% EER

4   Experient - Trajectory Based Models in Behavioural Authentication Scenario

To confirm that models of behavioural authentication can work on a large scale, an experiment (described in a master thesis [37]) was performed that utilized trajectory based model to build a behavioural authentication framework. The steps of this approach were as follows:

– The trajectory based model based on stay time extraction was provided that allowed for a representation of user's mobility,

- An approach for defining anomalous behaviour in **three main dimensions was proposed, including: geography, time and sequence,**
- Based on those measures, tests were run on a large scale sample of Poznan inhabitants - which were chosen based on important places identification approach [38]. The data was extracted from a BTS labelled CDR database consisting of more than 7 billion records describing the telecom activity of Orange S.A. clients in Poland over 6 months between February and July 2013,
- Instead of testing the user activities against a randomly chosen user, an approach based on classes, showcasing different levels of mobility similarity to the tested person's profile was applied[5],
- The model was successful in detecting in a short timespan of three activities batch length[6] and a month of learning data, with results presented in Table 2.

Table 2. Table showcasing the results of anomaly detection method with the use of 3 activities batch length. Source: Own work based on Poznan users data

	Value S_1	Value S_2	Value I_1	Value I_2	Value I_3
Approach	Static 90'th percentile		Iterative		
% of users rejected due to the unstable pattern	7%		0.8%		
Number of measures needed to classify an anomaly	1	2	1	2	3
Results					
Class	Measure (% of anomalies classified in)				
Random class	99,33%	85,16%	99,58%	99,57%	97,17%
Same town class	88,50%	72,32%	96,65%	**91,63%**	70,84%
Same home location class	60,40%	44,18%	70,17%	53,64%	37,29%
Same home and work location class	43,80%	26,04	53,21%	32,03%	20,09%
Same user class (FRR)	20,80%	8,83%	32,68%	**13,79%**	6,33%

The model was tested on a large sample of CDR telecom data and provided to be effective in dealing with sparse datasets. To classify whether tested activity is an anomaly model tests the observed values (between 0–1) for each batch of the activities. If at least one of them exceeds confidence interval for target threat, model marks this activity as an anomaly in this dimension. The confidence intervals (thresholds) were set as a 90'th percentile of the observed target threat in the validation phase. Whether one or more scores need to exceed the threshold to classify activity as an anomaly is a parameter in proposed model, influencing the FRR and accuracy ratio. To increase the method performance, an improvement was tested that decreased the values of thresholds iteratively by one percentile below 90 for the users that had too unpredictable patterns. This is showcased by the models with I identifier[7].

---

[5] Inspired by security domain informed/uninformed attacker scenario [39].

[6] Meaning the classification of anomaly was performed based on three consecutive activities.

[7] As in iterative.

Results prove that behavioural authentication is possible to be used even on a sparse dataset of CDR[8]. The results of the anomaly detection were satisfying in differentiating between users and the model was proven to be effective in detecting the possible theft scenarios - as presented by the same town class anomaly accuracy. The unpredictability of user movement - captured by the FRR was similar to the studies in the literature, based on the Table 1. Considering the results of the model, it achieved **about 97% accuracy, with the FRR staying close to 6% which presents a comparable method effectiveness.**

What is really more interesting, is showcased with the use of 2 measures for defining the anomaly. While increasing the FRR, we can achieve significant level of accuracy in theft scenario anomaly detection (same town class) while observing an acceptable false alarms ratio considering the sparsity of data source. This emphasizes the need to consider the movement dimensions for proper anomaly classification in those scenarios which could be useful for further studies. The modular design of the model, allows to change the measures used e.g. geographical measure to a SVM model based on coordinates if it would provide better overall result in the classification.

Differentiating between similar users proved to be difficult with the CDR data (same home and home and work class). Utilizing only mobility in this scenario may not be enough to differentiate between users living in close proximity. Nonetheless, the mobility pattern may be of use in a more complicated system utilizing more behavioural factors. The division on anomaly classes allowed to create a benchmark for the mobility based anomaly detection models considering the similarity of users.

4.1 Further Work

After focusing mainly on one aspect of behavioural biometry - mobility, there is still a room for improvement of the model. Developing methods that can better describe **similarity of trajectories** and including **less rigorous thresholds on time aspect** would definitely improve the performance of the model as it was observed during the experiment. Adding a **semantic aspect** on visited places could also improve the model. For example if a user is visiting a grocery store in a constant timeperiod, being in an unobserved location where the grocery store is located should not generate a high level of threat when we consider place semantics.

The proposed model is an example of authentication based only on behavioural profiling. **Extension of the model, working on a device-data based framework is the main focus of the further work also including another aspects like gait recognition, keystroke dynamics or touchscreen interaction profile into the model. User-application interaction model** could also be included as an another aspect of behavioural biometrics providing valuable insights.

---

[8] An average of 4 activities a day for a user on the sample tested.

Aggregating user behavioural data into the framework and allowing the user to chose whether he/she want to share this data with any application is a good introduction into raising user awareness considering the data value and a requirement for respecting user's privacy.

Another case would be studying the benefits of using behavioural profiling in providing **contextualization** to applications, enabling feedback for the used methods. Due to the fact, that current authentication and privileges systems do not fit the users needs, building a complete framework working on a mobile device backed up by a behavioural biometrics system would be a great example of the methods applicability in business.

References

1. Mobile cellular subscriptions (per 100 people) (2014). http://data.worldbank.org/indicator/IT.CEL.SETS.P2?end=2014&start=2014&view=bar. Accessed 19 July 2016
2. Aledavood, T., López, E., Roberts, S.G., Reed-Tsochas, F., Moro, E., Dunbar, R.I., Saramäki, J.: Daily rhythms in mobile telephone communication. PLoS ONE **10**(9), e0138098 (2015)
3. Fox, B., van den Dam, R., Shockley, R.: Analytics: Real-world use of big data in telecommunications. IBM Institute for Business Value (2013)
4. Hayashi, E., Riva, O., Strauss, K., Brush, A., Schechter, S.: Goldilocks and the two mobile devices: going beyond all-or-nothing access to a device's applications. In: Proceedings of the Eighth Symposium on Usable Privacy and Security, p. 2. ACM (2012)
5. Beyond the password: The future of account security (2016). https://www.telesign.com/wp-content/uploads/2016/06/Telesign-Report-Beyond-the-Password-June-2016-1.pdf. Accessed 10 Sept 2016
6. Muslukhov, I., Boshmaf, Y., Kuo, C., Lester, J., Beznosov, K.: Know your enemy: the risk of unauthorized access in smartphones by insiders. In: Proceedings of the 15th International Conference on Human-Computer Interaction with Mobile Devices and Services, pp. 271–280. ACM (2013)
7. Renaud, K.: Evaluating authentication mechanisms. In: Security and Usability, pp. 103–128 (2005)
8. Fridman, L., Weber, S., Greenstadt, R., Kam, M.: Active authentication on mobile devices via stylometry, application usage, web browsing, and GPS location (2015)
9. Market research - biometric smartphone model list (2016). http://www.acuity-mi.com/BSP.php. Accessed 19 July 2016
10. Saevanee, H., Clarke, N.L., Furnell, S.M.: Multi-modal behavioural biometric authentication for mobile devices. In: Gritzalis, D., Furnell, S., Theoharidou, M. (eds.) SEC 2012. IAICT, vol. 376, pp. 465–474. Springer, Heidelberg (2012). doi:10.1007/978-3-642-30436-1_38
11. Alzubaidi, A., Kalita, J.: Authentication of smartphone users using behavioral biometrics. IEEE Commun. Surv. Tutor. **18**(3), 1998–2026 (2016)
12. Crawford, H.A.: A framework for continuous, transparent authentication on mobile devices. Ph.D. thesis, University of Glasgow (2012)

13. Bo, C., Zhang, L., Li, X.Y., Huang, Q., Wang, Y.: Silentsense: silent user identification via touch and movement behavioral biometrics. In: Proceedings of the 19th Annual International Conference on Mobile Computing and Networking, pp. 187–190. ACM (2013)
14. Buthpitiya, S.: Modeling mobile user behavior for anomaly detection (2014)
15. Saevanee, H., Clarke, N., Furnell, S., Biscione, V.: Continuous user authentication using multi-modal biometrics. Comput. Secur. **53**, 234–246 (2015)
16. Li, F., Clarke, N., Papadaki, M., Dowland, P.: Active authentication for mobile devices utilising behaviour profiling. Int. J. Inf. Secur. **13**(3), 229–244 (2014)
17. Mazhelis, O., Puuronen, S.: A framework for behavior-based detection of user substitution in a mobile context. Comput. Secur. **26**(2), 154–176 (2007)
18. Boukerche, A., Notare, M.S.M.A.: Behavior-based intrusion detection in mobile phone systems. J. Parallel Distrib. Comput. **62**(9), 1476–1490 (2002)
19. Li, F., Clarke, N., Papadaki, M., Dowland, P.: Behaviour profiling for transparent authentication for mobile devices (2011)
20. Saramäki, J., Leicht, E.A., López, E., Roberts, S.G., Reed-Tsochas, F., Dunbar, R.I.: Persistence of social signatures in human communication. Proc. Nat. Acad. Sci. **111**(3), 942–947 (2014)
21. Gosnell, D.K.: Social fingerprinting: identifying users of social networks by their data footprint (2014)
22. Saevanee, H., Clarke, N., Furnell, S., Biscione, V.: Text-based active authentication for mobile devices. In: Cuppens-Boulahia, N., Cuppens, F., Jajodia, S., Abou El Kalam, A., Sans, T. (eds.) SEC 2014. IAICT, vol. 428, pp. 99–112. Springer, Heidelberg (2014). doi:10.1007/978-3-642-55415-5_9
23. Brocardo, M.L., Traore, I., Woungang, I.: Toward a framework for continuous authentication using stylometry. In: 2014 IEEE 28th International Conference on Advanced Information Networking and Applications, pp. 106–115. IEEE (2014)
24. Karnan, M., Akila, M., Krishnaraj, N.: Biometric personal authentication using keystroke dynamics: a review. Appl. Soft Comput. **11**(2), 1565–1573 (2011)
25. Gascon, H., Uellenbeck, S., Wolf, C., Rieck, K.: Continuous authentication on mobile devices by analysis of typing motion behavior. In: Sicherheit, pp. 1–12. Citeseer (2014)
26. Primo, A., Phoha, V.V., Kumar, R., Serwadda, A.: Context-aware active authentication using smartphone accelerometer measurements. In: Proceedings of the IEEE Conference on Computer Vision and Pattern Recognition Workshops, pp. 98–105 (2014)
27. Li, L., Zhao, X., Xue, G.: Unobservable re-authentication for smartphones. In: NDSS (2013)
28. Hilas, C.S., Sahalos, J.N.: User profiling for fraud detection in telecommunication networks. In: 5th International Conference on Technology and Automation, pp. 382–387 (2005)
29. Isaacman, S., Becker, R., Caceres, R., Kobourov, S., Martonosi, M., Rowland, J., Varshavsky, A.: Ranges of human mobility in Los Angeles and New York. In: 2011 IEEE International Conference on Pervasive Computing and Communications Workshops, PERCOM Workshops 2011, pp. 88–93 (2011)
30. Liu, F., Janssens, D., Cui, J., Wang, Y., Wets, G., Cools, M.: Building a validation measure for activity-based transportation models based on mobile phone data. Expert Syst. Appl. **41**(14), 6174–6189 (2014)
31. Çolak, S., Alexander, L.P., Alvim, B.G., Mehndiratta, S.R., González, M.C.: Analyzing cell phone location data for urban travel: current methods, limitations, and opportunities. Transp. Res. Rec.: J. Transp. Res. Board **2526**, 126–135 (2015)

32. Sun, B., Chen, Z., Wang, R., Yu, F., Leung, V.C.: Towards adaptive anomaly detection in cellular mobile networks. In: The IEEE Consumer Communications and Networking Conference, vol. 2, pp. 666–670 (2006)
33. Tandon, G., Chan, P.K.: Tracking user mobility to detect suspicious behavior. In: SDM, pp. 871–882. SIAM (2009)
34. Sun, B., Yu, F., Wu, K., Leung, V.: Mobility-based anomaly detection in cellular mobile networks. In: Proceedings of the 3rd ACM Workshop on Wireless Security, pp. 61–69. ACM (2004)
35. Yan, G., Eidenbenz, S., Sun, B.: Mobi-watchdog: you can steal, but you can't run!. In: Proceedings of the Second ACM Conference on Wireless Network Security, pp. 139–150. ACM (2009)
36. Yazji, S., Scheuermann, P., Dick, R.P., Trajcevski, G., Jin, R.: Efficient location aware intrusion detection to protect mobile devices. Pers. Ubiquit. Comput. 18(1), 143–162 (2014)
37. Kałużny, P.: Evaluation of trajectory based mobility profile in user behavioral authentication based on telecom data. Master thesis, Poznań University of Economics and Business, Poznań (2017)
38. Jankowiak, P., Kałużny, P.: Human mobility profiling based on call detail records analysis. Bachelor thesis, Poznań University of Economics and Business, Poznań (2015)
39. Kayacik, H.G., Just, M., Baillie, L., Aspinall, D., Micallef, N.: Data driven authentication: on the effectiveness of user behaviour modelling with mobile device sensors. arXiv preprint: arXiv:1410.7743 (2014)

Social Media – Profiling Users Movement Trajectory and Visited Places

Agata Szyszko[✉]

Poznan University of Economics and Business,
Ul. Towarowa 55, 61–896 Poznan, Poland
agata.szyszko@ue.poznan.pl

Abstract. The following article is an outline of the author's research on the profiling of social media users based on the places they visit. This is a preliminary research proposal because the author is currently in the first year of doctoral studies. The author in the article presented the reason for interest in social media. The article describes the definition of social media and its characteristics. It also describes some statistics related to mobile users along with a reason to show their importance for future research. In conclusion, the study proposal was described.

Keywords: Social media · User profiling · Trajectory · Geotagging · Geolocation

1 Social Media and Mobile Devices

1.1 Social Media – Definition

Social media is a highly interactive medium that uses widely available and comprehensive communication techniques. Social media is based on network as well as mobile technologies. They change the form of communication and emphasize the role of dialogue [4]. Kaplan and Haenlein [6] define social media as a group of applications which based on Web technology and Web 2.0 technology that allows users to create and exchange user-generated content. The Table 1 illustrates several definitions of social media. Notably, all definitions combine concepts such as communication, social community, creating public image or sharing information/content.

Social media are characterized by [3]:

- large–scale use,
- unrestricted access to create and edit information,
- contributing content accessible to all users,
- dissemination of information by the Internet users.

Characteristics above show that social media has two main functions, which is: information (sharing, extracting and extending knowledge) and social (building online societal relationship).

W. Abramowicz (Ed.): BIS 2017 Workshops, LNBIP 303, pp. 255–263, 2017.
https://doi.org/10.1007/978-3-319-69023-0_22

Table 1. Variety of social media definition.

Definition	Source
Websites and applications, that enable users to create and share content or to participate in social networking	Oxford living dictionaries[a]
Forms of electronic communication (as websites for social networking and microblogging) through, which users create online communities to share information, ideas, personal messages, and other content (as videos)	Merriam–Webster[b]
Websites and computer programs, that allow people to communicate and share information on the internet using a computer or mobile phone	Cambridge dictionary[c]

[a]https://en.oxforddictionaries.com/definition/social_media
[b]https://www.merriam-webster.com/dictionary/social%20media
[c]http://dictionary.cambridge.org/dictionary/english/social-media?fallbackFrom=engl
ish-polish

The popularity and rapid growth of social media enables to gather wide range of information about their users. Social media is readily used by marketers to conduct market analysis which also pursues marketing activities (campaign) [8]. Moreover, entrepreneurs are eager to use this type of media because they are attractive and have great potential for creating extra value for the organization. Social media and its use in the economy has gained particular importance. This is indicative of many studies, meetings and conferences which focus on the development of this phenomenon. Social media significantly and effectively changes many market relationships and ways of functioning businesses [9]. Entrepreneurs are keen to use social media to have a quick and easy contact with their consumers. They analyse the feelings associated with a particular marketing campaign, encourage discussion of branding issues as well as organize contests that engage clients so that they can feel valued and take an active part in brand building [10]. In addition, they can analyse user profiles in terms of their interests, visited places, or demographics (age, gender, etc.) [5].

1.2 Why Mobile Users?

Nowadays people use their smartphones for everything and everywhere. It's like a window to the world. Phone users exploit them during commuting distance, shopping, lunchtime and meals with others, before falling asleep or immediately after waking up. Many people can't imagine a day without a phone, in case if they forget to take the item or misplace it, they may feel uncomfortable, sick, panicked or even desperate [1]. The spectrum of smartphone applications is very broad, ranging from the taking pictures, playing music and watching movies (smartphone can be a handy TV), browsing the Internet, writing and reading e-mails or even using as a car navigation, up to the advanced features related to business [2,7]. Figure 1 depicts statistics of the total number of smartphone users worldwide from 2014 to 2020. It shows that the number of smartphone users increases annually – from 2014 to 2016 for around 0.53 billions users. The analysts predict that in 2020 there will be 2.87 billions smartphone users. The statistics confirm that the smartphone market will still increase and gain in value.

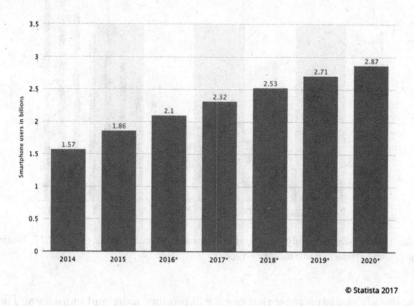

© Statista 2017

Fig. 1. Number of smartphone users worldwide from 2014 to 2020 (in billions). Source: https://www.statista.com

Furthermore, mobile data traffic is uninterruptedly growing. Figure 2 depicts total global monthly data and voice traffic from 2011 to 2017 (every year is divided into quarters). This increasing trend is caused by growing smartphone subscriptions and consequently an average data volume per subscription rises (individual data consumption). Year by year, data traffic increased around 50%, quarter by quarter around 10%. Researchers predict that from 2016 to 2020 global mobile traffic may increase by 8 times (Fig. 3).

The smartphones will generate around 90% of mobile data. It means that mobile users prefer to use mobile phones to browse the Internet or communicate via social networks, watch short videos, listen to music and share files, than tablets or laptops. All data, which is generated by mobile users, can be analysed and give opportunity to understand the reason for the appearance of a particular person in a particular place, profiling users or anticipating its every move. Moreover, users expect from mobile networks that they will adjust to their growing needs, resulting in increased data consumption.

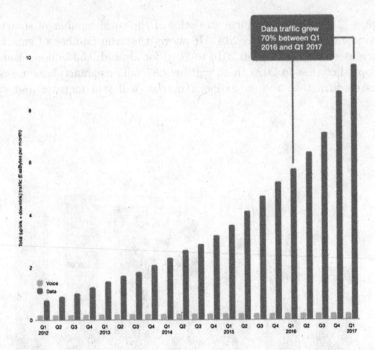

Fig. 2. Total global monthly data and voice traffic from Q1 2012 to Q1 2017. Source: https://www.ericsson.com/mobility-report

Above all, statistics show that users will produce more and more data. Thus, it enables a wider analysis of users profiles, primarily through the social networks. Social networks are still expanding and adding even more sophisticated functionalities to satisfy the needs of users and be competitive on the market. This trend will remain over the next few years.

In social media, users have comprehensive control over the public image creation, ranging from writing posts, adding photos and filling in their profile to sharing articles or videos. On the other hand, people create a (consciously or not) self-image in the way they want to be perceived by others. The main features of social networks are not only sharing photos or adding short text messages, but also adding geographical location to published posts. This annotation user can add manually or automatically based on the GPS location. The place which is marked in post can be defined as landmark.

The dictionaries give varied definitions of the word 'landmark'. It can be a building or an object which is used to depict surroundings to identify a location. In this instance, it could be a natural landmark like park, pond, lake or a static landmark like monuments, museums, operas etc., everything what is easily recognisable. Strikingly different definition of the landmark is an achievement, a discovery or an event (some point in history), which changed a state in the evolution of something or turned history around.

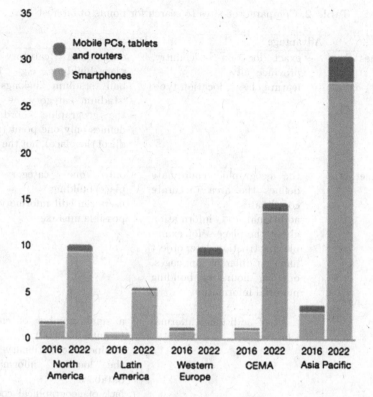

Fig. 3. Global mobile data traffic (ExaBytes per month). Source: https://www.ericsson.com/mobility-report

1.3 Proposed Research

Analysing the trajectory of the user's mobile phones can get information about the place and the time spent in a given location. The source of information about a particular place may be an accurate GPS location. Knowledge of latitude and longitude allows unambiguous determination of the whereabouts of the consumer. Information about the place can be obtained from the POI (point of interest). POI store information about the place name with its coordinates and type, eg. Cinema "Muza" or railway station "Poznań Główny". Additionally, other attributes are included such as contact information, address, reviews, category, etc. There are several websites that have information about a particular place. Each of the services has its advantages and drawbacks (Table 2 shows it). The combination of several sources would be the best solution, for example, geographic coordinates from OpenStreetMap, location information from GeoNames, and additional information (relations with place) from BabelNet.

The main disadvantage of this solution relates to its static form. For example, it does not provide for example the events that occur in the given place. The

Table 2. Compare web sites to search for points of interest

	Advantage	Drawback
GeoNames[a]	– exact location – country, province, city – feature class – location type	– only one category of place/building e.g. football stadium belongs to 'stadium' category – the geographic coordinate defines only one point (middle of the place), not the area
OpenStreetMap[b]	– the geographic coordinate defines the area (accurate coordinates) – additional information about the place – for example construction date, object name in different languages, opening hours or building material information	– only one category of place/building – users can edit information – possible mistake
WordNet[c]	– a lot of additional information	– a small number of entries (around 156 000) – reminds the dictionary than the location information database – lack of geographical coordinates
BabelNet[d]	– exact location – relations with place (stadium is related to football) – additional information – name in different language, photos or construction date	– lack of geographical coordinates

[a]http://www.geonames.org/
[b]https://www.openstreetmap.org/
[c]https://wordnet.princeton.edu/
[d]http://babelnet.org/

best example is the football stadium, which mainly belong to the sport category (football), but it should consider other events that may take place in it, e.g. concerts or sport events other than football. The semantic analysis of these landmarks from social media allows precise identification of user's arrival reasons to a specific location at a particular time. In this case, the main source is Twitter, because developers give access to Twitter's global stream of Tweet data. With the API for Developers, user can get recently added tweets from around the world. Additionally, user can specify restrictions, for example, only posts in English or in a definitive country, etc.

Statistics above are conducive to this solution, because a growing number of data can precisely define the subject of the research. Smartphone users are actively using social media, because they like to 'notify' friends about where they are and what they do. Figure 4 depicts the chart associated with active Twitter users and the most frequently chosen method to log in to Twitter account. About 80% of people use Twitter on mobile devices. It means that users add the new tweets not only from home or work, where they have access to a desktop PC/laptop, but also from any location.

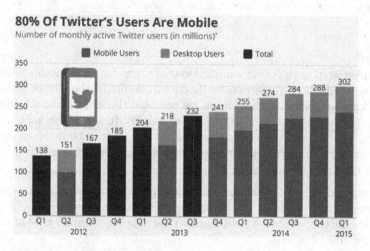

Fig. 4. Number of monthly active Twitter users (in millions) by devices. Source: https://www.statista.com (Color figure online)

The first step is to create a list of landmarks with geographic coordinates, a category to which they belong and the indexes, which would describe in detail the category (Table 3).

The analysis would allow to determine what is happening at a given place and at a given time at a particular landmark. This information can be obtained in two ways:

1. Create the tweets corpus which include the geolocation. It can be used to search for landmarks based on the coordinates from the Table 3. The next step would be to analyse the occurrences of keywords (the categories and the indexes) at different time periods. The increase in the number of individual words means, that at a given moment, in the specific landmark a particular event took place with the probability of XX%.

2. Create the tweets corpus based on the occurrences of keywords, which would be the names of landmarks. Subsequently, analysis of occurrences of keywords (indexes and categories) will be performed as in the previous method.

Table 3. The sample description of landmarks. Source: own elaboration.

Landmark	City	Coordinate	Category	Index
National stadium	Warsaw	N 52° 14.22′ E 21° 02.44′	Sport	Football, speedway, boxing, ice skating
			Music	Ballads, pop, rock, blues, disco, jazz, dubstep, reggae, funk, folk
			Leisure	A science fair, a book fair, skate park, bumber cars, curling
Stary Browar	Poznan	N 52° 24.07′ E 16° 55.35′	Leisure	Shopping
			Arts	Installation art, sculpture, exhibition

The next step is to collect sample tweets corpus for both methods, in order to compare, which of these two methods will result in the higher number of tweets. Another option is that, when we combine the results of both methods, we probably could gain even longer list of results. It should be kept in mind, that some of them may be in both groups, so they should be included once.

Finally, the knowledge about user's visited locations during specific events could be used for (by company):

- Personalised offer – company can receive an extra offer with additional bonuses, directly related to the user's interests, for example: a person, who goes to concerts, could get a discount on the ticket to a similar kind of concerts or group discount.
- Personalised advertising – customer gets only ads, that are related to his/her interests. This would enhance the accuracy of selection of offers appropriate to the customer. Consequently, it would reduce the costs of promotion and increase the probability of accepting the offer by the consumer.

Moreover, another suggestion could be an analysis of sentiment to specific places or events to improve the quality of services offered to consumers. A gathering of tweets related to the particular concert by a well-known musical group or musician, and an analysis of the sentimental/reflection on a given event, would help the event organizers to get a quick and clear view of the people who took part in the event. Feedback from the participants could help in the next organization of similar events and improve them.

2   Summary

This is a very early concept of research. The author is aware that the conceptual framework needs to be clarified. The article presents an idea for research and its vision. The author is at the initial stage of creating a point of interest database and preparing a corpus of data from Twitter.

References

1. Alkis, Y., Kadirhan, Z., Sat, M.: Development and validation of social anxiety scale for social media users. Comput. Hum. Behav. **72**, 296–303 (2017)
2. Chen, C.-Y., Chang, S.-L.: User-orientated perspective of social media used by campaigns. Telematics Infor. **34**(3), 811–820 (2017). Special Issue on Social Media in China
3. Dejnaka, A.: Portale spoecznościowe jako obszar komunikowania się na rynku B2C. Zeszyty Naukowe Uniwersytetu Ekonomicznego w Poznaniu (2011)
4. Dorenda-Zaborowicz, M.: Marketing w social media. Nowe Media. Czasopismo Nauk. **3**, 59–79 (2012)
5. He, W., Liu, H., He, J., Tang, S., Du, X.: Extracting interest tags for non-famous users in social network. In Proceedings of the 24th ACM International on Conference on Information and Knowledge Management, CIKM 2015, New York, NY, USA, pp. 861–870, ACM (2015)
6. Kaplan, A.M., Haenlein, M.: Users of the world, unite! The challenges and opportunities of social media. Bus. Horiz. **53**(1), 59–68 (2010)
7. Kietzmann, J.H., Hermkens, K., McCarthy, I.P., Silvestre, B.S.: Social media? Get serious! Understanding the functional building blocks of social media. Bus. Horiz. **54**(3), 241–251 (2011)
8. Mazurek, G.: Ewolucja wykorzystania mediów społecznościowych w marketingu (2016)
9. Nigel, M., Graham, J., Ant, H.: Social media. the complete guide to social media from the social media guys (2012)
10. Tuten, T.L., Solomon, M.R.: Social Media Marketing. Sage (2014)

Second National Congress
on Information Systems

Second Polish National Congress on Information Systems Chairs' Message

Jerzy Gołuchowski and Witold Abramowicz

The area of information systems and business informatics has been developing at Polish universities for more than 40 years. The researchers from this area are integrated within the Polish Scientific Society for Business Informatics. The goal of this organization is to conduct, initiate, and support research in the field of business informatics and to disseminate the practical application of research results in the economy and society. To this end, the society organizes the congress, whose aim is to promote business informatics among academia, industry, and administration environments, as well as to present the achievements of the leading Polish scientific centers.

The second edition of the congress focused on the topic of "Big Data Analytics for Business and Public Administration" and "Industry 4.0." It provided a forum where researchers can share their work and interact with others participants to receive valuable feedback on their work and find inspiration for further research. The congress was open to researchers and business practitioners from areas concerned with the analytics of large data sets, business processes and social media, management information systems, creative support systems, knowledge technologies, AI as well as education programs and methodology of business informations research.

The congress consisted of a set of events including a keynote speech, a discussion panel, as well as regular and poster sessions. There were 19 submissions. Each paper was evaluated by at least two Program Committee members. The 13 best articles were selected for presentation during the congress. Two presented articles were invited for publication in this volume. After the conference, the authors prepared improved versions of their articles, taking into account new insights and feedback received during the discussion in the sessions.

Overall, the Second National Congress on Information Systems established a valuable platform for presenting and exchanging knowledge of experts from the Polish Scientific Society of Business Informatics.

We would like to thank all the authors who submitted papers to the congress and the members of the Program Committee. We also thank the organizers of BIS 2017 for their effort and support.

Organization

Chairs

Jerzy Gołuchowski   University of Economics in Katowice, Poland
Witold Abramowicz   Poznan University of Economics and Business, Poland

Program Committee

Andrzej Bytniewski	Wrocław University of Economics, Poland
Helena Dudycz	Wrocław University of Economics, Poland
Agata Filipowska	Poznan University of Economics and Business, Poland
Dorota Jelonek	Czestochowa University of Technology, Poland
Jerzy Kisielnicki	University of Warsaw, Poland
Andrzej Kobyliński	Warsaw School of Economics, Poland
Jerzy Korczak	Wrocław University of Economics, Poland
Marian Niedźwiedziński	University of Lodz, Poland
Adam Nowicki	Wrocław University of Economics, Poland
Mieczysław Owoc	Wrocław University of Economics, Poland
Małgorzata Pańkowska	University of Economics in Katowice, Poland
Zbigniew Pastuszak	Maria Curie-Skłodowska University, Poland
Marcin Sikorski	Gdańsk University of Technology, Poland
Zdzisław Szyjewski	University of Szczecin, Poland
Janusz Wielki	Opole University of Technology, Poland
Stanisław Wrycza	University of Gdansk, Poland
Janusz Zawiła-Niedńwiecki	Warsaw University of Technology, Poland

Classification and Preprocessing in the Stock Data

Przemysław Juszczuk[✉] and Jan Kozak

Department of Knowledge Engineering, Faculty of Informatics and Communication,
University of Economics, Katowice, Poland
{przemyslaw.juszczuk,jan.kozak}@ue.katowice.pl

Abstract. In this paper we deal with the problem of assigning classes to the given market situation. We consider approach in which every market situation can be connected with one of the following decision classes: BUY, SELL or WAIT. Each of two classes: BUY and SELL can be assigned only on the basis of significant rises or drops of the given instrument. In all remaining cases WAIT class is assigned. Such approach allows to be independent of indicator values which nowadays are considered to have the significant prediction power. To achieve the goal we selected various stock instruments and with the use of the preprocessing and data discretization we generated decision tables for every considered datasets.

Furthermore, decision trees is built on the basis of generated decision tables. Decision trees are used in the process of classification of newly generated stock data. Presented approach is tested with the use of two independent sets: training set – used to built classifiers – decision classes, and test set – used to estimate accuracy of the generated decision trees. Finally we refer results to other approach in which forex data were used.

Keywords: Stock data · Machine learning · Decision trees · Data classification

1 Introduction

Automatic trading systems are one of the most important concepts used in the trading process with different instruments. Among the popular instruments we mention currency pairs on the forex market, futures contracts, stock instruments, binary options, global funds and more. Role of the human in the decision process seems to be marginalized due to use the concepts like high frequency trading, in which the decisions are made on the basis of complex procedures [4,10]. Other complex approaches include using the neural networks, or novel methods like genetic programming which are used in the process of generating new transaction rules [9], decision support systems based on set of indicators [11] as well as the multiagent systems based on the concept of consensus among agents [13].

Evolutionary computations along with the fuzzy systems are nowadays among the most popular methods allowing to expand the scope of the commonly

© Springer International Publishing AG 2017
W. Abramowicz (Ed.): BIS 2017 Workshops, LNBIP 303, pp. 269–281, 2017.
https://doi.org/10.1007/978-3-319-69023-0_23

used technical analysis indicators and the rule-based trading systems. First group of algorithms include the evolutionary algorithms [8], support vector machines [5], genetic programming [3] and more. Fuzzy systems can be especially useful in the case of the decision support systems [1]. However, for the best of authors knowledge, there is no articles related with the efficiency of above concepts in the case of different data. The most of these methods are used on the forex data, or in the case of selected stock data or whole market indexes [14]. At the same time the process of evaluation of the proposed strategy in the most cases is closely related with the concepts like expected return or maximal drawdown.

We propose methodology allowing to transform every single market situation into the fragment (row) of the decision table, where it will be described on the basis of technical analysis indicators (technical indicators). However the decision related to the particular market situation (BUY – for optimal buy signal, SELL – for optimal sell signal and WAIT – for indecision on the market) is not based on the values of technical analysis indicators, like it is usually solved, but on the price change of the given instrument in the following reading. To be more precise: in the case of significant price growth in the few successive readings this particular situation has the BUY signal assigned. Such approach ensure the sovereignty of the decision class and guarantees that it is not related with the values of indicators.

Crucial element of methodology introduced above will be its ability to estimate the effectiveness of the selected algorithm without need to include rules related with the technical indicators commonly used in the literature. It should be noted, that technical indicators and rules related with them were initially created to the very specific markets or even instruments. Thus it can be expected, that their efficiency with different instruments may differ.

In one of earlier articles [6] authors tested efficiency of such approach in the case of selected currency pairs. According to there previously presented experiments, it seems important, to answer the question, is there visible difference between effectiveness of commonly used machine learning algorithms in the case of different instruments. The research hypothesis given in this article is as follows: effectiveness of the decision tree-related algorithms is related with the type of the analyzed data. To confirm above hypothesis we proposed a novel method to assigning the decision classes to the market situations and we tested this method on the basis of the decision trees-related classifiers. Our results are referred to our previous articles in which we tested the possibility of using the C4.5 algorithm along with the CART algorithm in the process of assigning the decision classes in the case of forex data.

The whole article is divided into three main parts. First part deals with the problem of data acquisition and data preparation. We introduce method, which was used to transform stock data into the decision tables used in the classification process. The simple interval discretization is described as well. Second part of the article presents definitions along with description of algorithms used in the experiments. We focus on two very popular algorithms named CART and

C4.5. Finally, the last part presents detailed experiments conducted on different datasets with 3000 readings each. Results presented in numerical form are discussed and we finally conclude.

2 Methodology and Data Preparation

Stock data in general are exact example of temporal data. A time series may be described as:

$$\Xi = \{\Xi_t : t = 1, 2, \ldots, n\} \tag{1}$$

where n is the number of elements in the time series. Let's denote Υ as the sub-sequence of Ξ, if $\Upsilon = \{\Upsilon_t : t = i, i+1, \ldots, k\}$, and $k < n$. Now, two sub-sequences $\Xi = \{\Xi_t : t = i, i+1, \ldots, j\}$ and $\Upsilon = \{\Upsilon_t : t = k, k+1, \ldots, l\}$ are separable if $\nexists\ \Xi_t$ and $\Upsilon_{t'}$ that $t < t'$. Two sub-sequences Ξ and Υ overlap if $\exists$ Ξ_t and $\Upsilon_{t'}$ that $t > t'$. Every single element of the time series consist of price of the instrument as well as the set of indicators used in the prediction process.

$$\langle Price, Ind_1, Ind_2, \ldots, Ind_n \rangle \tag{2}$$

where these elements are: price of the instrument and values of the n indicators. We assume, that for a given sub-sequence Ξ with the length of n, the price value at the element Ξ_n can be determined on the basis of indicator values in the element Ξ_1. To be more specific: on the basis of the historical data for selected stock assets we have separated time series, with different length. For each time series we selected smaller sub-sequences, which were used to estimate the potential price movement and connect it with technical indicators values. The illustrative example of this method is presented on the Fig. 1.

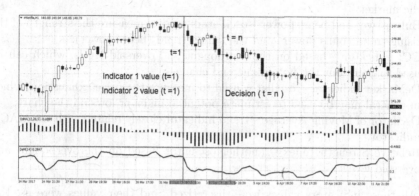

Fig. 1. Decision table creation on the basis of the time series

Indicator values are acquired from the chart in the time $t = 1$. Eventually, after n readings a decision related with these values is assigned on the basis of price movement.

In the first step of acquiring the data, a Υ which is sub-sequence of Ξ is selected. Moreover, cardinality of Υ is significantly smaller than the cardinality of Ξ. A first element of the sub-sequence Υ is selected and values of technical indicators are saved. In the second step of the procedure we assign one of the following decisions: BUY, SELL or WAIT to the values of technical indicators. We consider three possible scenarios:

- price of the asset increased during the sub-sequence Υ and the decision is set to BUY;
- price of the asset dropped below initial value observed in the Υ_1 and the decision is set to SELL;
- there is no significant difference between Υ_1 price and the Υ_n price, thus $|\Upsilon_1 - \Upsilon_n| < \epsilon$, where ϵ is initial threshold; and the decision is set to WAIT.

In the above context, both SELL and BUY decisions indicate the significant price movement, while the WAIT decision points to the indecision on the market.

To enable analysis with the use of the classical decision tree learning algorithms we transformed above data into the decision table. Decision table is one of the knowledge representation structures, which can be described as the ordered pair:

$$T = (X, A \cup d), \tag{3}$$

where X is set of all objects – in our case market situations, A will be the set of technical indicator values, and finally d will be the decision assigned to each object in the set X. To simplify our considerations we selected seven different indicators. An initial discretization of all indicators values was also done. Below we give some basic information about selected indicators:

- Standard deviation – indicator used to calculate the statistical volatility of the market;
- Bulls power and bears power – oscillators used to measure the strength of the rising trend (bulls power) and the falling trend (bears power);
- CCI indicator – based on the overbought and oversold levels, which can be used to point out the potential trend changes;
- DeMarker indicator – oscillator used to measure the price exhaustion, which in general may be used to estimate potential highs or lows on the chart;
- Oscilator of Moving Average – trend indicator closely related with the MACD indicator;
- Relative Strength Index – another oscillator based on the overbought and oversold levels.

All these indicators values were discretized, and their values were used as an attributes in the decision table. In the next section we shortly describe three machine learning algorithms used in the experiments section along with different measures of classification, which are especially useful in the case, where number of elements in decision classes is not uniform.

3   Decision Tree Learning Algorithms

As it was mentioned before, we used three algorithms: CART, C4.5 and Random Trees, which were described and used in the case of forex data in the [6]. Readers unfamiliar with basic features of decision trees should refer to [12]. Decision tree is constructed on the basis of the training set data which consists set of objects. In our case a training set was selected as a subset of the set X in the decision table T. Every considered object is labeled with one of the tree initially defined decision classes: BUY, SELL and WAIT. In the case of the decision tree, all nodes (with exclusion of leafs) contain splits – which are different in all considered algorithms. Arcs in the decision tree are labeled with distinct outcomes and eventually leafs in the tree have one single decision class.

The basic model in the case of constructing the decision trees is in general top-down, where an attribute is selected at each step of the algorithm. To simplify, in our methodology we selected algorithms which differ in the sense of the metrics. Random tree approach was used to achieve clear and easily understandable comparison between two classical methods: CART [2] and C4.5 [11]. In the case of the CART we used the classical Gini split criterion which was originally based on the measurement of the random variable concentration:

$$D_t = \sum_{i \neq j} \cdot p(i|t) \cdot p(j|t) = 1 - \sum_i p(i|t)^2 \qquad (4)$$

where: $p(i|t)$ is the probability of decision class i in node t; and eventually the binary classification tree was obtained.

In the case of the C4.5 algorithm a different splitting criterion was selected. In this method, the rule of relative profit calculated for every node was used:

$$Gain(S, A) = Entropy(S) - I(S, A) = Entropy(S) - \sum_i \frac{S_i}{S} \cdot Entropy(S_i) \quad (5)$$

where S is a set of examples and i is the number of subsets.

4   Experiments

Our goal is to compare effectiveness of three presented algorithms in the problem of data classification for different market instruments. We focused on three stock data (each divided into three different datasets). For each of them we used three different algorithms and different efficiency measures. To properly evaluate the efficiency of the proposed approach we compared results with the forex market data – three currency pairs, which were described in details in one of our previous article [6]. All calculations were conducted from the scratch for all considered data. In further part of this section we present short description of the analyzed data and results of conducted experiments. All experiments were conducted for the three algorithms (with default settings): the CART algorithm, the C4.5 algorithm and the Random Tree.

4.1   Data Selection and Preprocessing

We selected three independent stock companies: Apple, Netflix and Tripadvisor. These were examples of large, medium and small companies. All data collected from each company was divided into three distinct time series 3000 readings each. We used 1 h time window, where every new reading is calculated once per hour. Moreover, every reading (after the discretization process) has assigned one of the three decision classes: $BUY, SELL$ or $WAIT$. Due to specifics of these data, vast majority of elements belong to the class $WAIT$, which visibly increases difficulty of analyzed datasets. The ϵ value which was used to measure minimal price change in the given data was as follows:

– 2\$, 2.5\$, 3\$ for the Apple company;
– 3\$, 3.5\$, 4\$ for the Netflix company;
– 1.5\$, 2\$, 2.5\$ for the TripAdvisor company,

where length of the sub-sequence Υ for all data was equal to 3 (for the smallest ϵ), 5 (for the medium ϵ) and 7 for the largest ϵ values. Details related with the cardinality of all decision classes was presented in the Table 1. All datasets were randomly divided with the use of the sampling without replacement into training and test sets. In all cases we considered data with 7 numeric attributes and one decision attribute (decision class).

Table 1. Cardinality of decision classes for different datasets.

Dataset	Train set			Test set		
	SELL	BUY	WAIT	SELL	BUY	WAIT
Apple 1	93(4.1%)	95(4.2%)	2062(91.6%)	23(3.1%)	35(4.7%)	692(92.3%)
Apple 2	107(4.8%)	95(4.2%)	2048(91.0%)	27(3.6%)	42(5.6%)	681(90.8%)
Apple 3	103(4.6%)	86(3.8%)	2061(91.6%)	21(2.8%)	42(5.6%)	687(91.6%)
Netflix 1	154(6.8%)	117(5.2%)	1979(88.0%)	49(6.5%)	46(6.1%)	655(87.3%)
Netflix 2	183(8.1%)	154(6.8%)	1913(85.0%)	59(7.9%)	49(6.5%)	642(85.6%)
Netflix 3	189(8.4%)	174(7.7%)	1887(83.9%)	58(7.7%)	48(6.4%)	644(85.9%)
TripAdvisor 1	148(6.6%)	166(7.4%)	1936(86.0%)	53(7.1%)	53(7.1%)	644(85.9%)
TripAdvisor 2	127(5.6%)	157(7.0%)	1966(87.4%)	29(3.9%)	43(5.7%)	678(90.4%)
TripAdvisor 3	110(4.9%)	151(6.7%)	1989(88.4%)	30(4.0%)	44(5.9%)	676(90.1%)
EURUSD 30	509(5.6%)	600(6.7%)	7891(87.7%)	87(2.9%)	83(2.8%)	2828(94.3%)
EURUSD 45	234(2.6%)	240(2.7%)	8526(94.7%)	35(1.2%)	31(1.0%)	2932(97.8%)
EURUSD 60	112(1.3%)	96(1.1%)	8792(97.7%)	15(0.5%)	13(0.4%)	2970(99.1%)
GPBUSD 30	660(7.3%)	607(6.7%)	7733(85.9%)	205(6.8%)	225(7.5%)	2568(85.7%)
GPBUSD 45	274(3.0%)	260(2.9%)	8466(94.1%)	88(2.9%)	91(3.0%)	2819(94.0%)
GPBUSD 60	118(1.3%)	125(1.4%)	8757(97.3%)	46(1.5%)	41(1.4%)	2911(97.1%)
USDJPY 30	471(5.2%)	514(5.7%)	8015(89.1%)	131(4.4%)	95(3.2%)	2772(92.5%)
USDJPY 45	196(2.2%)	216(2.4%)	8588(95.4%)	50(1.7%)	28(0.9%)	2920(97.4%)
USDJPY 60	101(1.1%)	90(1.0%)	8809(97.9%)	18(0.6%)	13(0.4%)	2967(99.0%)

From the forex market we selected 9 real-world data, which included three different currency pairs. For every considered currency pair we prepared sets depending on the number of pips, accordingly: 30, 45 and 60. It should be noted, that in the case of every dataset there were three decision classes as well: $BUY, SELL$ and $WAIT$, while the cardinality of decision classes was not equal (similarly to the case of the stock data, cardinality of the $WAIT$ class was significantly higher than two remaining decision classes). In this particular case the whole set consisted of 8 numeric attributes and the decision class (nominal). Conditional attributes were as follows: Alligator, bulls power, bears power, CCI, Demarker, RSI, Stochastic Oscillator and Williams indicator.

Exact parameters of all datasets were given in the second part of the Table 1. Information included division of the dataset (cardinality of the training set was equal to the 75% of whole dataset) along with information related with the cardinality of every decision class.

4.2 Results of Experiments

During the analysis overall 54 different experiments were conducted. In the case of decomposition it was over 150 different features that were analyzed. In this section we present selected results which were representative for the remaining results. Comments to the remaining observations were added as well.

In the Table 2 an accuracy of the classification for all considered algorithms was presented. It was calculated in the classical way (Eq. (6)) and without the $WAIT$ class which for these particular data can be omitted. In such case all objects, which were in the case $WAIT$ or during the algorithm run were assigned to the $WAIT$ class are excluded from the analysis. As it can be easily seen, the Random Tree algorithm is visibly worse in comparison to the remaining algorithms, which confirms, that it is not effective algorithm for the classification problem. Moreover, it also confirms, that the use of the CART algorithm and the C4.5 algorithms brings positive results (in this particular case the Random Tree was used to confirm, that the results are not random).

It can be seen, that the classification relates with the $WAIT$ class presents very good results in the case of the stock companies and the currency pairs. It means, that treating the classifier as a tool allowing to point out strong $SELL$ and BUY signal, at the same time no losses related with the operations related with the $WAIT$ class in many cases brings error-less classification.

For the more precise analysis of obtained results we used different measures of classification effectiveness. In this particular case the precision along with the recall measure for the class $SELL$ and BUY was used. We did not analyzed the $WAIT$ signal. Moreover, due to weak results, in this article we did not presented results obtained for the Random Tree algorithm. However conducted experiments confirm, that in the case of analyzed measures the Random Tree algorithm allowed to obtained visibly worse results that it was possible in the case of the CART and the C4.5.

In the Table 4 we present results for the precision and the recall, first for the $SELL$ and next for the BUY. These are results included also classification with the $WAIT$ signal. While the results with omitting the $WAIT$ signal and objects classified as the $WAIT$ are presented in the Table 5. Presented measures of classification efficiency were calculated on the basis of equations: precision (8) and recall (7) according to the notation from the Table 3.

$$Acc = \frac{TP + TN}{TP + TN + FP + FN}. \tag{6}$$

$$Recall = \frac{TP}{TP + FN}. \tag{7}$$

$$Precision = \frac{TP}{TP + FP}. \tag{8}$$

Table 2. Comparative study – accuracy rate.

| Data set | CART | C4.5 | RT | Without WAIT | | |
| | | | | CART | C4.5 | RT |
	acc	acc	acc	acc	acc	acc
Apple 1	**0.9187**	**0.9187**	0.8787	0.9474	**0.9500**	0.8065
Apple 2	**0.9227**	**0.9227**	0.8960	1.0000	1.0000	1.0000
Apple 3	0.9400	**0.9480**	0.9120	1.0000	1.0000	0.9706
Netflix 1	0.8933	**0.8987**	0.8547	**0.9643**	0.9231	0.9167
Netflix 2	**0.8867**	0.8853	0.8613	1.0000	0.9773	0.9808
Netflix 3	0.9160	**0.9173**	0.8813	1.0000	1.0000	0.9848
TripAdvisor 1	**0.8627**	0.8587	0.8080	0.8889	**0.9200**	0.8929
TripAdvisor 2	0.9213	**0.9253**	0.8867	0.9730	**1.0000**	0.9487
TripAdvisor 3	0.9213	**0.9293**	0.8933	0.9722	**0.9730**	0.9714
EURUSD 30	**0.9473**	0.9426	0.8726	0.8750	**0.9167**	0.8600
EURUSD 45	**0.9803**	0.9793	0.9426	1.0000	1.0000	0.9167
EURUSD 60	**0.9703**	0.9650	0.9503	1.0000	1.0000	0.7895
GPBUSD 30	**0.8609**	0.8572	0.7748	**0.9302**	0.8308	0.7064
GPBUSD 45	**0.9410**	0.9383	0.9030	1.0000	1.0000	0.8947
GPBUSD 60	0.9710	**0.9720**	0.9500	1.0000	1.0000	0.9091
USDJPY 30	**0.9250**	0.9246	0.8482	1.0000	0.0000	0.8000
USDJPY 45	**0.9740**	0.9730	0.9293	0.0000	**1.0000**	0.5000
USDJPY 60	**0.9897**	0.9877	0.9656	0.0000	**1.0000**	1.0000

Abbrev.: acc – accuracy rate.

Table 3. Confusion matrix

	Predicted positive	Predicted negative
Positive examples	True positive (TP)	False negative (FN)
Negative examples	False positive (FP)	True negative (TN)

Table 4. Comparative study – precision and recall.

Data set	SELL CART		C4.5		BUY CART		C4.5	
	prec	rec	prec	rec	prec	rec	prec	rec
Apple 1	0.3125	0.2174	0.5714	0.1739	0.5417	0.3714	0.4286	0.4286
Apple 2	0.6250	0.3704	0.6111	0.4074	0.6522	0.3571	0.6296	0.4048
Apple 3	0.7778	0.3333	0.6842	0.6190	0.7600	0.4524	0.8696	0.4762
Netflix 1	0.6500	0.2653	1.0000	0.2041	0.7000	0.3043	0.6667	0.3043
Netflix 2	0.7179	0.4746	0.7353	0.4237	0.5833	0.4286	0.5806	0.3673
Netflix 3	0.8537	0.6034	0.8333	0.6034	0.6944	0.5208	0.7000	0.5833
TripAdvisor 1	0.5385	0.1321	0.6000	0.1698	0.5000	0.1698	0.4242	0.2642
TripAdvisor 2	0.6667	0.5517	0.7500	0.6207	0.5556	0.4651	0.5909	0.3023
TripAdvisor 3	0.7200	0.6000	0.7097	0.7333	0.5484	0.3864	0.6667	0.3182
EURUSD 30	0.5294	0.1034	0.4000	0.1149	0.7500	0.1446	0.5217	0.1446
EURUSD 45	0.8000	0.1143	0.5000	0.1143	0.8333	0.1613	0.8333	0.1613
EURUSD 60	0.5000	0.0217	0.1600	0.0870	0.4000	0.0976	0.4667	0.1707
GPBUSD 30	0.7000	0.1024	0.5625	0.1317	0.4750	0.0844	0.3913	0.1200
GPBUSD 45	0.0000	0.0000	0.6250	0.1136	0.6250	0.0549	0.3611	0.1429
GPBUSD 60	1.0000	0.0435	0.0000	0.0000	0.3750	0.0732	0.6364	0.1707
USDJPY 30	0.0000	0.0000	0.0000	0.0000	0.5714	0.0421	0.0000	0.0000
USDJPY 45	0.0000	0.0000	0.3333	0.0200	0.0000	0.0000	0.3333	0.0714
USDJPY 60	0.0000	0.0000	0.0000	0.0000	0.0000	0.0000	1.0000	0.0769

Abbrev.: prec – precision; rec – recall.

In this case it can bee seen, that application of these algorithms in the case of the forex data not always brings good results. In the case of many currency pairs with different number of pips, the precision measure or the recall measure is often equal to 0.0. It means that in the case of the *SELL* or *BUY* these objects were not classified at all and the high accuracy values results from the proper recognition of the *WAIT* signals, which were the most common in these datasets. Especially interesting is the situation related with the stock data. In this case there is no situation, in which there is lack of recognized signals, and these recognized have high values. It means, that in the case of the high precision for the *SELL*, *SELL* decision for the classifier is strong signal which should be considered (and similar is observed for the *BUY*). While the recall ensures the decision maker, how many *SELL* or *BUY* signals could be estimated by the algorithms. It can be noticed, that in the case of the CART and the C4.5 algorithms these results are good, but not always different. It can indicate necessity of classification with the use of both algorithms and eventually settle the collective decision.

Table 5. Comparative study without WAIT – precision and recall.

Data set	SELL				BUY			
	CART		C4.5		CART		C4.5	
	prec	rec	prec	rec	prec	rec	prec	rec
Apple 1	1.0000	0.8333	1.0000	0.8000	0.9286	1.0000	0.9375	1.0000
Apple 2	1.0000	1.0000	1.0000	1.0000	1.0000	1.0000	1.0000	1.0000
Apple 3	1.0000	1.0000	1.0000	1.0000	1.0000	1.0000	1.0000	1.0000
Netflix 1	1.0000	0.9286	1.0000	0.8333	0.9333	1.0000	0.8750	1.0000
Netflix 2	1.0000	1.0000	1.0000	0.9615	1.0000	1.0000	0.9474	1.0000
Netflix 3	1.0000	1.0000	1.0000	1.0000	1.0000	1.0000	1.0000	1.0000
TripAdvisor 1	0.7778	1.0000	0.8182	1.0000	1.0000	0.8182	1.0000	0.8750
TripAdvisor 2	0.9412	1.0000	1.0000	1.0000	1.0000	0.9524	1.0000	1.0000
TripAdvisor 3	0.9474	1.0000	0.9565	1.0000	1.0000	0.9444	1.0000	0.9333
EURUSD 30	0.9000	0.8182	0.8333	1.0000	0.8571	0.9231	1.0000	0.8571
EURUSD 45	1.0000	1.0000	1.0000	1.0000	1.0000	1.0000	1.0000	1.0000
EURUSD 60	1.0000	1.0000	1.0000	1.0000	1.0000	1.0000	1.0000	1.0000
GPBUSD 30	0.9545	0.9130	0.8710	0.7941	0.9048	0.9500	0.7941	0.8710
GPBUSD 45	0.0000	0.0000	1.0000	1.0000	1.0000	1.0000	1.0000	1.0000
GPBUSD 60	1.0000	1.0000	0.0000	0.0000	1.0000	1.0000	1.0000	1.0000
USDJPY 30	0.0000	0.0000	0.0000	0.0000	1.0000	1.0000	0.0000	0.0000
USDJPY 45	0.0000	0.0000	1.0000	1.0000	0.0000	0.0000	1.0000	1.0000
USDJPY 60	0.0000	0.0000	0.0000	0.0000	0.0000	0.0000	1.0000	1.0000

Abbrev.: prec – precision; rec – recall.

On the Figs. 2 and 3 we can see supplementary results related with the analyzed data, which allows to visualize decisions achieved by the classifier from the point of the view of the good decision *SELL* or *BUY*. On the Fig. 2 we present the percent of properly classified *SELL*, the properly classified *BUY* along with the percent of strong errors – which can be understand as a classification of the *SELL* signal as the *BUY* signal or the opposite. Similar juxtaposition is presented on the Fig. 3, however in this particular case, the *WAIT* class was omitted in the analysis. All figures were presented for the CART algorithm, because the similar situation observed in the case of the C4.5 algorithm allows to observe similar features.

In this case it can be noticed, that the application of the decision trees in the case of similar solutions allows to achieve good results for the stock data, while the forex market is inclined towards less stability and the results are not always so good (at least in the case of keeping the *WAIT* class). However very interesting results can be obtained in the case of omitting the *WAIT* class. On the Fig. 3 it can be seen, that the percent of errors between classes *SELL* and

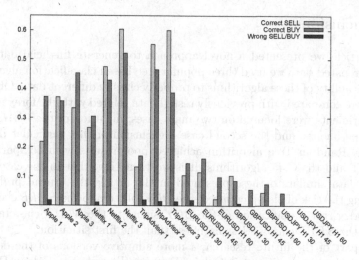

Fig. 2. Percent of properly classified SELL and BUY signals and percent of SELL classified as the BUY (or the BUY signals classified as the SELL

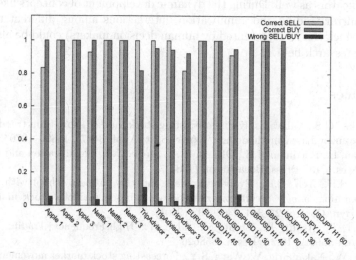

Fig. 3. Results with omitting the WAIT class and classifying to the WAIT class - percent of properly classified SELL, BUY along with the percent of SELL classified as the BUY (or the BUY classified as the SELL

BUY is very low, while the predictability of both classes is very high (although higher in the case of the BUY class). This case can be observed also for the forex market, because omitting the *WAIT* class leads to situation, where remaining classes have very small cardinality or all of them are classified properly.

5   Conclusions

In this article we presented a novel approach to generate financial data sets. For the prepared data we used three popular tree-based classification algorithms and testes ability of these algorithms to properly classify different data. Obtained results were compared with previously tested data related with the forex market. Our experiments were focused on two main cases: inclusion of the $WAIT$ class in the experiments, and the second case – exclusion of this particular decision class. The Random Tree algorithm achieved poor results with comparison to the CART and the C.45 algorithms. It is worth noting, that in the case of the financial data similar to these presented in the article the crucial problem is minimizing the risk of classification of the BUY objects to the $SELL$ class (and vice versa). Error classification of the BUY signal to the $WAIT$ class (and the same for the $SELL$ class) is less harmless than the first situation.

As a part of the future research, a more adaptive versions of the decision-tree based algorithms (like Ant Colony Decision Tree or Ant Colony Decision Forrest) should be checked. Second direction of the research should include the concepts related not only with the technical analysis indicators, but the fundamental indicators as well. During the dynamic development of concepts like social trading, mirror trading and gamification, interactions among different trading systems (which can be represented by human decision makers) could be also very promising research field.

References

1. Atsalakis, G.S., Valavanis, K.P.: Forecasting stock market short-term trends using a neuro-fuzzy based methodology. Expert Syst. Appl. **36**(7), 10696–10707 (2009)
2. Breiman, L., Friedman, J.H., Olshen, R.A., Stone, C.J.: Classification and Regression Trees. CRC Press, Boca Raton (1984)
3. Chena, S.H., Yeh, C.H.: Evolving traders and the business school with genetic programming: a new architecture of the agent-based artificial stock market. J. Econ. Dyn. Control **25**(3–4), 363–393 (2001)
4. Gomber, P., Arndt, B., Lutat, M., Uhle, T.: High-Frequency Trading (2011). http://dx.doi.org/10.2139/ssrn.1858626
5. Huang, W., Nakamoria, Y., Wang, S.Y.: Forecasting stock market movement direction with support vector machine. Comput. Oper. Res. **32**(10), 2513–2522 (2005)
6. Przemyslaw, J., Jan, K., Katarzyna, T.: Decision trees on the foreign exchange market. In: Czarnowski, I., Caballero, A.M., Howlett, R.J., Jain, L.C. (eds.) Intelligent Decision Technologies 2016. SIST, vol. 57, pp. 127–138. Springer, Cham (2016). doi:10.1007/978-3-319-39627-9_12
7. Korczak, J., Hernes, M., Bac, M.: Risk avoiding strategy in multi-agent trading system. In: Proceedings of Federated Conference Computer Science and Information Systems (FedCSIS), pp. 1119–1126 (2013)
8. Kuo, R.J., Chen, C.H., Hwang, Y.C.: An intelligent stock trading decision support system through integration of genetic algorithm based fuzzy neural network and artificial neural network. Fuzzy Sets Syst. **118**(1), 21–45 (2001)

9. Lai, K.K., Yu, L., Wang, S.: A neural network and web-based decision support system for forex forecasting and trading. Data Min. Knowl. Manag. **3327**, 243–253 (2005)

10. Menkveld, A.J.: High frequency trading and the new market makers. J. Financ. Markets **16**(4), 712–740 (2013)

11. Quinlan, J.R.: Induction of decision trees. Mach. Learn. **1**(1), 81–106 (1986)

12. Safavin, S., Landgrebe, R.D.: A survey of decision tree classiffier methodology. IEEE Trans. Syst. **21**(3), 660–674 (1991)

13. Samaras, G.D., Matsatsinis, N.F., Zopounidis, C.: A multicriteria DSS for stock evaluation using fundamental analysis. Eur. J. Oper. Res. **187**(3), 1380–1401 (2008)

14. Woodside-Oriakhi, M., Lucas, C., Beasley, J.E.: Heuristic algorithms for the cardinality constrained efficient frontier. Eur. J. Oper. Res. **213**(3), 538–550 (2011)

Relative Quality Assessment of Wikipedia Articles in Different Languages Using Synthetic Measure

Włodzimierz Lewoniewski$^{(\boxtimes)}$ and Krzysztof Węcel

Poznań University of Economics and Business, Poznań, Poland
{wlodzimierz.lewoniewski,krzysztof.wecel}@ue.poznan.pl

Abstract. Online encyclopedia Wikipedia is one of the most popular sources of knowledge. It is often criticized for poor information quality. Articles can be created and edited even by anonymous users independently in almost 300 languages. Therefore, a difference in the information quality in various language versions on the same topic is observed. The Wikipedia community has created a system for assessing the quality of articles, which can be helpful in deciding which language version is more complete and correct. There are several issues: each Wikipedia language can use own grading scheme and there is usually a large number of unevaluated articles. In this paper, we propose to use a synthetic measure for automatic quality evaluation of the articles in different languages based on important features.

Keywords: Wikipedia · Article quality · Synthetic measure · Wikirank

1 Introduction

The social nature of Web 2.0 services offers almost all users the same freedom to contribute. Wikipedia one of the best examples of online collaborative human knowledge on the Web. This online encyclopedia has more than 44 million articles in almost 300 language editions.[1] English version is the biggest and have more than 5.4 million articles. There are other language versions, which consist over million articles, e.g. German, French, Russian, Polish.

There are systems of grades for article quality in Wikipedia and particular language version can use own assessment standard [1]. Each language version have special awards for articles with the best quality. In English version such articles are called "Featured articles" (FA). In German Wikipedia articles with the highest quality have name "Exzellente Artikel", what is essentially equivalent to FA grade in English. Such articles should be well written, in particular fulfil certain criteria. Articles that meet a core set of editorial standards but are not featured articles, qualify as "Good articles" (GA); in German language – "Lesenswerte Artikel". There also other lower quality grades. In English Wikipedia A-class, B-class, C-class, Start and Stub articles. However,

---

[1] https://meta.wikimedia.org/wiki/List_of_Wikipedias.

W. Abramowicz (Ed.): BIS 2017 Workshops, LNBIP 303, pp. 282–292, 2017.
https://doi.org/10.1007/978-3-319-69023-0_24

quality grade scheme depends on language version. For example, German Wikipedia not use other grades than FA and GA, Belarusian Wikipedia use only 3 grades (FA, GA, Stub).

Usually in each language version of Wikipedia there are only about 0.4–0.6% of high-quality articles (marked as FA or GA). Other articles can get lower quality grades but still most of the articles are unevaluated. For example, in Polish Wikipedia the share of articles without quality grade is about 99%. This number could be lowered by involving more experienced users and experts from different disciplines. Unfortunately, such experts are not always available.

Most of existing studies build quality models based on binary classification, which is limited in comparing articles on similar quality. In this work we propose to use synthetic measure to assess the quality of articles as continuous variable.

2 Related Work

There are number of studies, which describes various ways to predict the quality of the Wikipedia articles. Some of them determine the quality based on article's content, another uses the edit history, the article's talk page and other sources. In general, we can divide related studies into the two groups: content-based and user-based approaches. Existing research works proposed different feature sets for measuring quality of Wikipedia articles.

Let's start by looking at scientific works analyzed the article content. One of the first studies showed that longer articles in Wikipedia often had higher quality grades [2]. Later works identified other features related to various constituents of the article: the best articles have more images, sections, use bigger number of references than articles with lower quality [1, 3, 4]. Special quality flaw templates can also help in articles assessment in Wikipedia [5].

In scientific works, attention is paid to writing style of articles, which depends on the language characteristics. High quality articles cover more concepts, objects and facts than weaker counterparts [6, 7]. Thus, bigger relative number of facts in a document can indicate its higher informativeness. Character trigram feature can be used to analyze article writing style [8]. Another study used some basic lexical metrics derived from the statistic on word usages in Wikipedia articles as the factors that can reflect its quality [9]. Therefore, we can expect that high-quality articles use more nouns and verbs and less adjectives.

Other group of studies - works related to editor's behavior, explore how the users experience and coordinate their activities in relation to article quality. These approaches use various characteristics related to a user reputation and changes that they made [10, 11]. Usually high quality articles have a large number of editors and edits [12]. Interaction among editors and articles can be visualized as a network, and using graph theory structural features associated to articles quality can be determined [13]. There is also artificial intelligence service involved to discover damaging edits, which can be used to immediately score the quality [14]. However, such user-based methods often require complex calculations and they do not analyze article itself, which would indicate what needs to be changed to improve its quality.

There are also a few works, that try to combine features from edition history and articles content [15, 16].

Concluding, existing studies propose different feature sets for assessing quality of articles in Wikipedia. However, there is no single universal feature set for doing it [16], especially if we consider different language versions [1, 3]. It must also be taken into account that extraction and analysis of some features (e.g. lexical) depend on the language version [6, 7, 9].

We decided to consider only content-based features, because they can also show to Wikipedia contributors what can be changed in the article to improve it quality.

Majority of studies solve the problem of automatic quality assessment of articles as classification task: articles can be marked as Complete or Incomplete [1, 3, 4, 6, 7, 9]. However, this approach is not able to show in what degree the article is better or worse than the other, if both are marked as the same class (e.g. Incomplete). An additional problem is caused by different standards in the quality grades between Wikipedia language editions.

Our work proposes to use synthetic measure to assess the articles' quality in different Wikipedia languages as a continuous variable. We verified our method on articles in 7 languages: Belarussian (BE), German (DE), English (EN), French (FR), Polish (PL), Russian (RU), Ukrainian (UK).

3 Building a Synthetic Measure

Proposed quality synthetic measure should be expressed as a real number between 0 and 100. So, the measure will cover the whole quality spectrum and relate quality to the highest quality class.

In order to build the synthetic measure we chose 5 important features, which were used in studies:

- Article length (in bytes)
- Number of references
- Number of images
- Headers 1st and 2nd level
- The ratio of number of references and article length.

As we mention before, in some Wikipedia language versions there are developed scale of grades. Often we can observe a positive correlation between the article quality and the value of each features. In English Wikipedia generally, the following quality classes are distinguished (from the highest): FA, GA, B, C, Start, Stub. Distribution of articles features of each quality class is shown in Fig. 1. To build this chart we use randomly chosen 1000 articles from each quality class.

For any given feature and given language we calculate the median value in the highest quality class (FA). This value is used as a threshold. Medians for each considered feature and language versions are shown in Table 1.

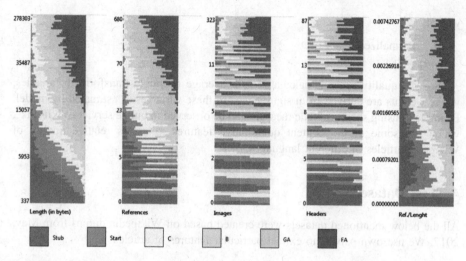

Fig. 1. Distribution of features in articles of each quality class in English Wikipedia. Source: own calculation. (Color figure online)

Table 1. Median feature values in the highest quality class in different Wikipedia languages. Source: own calculation.

Lang.	Length	References	Images	Headers	Ref./Len.
BE	198 365	210	36	27	0.001106
DE	56 238	55	17	21	0.000952
EN	49 038	115	13	14	0.002364
FR	91 004	185	29	26	0.002100
PL	59 672	96	17	17	0.001663
RU	139 415	163	24	22	0.001169
UK	82 371.5	40.5	24.5	21	0.000491

Based on the presented medians we can normalize each feature in particular Wikipedia language version according to the following rule: if the value of the given feature in given language exceeds the threshold, it is set to 100 points, otherwise its value is linearly scaled to reflect the relation of the value to the median value. Let us assume that the median for the number of images in the highest class is 32. Any article with higher number of articles will score 100 for this feature; article with 16 images will get proportionally 50 points after normalizing.

We assume that all features can have the same effect on the value of our measure, therefore articles quality can be calculated according to the following formula:

$$Quality\,Score = \frac{1}{c}\sum_{i=1}^{c} nf_i$$

where:

nf_i – normalized feature i,

c – number of features.

So, she quality score is calculated as a average of single transformed variables, where weights are derived from significance of these variables as estimated by model. Example of using such synthetic measure can be observed in online service WikiRank[2], which use some of the content quantitative features to assess relative quality of Wikipedia articles in different languages.

4   Test Datasets

All the below mentioned datasets were created based on Wikipedia dumps from May, 2017. We use own parsers to extract particular features of articles.

4.1   LS

We decided to choose 3 datasets, which describe cities in selected countries: Poland, Germany, and France. Cities are usually best described in a mother tongue, therefore we call them language-sensitive (LS). For verification we choose cities, which are described in at least 5 languages: DE, EN, FR, PL, and RU. Therefore, we choose articles about 10516 German cities, 10092 French cities, 904 Polish cities.

In each LS dataset we count articles that have the highest particular feature and the highest quality score. Share of the best articles count is shown below.

German Cities

Table 2. Share of articles with the highest value of quality score and particular feature in various languages of Wikipedia in German cities dataset. Source: own calculation.

	Length	References	Images	Headers	Ref./Len.	Score
DE	91.73%	96.87%	52.21%	80.88%	89.07%	95.49%
EN	7.00%	1.95%	18.70%	11.26%	0.78%	4.14%
FR	0.03%	0.56%	0.94%	0.03%	2.81%	0.26%
PL	0.79%	0.51%	11.11%	0.10%	4.72%	0.10%
RU	0.01%	0.06%	0.66%	0.01%	2.31%	0.02%

According to Table 2, more than 95% German cities are best described in German Wikipedia. If we consider individual features, it is noticeable that the images count is relatively the worst predictor among features of language affiliation of the selected articles – only about half of the articles that describe cities in Germany have the highest number of images in their own language. Much better result shows number of references – that feature has even better prediction than quality score.

---

[2] http://wikirank.net.

French Cities

Table 3. Share of articles with the highest value of quality score and particular feature in various languages of Wikipedia in French cities dataset. Source: own calculation.

	Length	References	Images	Headers	Ref./Len.	Score
DE	12.50%	16.57%	0.37%	0.20%	23.47%	9.24%
EN	5.23%	4.11%	52.80%	3.77%	3.29%	5.44%
FR	73.50%	57.68%	39.32%	92.14%	36.84%	79.41%
PL	0.44%	0.93%	2.92%	0.00%	2.00%	0.28%
RU	7.95%	19.72%	0.15%	0.02%	30.84%	5.62%

Table 3 shows that almost 80% of French cities are the best described in their native language according to our synthetic measure. Similarly to the case of German cities, the number of images shows relatively low prediction – only less than 40% of articles that describe cities in France have the highest value of this feature in their own language. Moreover, over half of the articles in another language version (English) that describe French cities have the highest number of images value. It should be noted that in this dataset references to length ratio is the worst predictor in contrast to German cities dataset, where this feature shows over 80% prediction. Slightly less number of articles in another language versions (Russian) has also the one of the highest value of this feature. In French cities dataset, the number of headers has better predictive power than quality score– over 90% of articles about French cities have the highest value of that feature in their own language version. So, almost all articles of this dataset have larger number of sections in French Wikipedia, which may indicate a more comprehensive description of cities in comparison with other considered language versions.

Polish Cities

Table 4. Share of articles with the highest value of quality score and particular feature in various languages of Wikipedia in Polish cities dataset. Source: own calculation.

	Length	References	Images	Headers	Ref./Len.	Score
DE	12.94%	31.42%	0.00%	5.86%	59.51%	13.94%
EN	1.33%	1.33%	0.22%	0.44%	3.21%	1.22%
FR	0.00%	0.00%	0.00%	0.22%	2.65%	0.00%
PL	83.41%	66.37%	70.13%	82.08%	29.98%	84.85%
RU	0.00%	0.11%	0.00%	0.00%	2.99%	0.00%

According to Table 4, the Polish dataset quality score has the highest prediction of language affiliation of considered articles than each individual feature. It is noticeable that according to this score almost 14% Polish cities are described better in German Wikipedia that in others languages. That can be explained by geographical location and relatively large popularity of some of these cities among German people. If we consider individual features with high precision ability, we can distinguish two of them: articles length and headers count. Like quality score these features separately predict almost the same number of articles in the Polish version. However, in much more articles in German version of this dataset have the highest value of references to length ratio than in Polish language - the difference is about twice.

In LS datasets quality score calculated by proposed method shows high precision. Depending on topic individual parameters can also show even higher precision than synthetic measure. However, there is no universal parameter for all presented topics that solve this task. Therefore, synthetic measure use different features for quality assessment.

Now, let's try to assess the quality of articles that are presented in different language versions of Wikipedia and don't have distinct topic or language affiliation.

4.2   5L Dataset

In this dataset we chose 273 878 articles, written in at least 5 languages: DE, EN, FR, PL, RU. According to Table 5 we see, that the largest number of the best quality articles is in English version - slightly more than half of the considered titles.

Table 5. Share of articles with the highest value of quality score and particular feature in various languages of Wikipedia in 5L dataset. Source: own calculation.

	Length	References	Images	Headers	Ref./Len.	Score
DE	19.59%	31.17%	9.56%	12.41%	38.81%	22.58%
EN	61.46%	41.70%	46.73%	57.95%	17.71%	53.34%
FR	7.33%	8.59%	16.38%	12.80%	10.04%	11.52%
PL	5.31%	6.69%	7.70%	5.26%	9.72%	6.36%
RU	4.40%	5.95%	9.11%	5.18%	10.74%	6.10%

English version also have the largest number of articles with the highest value of individual features except for the references to length ratio, which has highest value in almost 40% of German version. According to these indicators we can conclude, that the greater number of articles from English and German Wikipedia are more developed among 5 considered languages.

4.3   7L Dataset

In this dataset we choose 46 957 articles, written in at least 7 languages: BE, DE, EN, FR, PL, RU, UK. From Table 6 we can confirm the findings of previous 5L dataset on the share of articles with highest values of features and quality score.

Results from 7L and 5L dataset lead to general conclusion: English version of Wikipedia has the largest share of articles with the relatively better quality than other languages. German Wikipedia is in the second place by general relative quality of articles. This fact is also confirmed by other indicators of these language versions of

Wikipedia – they have the largest quantity of edits and the greatest number of active users[3]. However, this rule does not apply to the Ukrainian Wikipedia, which has about 12% of articles with the highest quality score in 7L dataset despite the fact that this language version is less developed than French, Polish and Russian Wikipedia.

Table 6. Share of articles with the highest value of quality score and particular feature in various languages of Wikipedia in 7L dataset. Source: own calculation.

	Length	References	Images	Headers	Ref./Len.	Score
BE	0.10%	0.24%	0.10%	0.21%	2.11%	0.23%
DE	14.86%	20.38%	11.17%	7.59%	23.74%	17.15%
EN	57.32%	38.56%	43.55%	50.75%	14.87%	49.99%
FR	5.71%	10.29%	10.79%	13.18%	10.65%	9.77%
PL	4.21%	4.00%	4.63%	4.56%	6.10%	4.13%
RU	6.79%	5.06%	7.51%	5.51%	6.18%	6.08%
UK	4.36%	15.74%	2.65%	2.40%	19.15%	12.19%

5 Articles Assessment

In this section we present the results of assessing over 10 million articles in 7 language versions based on Wikipedia dumps from May, 2017. Table 7 presents share of articles whose quality score falls within the specified interval.

Table 7. Share of Wikipedia articles whose quality score falls within the specified interval in each of seven language versions. Source: own calculation.

Score interval	BE	DE	EN	FR	PL	RU	UK
[0, 10)	72.29%	56.90%	30.35%	41.13%	49.88%	60.80%	59.31%
[10, 20)	20.11%	7.65%	27.51%	30.25%	22.85%	20.30%	10.15%
[20, 30)	5.95%	19.88%	22.23%	18.14%	18.17%	12.34%	16.96%
[30, 40)	0.96%	10.10%	10.55%	6.92%	6.19%	4.43%	10.50%
[40, 50)	0.36%	3.02%	4.50%	1.90%	1.68%	1.17%	1.66%
[50, 60)	0.14%	1.19%	2.17%	0.80%	0.61%	0.47%	0.68%
[60, 70)	0.07%	0.59%	1.18%	0.38%	0.30%	0.22%	0.32%
[70, 80)	0.04%	0.30%	0.66%	0.20%	0.14%	0.11%	0.19%
[80, 90)	0.04%	0.19%	0.45%	0.14%	0.09%	0.08%	0.13%
[90, 100)	0.04%	0.18%	0.40%	0.13%	0.09%	0.07%	0.11%

Results shows that in all language versions more than 90% of articles have quality score less than 40. The greatest number of articles that have quality score 40 and more is English and German Wikipedia.

---

[3] https://en.wikipedia.org/wiki/List_of_Wikipedias.

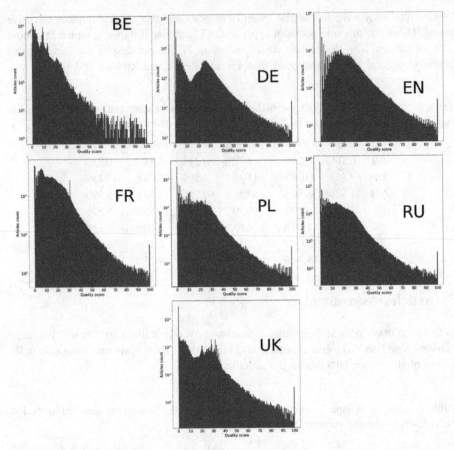

Fig. 2. Distribution of articles with assessed quality score using synthetic measure. Source: own calculation.

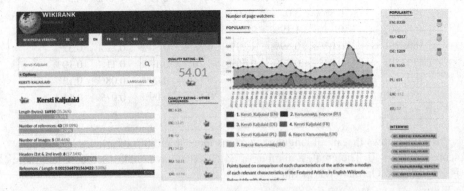

Fig. 3. Quality and popularity comparison. Source: http://wikirank.net/en/Kersti_Kaljulaid

More clear distribution of quality score is presented in Fig. 2. We can see that articles whose quality score falls within the highest interval [90, 100) usually have maximum value of synthetic measure.

6 Conclusions and Future Work

Synthetic measure can help to assess the quality of articles in different Wikipedia languages. In language-sensitive topics our approach can achieve precision over 90%. Differences between predicting ability of the individual features depending on topic shows that it is necessary to provide different weight for each component of the synthetic measure in each language version. In future we plan to extend the number of features and take into account their importance in particular language.

Quality assessment model can be applied in evaluation of the data quality placed in infoboxes.

One of the interesting directions of research is to examine the quality of information in relation to demand. It can be expected that the bigger the number of users reading a Wikipedia article, the bigger number of people interested in improving the content. So, the most popular language version can have also the best quality. Figure 3 presents example of comparison of popularity and quality of article about Kersti Kaljulaid in service WikiRank.

References

1. Węcel, K., Lewoniewski, W.: Modelling the quality of attributes in Wikipedia infoboxes. In: Abramowicz, W. (ed.) BIS 2015. LNBIP, vol. 228, pp. 308–320. Springer, Cham (2015). doi:10.1007/978-3-319-26762-3_27
2. Blumenstock, J.: Size matters: word count as a measure of quality on Wikipedia. In: Proceedings of the 17th International Conference on World Wide Web, pp. 1095–1096. ACM (2008)
3. Lewoniewski, W., Węcel, K., Abramowicz, W.: Quality and importance of Wikipedia articles in different languages. In: Dregvaite, G., Damasevicius, R. (eds.) ICIST 2016. CCIS, vol. 639, pp. 613–624. Springer, Cham (2016). doi:10.1007/978-3-319-46254-7_50
4. Warncke-Wang, M., Cosley, D., Riedl, J.: Tell me more: an actionable quality model for Wikipedia. In: Proceedings of the 9th International Symposium on Open Collaboration, p. 8. ACM, August 2013
5. Anderka, M.: Analyzing and predicting quality flaws in user-generated content: the case of Wikipedia. Ph.D., Bauhaus-Universitaet, Weimar, Germany (2013)
6. Lex, E., et al.: Measuring the quality of web content using factual information. In: Proceedings of the 2nd Joint WICOW/AIRWeb Workshop on Web Quality, pp. 7–10. ACM (2012)
7. Khairova, N., Lewoniewski, W., Węcel, K.: Estimating the quality of articles in Russian Wikipedia using the logical-linguistic model of fact extraction. In: Abramowicz, W. (ed.) Business Information Systems, BIS 2017. LNBIP, vol. 288, pp. 28–40. Springer, Cham (2017). doi:10.1007/978-3-319-59336-4_3

8. Lipka, N., Stein, B.: Identifying featured articles in Wikipedia: writing style matters. In: Proceedings of the 19th International Conference on World Wide Web, pp. 1147–1148. ACM (2010)

9. Xu, Y., Luo, T.: Measuring article quality in Wikipedia: lexical clue model. In: 2011 3rd Symposium on Web Society (SWS), pp. 141–146. IEEE (2011)

10. Wu, G., Harrigan, M., Cunningham, P.: Characterizing Wikipedia pages using edit network motif profiles. In: Proceedings of the 3rd International Workshop on Search and Mining User-Generated Contents, pp. 45–52. ACM (2011)

11. Suzuki, Y., Nakamura, S.: Assessing the quality of Wikipedia editors through crowdsourcing. In: Proceedings of the 25th International Conference Companion on World Wide Web, pp. 1001–1006. International World Wide Web Conferences Steering Committee (2016)

12. Wilkinson, D.M., Huberman, B.A.: Cooperation and quality in Wikipedia. In: Proceedings of the 2007 International Symposium on Wikis, pp. 157–164. ACM (2007)

13. Ingawale, M., Dutta, A., Roy, R., Seetharaman, P.: Network analysis of user generated content quality in Wikipedia. Online Inf. Rev. 37(4), 602–619 (2013)

14. Halfaker, A., Taraborelli, D.: Artificial intelligence service gives Wikipedians 'x-ray specs' to see through bad edits (2015). https://blog.wikimedia.org/2015/11/30/artificial-intelligence-x-ray-specs. Accessed 25 April 2017

15. Dalip, D.H., Lima, H., Gonçalves, M.A., Cristo, M., Calado, P.: Quality assessment of collaborative content with minimal information. In: 2014 IEEE/ACM Joint Conference on Digital Libraries (JCDL), pp. 201–210. IEEE (2014)

16. Dang, Q.V., Ignat, C.L.: Quality assessment of Wikipedia articles without feature engineering. In: 2016 IEEE/ACM Joint Conference on Digital Libraries (JCDL), pp. 27–30. IEEE (2016)

The Evolution of Business Information Systems and the BIS

Completeness and Reliability of Wikipedia Infoboxes in Various Languages

Włodzimierz Lewoniewski[✉]

Poznań University of Economics and Business, Poznań, Poland
wlodzimierz.lewoniewski@ue.poznan.pl

Abstract. Despite its popularity, Wikipedia is often criticized for poor information quality. Currently this online knowledge base consist over 45 million articles in almost 300 various languages. Articles in Wikipedia often includes special tables which present shortly important information about persons, places, products, organizations and other subjects. This table is usually placed in a visible part of the article and Wikipedia community called it "infobox". These infoboxes contains information in a structured form that allows automatically enrich popular public databases such as DBpedia. Wikipedia users can edit infoboxes in different languages independently. So, quality of information about the same thing may differ between various language versions. This article will examine the completeness and reliability of infoboxes about different topics in seven language versions of Wikipedia: English, German, French, Polish, Russian, Ukrainian and Belarussian. The results of the study can be used for automatic assessing and improving the quality of information in Wikipedia as well as in other public knowledge bases.

Keywords: Wikipedia · Infobox quality · Reliability · Completeness · DBpedia

1 Introduction

Wikipedia is on 5th place in the ranking of the most popular websites in the world[1]. Nowadays it is one of the most popular sources of knowledge and it allows everyone to participate in the content contribution in over 280 languages[2]. The largest English language version of Wikipedia over 5, 4 million articles. Among language versions, which have more than 1 million articles are German, French, Russian and Polish.

Articles related to various topics in different languages can be created and edited even by anonymous users Wikipedia. The contributors of this encyclopedia do not have to formally demonstrate their competences or skills in a specific area. Often changes in articles are immediately available online to wide audience. These and other reasons allows criticizing Wikipedia for poor quality of information. However, some articles in can provide valuable information.

---

[1] http://www.alexa.com/siteinfo/wikipedia.org.
[2] https://meta.wikimedia.org/wiki/List_of_Wikipedias.

W. Abramowicz (Ed.): BIS 2017 Workshops, LNBIP 303, pp. 295–305, 2017.
https://doi.org/10.1007/978-3-319-69023-0_25

Wikipedia articles can includes dedicated table with main facts about the subject – so called "infobox". As one of the most important elements of the article, infobox usually placed on a visible part - top right-hand corner of article. That one of the most important elements. Infobox is in fact a Wikipedia template that contains list of items "parameter = value" in a wiki markup. Additionally, values of parameters can also be inserted from Tabular Data[3] or WikiData[4]. Example of such infobox with its sources is shown in Fig. 1.

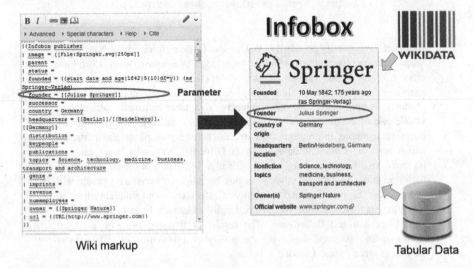

Wiki markup   Tabular Data

Fig. 1. Infobox with its data sources in English Wikipedia about publisher in article "Springer Science + Business Media".

Depending on the topic infoboxes have a different name, appearance and a strictly defined set of parameters. The structure of the infobox allows others public knowledge bases to extract the data. Among such projects, one of the most popular is DBpedia[5]. This crowd-sourced community effort uses a special framework[6] to extract information from these infoboxes and makes its available on the Web.

Infoboxes describing the same topics exist in different Wikipedia languages. Each language version of infobox can have its own set of parameters and parameters describing the same facts can be written differently. Therefore, DBpedia Extraction Framework uses the mappings defined by the community[7] to homogenize information extracted from Wikipedia in various languages. This makes possible to compare the filled parameters having different spellings. Later we can use this to determine which parameters are missing in certain language versions and automatically transfer them.

---

[3] https://en.wikipedia.org/wiki/Wikipedia:WikiProject_Tabular_Data.

[4] https://www.wikidata.org.

[5] http://wiki.dbpedia.org/.

[6] https://github.com/dbpedia/extraction-framework.

[7] http://mappings.dbpedia.org.

One of the features of Wikipedia is that information about the same subject created in different languages often independently of each other. Therefore, an important issue is to identify the language version (or versions) with infoboxes that contains more complete and reliable data. In this paper presents an analysis of these two quality dimensions of infoboxes describing different topics in seven language versions of Wikipedia: English (EN), German (GE), French (FR), Russian (RU), Polish (PL), Ukrainian (UK), Belarussian (BE).

2 Related Work

In Wikipedia, there is a system for assessing the quality of articles by community in particular language versions. However, a large number of articles have not yet been evaluated [1]. Therefore, automatic assessment of Wikipedia articles is a well-known and developed topic in scientific works. Such articles features as text length, number of references, images, sections can help in assessing Wikipedia articles [1–3]. Additionally for this purpose it is possible to analyze authors' reputation and articles edit history [4, 5], in some cases natural language processing techniques can be useful [6]. At the same time, each language version of Wikipedia can have its own quality model [1, 2]. Some of the proposed features used in online service WikiRank[8] to compare quality and popularity of articles in different languages. Those researches mainly focused on the analysis of the quality of articles as whole, not its individual elements such are infoboxes.

Preliminary experiments have shown that the articles evaluated with the highest grade by Wikipedia community in one language do not always contains infoboxes with the highest quality in comparison to other language versions, where articles received lower grades. Therefore, it is also necessary to be able to evaluate the quality of data in infoboxes taken into the account other measures.

As mentioned earlier, DBpedia extracts the information of the Wikipedia infoboxes. There are different approaches and tools to assess quality in this semantic database. RDFUnit uses pre-defined quality test patterns based on a SPARQL query template to analyze integrity constraints of dataset [7]. In contrast to the RDFUnit, ontology driven framework Luzzu allows implementation of different metrics without SPARQL querying [8]. Since DBpedia is the representative of Linked Open Data (LOD), in the area of fusion of data from different languages, Sieve framework can be used [9]. There are also algorithms that can identify missing type statements, and identifies faulty statements in LOD [10]. However, these approaches require domain experts to identify quality assessment metrics in a schema layer and for a more in-depth analysis of quality of the LOD it is necessary to take into account additional quality dimensions [11].

This paper proposed method to evaluate completeness and reliability of infoboxes that's describes companies, universities, films, albums and video games in seven language versions.

---

[8] http://wikirank.net.

3 Dataset

The results presented in the paper were carried out on Wikipedia dumps on May, 2017. First, articles with infoboxes on each topic in different languages were found. The number of such articles shown in the Table 1.

Table 1. Number of articles with infoboxes in particular topic in different Wikipedia languages. Source: own calculation in May, 2017.

Topic	BE	DE	EN	FR	PL	RU	UK
Album	130	8 348	137 972	36 379	22 026	14 144	6 522
Companies	371	21 703	56 678	15 427	4 660	9 449	3 628
Films	212	32 327	114 727	35 063	18 654	25 615	12 879
Universities	244	3 406	20 421	4 109	2 175	2 320	1 082
Video games	51	2 839	20 685	11 096	2 924	5 492	1 341

It is easy to see that the largest English Wikipedia has the largest number of articles in each considered topic. The analysis of articles in this dataset also showed that only a small part of the articles are presented in all language versions. Figure 2 presents the coverage of articles in three topics in some language versions of Wikipedia.

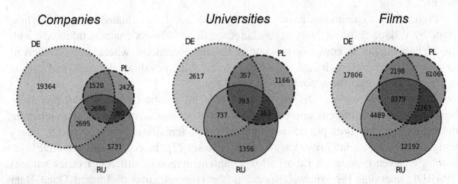

Fig. 2. Coverage of Wikipedia articles about companies, universities and films in German (DE), Polish (PL) and Russian (RU) language. Source: own calculations in May, 2017.

To calculate quality metrics presented in this work, parameters of infoboxes were extracted using own parser. The article will use such concepts as number of filled parameters, number of references, number of unique references. For a more visual understanding, Fig. 3 shows an example of an infobox with this metrics.

Fig. 3. Example of the infobox about film and some of its metrics.

4   Completeness of Infoboxes

Often users of Wikipedia do not fill in all the parameters of infoboxes. When calculating all presented in this paper metrics, the infoboxes parameters that Wikipedia users entered by mistake were ignored. Such incorrect parameters can easily be identified - as mentioned earlier, each infobox contains a certain set of predefined parameters names.

There are parameters that are filled more often than others. Figure 4 shows the top 20 most frequently filled parameters in the two selected infoboxes in English Wikipedia.

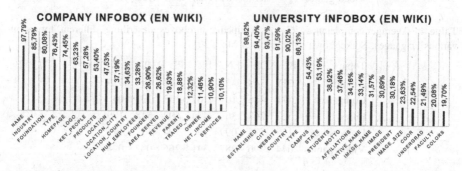

Fig. 4. The top 20 most frequently filled parameters in the company and university infoboxes in English Wikipedia. Source: own calculations.

It should be noted that the frequency of filling the same parameters in different language versions is vary. Table 2 presents filling frequency of some parameters if infoboxes that describes companies in particular Wikipedia language edition. It is also important that in some language versions certain infoboxes do not use parameters that are used by other Wikipedia languages.

Table 2. Filling frequency of some parameters of company infoboxes in different languages of Wikipedia. Source: own calculation in May, 2017.

Parameter	BE	DE	EN	FR	PL	RU	UK
Name	75.76%	91.57%	97.79%	88.17%	99.87%	93.23%	78.00%
Industry	61.74%	91.22%	85.79%	78.81%	82.14%	79.04%	67.47%
Foundation	70.45%	93.14%	80.08%	87.46%	89.27%	87.29%	52.04%
Type	64.02%	85.01%	76.43%	47.79%	65.95%	70.97%	53.99%
Homepage	70.08%	74.86%	74.45%	79.96%	81.34%	75.70%	62.28%

In this work completeness of infoboxes measured by two metrics. The completeness C_1 of infobox calculated as the ratio of the number of parameter values to the number of all defined parameters in the infobox of a given type:

$$C_1 = \frac{FP}{AP},$$

where FP – number of filled parameters, AP – number of all defined parameters in considered infobox.

Table 3. Average completeness C_1 of Wikipedia infoboxes describing different topics in various languages. Source: own calculation in May, 2017.

Topic	BE	DE	EN	FR	PL	RU	UK
Album	.339	.423	.533	.336	.432	.611	.415
Companies	.162	.589	.2	.295	.288	.221	.105
Films	.647	.399	.479	.509	.525	.617	.313
Universities	.284	.46	.186	.304	.347	.329	.213
Video games	.14	.418	.381	.434	.371	.153	.149

Table 4. Average completeness C_2 of Wikipedia infoboxes describing different topics in various languages. Source: own calculation in May, 2017.

Topic	BE	DE	EN	FR	PL	RU	UK
Album	.217	.343	.452	.223	.341	.474	.329
Companies	.071	.446	.107	.167	.153	.131	.04
Films	.527	.268	.36	.414	.402	.518	.199
Universities	.158	.335	.099	.19	.204	.19	.114
Video games	.044	.296	.287	.341	.266	.043	.048

Second method of measuring completeness based on the previous one with considering weights for each filled parameter:

$$C_2 = \frac{\sum_{i=1}^{FP} WP_i}{AP},$$

where FP – number of filled parameters, WP_i – weight of the parameter P_i, AP – number of all defined parameters in considered infobox.

Weight is based on the frequency of filling this parameter. For example for university infobox in English Wikipedia weight of parameter "city" is 0.9347 (see Fig. 3).

The results of calculating the average value of completeness are presented in Tables 3 and 4. Depending on the counting method we got different values on the same topics and languages. However, similarity in trends can be observed.

Figure 5 shows distribution of completeness C_1 and C_2 of infoboxes that describes different topics in particular language versions of Wikipedia. In presented boxplots the central box represents the middle 50% of the considered infoboxes in particular Wikipedia language, the central bar is the median and the bars at the end of the dotted lines (circles) close the most of the observations. Circles that lie beyond the end of the whiskers are data points that may be outliers.

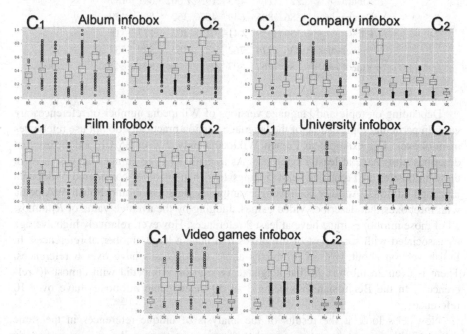

Fig. 5. Distribution of completeness C_1 and C_2 of infoboxes that describes different topics in particular language version of Wikipedia. Source: own calculations using pandas library (http://pandas.pydata.org)

Differences between completeness of the same infoboxes in various languages occurs due different sets of predefined parameters. For example in German Wikipedia infobox about company can have only 14 parameters while such infobox in Ukrainian edition can have over 40.

5   Reliability of Infoboxes

One of the convenient ways to verify the reliability of information in Wikipedia is to check the sources (if they exist). So, to measure reliability of infoboxes the following metrics are used in this paper: number of references (R_1), number of unique references (R_2), references to filled parameters ratio R_3 calculated by the formula:

$$R_3 = \frac{R_1}{FP},$$

where R_1 – number of references in the infobox, FP – number of filled parameters.

Table 5 presents the results of average number of references R_1 in Wikipedia infoboxes describing different topics in various languages.

Table 5. Average number of references R_1 of Wikipedia infoboxes describing different topics in various languages. Source: own calculation in May, 2017.

Topic	BE	DE	EN	FR	PL	RU	UK
Album	.22	.1	.153	.195	1.002	.641	.187
Companies	.386	.803	.649	.457	.352	.56	.459
Films	.553	.059	.441	.01	.403	.177	.316
Universities	.236	.774	.762	.47	.363	.329	.337
Video games	1.8	.467	.807	.278	1.944	.874	.641

Depending on topic and language versions of Wikipedia number of references are vary. In particular topics some of the language version practically do not use references in infoboxes. For example in French Wikipedia only 277 of 35 013 infoboxes that describes films have at least 1 reference. As a result, average number of references in these infoboxes in French at least 5 times less than in other considered Wikipedia language editions. Another interesting example is Belarussian and Polish Wikipedia with infoboxes that describes video games. Judging by the average value of R_1 almost all of those infoboxes must have at least 2 references. However, relatively high average R_1 associated with some part of infoboxes that have a large number of references. In Polish version about 10% of infoboxes about video games have over 6 references. There is even an infobox in that language version of Wikipedia with almost 40 references[9]. In the Belarusian Wikipedia 3 of 50 video game infoboxes have over 10 references.

Now let's look at the results of the analysis of unique references in the same dataset. Table 6 presents average number of unique references R_2.

Table 6. Average number of unique references R_2 of Wikipedia infoboxes describing different topics in various languages. Source: own calculation in May, 2017.

Topic	BE	DE	EN	FR	PL	RU	UK
Album	.22	.086	.119	.169	.952	.567	.176
Companies	.273	.52	.335	.258	.247	.304	.248
Films	.398	.052	.329	.008	.131	.135	.284
Universities	.194	.554	.526	.33	.29	.23	.255
Video games	1.66	.367	.54	.2	.876	.656	.526

---

[9] https://pl.wikipedia.org/wiki/StarCraft_II:_Wings_of_Liberty.

Comparing with the results of the calculation of average R_1, Table 5 shows lower values. This difference is due to the fact, that sometimes two or more parameters of particular infobox can have common source as a reference. Difference between Tables 4 and 5 also shows how often do Wikipedia community use common source to describe different parameters of particular infobox in each language. For example in Polish Wikipedia infoboxes about video games in average one source can occur as 2 references in particular infobox. However, there are also such cases, where every or almost all references within particular infobox are unique. This concerns album and university infobox in Belarusian language, film infobox in French, German, and Russian Wikipedia.

In the previous section, the results of the measurement of completeness were considered. Table 7 shows how the infobox parameters supported by references through counting average references to filled parameters ratio R_3.

Table 7. Average references to filled parameters ratio R_3 of Wikipedia infoboxes describing different topics in various languages. Source: own calculation in May, 2017.

Topic	BE	DE	EN	FR	PL	RU	UK
Album	.039	.009	.015	.023	.098	.054	.019
Companies	.076	.115	.106	.065	.051	.121	.249
Films	.04	.013	.041	.001	.035	.014	.034
Universities	.03	.11	.095	.048	.04	.036	.054
Video games	.402	.052	.103	.032	.214	.218	.159

The results show, that relatively more often Wikipedia users inserts references to parameters of infoboxes about video games (especially in Belarussian, Polish and Russian) and companies (especially in Ukrainian).

6 Conclusions and Future Work

In this paper were introduced quality metrics of infoboxes related to completeness and reliability. Result of the analysis shows, that depending on the Wikipedia language version and described topic there different completeness of infoboxes. According to research can be observed a different culture of filling the parameters in infoboxes – in specified languages there are parameters usually filled by users more often than their counterparts in other language versions of Wikipedia. Additionally, some infoboxes in certain languages may not use parameters that are commonly used in other language versions. Therefore, some facts presented in infoboxes describing certain topics may be particularly important (or not important) for separate Wikipedia language community.

The methods proposed in the article for evaluating completeness and reliability can be used in other models to determine infobox with the best quality of data across language versions of Wikipedia. Using these quality models together with techniques of parameters unification it is possible to improve the quality of data in multilingual

Wikipedia and other knowledge bases. Figure 6 presents example of extracting the parameters from company infobox in different languages and unification to common property names in DBpedia.

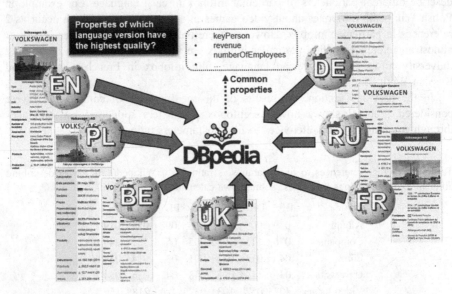

Fig. 6. Extracting the parameters from company infobox in different languages of Wikipedia and unification to common property names in DBpedia.

Each Wikipedia article in certain language version without an infobox can be enriched potentially from other language versions. Presented in paper metrics with other quality models can help determine such language version (versions). Despite the fact that Wikipedia is the largest, it can be enriched by other language versions. Table 8 presents potential number of articles in each language and each topic that can be created or enriched using infoboxes from other language version of Wikipedia.

Table 8. Number of Wikipedia articles that can be created or enriched using infoboxes from other languages. Source: own calculation in May, 2017.

Topic	BE	DE	EN	FR	PL	RU	UK
Album	170 793	157 925	22 538	130 712	143 118	151 548	162 086
Companies	83 829	58 169	22 783	65 154	77 409	72 932	79 470
Films	146 876	114 263	28 355	100 265	128 189	119 812	133 739
Universities	24 325	20 273	3 420	19 804	22 298	21 728	23 072
Video games	24 325	21 184	2 924	12 953	21 245	18 559	22 917

Future works will continue researches in the field of quality measurement of Wikipedia infoboxes. Through research new metrics will be developed. For example, for research on reliability of infoboxes in various languages of Wikipedia it is planned to take into account similarities of the references [12].

References

1. Lewoniewski, W., Węcel, K., Abramowicz, W.: Quality and importance of Wikipedia articles in different languages. In: Dregvaite, G., Damasevicius, R. (eds.) ICIST 2016. CCIS, vol. 639, pp. 613–624. Springer, Cham (2016). doi:10.1007/978-3-319-46254-7_50
2. Warncke-Wang, M., Cosley, D., Riedl, J.: Tell me more: an actionable quality model for Wikipedia. In: Proceedings of the 9th International Symposium on Open Collaboration, p. 8. ACM (2013)
3. Węcel, K., Lewoniewski, W.: Modelling the quality of attributes in Wikipedia infoboxes. In: Abramowicz, W. (ed.) BIS 2015. LNBIP, vol. 228, pp. 308–320. Springer, Cham (2015). doi:10.1007/978-3-319-26762-3_27
4. Suzuki, Y., Nakamura, S.: Assessing the quality of Wikipedia editors through crowdsourcing. In: Proceedings of the 25th International Conference Companion on World Wide Web, pp. 1001–1006. International World Wide Web Conferences Steering Committee (2016)
5. Ingawale, M., Dutta, A., Roy, R., Seetharaman, P.: Network analysis of user generated content quality in Wikipedia. Online Inf. Rev. **37**(4), 602–619 (2013)
6. Khairova, N., Lewoniewski, W., Węcel, K.: Estimating the quality of articles in Russian Wikipedia using the logical-linguistic model of fact extraction. In: Abramowicz, W. (ed.) BIS 2017. LNBIP, vol. 288, pp. 28–40. Springer, Cham (2017). doi:10.1007/978-3-319-59336-4_3
7. Kontokostas, D., Westphal, P., Auer, S., Hellmann, S., Lehmann, J., Cornelissen, R., Zaveri, A.: Test-driven evaluation of linked data quality. In: Proceedings of the 23rd International Conference on World Wide Web, pp. 747–758. ACM (2014)
8. Debattista, J., Auer, S., Lange, C.: Luzzu - a framework for linked data quality assessment. In: 2016 IEEE Tenth International Conference on Semantic Computing (ICSC), pp. 124–131. IEEE (2016)
9. Mendes, P.N., Mühleisen, H., Bizer, C.: Sieve: linked data quality assessment and fusion. In: Proceedings of the 2012 Joint EDBT/ICDT Workshops, EDBT-ICDT 2012, New York, NY, USA, pp. 116–123. ACM (2012)
10. Paulheim, H., Bizer, C.: Improving the quality of linked data using statistical distributions. Int. J. Semant. Web Inf. Syst. (IJSWIS) **10**(2), 63–86 (2014)
11. Zaveri, A., Rula, A., Maurino, A., Pietrobon, R., Lehmann, J., Auer, S.: Quality assessment for linked data: a survey. Semant. Web **7**(1), 63–93 (2016)
12. Lewoniewski, W., Węcel, K., Abramowicz, W.: Analysis of references across Wikipedia languages. In: The 23rd International Conference on Information and Software Technologies (2017). https://link.springer.com/chapter/10.1007/978-3-319-67642-5_47

Author Index

Printed in the United States
By Bookmasters